HOUSTON

ON THE MOVE

FOCUS ON AMERICAN HISTORY SERIES
The Dolph Briscoe Center for American History

University of Texas at Austin
Don Carleton, Editor

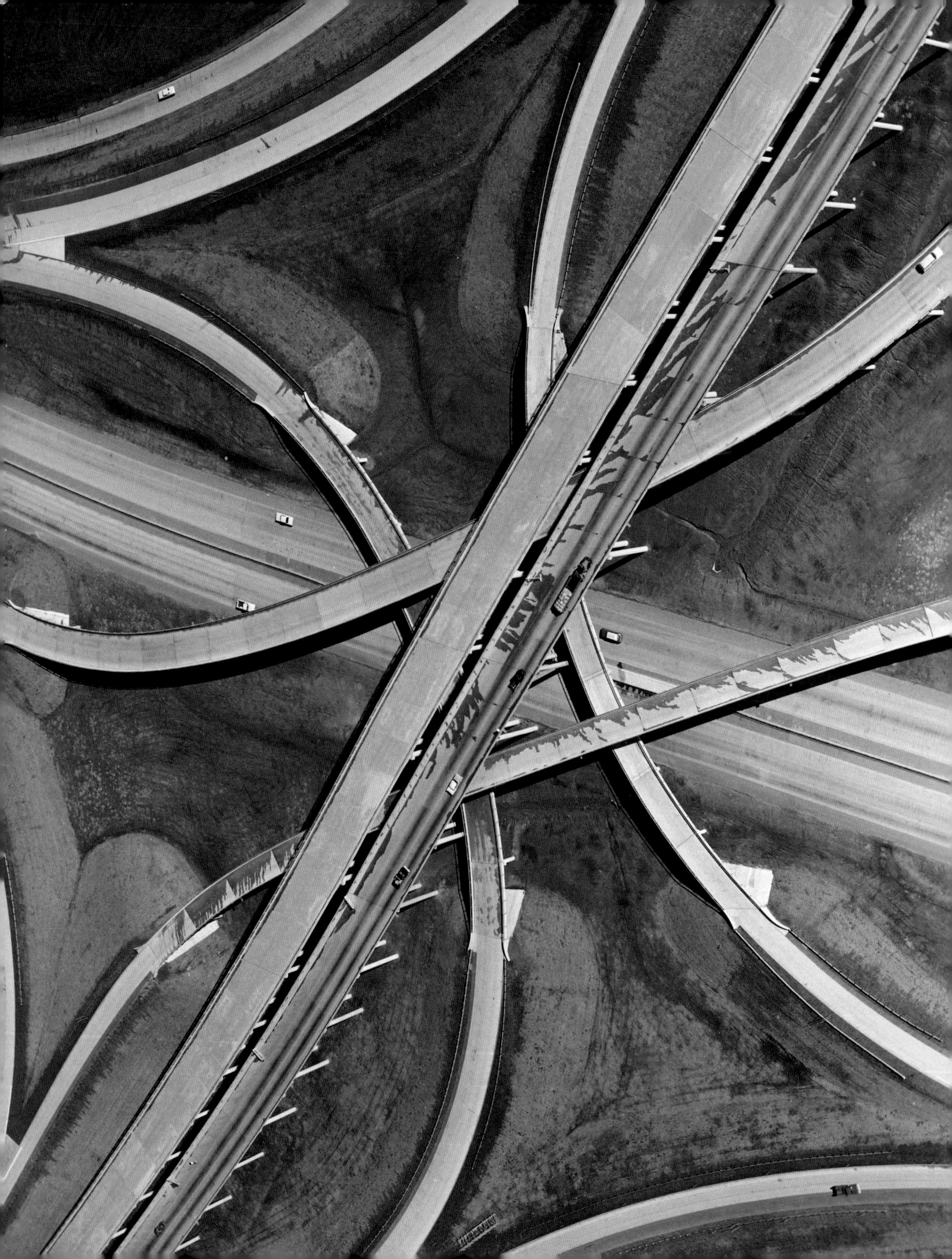

A PHOTOGRAPHIC HISTORY

HOUSTON

ON THE MOVE

STEVEN R. STROM

PHOTOGRAPHS BY BOB BAILEY STUDIOS

UNIVERSITY OF TEXAS PRESS
AUSTIN

BRISCOE CENTER
FOR AMERICAN HISTORY

Publication of this book was made possible in part by support from Clifton and Shirley Caldwell and a challenge grant from the National Endowment for the Humanities.

Printed in USA
First edition, 2016

The paper used in this book meets the minimum requirements of ANSI/NISO Z39.48-1992 (R1997) (Permanence of Paper). ♾

Design by Lindsay Starr

Library of Congress Cataloging-in-Publication Data

Names: Strom, Steven R., author. Bob Bailey Studios, photographs.
Title: Houston on the move : a photographic history / Steven R. Strom ; photographs by Bob Bailey Studios.
Other titles: Focus on American history series.
Series: Focus on American history series
Description: First edition. Austin : University of Texas Press, 2016. Includes bibliographical references and index.
Identifiers: LCCN 2016012908 (print) LCCN 2016015084 (ebook)
ISBN 9781477310946 (cloth : alk. paper)
ISBN 9781477310953 (library e-book)
ISBN 9781477310960 (non-library e-book)
Subjects: LCSH: Houston (Tex.)—Pictorial works. Houston (Tex.)—History.
Classification: LCC F394.H8 S84 2016 (print) LCC F394.H8 (ebook)
DDC 976.4/141100222—dc23
LC record available at http://lccn.loc.gov/2016012908

doi: 10.7560/310946

CONTENTS

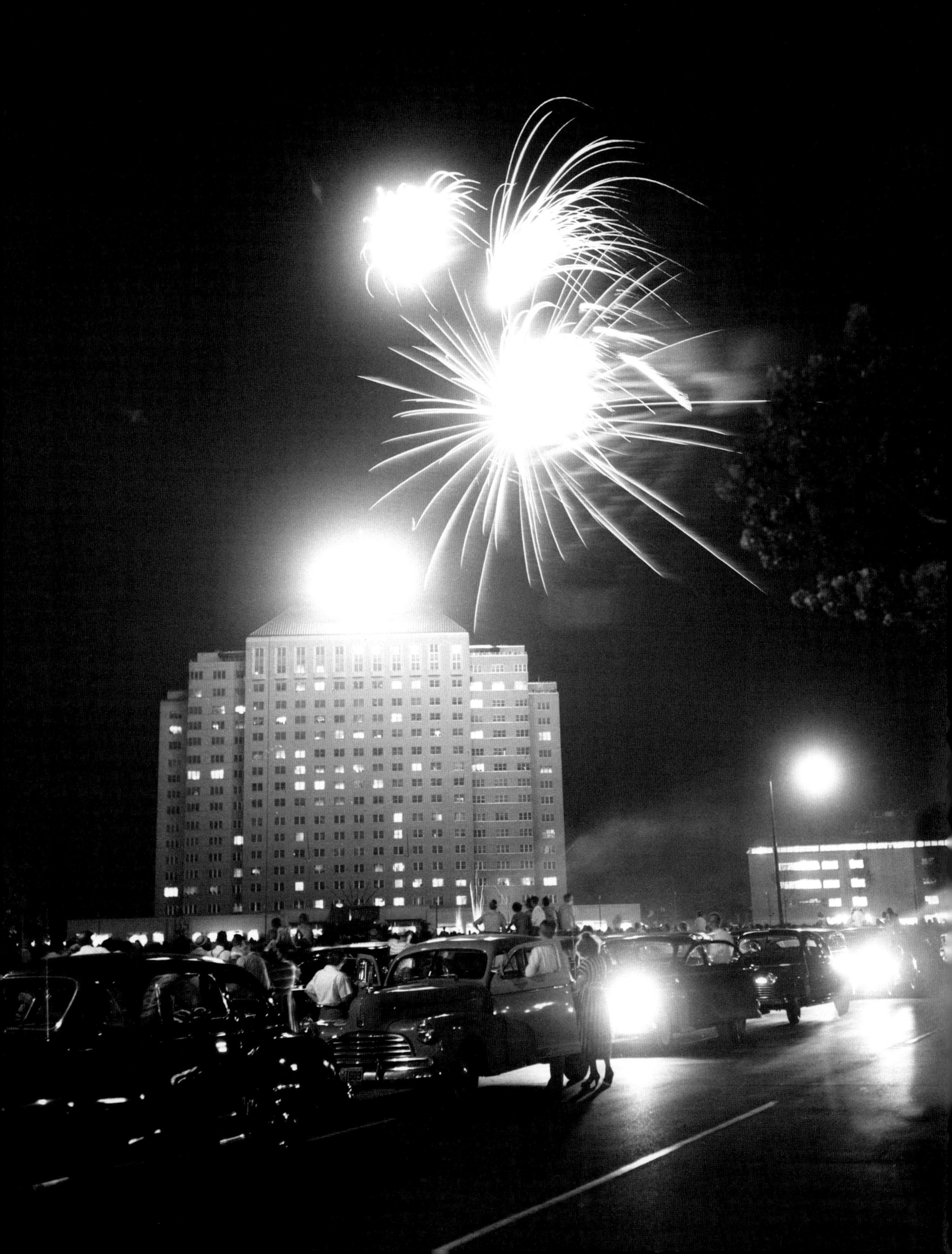

ACKNOWLEDGMENTS

The primary thanks for the production of this book must go to Executive Director of the Dolph Briscoe Center for American History, University of Texas at Austin, Dr. Don Carleton, who generously allowed me to utilize the Bob Bailey Studios Photographic Archive and approved and cosponsored the book's creation. This book appears as one of an ongoing historical series that is a collaboration between the Briscoe Center and the University of Texas Press. Dr. Carleton had the foresight to recognize the immense historical value of the Bailey collection and was responsible for its acquisition for the Briscoe Center in 1998. Dr. Carleton's appreciation for the value of the Bailey Studios collection has preserved an invaluable historical resource for the public's use.

The completion of this book would not have been possible without the participation and contributions of Bob Bailey's nephew, Jim Bailey. Jim worked at the Bailey Studios as a young man, and is currently an award-winning documentary film producer in Houston. Jim not only consented to an interview, but also loaned crucial family photographs and documents, as well as newspaper clippings and press releases about Bob Bailey and his work. Without Jim's invaluable input and assistance, a genuine sense of Bob Bailey's life and contributions would have been difficult to properly portray.

The Briscoe Center's Editor and Head of Publications Dr. Holly Taylor, assisted the project with multiple reviews and edits of the manuscript. Many thanks to Photo Archivist Amy Bowman, who provided research assistance, helped with the selection of photographs, answered hundreds of my questions, assisted the book's production with her organizational skills, and ensured that my research experiences at the Briscoe Center ran smoothly. Ellie Dickson, a former graduate student assistant to Amy, provided detailed reference assistance during the research phase of the book and was able to assist me with the knowledge of the collection that she had gained from her reference work with the Bailey photographs. The Briscoe Center's Photography Services Coordinator Aryn Glazier ably assisted the project with his technical skills. Also at the Briscoe Center, Digital Projects Coordinator Hal Richardson worked on the scans of the Bailey photos, preparing them for publication, while Audiovisual Archivist Justin Kovar prepared some of the film files for publicaiton.

I must also thank Amy Bowman's predecessor as photo archivist, Linda Peterson. In 1998, when the transfer of the Bailey photos from Houston to Austin was not yet completed, Dr. Carleton gave his permission for me to access the uncataloged Bailey photos. Dr. Carleton granted the access in response to a request from Houston Mayor Lee Brown to allow me to search for photos of the interior of Houston's City Hall, in an attempt to restore the building's interior to its original condition when it was completed in 1939. Linda helped me to locate numerous photos that were extremely useful to the restoration project. Later, she also assisted me when some of the Bailey photos were published in a *Cite* magazine article I wrote which stressed the collection's importance to Houston and Texas history.

At the University of Texas Press, great gratitude is due to Senior Editor Jim Burr, who skillfully shepherded the book from the proposal stage to its publication. Many thanks go to Manuscript Editor Victoria Davis and Editorial Fellow Amanda Frost, who showed infinite patience when working with my writing, and whose editing skills greatly improved the manuscript.

Additional specialized research assistance was provided in both Austin and Houston by Bob Bauer, Martha Bauer, and Ken Hammond. Ken also shared his stories with me of his own involvement with the April 16, 1947, Texas City Disaster, which Bob Bailey so ably chronicled. He was working for Southwestern Bell Telephone on the morning of the disaster, and raced with a coworker to the Texas City Southwestern Bell office to keep the switchboard open at a time when maintaining outside communications was absolutely vital for the ongoing emergency operations.

My father, Leo Strom, was working in Texas City at the Amoco Oil Company plant on the morning of the disaster, and volunteered with some of his coworkers to help work the many fire hoses in use that day, vital work since twenty-eight of the twenty-nine members of the Texas City Fire Department were killed following the first of two explosions onboard two anchored ships in the port of Texas City.

This book is dedicated to my grandfather, B. D. Jones, who left his home in Dickinson, Texas, on the morning of April 16, in a carpool with three other men, for his job at the Monsanto Chemical Company plant in Texas City. His office was adjacent to the docks where the two ship explosions occurred. Following the disaster that morning, he returned home later that day, badly injured, but still alive. It took more than five years for my grandmother, Lucille Jones, and his daughters, Aunt Faye and my mother Bernice, to help slowly remove most of the slivers of glass that the initial explosion had embedded into his body. The other men in his carpool were all killed. My grandfather's stories of growing up in rural East Texas and his later life on the Gulf Coast inspired me with a lifelong love for the history of Texas.

HOUSTON

ON THE MOVE

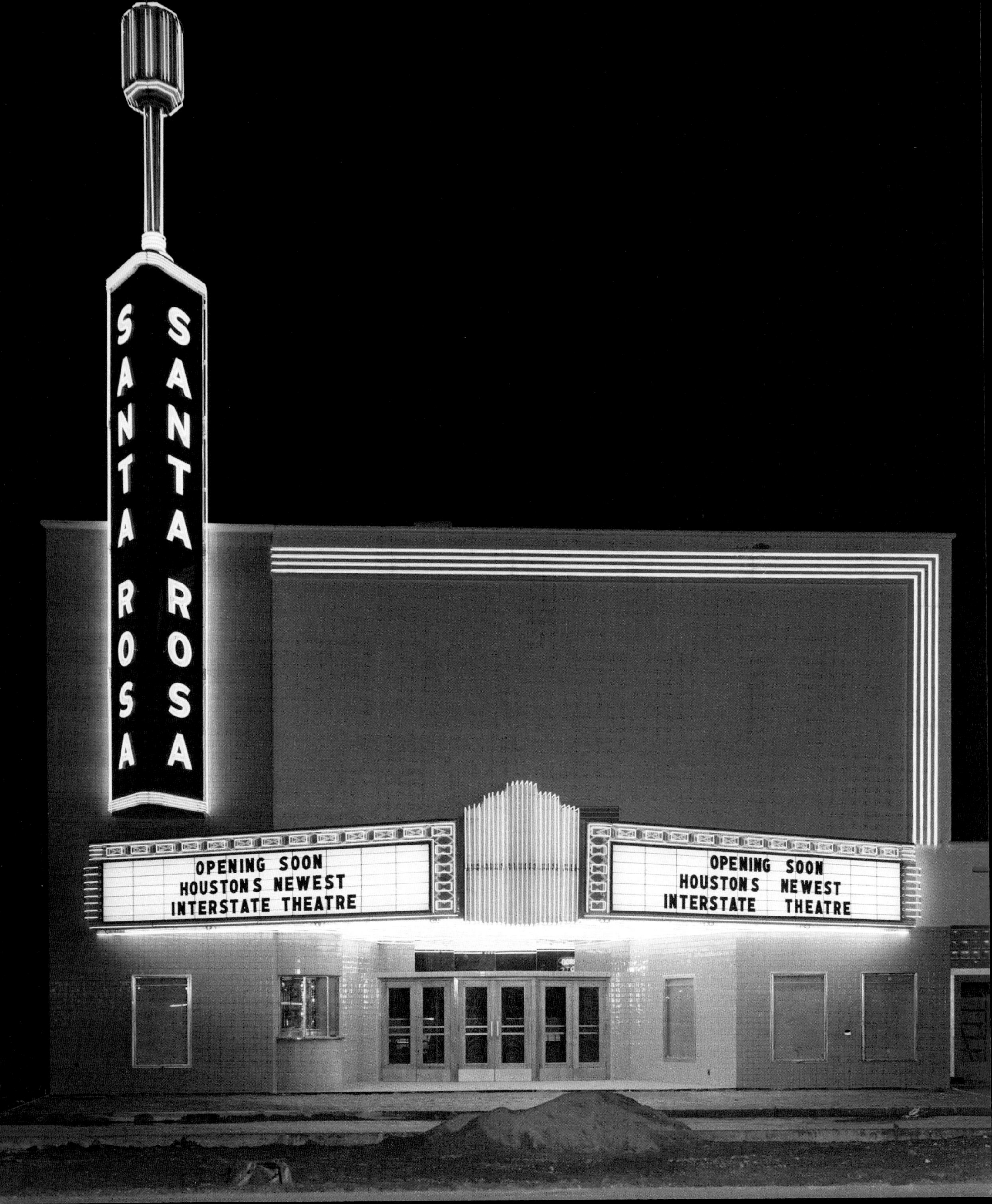

SANTA ROSA
SANTA ROSA
OPENING SOON
HOUSTONS NEWEST
INTERSTATE THEATRE
OPENING SOON
HOUSTONS NEWEST
INTERSTATE THEATRE

INTRODUCTION

A photograph acquires something of the dignity which it ordinarily lacks when it ceases to be a reproduction of reality and shows us things that no longer exist.

MARCEL PROUST
Remembrance of Things Past

•••

IN ONE OF THE VERY FEW TIMES that French novelist Marcel Proust, generally considered to be the greatest re-creator of lost time in the history of literature, was ever succinct about anything, he described the past as something that belonged "to a mysterious world to which one never may return again once its doors are closed." Fortunately, Bob Bailey and the photography studio he created in 1929 chronicled the existence of Houston, Texas, with cameras for more than six decades.

Browsing through the images contained in the Bob Bailey Studios Photographic Archive, now housed at the University of Texas's Dolph Briscoe Center for American History, is the closest that any of us can ever come to visiting the Houston of the vanished twentieth-century past—a Houston that still lives fondly in so many people's memories. As Briscoe Center photographs archivist Amy Bowman explains, "The studio's photographs of the city are often profoundly moving to longtime Houstonians. Many of our patrons have thought that their memories were the only record left of the demolished buildings and city landmarks shown in the archive." The Bob Bailey Studios Photographic Archive comes as close as any single archival collection to representing a comprehensive survey of Houston during the studio's active years; as a result, the Bailey Studios photographs and Houston are inseparable in the minds of many Houstonians.

To many people who are familiar with the work of Bob Bailey and the studio he founded, his body of work seems to have sprung from his native Texas roots almost *sui generis*. However, his career does in fact fit in well with developments in the history of photography as they occurred in both the United States and Western Europe. By placing Bailey's work in the context of the overall history of photography, it becomes clear that the photographic archive is not simply an important resource for Houstonians and Texans; it is a national treasure that can now be shared by all, thanks to the acquisition and preservation of the Bailey Studios images at the Briscoe Center.

Bailey opened his studio only ninety years after the first successful demonstration of the daguerreotype in France. A great deal of excitement and novelty still surrounded the relatively young field of photography, which was undergoing constant experimentation and technical advances when Bailey entered the field. Although people likely always fantasized about preserving their favorite memories, there was no technical way to achieve such preservation prior to the nineteenth century; memories remained only in the enclosed world of the individual mind, except for a minute number of specially commissioned paintings, drawings, and sculptures created for the upper classes. It was the introduction of the first daguerreotype in 1839 by Louis Daguerre and the exponential expansion of photographs by the late nineteenth century that largely, and democratically, erased any such obstacles to memory aids.

By the close of the 1840s, some three million daguerreotypes were already being purchased annually by Americans. In New York City alone, there were approximately one hundred commercial photography studios by 1853. Commercial photography's first widely known establishment was Mathew Brady's, whose New York City salon was already fashionably famous in the 1850s, a decade before Brady made his haunting photographs of the Civil War. By this time, the use of a combination of collodion-on-glass negatives and albumen prints was being perfected, allowing photographers to take consistently sharp and reproducible images. As a result, contact prints gradually replaced one-of-a-kind daguerreotypes. Making contact prints also simplified the photographic process—a welcome advance since the technology of creating daguerreotypes was hard to master, and handling and developing the plates was both tiresome and technically difficult.

Although early commercial photographers in America's large cities often sought to cement their status by photographing celebrities, the trendiness of having one's photo taken quickly spread from the upper-middle and upper classes to the expanding middle class and even to the working class, thereby ensuring the business success of the new technology. The high volume of sales encouraged commercial photographers to improve photographic technology, including cameras, equipment, negatives, and reproduction techniques in an effort to lower costs and increase profits. By the latter part of the nineteenth century, all of the large as well as most mid-sized cities in the United States had their own commercial studios. The photography business soon spread beyond America's urban areas. In rural and undeveloped frontier areas, the traveling itinerant photographer quickly became an established profession, and these photographers became a fixture as they made their annual rounds of farms and small towns.

With the development of flexible roll film by Eastman Kodak and the introduction of the personal "box" camera by that company in 1888, millions of people soon had the ability to create their own photographs. However, many Americans continued to want professionally shot photos of their families and family events, such as birthdays, weddings, and anniversaries, to preserve as familial memories and records. Businesses and advertisers also needed professional-quality photographs of their buildings, stores, billboards, merchandise, and signage. The quality of amateur photographs simply could not fulfill this demand, and professional photographers sought to differentiate themselves from amateurs by stressing the artistry and craftsmanship of their work in an effort to regain some of the business they had lost to amateurs. A further distinction in the production of photographs—this time within professional photography itself—arose during the late 1890s, when photographer Alfred Stieglitz began to formulate a philosophy that classified photography, previously viewed by most people as a mere mechanical reproduction of reality,

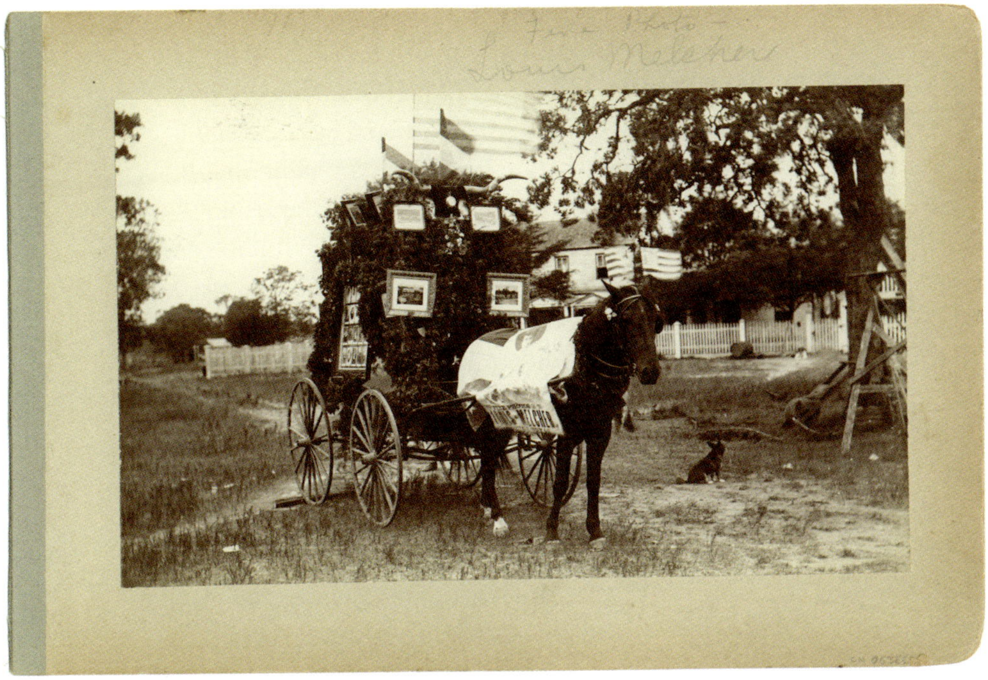

Horse with carriage advertising the Melcher photography studio, Texas, ca. 1900. Louis Melcher Photograph Collection, di_06454, Dolph Briscoe Center for American History, the University of Texas at Austin

as one of the fine arts. In the United States, Stieglitz's coterie of followers was designated the Photo-Secession, which promoted fine art photography and the accompanying pictorialist movement. By about 1915, professional photography was divided between a very small group of artistic photographers and an overwhelming majority of commercial photographers. Although by no means opposed to the creation of quality photos, the latter had to earn a living and relied on clients who decided their subject matter and generally did not appreciate "artsy" photographs.

It was in this divided atmosphere that Bob Bailey began his commercial photography career in 1929. One of the purposes of this book is to show that in the Bailey Studios' body of commercial work the two factions were not at all exclusive. In fact, many of Bailey's photos reveal not only an overlap of styles but also numerous purely artistic images. Bailey's photographs defy any simplistic labeling; each of his images must be read and interpreted on its own merits. Former Briscoe Center photographic archivist Linda Peterson has ably summarized the studio's achievements: "The Baileys were able to push their equipment in new and exciting ways that document in an historic sense, as well as an artistic sense. Their collection is astonishing both in the range of its subject matter and the artistry of its visual style."

One of the key facets of Bob Bailey's photographic artistry was shared with some of our greatest painters: the ability to transform seemingly mundane, commonplace scenes and subjects into something extraordinary, guaranteed to attract the viewer's attention. Bob's nephew Jim Bailey, the son of Bob's brother Milton, says that his uncle "looked at life with an 8 × 10 camera, while everyone else was looking at a 35mm . . . he saw the big picture."

The novelist Andre Gide described this type of artistic ability, which is also completely applicable to great photographers: "I have always believed that the great artists are those who dare to portray as beautiful a thing which is so natural that anyone seeing it afterwards would say, 'Why have I never noticed how beautiful this is?'" Bailey's viewers may have walked past the same building, stared at the same shop window, or crossed the same intersection many times without having seen the beauty Bailey saw in the exact same location.

If Bob Bailey had worked in the Northeast or on the West Coast, particularly in New York City, Los Angeles, or San Francisco, nearer to the primary media and intellectual centers of his time, he would be recognized and known today as a great photographer, possibly even defying the strictly "commercial" label. As it was, Bailey's photography career was largely confined to Houston, Texas, and the immediate surrounding area, where he was locally well known and highly acclaimed for his work, both by his clients and by the general public. The studio's local reputation was given an additional boost by the publication and sale of calendars from 1990 until 2002, featuring images from the studio's archive. It was through these calendars that many younger Houstonians came to know and admire the Bailey Studios' photographs, many years after Bob Bailey's death.

Biographical details regarding Bob Bailey are fairly sparse; his story in many ways is that of the "everyman." He did not leave voluminous amounts of correspondence behind, nor did he write and publish books and articles. Rather, Bailey's life is primarily revealed in his amazing, enormous body of work that was completed in a period of over four

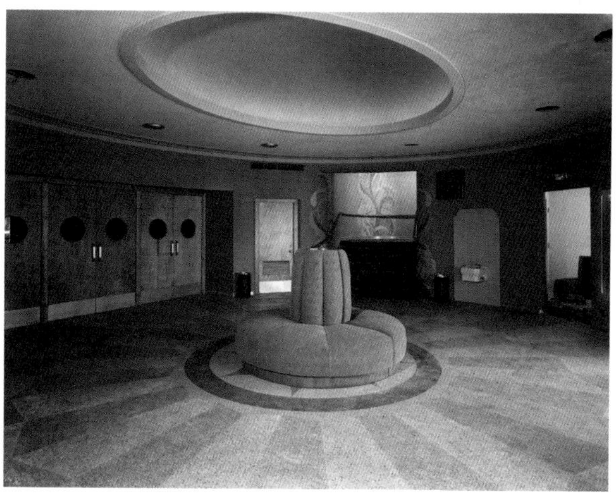

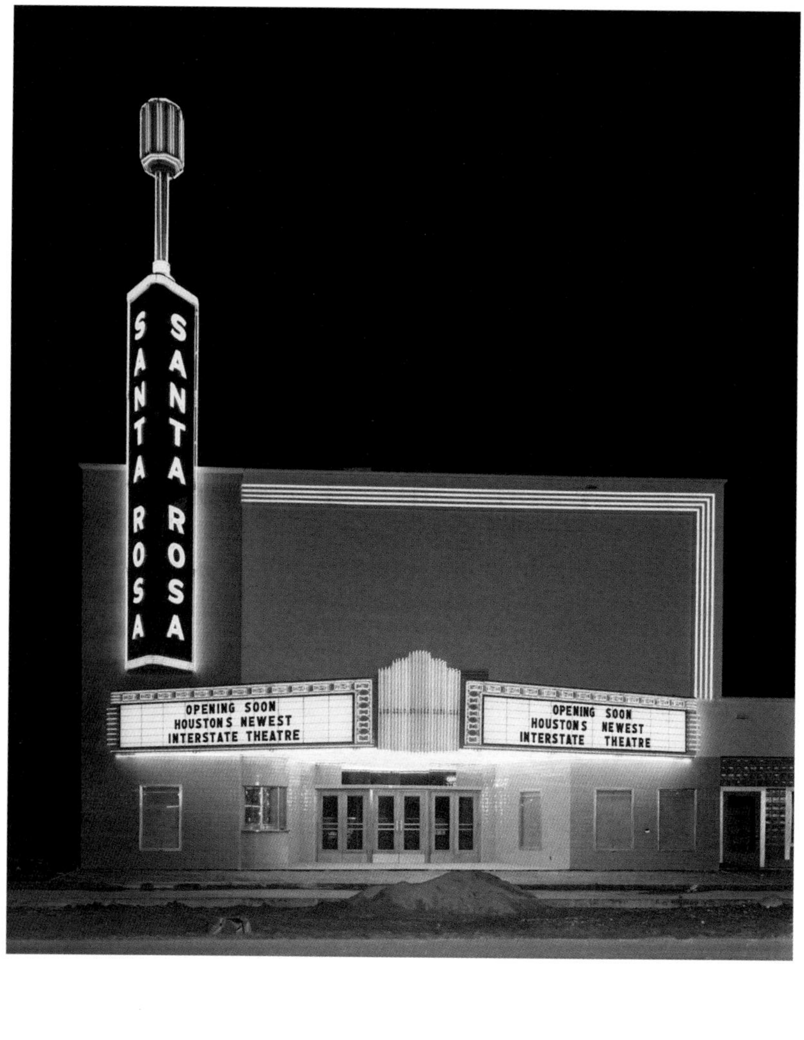

Photographs of the Santa Rosa Theater, November 1946. Bob Bailey Studios Photographic Archive, e_bb_1775 and e_bb_1886, Dolph Briscoe Center for American History, the University of Texas at Austin

decades; there are more than 500,000 photos in the Bailey Studios collection and some fifty-two 16 mm films, comprising at least eighty-five reels.

Robert H. Bailey was born in Fort Worth, Texas, on September 3, 1909, the son of Walter and Mary Lou Bailey. Bob was the oldest of three boys; Marvin was born next, and Milton was Bob's youngest brother.

At some point in the early 1920s, Walter, like so many other Americans, decided to move his entire family to Los Angeles in search of better job opportunities. While details about the Baileys' stay in Los Angeles are scarce, it is not difficult to surmise that Bob, like so many other young men at the time, was fascinated by the amazing technical developments of the early twentieth century and certainly would have been influenced by living in what was then the heart of the motion picture industry. It is even worthwhile to speculate that his California sojourn may well have been the source of Bob's later interest in filmmaking.

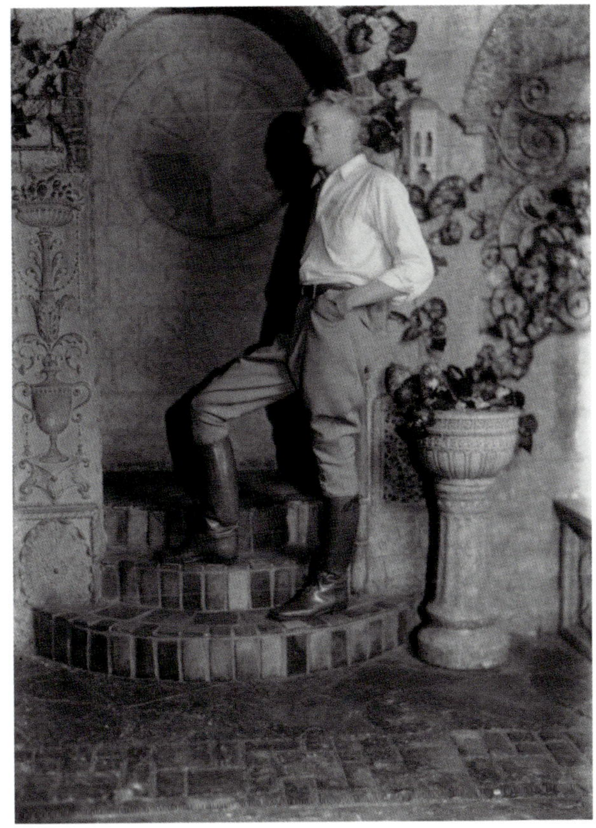

Bob Bailey, ca. 1927. This photo was possibly taken in California during the Bailey family's stay in Los Angeles. Photograph courtesy of the Bailey family.

After remaining in Los Angeles for only a few years, Walter moved the Bailey family back to Houston, their original home. Following the family's return from California, Bob graduated from Sam Houston High School and then began working in Cecil M. Thomson's successful Houston commercial photographic studio in 1928. Almost immediately, Bob knew that he wanted to be a professional photographer and also that he did not want to work for someone else. In 1929, after only about a year with Thomson Studios, Bob opened his first photography studio in Houston. No one today knows why Bob decided so quickly on a photography career nor where he learned his skills. Jim Bailey recalls that Bob was always confident, always in charge, and never looked back on any decision. What is definitely known is that by the time Bob began his own business, he was already a highly skilled photographer. The quality and careful composition of his photographs almost immediately gained him a large following of regular clients. Interestingly, Bob never printed any business cards during his career; he felt that the quality of his work spoke for itself, and he relied on satisfied customers to spread the word to other potential clients. Evidence from the Bailey archive shows that even at the outset of his career, Bob clearly never lacked clients and assignments.

Bailey's first studio business was known as Etchcraft Studio and was located in the Marine Bank Building at 1116-1120 Texas Avenue. By 1934, Bailey had moved his studio to the Guaranty Building, at 1302 Rusk, where he remained for many years. In the 1941 *Houston City Directory*, Bailey's business was listed for the first time as the Bob Bailey Studios. In 1952, Bailey moved to his own studio, which was built in an Art Moderne style, at 515 Taft and Allen Parkway. The building still stands but has been altered almost beyond recognition. Bob made one more studio move during his lifetime when he moved his operations to a studio located at 3931 Feagan Street in 1965. In 1972, following Bob's death, the studio made its final move to 931 Yale Street.

As his business rapidly developed and grew, Bob became known for his composition and lighting skills. His brother Marvin started working in the studio in the late 1930s, and together the two brothers formed a remarkable working partnership. However, Marvin was not the only other Bailey who helped at the studio over the years. At one time, the entire immediate family worked at Bob Bailey Studios in varying capacities. Bob's nephew Jim started working at the studio when he was only in the ninth grade. In addition to helping with photography assignments, Jim catalogued the photos, kept the ledger books up to date, and later assisted in producing some of the commercial films that Bob made, once even driving cross-country from the West Coast on an assignment while Bob flew across the country to New York.

Bob Bailey seems to have had an innate ability for photographic composition that often lent a certain dramatic flair to some of his photos. Jim Bailey remembers that one of the earliest and most important lessons that Bob taught him was: "Shoot a photograph from an angle whenever possible. The proportions always look better, and the composition is easier." It was such techniques that helped to differentiate so many of Bailey's photographs from those of many of his contemporaries, sometimes

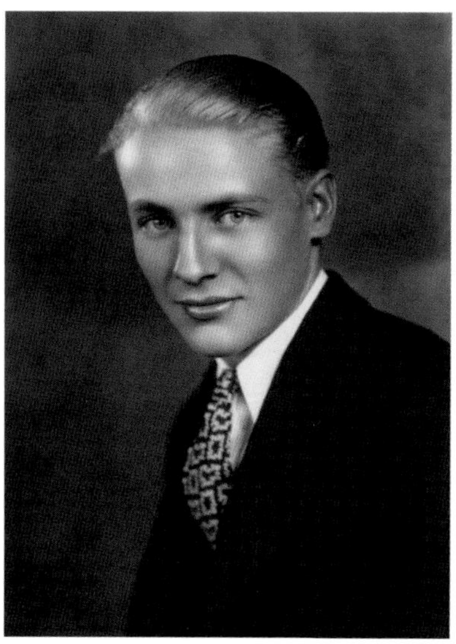

Bob Bailey had his portrait taken at Cecil Thomson Studios, ca. 1928, shortly before he opened his own business. Photograph courtesy of the Bailey family.

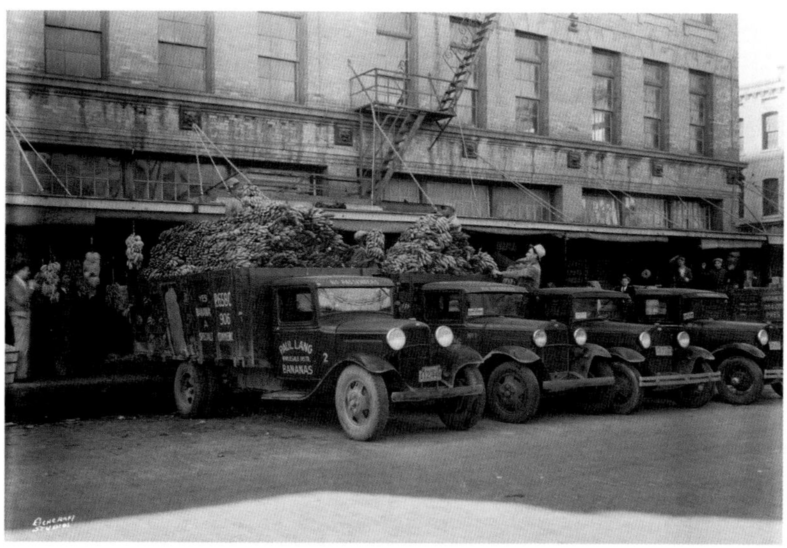

Banana shipments being loaded onto trucks belonging to Paul Lang Wholesale Distributor, January 1933. This photo was taken during Bailey's Etchcraft Studio period. Bob Bailey Studios Photographic Archive, e_bb_5969, Dolph Briscoe Center for American History, the University of Texas at Austin

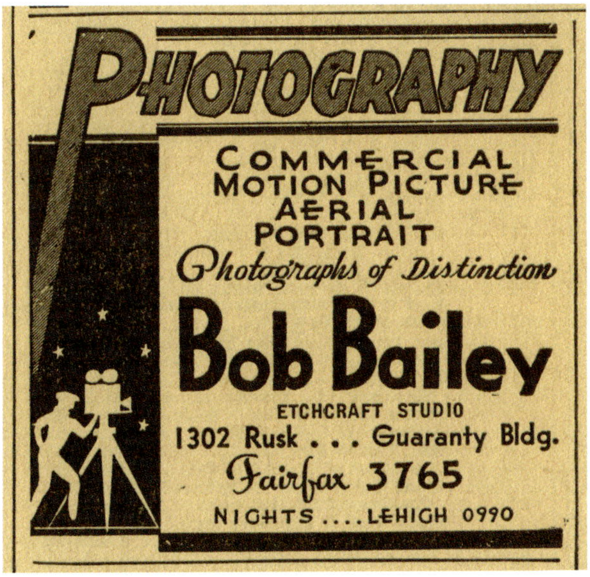

An early ad for Bailey's Etchcraft Studio that appeared in the 1935 Houston telephone directory. Texas Directory Collection, di_08716, Dolph Briscoe Center for American History, the University of Texas at Austin

imparting stylishness and originality to even the most ordinary subjects. Another appealing quality about the Bailey photos is the sheer visual clarity of most of the images. Ironically, the almost flawless quality of the early photographs resulted from a now-outmoded technical necessity: until the 1950s, each camera used by the Baileys could only hold two 8×10 negatives. The large negatives almost guaranteed a high level of definition in the photos, allowing the images to capture the numerous details that people still enjoy seeing. The Bailey Studios later switched to 4×5-inch negatives, which, along with 35 mm film, were used for the remainder of the studio's existence.

Not long after Etchcraft Studio opened, Bailey's new business received a jumpstart when he was hired to film newsreel footage for Fox Movietone News and Pathé News, two of the movie industry's largest producers and distributors of newsreels. Bailey maintained this business relationship through the 1950s and 1960s, when competition from television news programs killed off the newsreel business. Newsreels were not the sole output of the studio's motion-picture work; in the early 1930s, Bob was hired by Rice Institute to film their football games and other sports events, making him a pioneer in the field of sports films. This successful work led to Bailey later taking game films for the Houston Oilers, Texas A&M, and some Houston high schools. Over the years, Bob became increasingly dedicated to making industrial and promotional films to the point where, in 1960, he divided his operations into film production and still photography components: Bob Bailey Productions and Bob Bailey Studios, Inc. Bob only worked on films from that time on, while Marvin assumed responsibility for the photography division. By this time, Marvin specialized in aerial photography, photographing large construction projects, and Sakowitz Department Store shoots. Bob even built his own film-processing machine, and his filmmaking took him on assignments all across the United States as he carved a niche for himself making specialty films, often for energy companies, including promotional and educational industrial films. According to Jim Bailey, Bob personally approved every scene in any movie he directed as well as the music and the voice talent.

Some of his major film clients included Houston's Cameron Iron Works, the Houston Chamber of Commerce, the Southern Gas Association, and almost all of the major oil companies. Bailey's production titled *Everybody Knows Brooklyn*, produced by the Brooklyn Chamber of Commerce in 1964, was shown in 35 mm format in many Loew's theaters across the country. In an era before the nation was swamped by cable television "how-to" programming, he received a special award in December 1966 from the American Gas Association "for competence and artistry in the production of cooking films." By that time, Bailey had produced five films on cooking using natural gas appliances, and more than one thousand prints of those films were in circulation around the country. Among his many other film awards, Bailey received a Distinguished American Citizen Award, which was granted to him by Harding College in Arkansas for his civic and patriotic efforts as expressed in his film *Republic of Apathy*. During the 1960s, Bailey was also shooting film assignments in a number of locations around the world.

Bob was thoroughly dedicated to his profession, but he enjoyed his world away from work as well. In the midst of establishing his business, for instance, Bob attended and graduated from South Texas College of Law in 1937. Bob never practiced law but had always wanted to have a law degree, so he earned one despite his busy schedule. Bob loved the water, and much of his recreational time was spent on his yacht. In the early 1950s, he built a home along Clear Lake at 303 Lakeside Lane near the present-day city of Nassau Bay, an area that would soon be very near the Manned Spacecraft Center (today's Lyndon B. Johnson Space Center). His beautiful residence was designed by modernist architect Lucian Hood, and

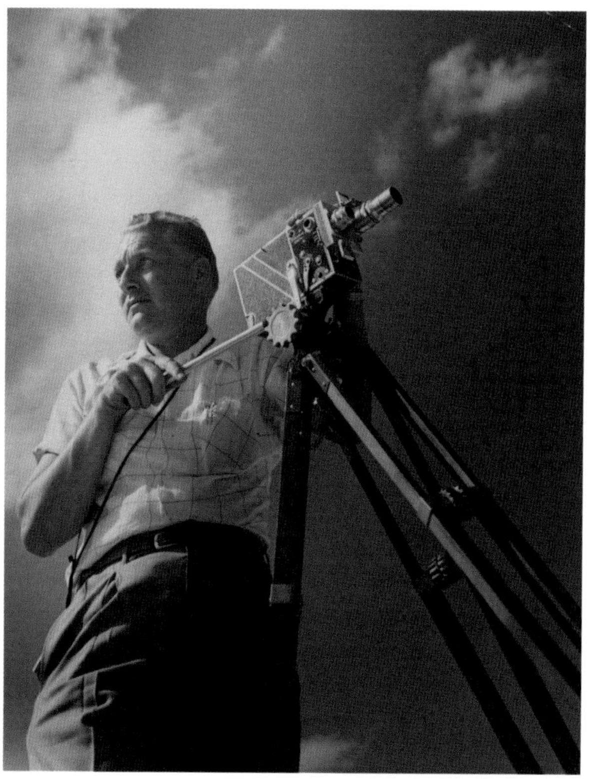

Bob Bailey with his 16 mm film camera, ca. 1960. Bob always preferred to use a Linhof Rollex camera when making his films. Photograph courtesy of the Bailey family.

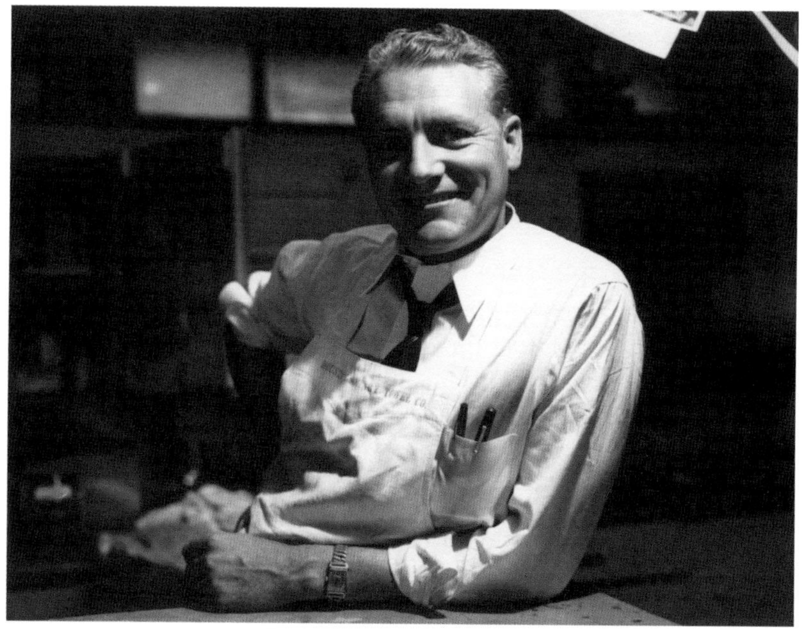

Bob Bailey in his studio, ca. 1960. Photograph courtesy of the Bailey family.

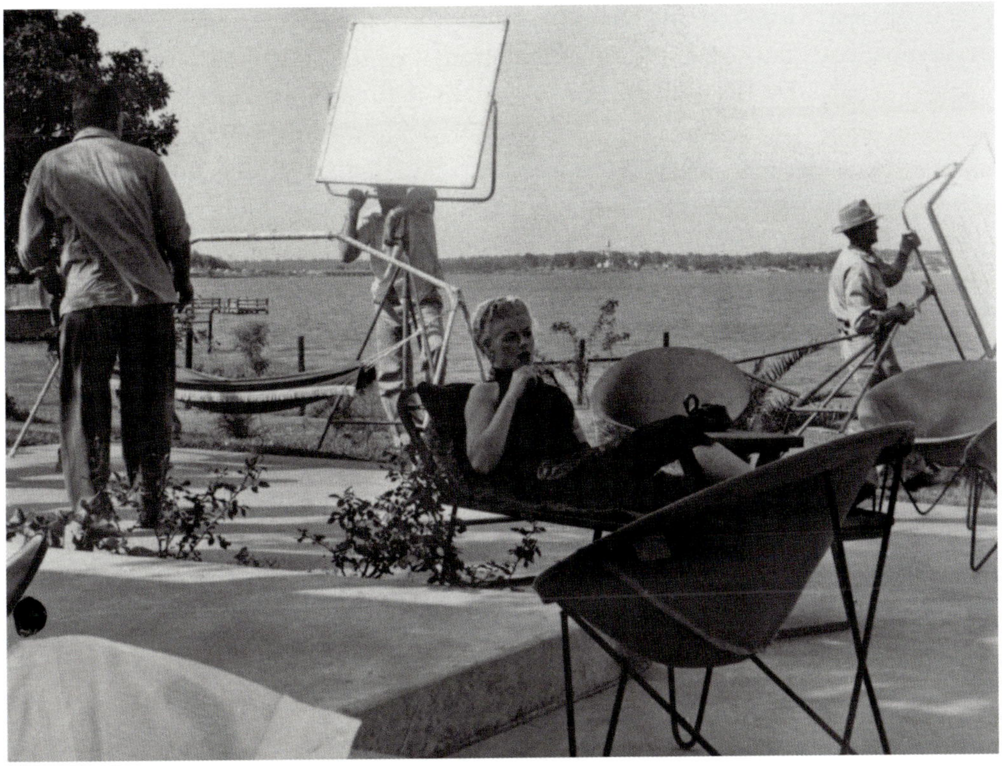

Actress Barbara Hale lounges between takes during the filming of *The Houston Story*, ca. 1956. Location shots for the film were photographed at Bailey's residence, located at 303 Lakeside Lane along Clear Lake, which is visible in the background. Photograph courtesy of the Bailey family.

it was used for location shooting for the 1956 film *The Houston Story*, directed by William Castle and starring Gene Barry and Barbara Hale. Bob's yacht, the *Sundown*, was moored at a dock adjacent to his home. He helped organize the first Galveston Bay Power Squadron and once served as commodore of the Lakewood Yacht Club.

Bob became ill while working on an industrial film about a pipeline under construction by Texaco and Gulf Oil over the Andes Mountains in Ecuador. The film was being shot at an altitude of some thirteen thousand feet, causing Bob heart problems. Following his return to Houston, he was hospitalized and required heart surgery. He died April 20, 1971, at the age of sixty-one, while undergoing surgery at Methodist Hospital. The last film that Bailey completed was titled *Tenneco and the 200 Million*, but he died before he could view his final production. Bob was survived by his wife Mary and his brothers.

Marvin assumed control of the business with Jim Rankin, another Bailey Studios employee, and continued photographing stills for the studio until the mid-1990s. Jim Bailey also continued his film work for the studio following Bob's death, creating films for Bailey Productions until about 1985; he would later go on to become a successful documentarian and filmmaker in his own right. One of Marvin Bailey's last major commissions was recording the construction and completion of the Sam Houston Race Park, which opened in 1994. Marvin died on July 29, 1998, and following his death, the studio was closed.

The uniqueness of the body of work left behind by Bob Bailey's studio is amazing, given the fact that he never belonged to any photography society, local or national, and neither subscribed to nor kept abreast of trade periodicals. Despite Bailey's apparent lack of knowledge about what was going on in the broader field of photography outside of Houston, his work bears some resemblance to many of the photographic greats of his time, and he achieved for Houston what other well-known photographers achieved for their own cities. In the United States, Bailey's career perhaps most closely resembles that of Berenice Abbott, who single-handedly devoted herself to cataloging the rapidly disappearing buildings of her native New York City. Abbott began her project in the early 1930s, and first worked with no outside financial assistance, then continued her photographic documentation after she was hired by the Federal Art Project in 1935. Abbott consequently created visual documentation of portions of New York before the construction of more skyscrapers eliminated so many long-standing buildings.

Some of Bailey's work also bears similarities to Charles Sheeler and Esther Bubley, who both excelled in taking industrial photographs that celebrated the progress of American technology and industry. In fact, one of Bubley's most famous photos was taken in 1945 in Tomball, Texas, near Houston. Titled *Tomball Gasoline Plant*, Bubley achieved the

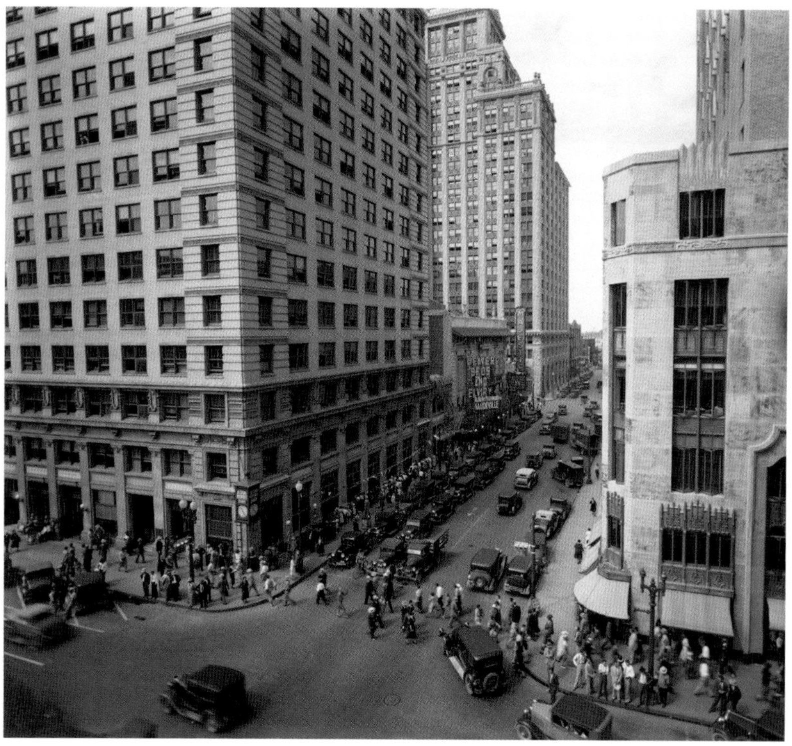

Corner of Main and Rusk, Houston, September 1932. Bob Bailey Studios Photographic Archive, e_bb_0826, Dolph Briscoe Center for American History, the University of Texas at Austin

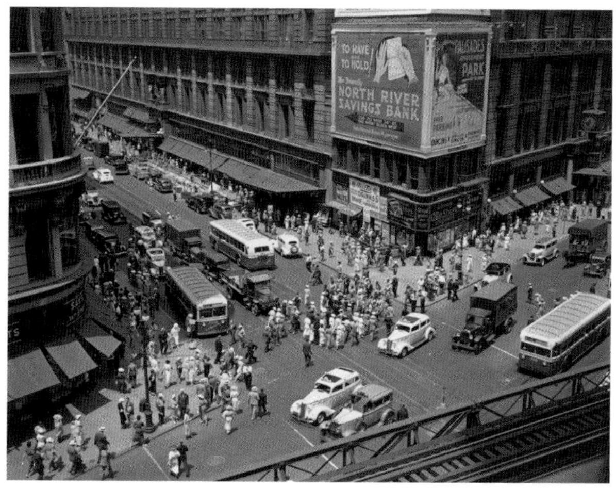

Herald Square, 34th and Broadway, Manhattan, July 16, 1936, by Berenice Abbott. From *Changing New York*, part of the Works Progress Administration's Federal Art Project. Courtesy: Photography Collection, Miriam and Ira D. Wallach Division of Arts, Prints and Photographs, New York Public Library, Astor, Lenox and Tilden Foundations.

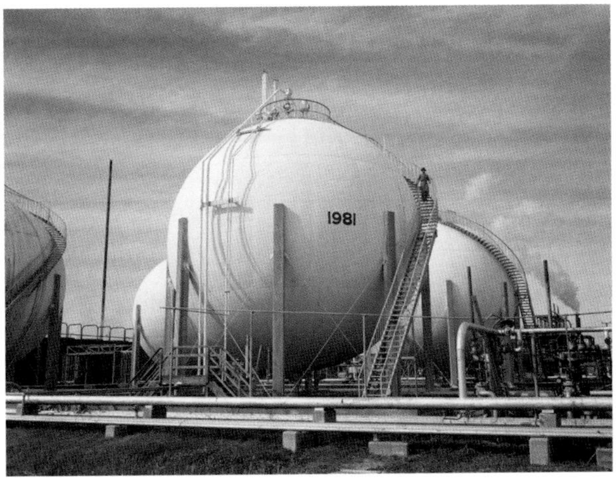

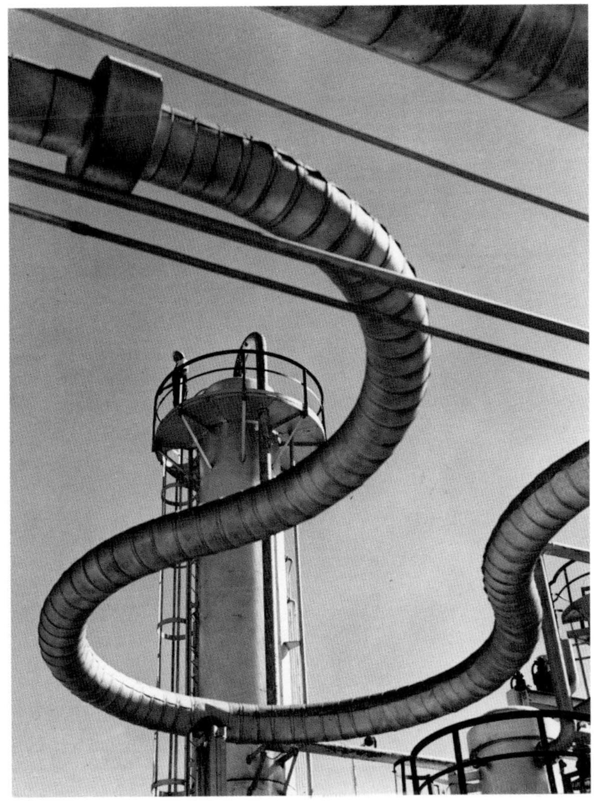

Above: Oil storage tank, ca. 1936. Bob Bailey Studios Photographic Archive, e_bb_2087, Dolph Briscoe Center for American History, the University of Texas at Austin

Right: Tomball gasoline plant, photographed by Esther Bubley for the Standard Oil of New Jersey photography project, June 1945. ExxonMobil Historical Collection, e_sonj_0125, Dolph Briscoe Center for American History, the University of Texas at Austin

integration of her human subjects with the complicated components of a modern industrial facility.

Among European photographers, Eugene Atget's career closely paralleled the direction that Bailey's work would later achieve. From 1900 to 1927, Atget worked in Paris as a commercial photographer to earn a living but used much of his own time to document the Paris of his youth that he loved so well, a Paris that was rapidly being destroyed and remade in the name of modernity. Some of Bailey's industrial and building photos bear similarities to the industrial and architectural photographs of Bauhaus-influenced Werner Mantz, who was doing much of his most artistic work in Germany during the 1920s and early 1930s.

Bailey's forty-year career coincided with some of the major twentieth-century developments in the history of photography. His photos of Houston life also reflect some of this country's important economic movements and social trends. As an example, some of the Bailey Studios' early photos parallel the fascination with nighttime photography that was held by so many other photographers in the early twentieth century. With the rapid introduction of electric lighting in the early decades of the century, it was the first time in history that cities were well lit after dark, and photographers were fascinated with the possibilities of utilizing artificial lighting for taking photos after dark. It was literally the first time in the young history of photography that a nighttime shot could be taken with any clarity. The introduction and rapid expansion in the 1920s of neon lighting for advertising gave nighttime photographers an additional type of lighting to utilize in their photo compositions.

The photos of billboards and signage that were documented by the Bailey Studios are also a reminder of a great ongoing "war" that was being conducted for advertisers' dollars at the time between newspapers and advocates of outdoor advertising. A great deal can be discerned about a city by reviewing the history of its billboards and signage. Although the studio was shooting signage for clients, who likely wanted a street or car-level view of what their billboards and signs looked like to potential consumers, the photographs also inadvertently captured the rapidly changing landscape of American consumerism and advertising. Today, researchers are often able to date an undated photograph by the type of billboard or sign shown in the picture or by the product being advertised. The products and goods being displayed also give clues regarding what the city's mores and interests were at the time. These outdoor signs reveal Houston's material aspirations and desires, sometimes with garish images that appear as though they were about to leap into passing cars.

The growth of Bob Bailey's photography business also accompanied the rapid development of the cult of celebrity. Advances in photography and the availability of cameras increased in tandem with the development of the newly emerging motion-picture and radio industries. Celebrities had long been used in American advertising, but

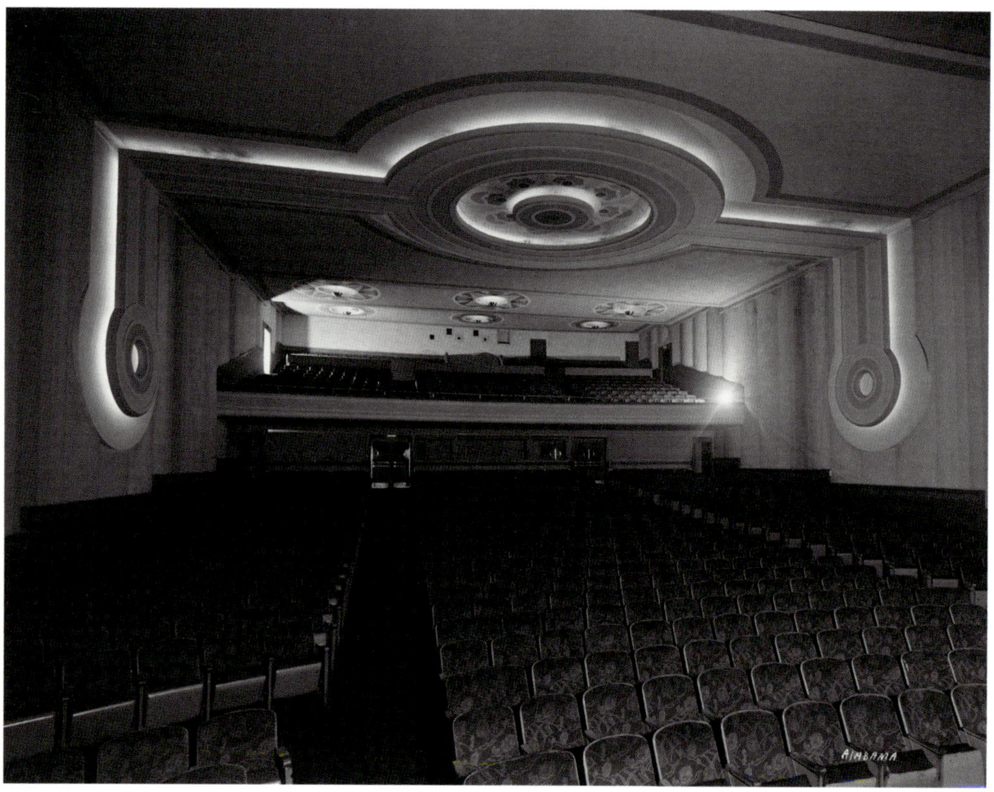

Alabama Theatre, 1950. Bailey's photographs of Houston theaters bear a striking resemblance to the architectural photography of German photographer Werner Mantz. Bob Bailey Studios Photographic Archive, e_bb_1494, Dolph Briscoe Center for American History, the University of Texas at Austin

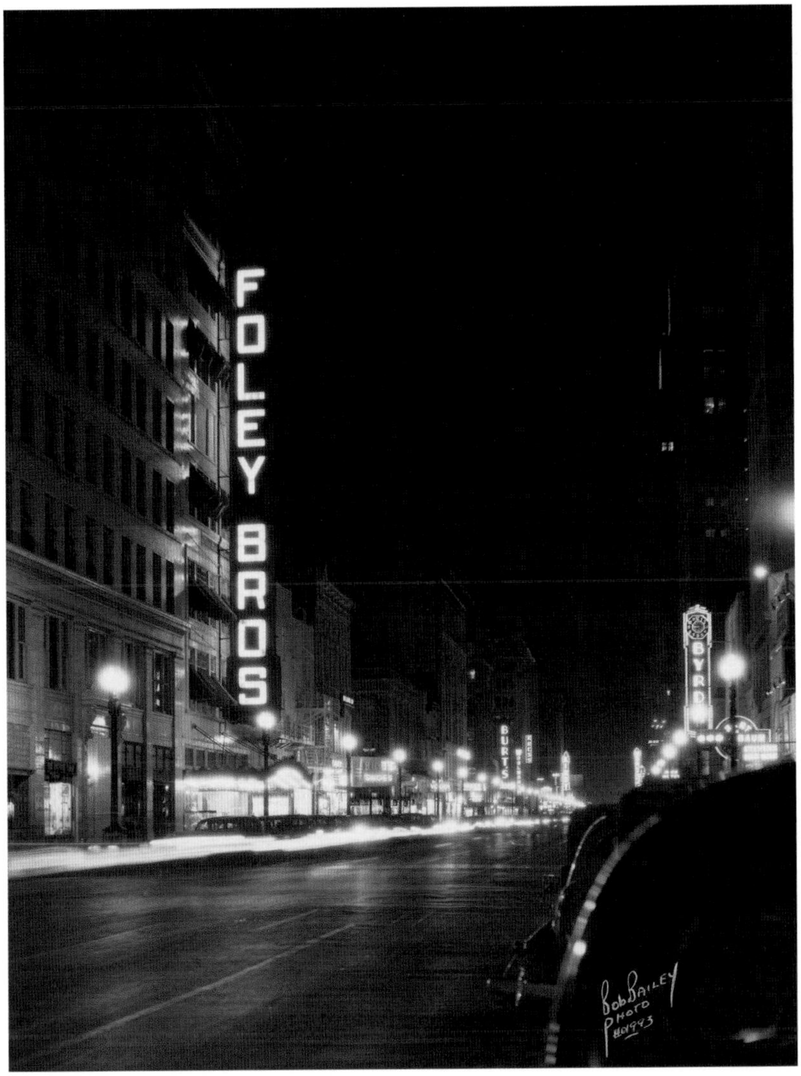

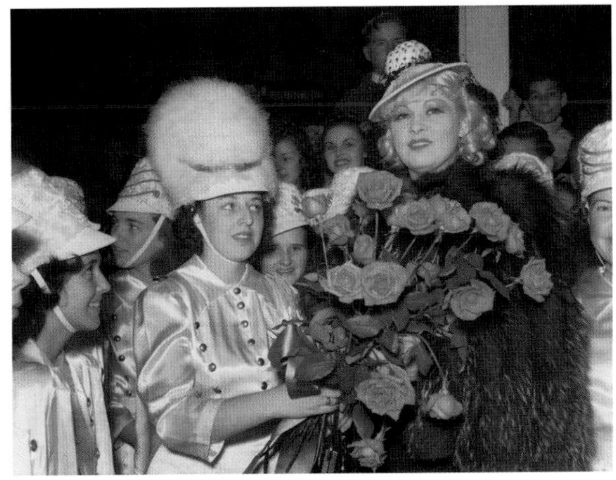

Left: A nighttime view of Foley's Department Store in downtown Houston, ca. 1935. Bob Bailey Studios Photographic Archive, e_bb_0074, Dolph Briscoe Center for American History, the University of Texas at Austin

Above: During her 1939 visit to Houston, Mae West was greeted with a bouquet of roses by an unidentified delegation, probably from a Houston high school girls' drum and bugle corps. It is difficult to tell who had the most awkward smile—the drum majorette, looking simultaneously awestruck and puzzled as she hands the bouquet to an already aging West, or West herself, managing to smile through yet another personal appearance. Bob Bailey Studios Photographic Archive, e_bb_2332, Dolph Briscoe Center for American History, the University of Texas at Austin

the "stars" were largely confined to sports figures and a few major entertainment personalities, frequently stage stars and singers, who made limited appearances in newspapers and magazines of the day. But as films became America's primary form of entertainment, their actors quickly gained the status of celebrity gods and goddesses, with an audience craving more photographs of their favorite stars. The insatiable camera placed a heavy emphasis on looks and appearance, which tied in perfectly with the "dream factories" of the film studios that churned out millions of heavily retouched photos of their stars for adoring fans.

Because of the Baileys' work for the Interstate Theatre chain and Loew's State Theatre, the studio was able to photograph publicity shots of the many film celebrities who visited Houston, particularly from the 1930s to 1950s, when the movie studios were at the height of their power. Stars' contracts often stipulated requirements to make cross-country tours and personal appearances to promote their latest films, and Houston was a frequent stop. The annual Houston Rodeo was another event that enabled the studio to shoot stars, which, by the 1950s, included major celebrities from the new medium of television. In addition, the Baileys shot every aspect of each new Interstate theater's construction and followed those with regular interior and exterior photos for insurance purposes. They had a similar assignment for Loew's State Theatre, which was located downtown and one of Houston's great movie palaces.

The Bailey Studios' founding and subsequent success occurred in tandem with the rapid acceleration of America's commercial culture; the material culture of "things" was ascendant in the early twentieth century and very soon was almost totally dominant. The goods produced by America's vast factory system flooded the everyday lives of almost all Americans, and virtually everyone wanted to possess them. In order to deal with the selling of these rapidly increasing varieties of goods to American consumers, most stores, and particularly department stores, were forced to develop new ways of displaying these goods; thus the development of display or show windows in the larger towns and cities of America. A dream culture quickly emerged in which the minds of waking Americans were flooded with images and fantasies of desirable consumer goods that often occupied some portion of their subconscious, and often fully conscious, thoughts even while they went about their most ordinary daily activities.

Bob Bailey had the remarkable opportunity to document these display windows as they came to play a major role in Houston's downtown scene. Although Bailey was primarily taking these photographs for client department and display supply stores that wanted to document their elaborate displays, he was also able to impart a particularly dreamlike, otherworldly quality to his photos of show windows that went far beyond mere documentation and frequently imparted the very surreal quality that stores were hoping to implant in the minds of prospective consumers. While Bailey's photos of mannequins and displays were more technically advanced, he shared a kinship with Eugene Atget, who documented many of Paris's store window displays, sometimes giving particular attention to those using mannequins. The efforts of store window dressers sometimes to create a surrealistic quality to their displays conveniently merged with the early twentieth-century movement of surrealism, which had a special place in its philosophy for mannequins. To some of the surrealists, mannequins occupied the role of being intermediary figures between the everyday world and the world of the subconscious, since they eerily represented a state between inanimate and living objects.

Considering the fact that in 1900 Houston had only a handful of buildings that qualified as skyscrapers, the city's downtown area must have seemed nothing less than miraculous to Houstonians only three or four decades later, by which time the city even had a few genuine skyscraper "canyons." Houston contained no skyscraper until the construction of the six-story Binz Building in 1898; by the end of the 1920s, the boom of that decade had provided Houston with a number of them, including the tallest building in the entire South, the Gulf Building. While never coming close to the number of skyscrapers in a larger city like Chicago, by 1930 Houston had a large and impressive number of buildings in the city's downtown core certain to give any civic booster a justifiable amount of pride. To the incoming shoppers and visitors from surrounding small towns and rural areas, downtown Houston must have seemed at times as though it were an entirely different world, with the densely packed large buildings and skyscrapers,

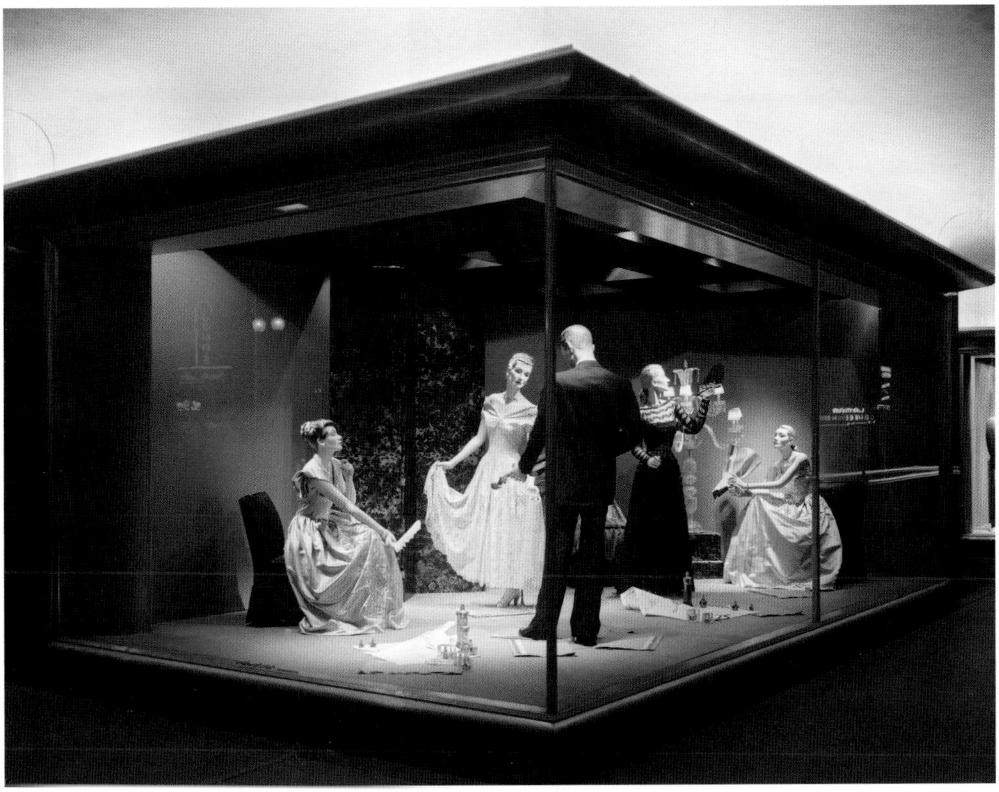

A Foley's display window photographed in 1947. Between the artistry of the display itself, complete with miniature-scale buildings placed near the mannequins to add to the surreal dreamlike quality of the display, and Bailey's skill in composition, with the store's corner angle as the center of the image, this shot is an excellent example of Bailey's artistry. Bailey took the time to shoot this nighttime image in an unusual way and at an unusual angle, when it could have been a very ordinary front-on shot of the display. Bob Bailey Studios Photographic Archive, e_bb_4912, Dolph Briscoe Center for American History, the University of Texas at Austin

huge crowds, the high noise levels accompanying any large urban area, and the large volume of traffic that plagued Houston almost from the very beginning of the automobile age. As architectural illustrator Hugh Ferriss wrote in 1929, summarizing the feelings of a nation that was overwhelmingly rural only a few decades earlier, "Going down into the streets of a modern city must seem a little like Dante's descent into Hades."

Bailey's action photos of Houston's downtown, that is to say shots that included people going about their business as opposed to photos taken only of buildings, were taken in natural space, with people moving along the sidewalks or on the streets and buildings, display windows, and walls in the background. His assignments led to his eventual creation of a chronicle of Houston's downtown activities during the four decades that he was active. This period was, however, the high-water mark of America's downtowns and the important role that they had always played in the lives of most cities and towns. One glance at any of the street scenes taken during these decades reveals that downtown Houston was the place to be, not only for work on weekdays but also for entertainment of all sorts on weekends and holidays. Bailey's death in 1971 coincided with the death knell of the great majority of America's downtown areas, most of them having given way to the effects caused by suburban sprawl, which pulled businesses away to the suburbs. By the time of Bailey's own death, the fate of America's large urban-area downtowns was already sealed.

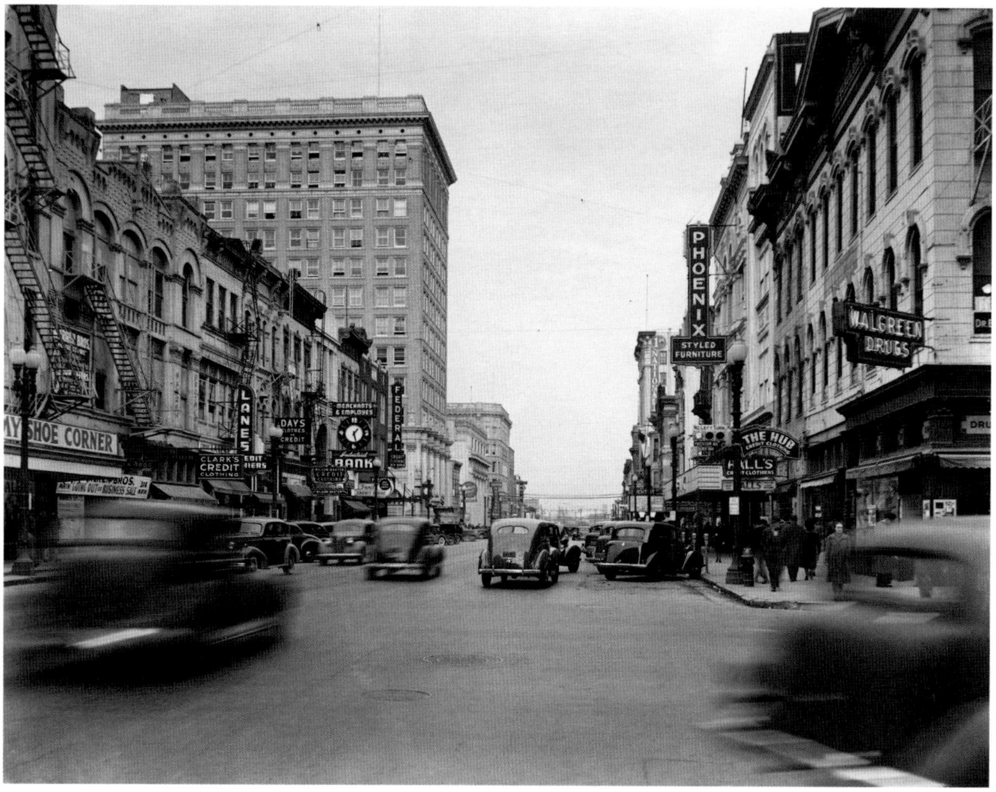

300 block of Main Street, Houston, circa 1940. Bob Bailey Studios Photographic Archive, e_bb_1270, Dolph Briscoe Center for American History, the University of Texas at Austin

Some of the additional Houston developments photographed by the Bailey Studios include the contributions that Houston made during World War II as part of the home-front drive to help defeat the Axis powers; the incredibly rapid changes Houston underwent during the 1960s in its transformation from an oil industry and cattle town to Space City and its association with modernity; the evolution of Houston's transportation systems and the glorification of America's car culture; and Houston's shaping by its natural water networks and weather events, such as the 1935 Buffalo Bayou flood and Hurricane Carla's devastation of the Texas Gulf Coast in September 1961.

Bailey also recorded some of the major events and changes in a few of Houston's neighboring communities. One of the many unique strengths of the Bailey Studios Photographic Archive is its coverage of the Texas City Disaster of April 16, 1947. To this day, that disaster remains the largest and deadliest industrial accident in the history of the United States, yet few people today are aware of it outside of Texas, and even in Texas the memory of it continues to recede with the passage of time. The disaster began adjacent to Texas City's Monsanto chemical plant, where a docked ship packed with ammonium nitrate exploded, causing a chain reaction of exploding ships, spreading fires that reached plant facilities. Five hundred and eighty-one people were killed. One hundred and twenty-one were listed as missing, since not a single body part was ever located, and more than five thousand people were

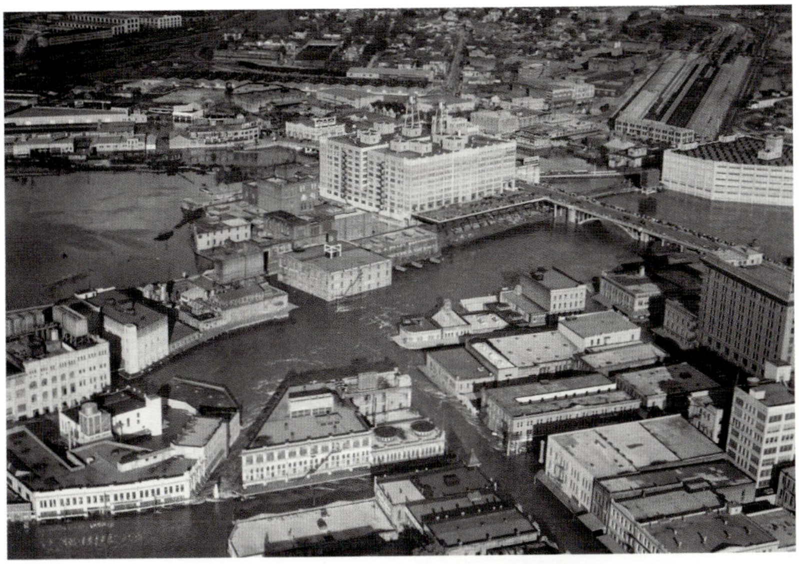

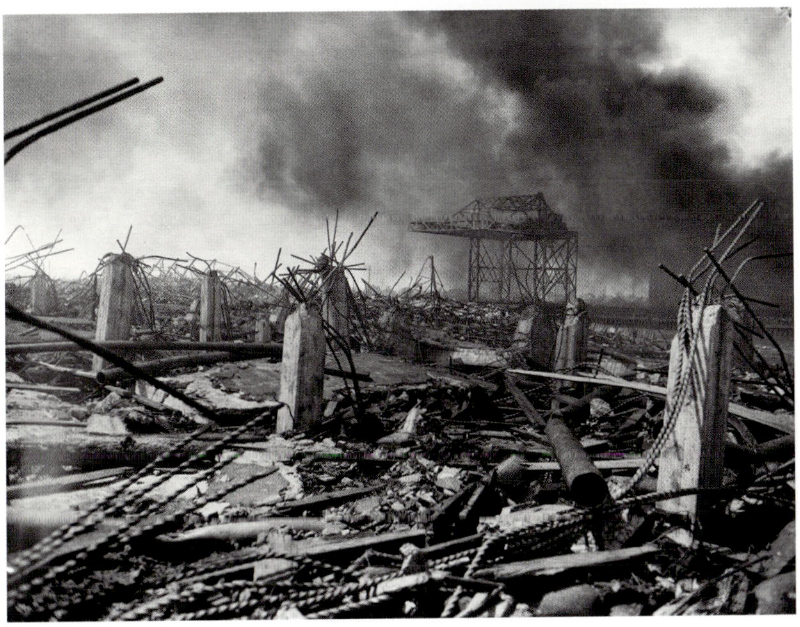

Top: View of flooded streets in downtown Houston, with the Merchandise Mart (used today as part of the campus for the University of Houston) in center background, December 1935. Twenty-five blocks of the downtown area were flooded. The 1935 flood resulted in seven deaths and nearly three million dollars in property damage, which spurred the creation of the intricate flood control system still in use today. Bob Bailey Studios Photographic Archive, e_bb_2467, Dolph Briscoe Center for American History, the University of Texas at Austin

Bottom: View of the destruction following the explosion and fires of the Texas City Disaster, 1947. The scene, in which all that remains of an industrial area are twisted pieces of iron and a few concrete pylons, appears more like photos of the nuclear devastation of Hiroshima or Nagasaki than any American city at the time. Bob Bailey Studios Photographic Archive, e_bb_0986. Dolph Briscoe Center for American History, the University of Texas at Austin

injured in some way, with many of them receiving wounds that left them physically disabled for the rest of their lives. The nearby town of Texas City, with a population of about eight thousand, was almost leveled.

Bailey was hired by one of the news services to cover the disaster, and he raced to Texas City the day the disaster occurred. He appears to have remained on site for at least a few days, allowing him to take a large number of photos chronicling the devastation. Bailey liked to experiment with color film, and he shot color motion picture footage of the disaster's aftermath. The color images taken from that film that appear in this book are likely the first color scenes ever published of the Texas City explosion.

The photographs that follow in this book represent only the smallest fraction of the images that comprise the Bailey Studios Photographic Archive. It is worth keeping in mind that Bob Bailey's

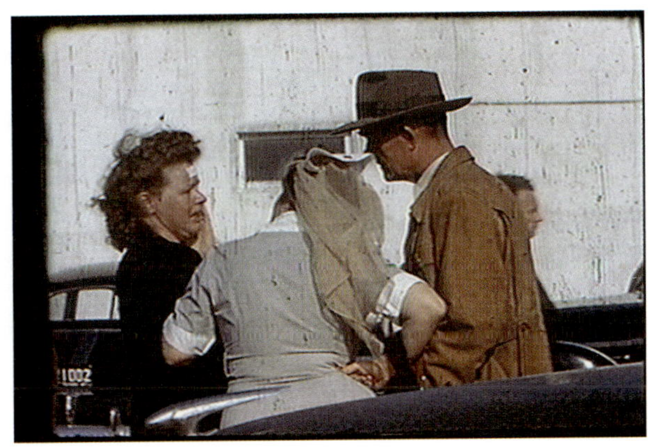

Film still from Bailey's color footage of the Texas City Disaster, 1947. Bob Bailey Studios Photographic Archive, e_bb_6418, Dolph Briscoe Center for American History, the University of Texas at Austin

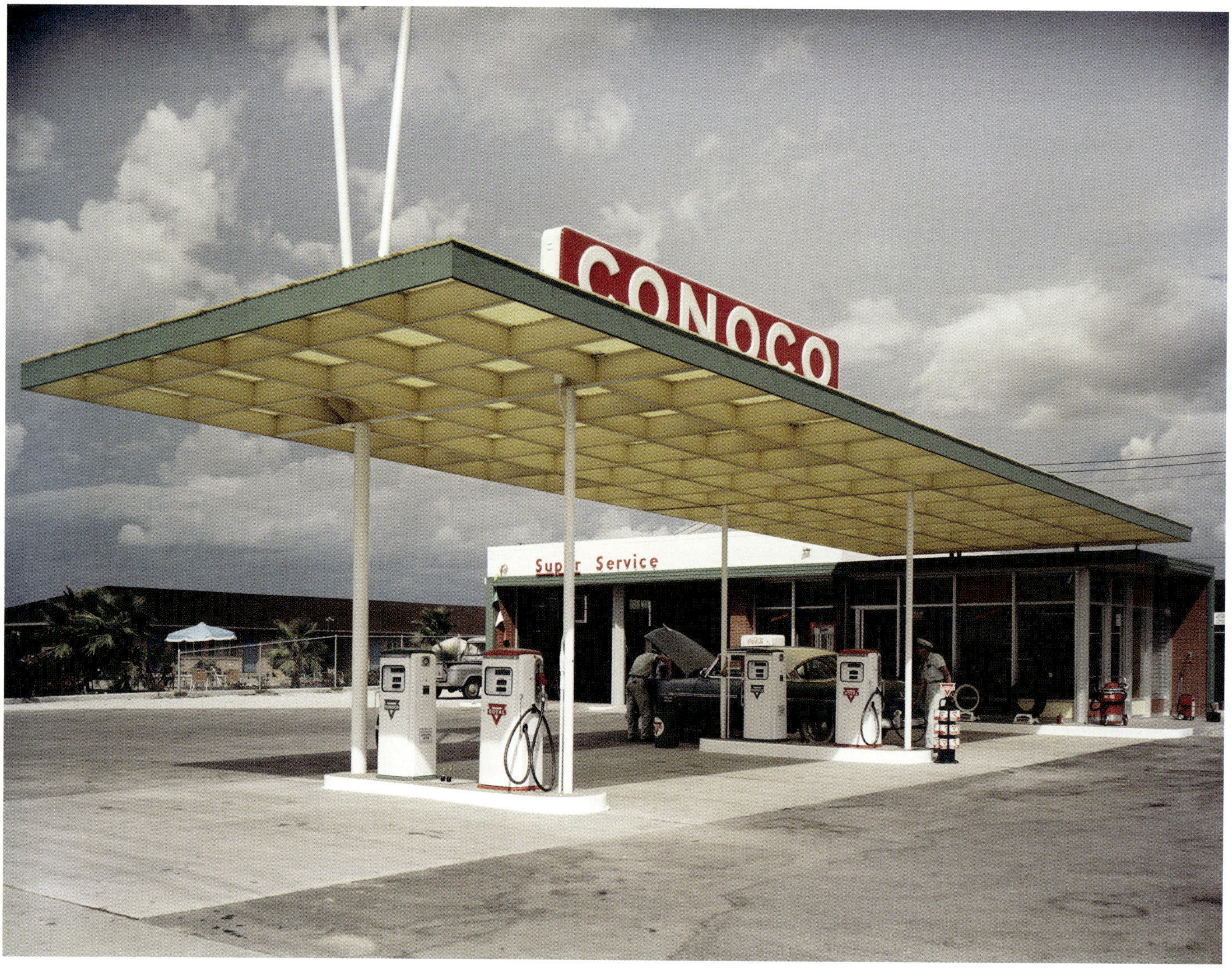

Conoco gas station, November 1958. Bob Bailey Studios Photographic Archive, e_bb_1950, Dolph Briscoe Center for American History, the University of Texas at Austin

subjects were determined by his paying clients. However artistic many of his photographs are, he was taking these photos for commercial reasons. Therefore, the archive includes thousands of photos of movie theaters and film celebrities from Bailey's work for the Interstate Theatre chain and Loew's State Theatre, two of his biggest clients; many, many pictures of Foley's Department Store, a mainstay Bailey customer for decades; photographs of gas station openings and oil-related scenes, due to his work for the oil industry; and countless images of the city's office buildings for corporate clients. Above all, the archive contains an enormous number of one of the largest group of subjects that Bailey ever photographed: industrial parts, equipment, and tools for Houston industrial giants, including the Hughes Tool Company. The number of differing subjects that Bailey shot is one of the key facets that make the collection so important to such a wide variety of historians and other researchers. Briscoe archivist Amy Bowman comments that, "I'm continually surprised by the new ways our researchers approach the archive—it's a testament to the diversity of its subject matter. Just in the past year our researchers have included everyone from a historian documenting the growth of suburbs during the late-twentieth century to a jukebox aficionado investigating early machine models."

Each Bailey image of Houston is a single moment of the city frozen in time, but collectively they present an overall picture of a great city in the making: a downtown striving to be the best, biggest, and tallest; birthday parties, snow days, celebrations, and rodeos; opulent department stores; Hollywood stars descending into town; amazingly rapid industrial and commercial growth; and the inexorable march of the suburbs. In gazing at these photos, starkly realistic images are intermingled with our sometimes hazy, stylized memories and dreams of the past. The photographs will elicit different responses from different viewers, but all of the images will revive and strengthen existing memories while kindling new discoveries. Because of photography's ability to convey the common experiences shared by all of us, these photos will appeal not only to those readers who carry nostalgia for the Houston of the past but also will resonate with people who never lived in Houston and present-day Houstonians too young to have lived during the times chronicled by Bob Bailey and his studio. For those who grew up or lived in Houston from the 1930s through the 1990s, viewing the Bailey photographs included in this book will provide a glimpse into Houston's shared collective memory, while also evoking singularly personal recollections.

1 Epigraph: Proust, *Remembrance of Things Past*, 693.

1 *once its doors are closed*: Proust quoted in Hudson, *Marcel Proust*, 302.

2 *one hundred commercial photography studios by 1853*: Carroll, *Popular Modernity in America*, 90.

2 *tiresome and technically difficult*: Goldberg and Silberman, *American Photography*, 15–19.

There is a good summary of America's infatuation with daguerreotype portraits in Rosenblum, *A History of World Photography*, 45–52.

2 *the traveling itinerant photographer*: Larkin, *Where We Worked*, 29; "Portraits in the Open Air: The Rise of the Itinerant Photographer," *Picturing the Family*, accessed September 4, 2015, http://www.open.edu/openlearn/history-the-arts/culture/visual-art/picturing-the-family/content-section-0.

2 *classified photography . . . as one of the fine arts*: Goldberg and Silberman, 21–25; Rosenblum, 325–337, 413–422.

4 Andre Gide, *The Immoralist*, 191.

5 *Bob's later interest in filmmaking*: Jim Bailey, interview by Steven Strom, Houston, Texas, June 14, 2013.

5 *never lacked clients and assignments*: Ibid.

6 *Jim started working at the studio*: Ibid.

6 *an innate ability for photographic composition*: Ibid.

8 *locations around the world*: Ibid; "Space Center Hospital Opens Bob Bailey Room," *Spaceland News Citizen* (Houston, TX), May 8, 1971.

9 *The Houston Story*: "The Houston Story," Internet Movie Database, accessed June 30, 2015.

9 *He died April 20, 1971*: "R. H. Bailey Services Set For Friday," *Houston Chronicle*, April 28, 1971; "Bob Bailey Services Set at 1:30 Today," *Houston Post*, April 30, 1971.

9 *documentarian and filmmaker in his own right*: Jim Bailey interview.

10 *abreast of trade periodicals*: Ibid.

11 *a modern industrial facility*: For photographic work by Berenice Abbott and Esther Bubley, see Yochelson and Schmid, *Esther Bubley* and Greene, *The Photographs of Esther Bubley*.

11 *remade in the name of modernity*: For Eugene Atget's work in Paris, see *Atget: The Art of Documentary Photography*, National Gallery of Art, Washington, DC, accessed June 29, 2015, http://www.nga.gov/feature/atget/bio.shtm.

12 *about to leap into passing cars*: "History of Billboard Advertising," Capitol Outdoor Advertising, accessed July 30, 2015, http://www.capitoloutdoor.com/ooh-media/billboard-advertising/history-billboard-ad vertising/history-billboard-advertising

14 *one of Houston's great movie palaces*: Eric Hanson, "Remember When," 9.

14 *A dream culture quickly emerged*: For information on the rise of the consumer culture in America, see Lizabeth Cohen, *A Consumer's Republic* and Gabrielle Esperdy, *Modernizing Main Street*.

14 *a state between inanimate and living objects*: Laura Muir, *Lionel Feininger*, 38–40.

15 *"like Dante's descent into Hades"*: Hugh Ferriss, *The Metropolis of Tomorrow*, 18.

16 *Texas City Disaster of April 16, 1947*: Tess Arrington et al. *We Were There*, iv–xi.

17 *Photo, top*: "Houston's Devastating Flood of 1935," *Houston Chronicle*, June 2, 2015, accessed July 23, 2015, http://www.houstonchronicle.com/local/bayou-city-history/article/Houston-s-devastating-flood-of-1935-6293100.php

PLATES

1930 TO 1945

A CITY COMES OF AGE

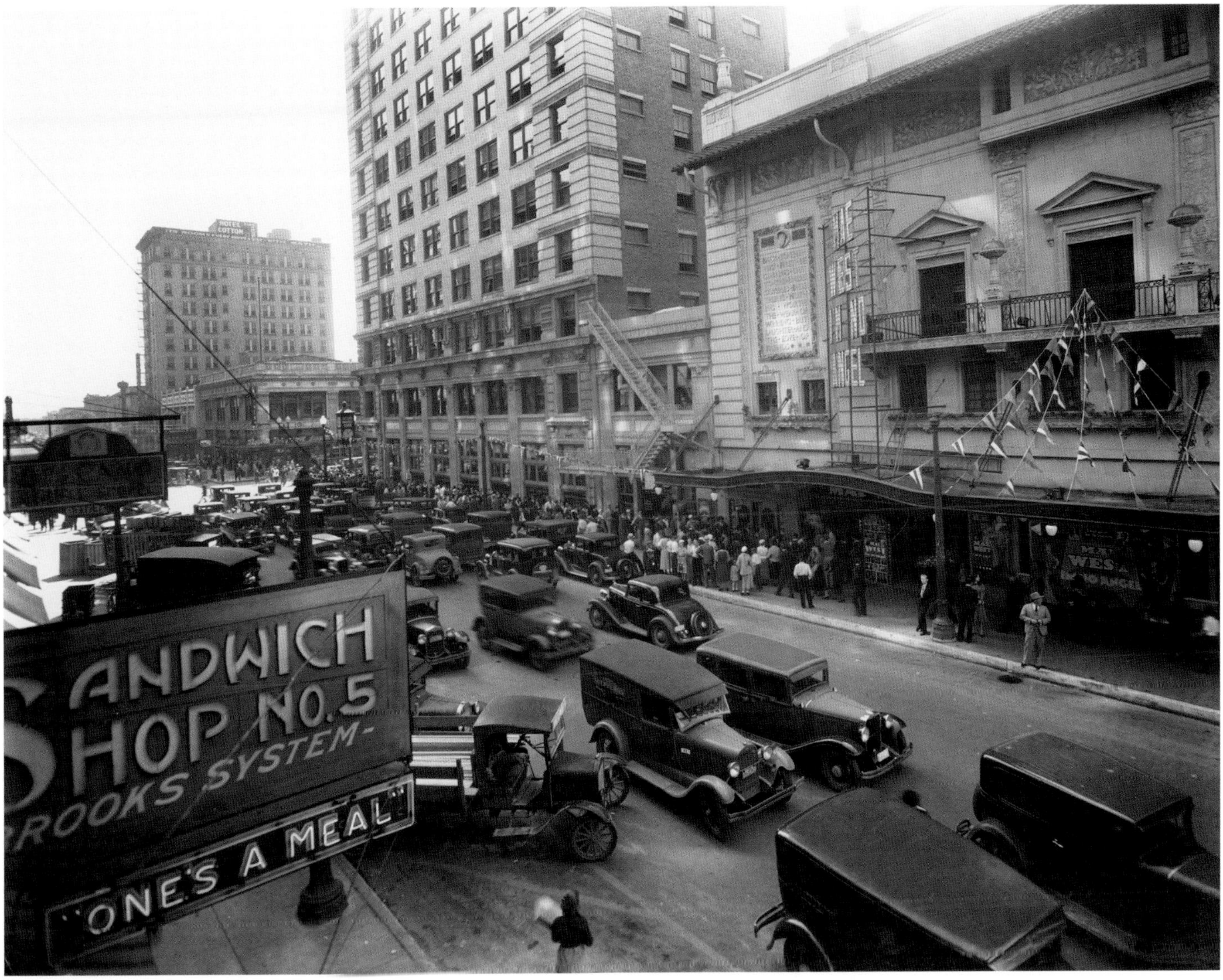

This photo shows the 900 block of Rusk Street in December 1933, with the Majestic Theatre on the right. Despite the fact that Houston was still in the early stages of America's emerging car culture, the city's streets were already jammed with considerable traffic. In 1908, only about eighty cars were registered in the city.

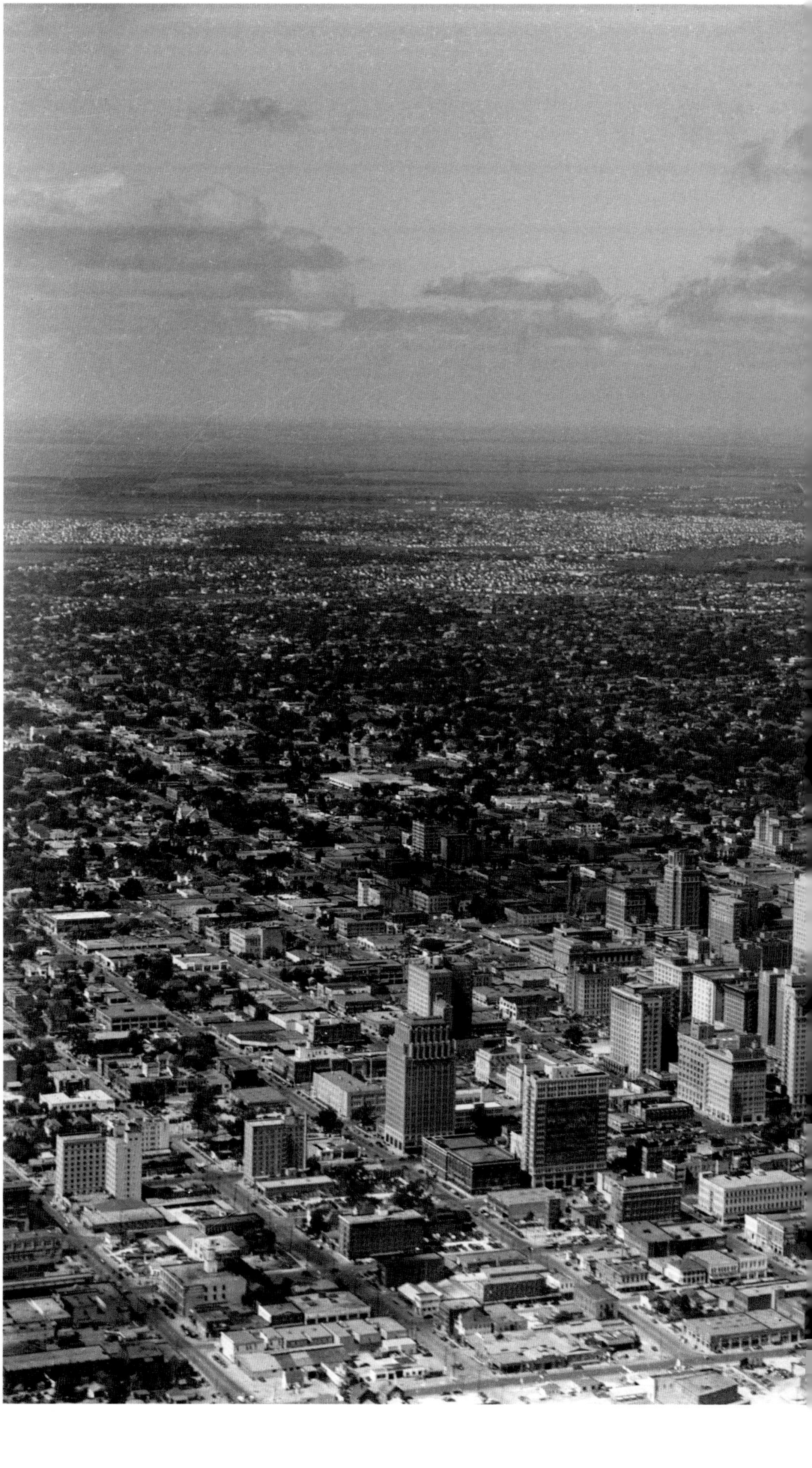

Aerial view of Houston, ca. 1934. Bob Bailey was an early aerial photographer in the Houston commercial photography market, and it soon became one of his best-known specialties.

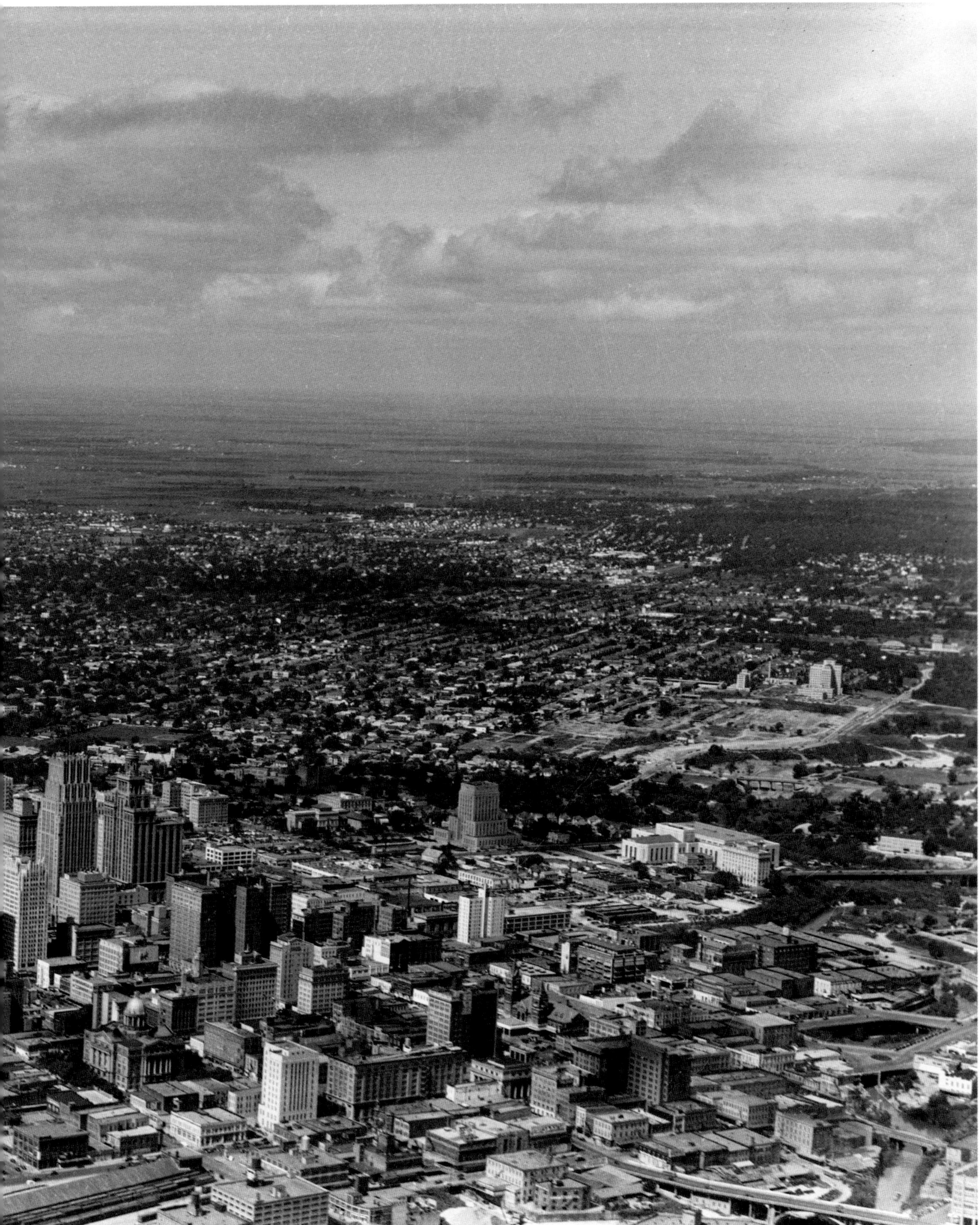

View of Main Street with San Jacinto Hotel, located at Main and Walker, in center foreground, ca. 1940. When the ten-story hotel opened in 1911, it was another addition to Houston's burgeoning skyline, and its elaborate ornamentation added a touch of class to Houston's principal commercial corridor. The hotel was converted to an office building in 1950.

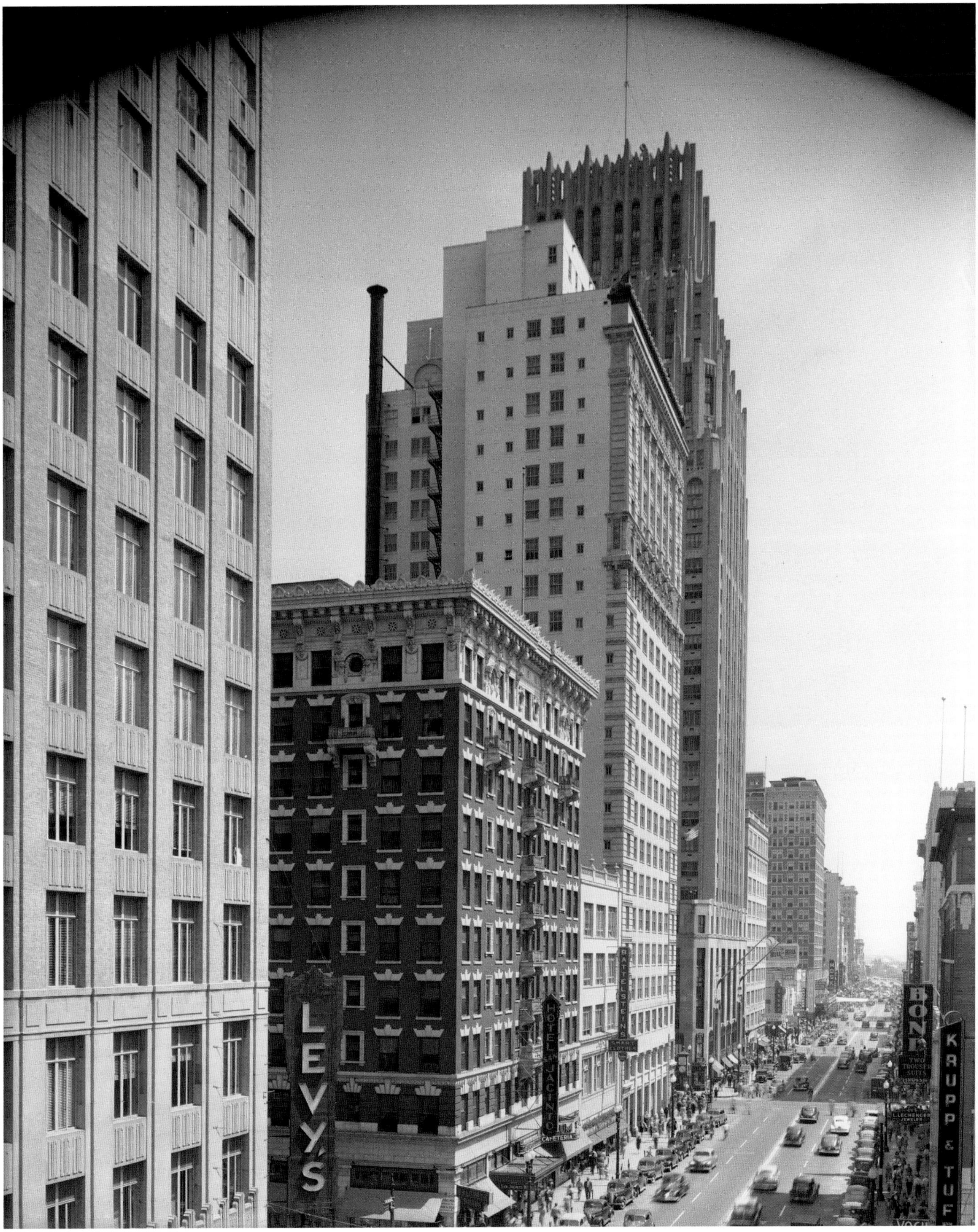
LEVY'S
CAFETERIA
KRUPP & TUF

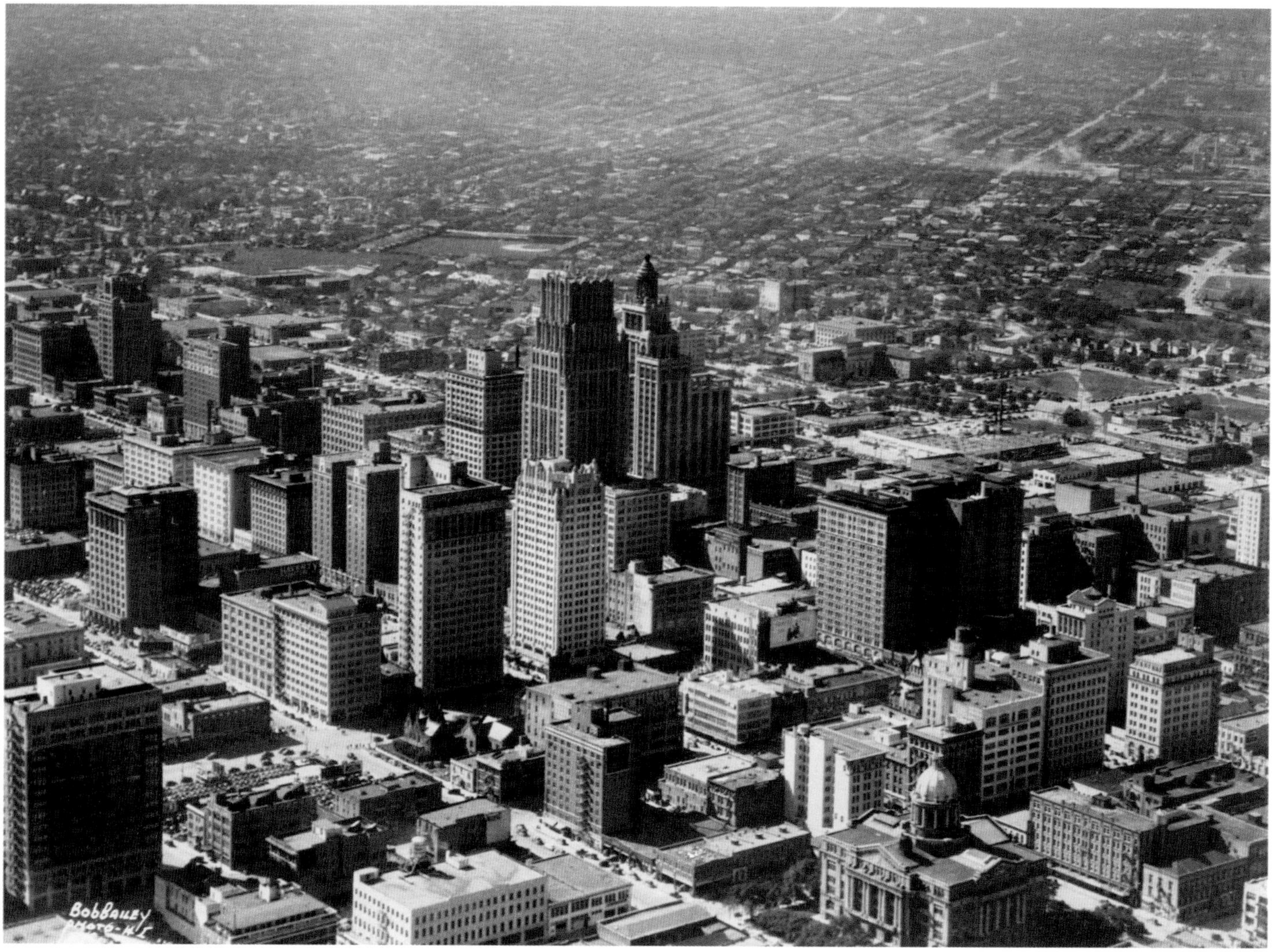

A closer aerial view of downtown Houston, ca. 1935, with Harris County Courthouse at lower right, and the Gulf and Esperson buildings at center.

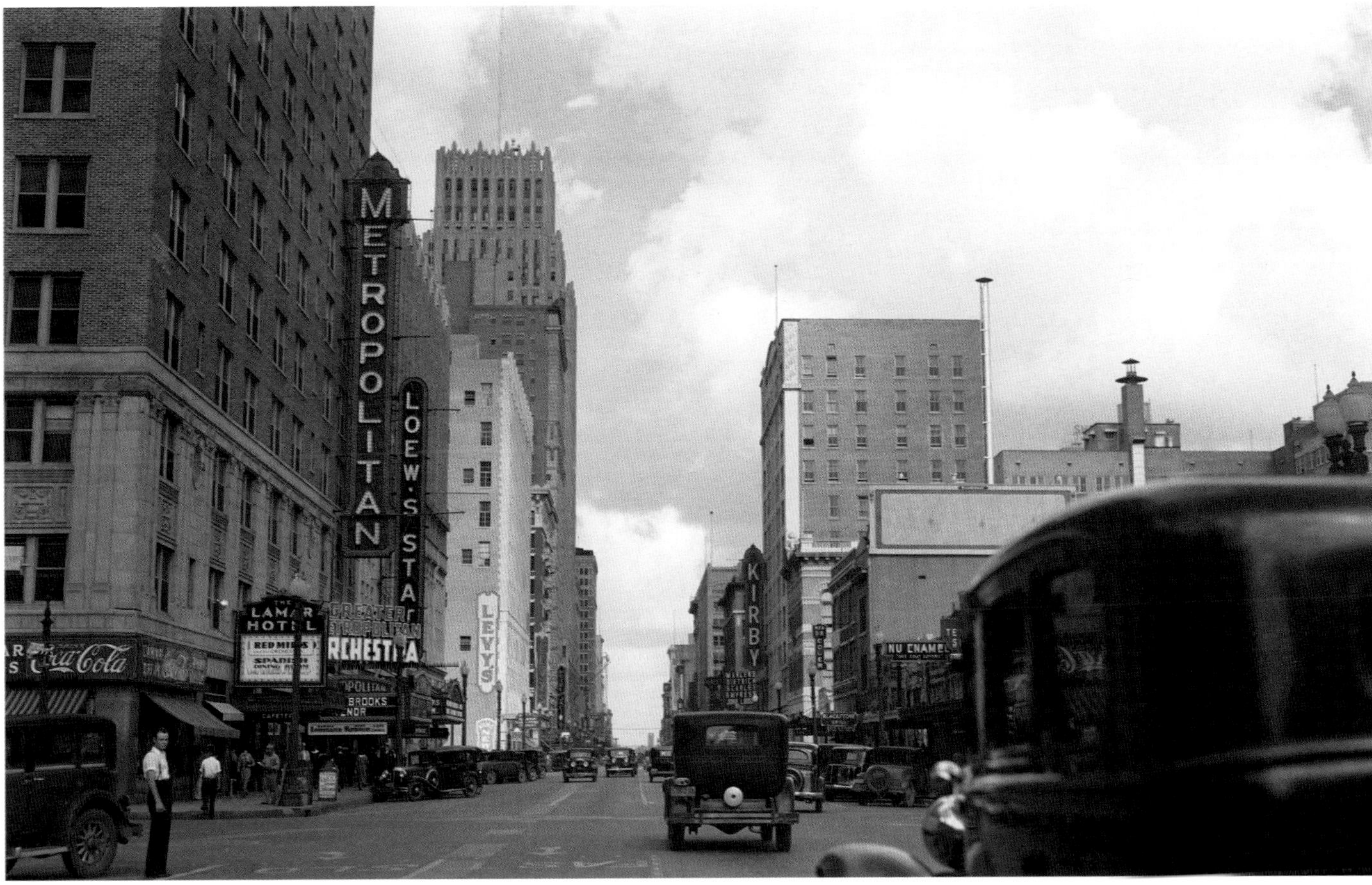

Street-level view of Main Street, looking north from Lamar Avenue up Theatre Row, 1934. The Lamar Hotel is at the far left.

Another view of Main Street, looking north from Loew's State Theatre toward Levy's and Foley Brothers Department Stores. This photo was taken for the Houston Chamber of Commerce in October 1940. Much of the area was known as Theatre Row, Houston's primary entertainment district, the place to see and be seen on Friday and Saturday nights.

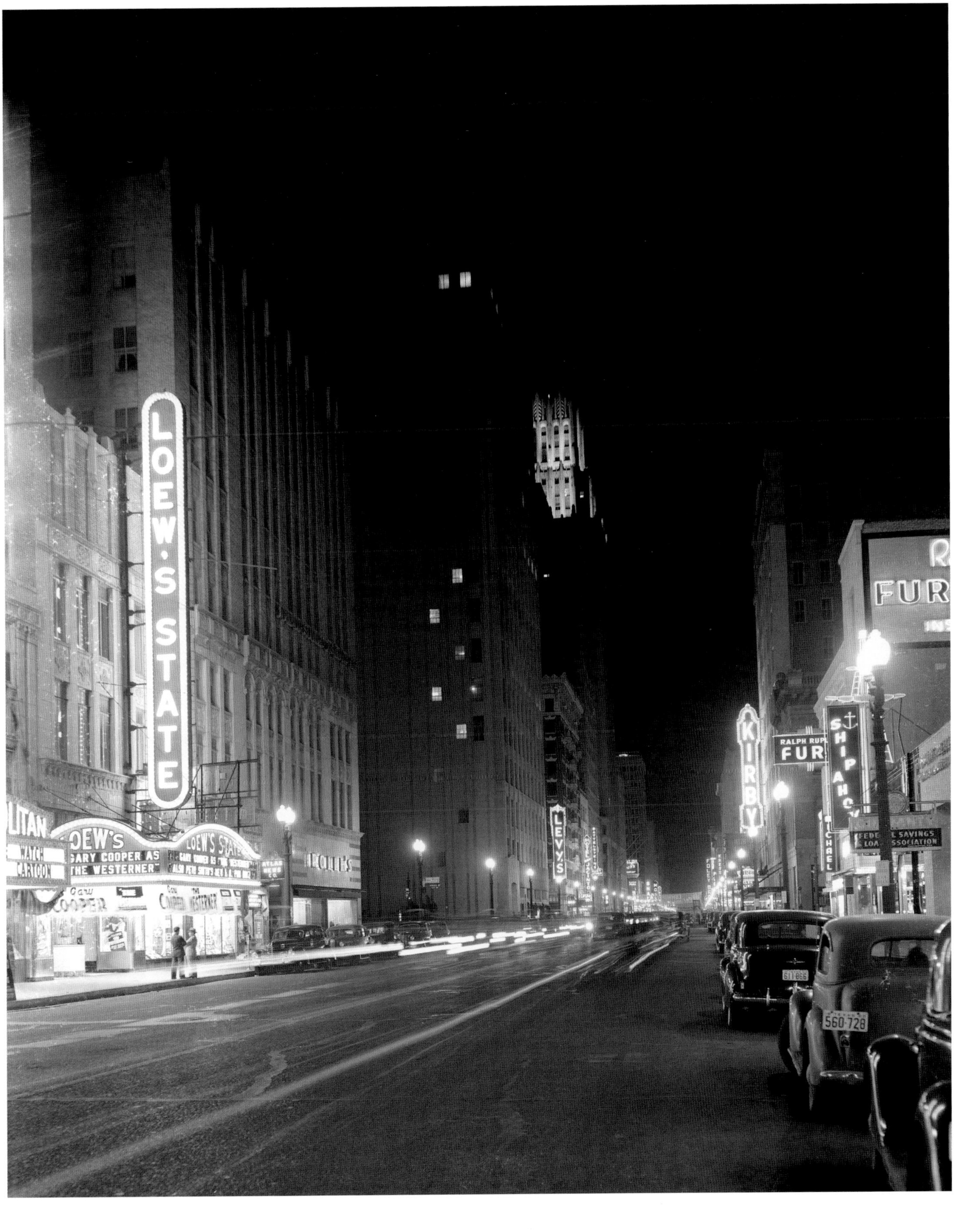
LOEW'S STATE
LOEW'S
GARY COOPER AS
"THE WESTERNER"
WATCH
CARTOON
LEVY'S
KIRBY
SHIP AHOY

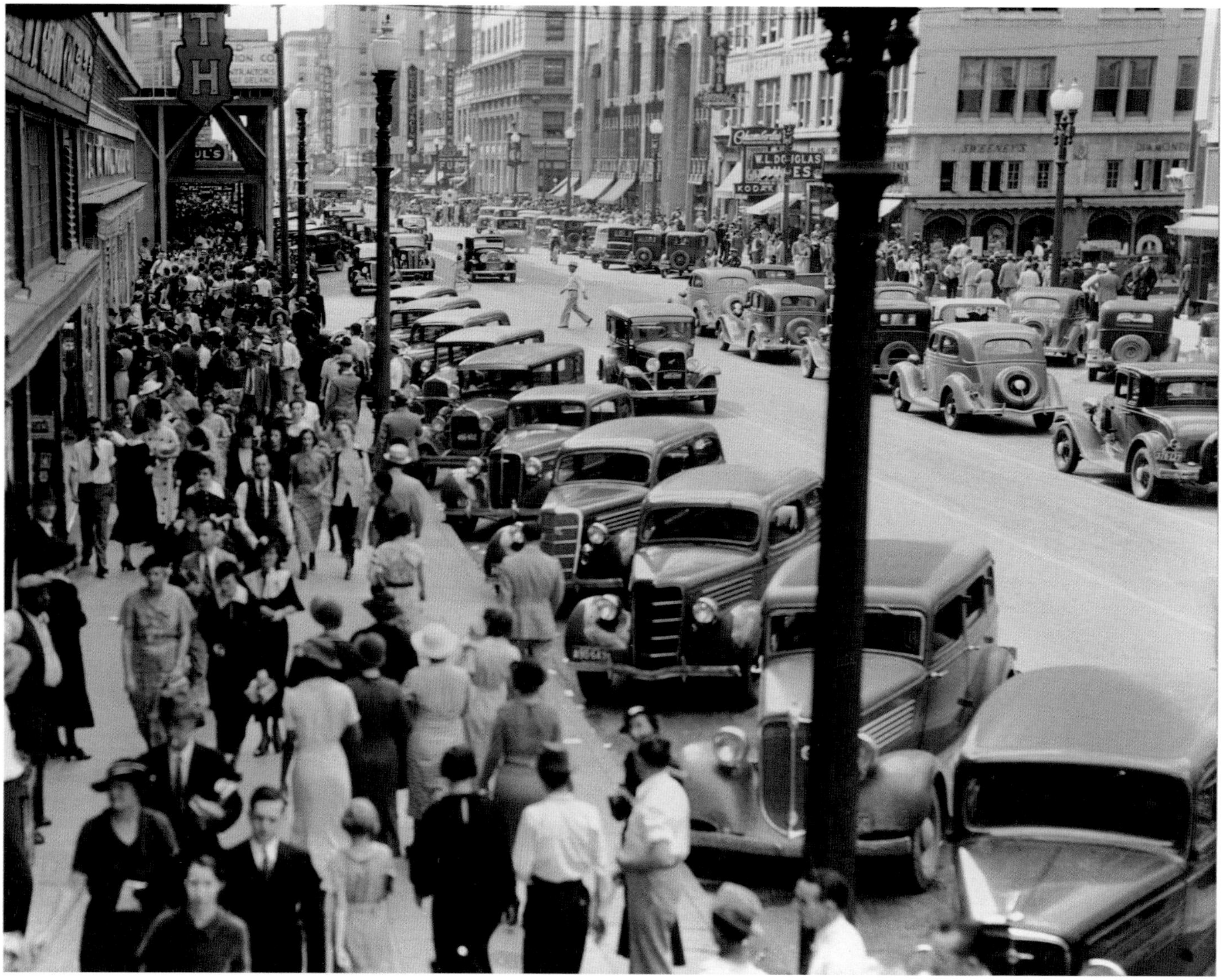

Main Street scene taken in 1935. This shot shows the typical throngs of people and automobiles that jammed Houston's downtown core prior to the city's suburban expansion and the development of the extensive tunnel system, which virtually removed pedestrians from downtown streets.

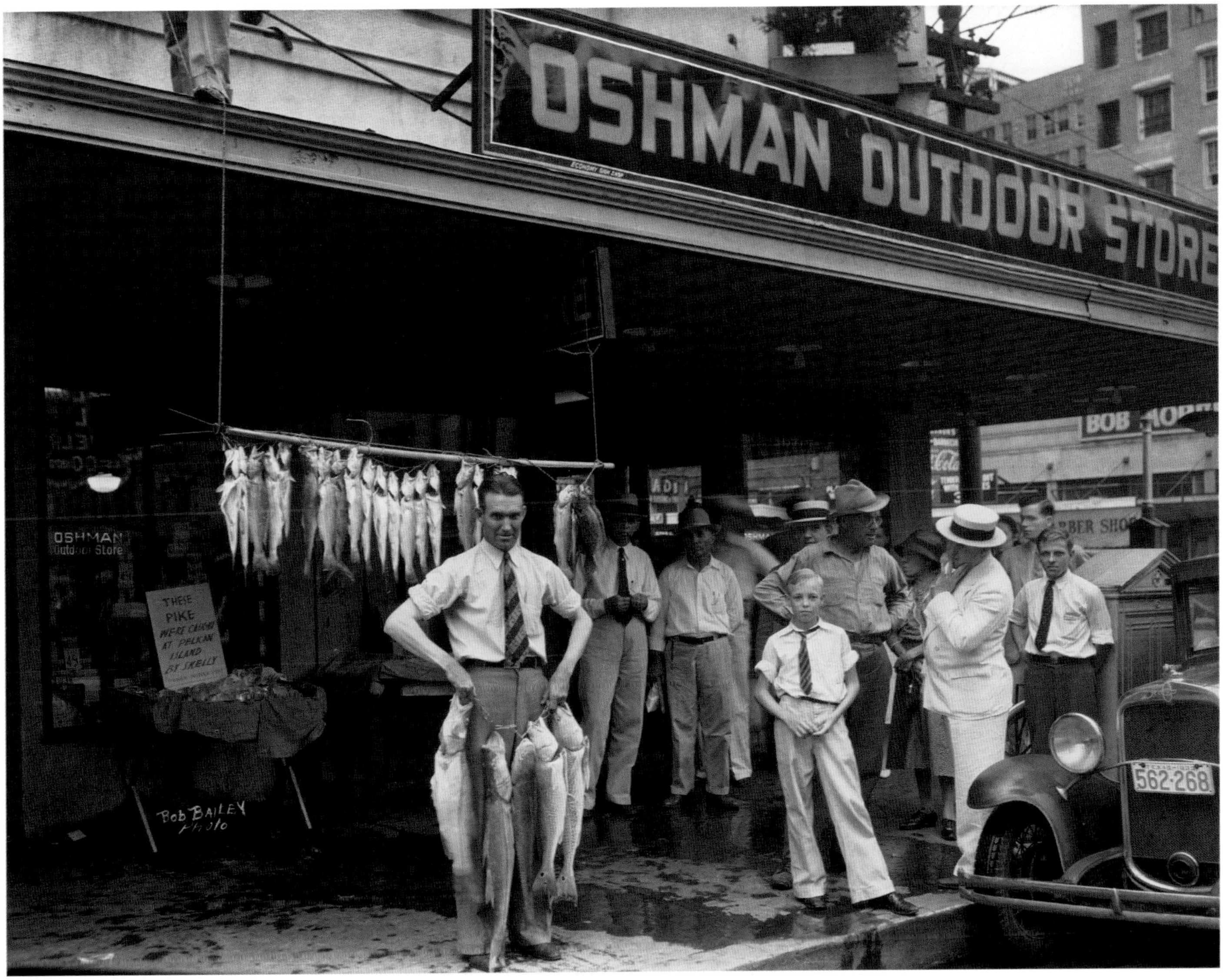

A man displays his catch in front of Oshman's Outdoor Store in June 1933. The group of onlookers included Bob Bailey's younger brother Marvin, who is the small boy standing to the fisherman's left at the near-center of the photograph.

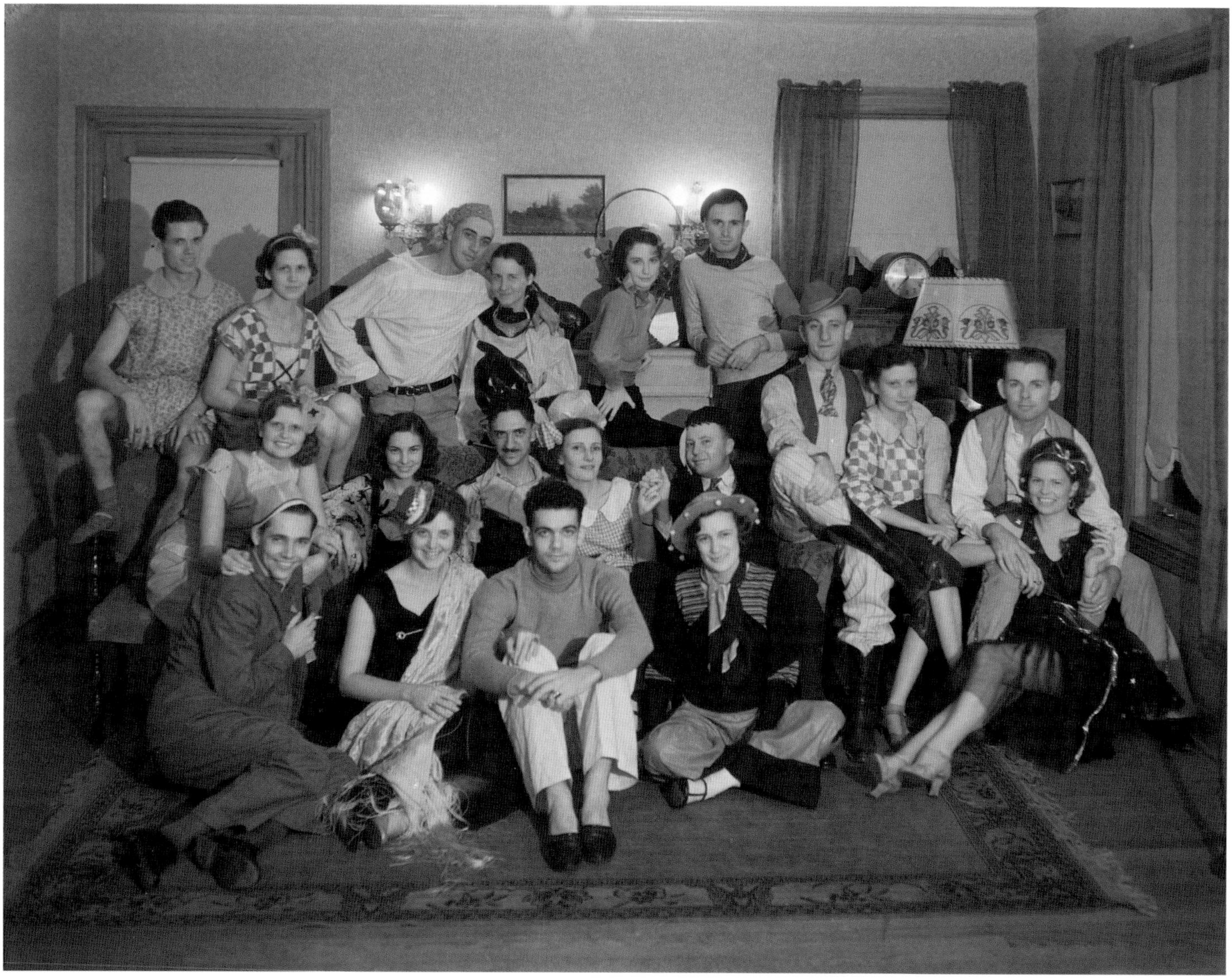

Above: Houstonian Everett Rodgers held this Halloween costume party in his home on October 31, 1932. Despite much recent news coverage of Halloween turning into an adult festival and away from children, some adults have clearly always had a fondness for the holiday.

Facing: Hill Billie's Band performed at the Texan Theatre in 1934, probably as part of the pre-film entertainment that theaters once provided for their audiences. With such a large segment of Houston's population comprised of formerly rural people, "hillbilly" and country and western bands and music were staples of local entertainment venues.

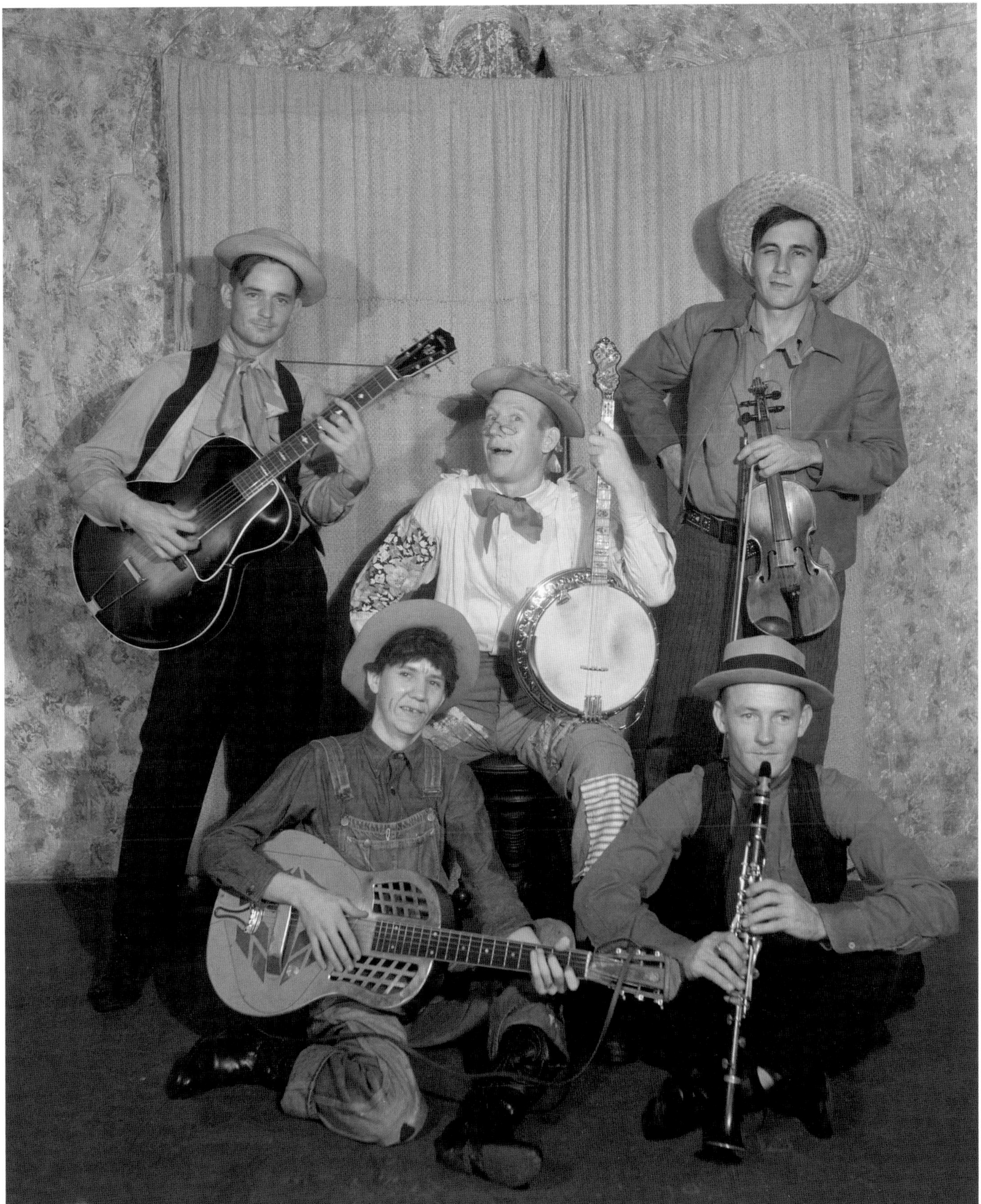

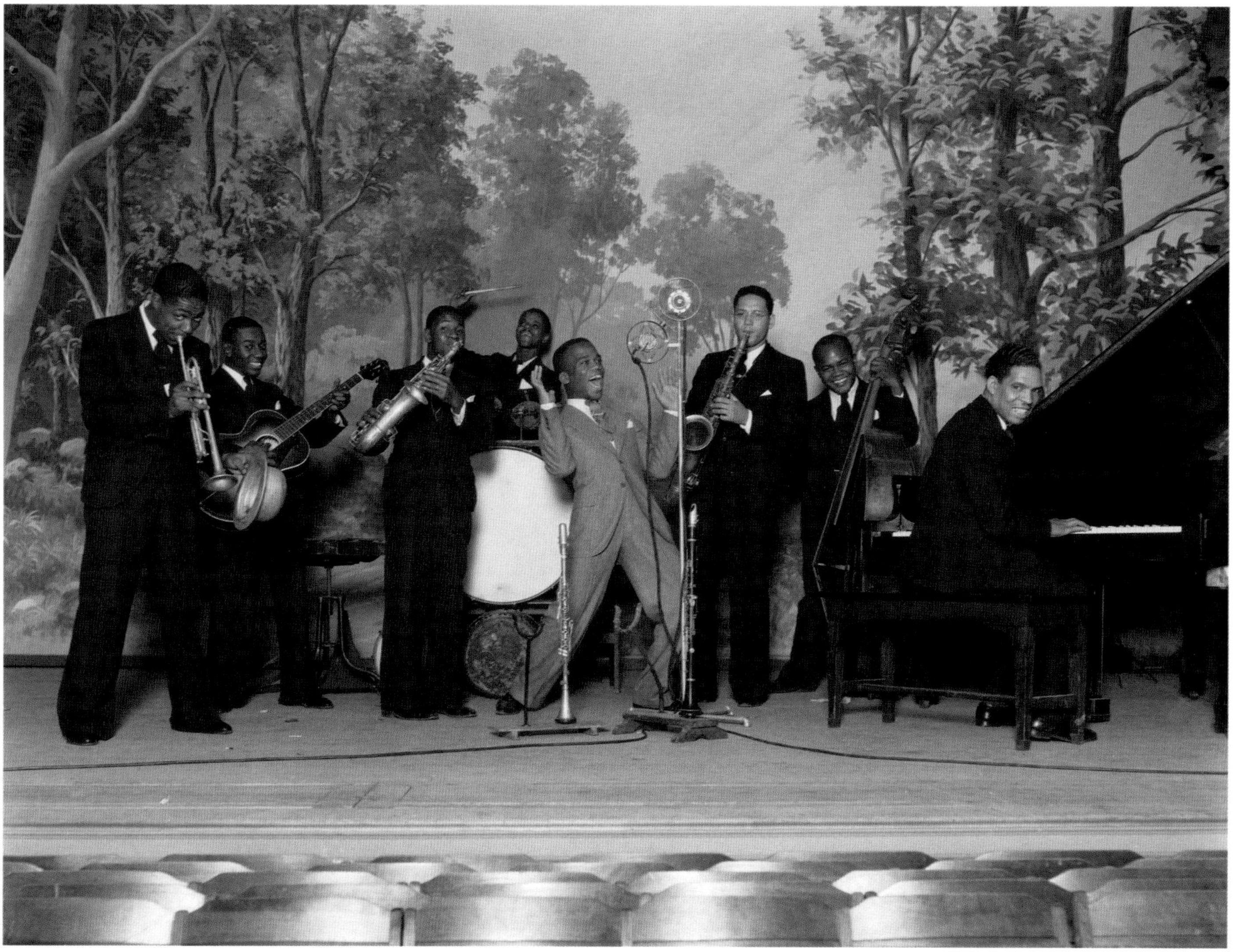

The Sunset Royals performing at the Harlem Grill in October 1934. The Royals may have served for a time as the in-house orchestra of the popular Harlem Grill nightclub. The club was located at the intersection of West Dallas and Heiner, on the northwest corner. West Dallas was the center of the thriving commercial and entertainment district for African Americans who had lived in the Fourth Ward's Freedmen's Town community since the abolition of slavery. Freedmen's Town was eventually destroyed by the construction of I-45 through the heart of the area, in tandem with some "development" projects that failed to include the input or participation of the community's African American residents and business owners.

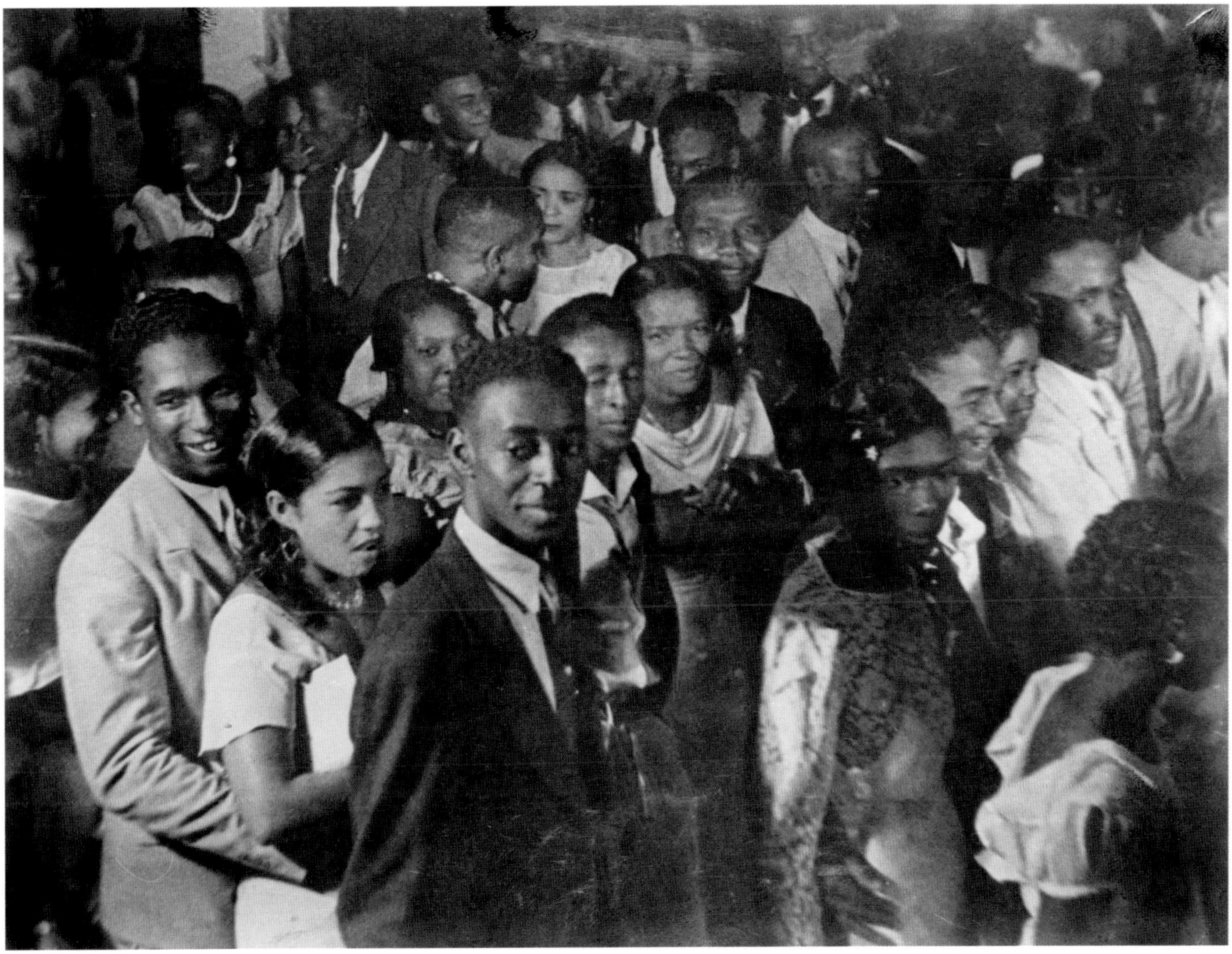

Part of the crowd who came to hear the Harlem Grill orchestra in October 1934.

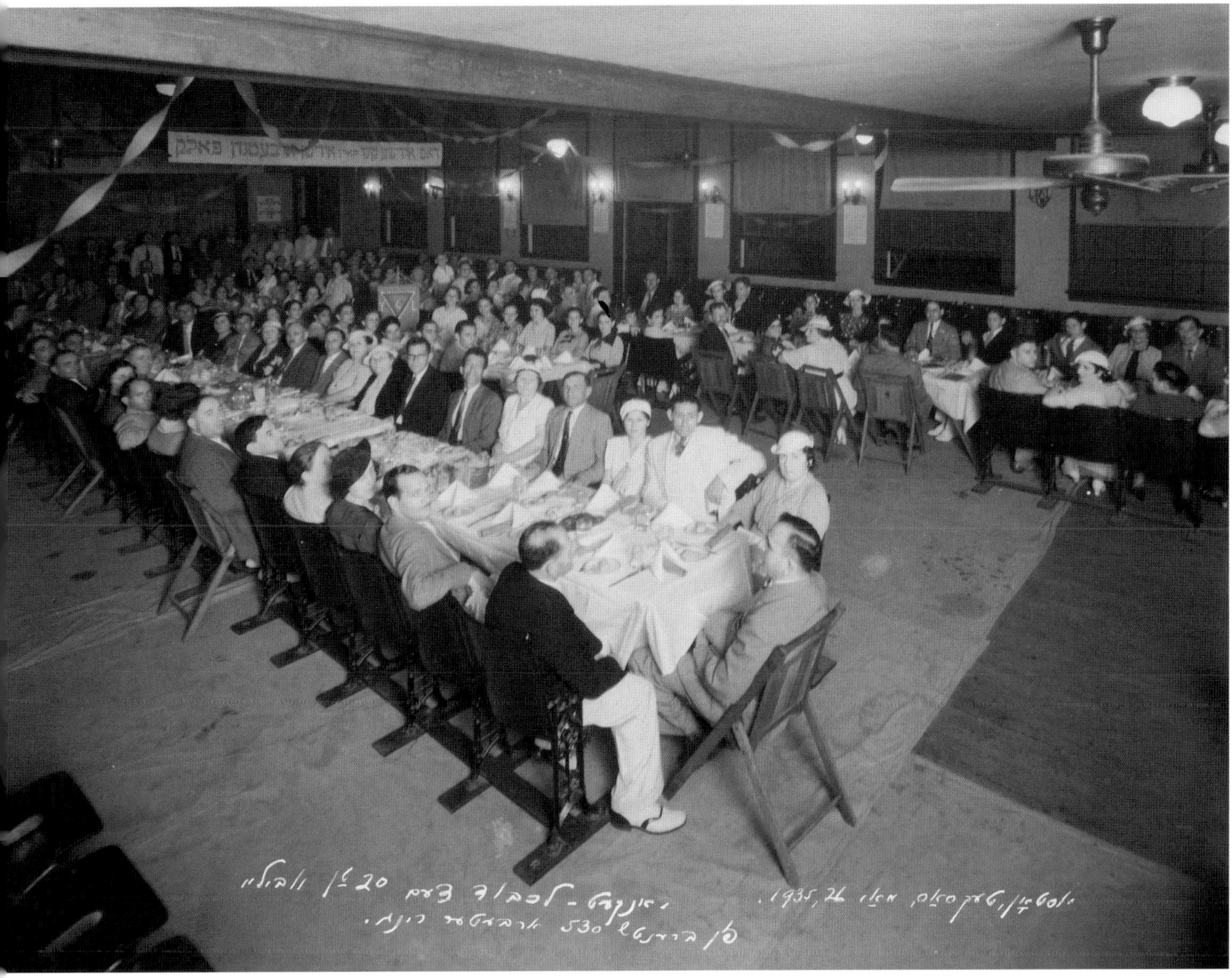

The Kessler family hired Bailey to photograph this birthday gathering on May 26, 1935. The banner stretched across the rear of the meeting hall is in Hebrew. Bailey photographed hundreds of meetings, receptions, and celebrations during his career.

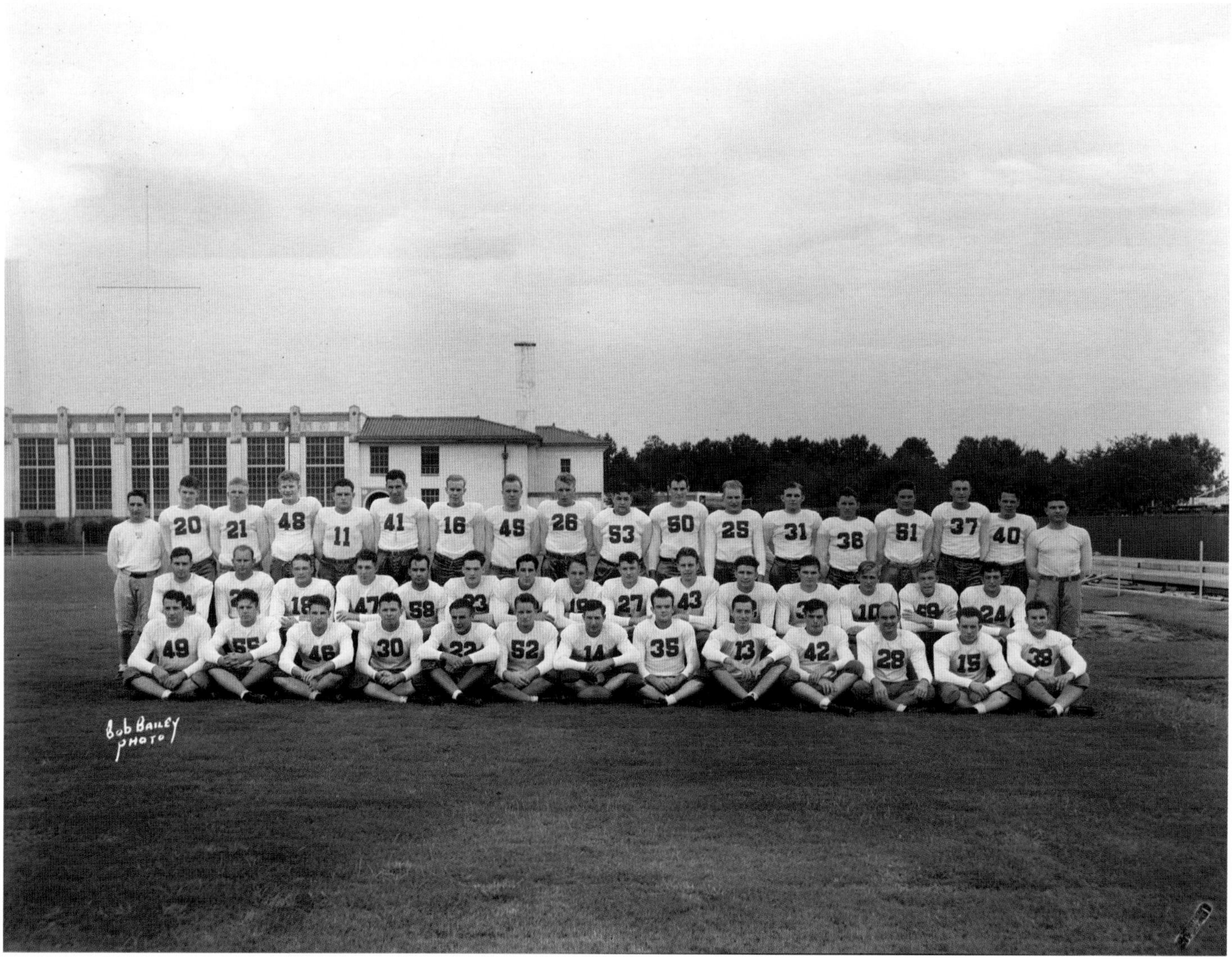

Rice Institute's football team for 1935. Team member Bill Wallace was named All American Halfback and Outstanding Back of the Southwest Conference that year. Bob Bailey had a long-standing relationship with Rice Institute, which changed its name to Rice University in 1960, and its sports department. As Rice's official sports photographer, he was a member of Rice's football traveling party. Bailey also filmed Rice football games beginning in the 1930s, something that was unusual for the time.

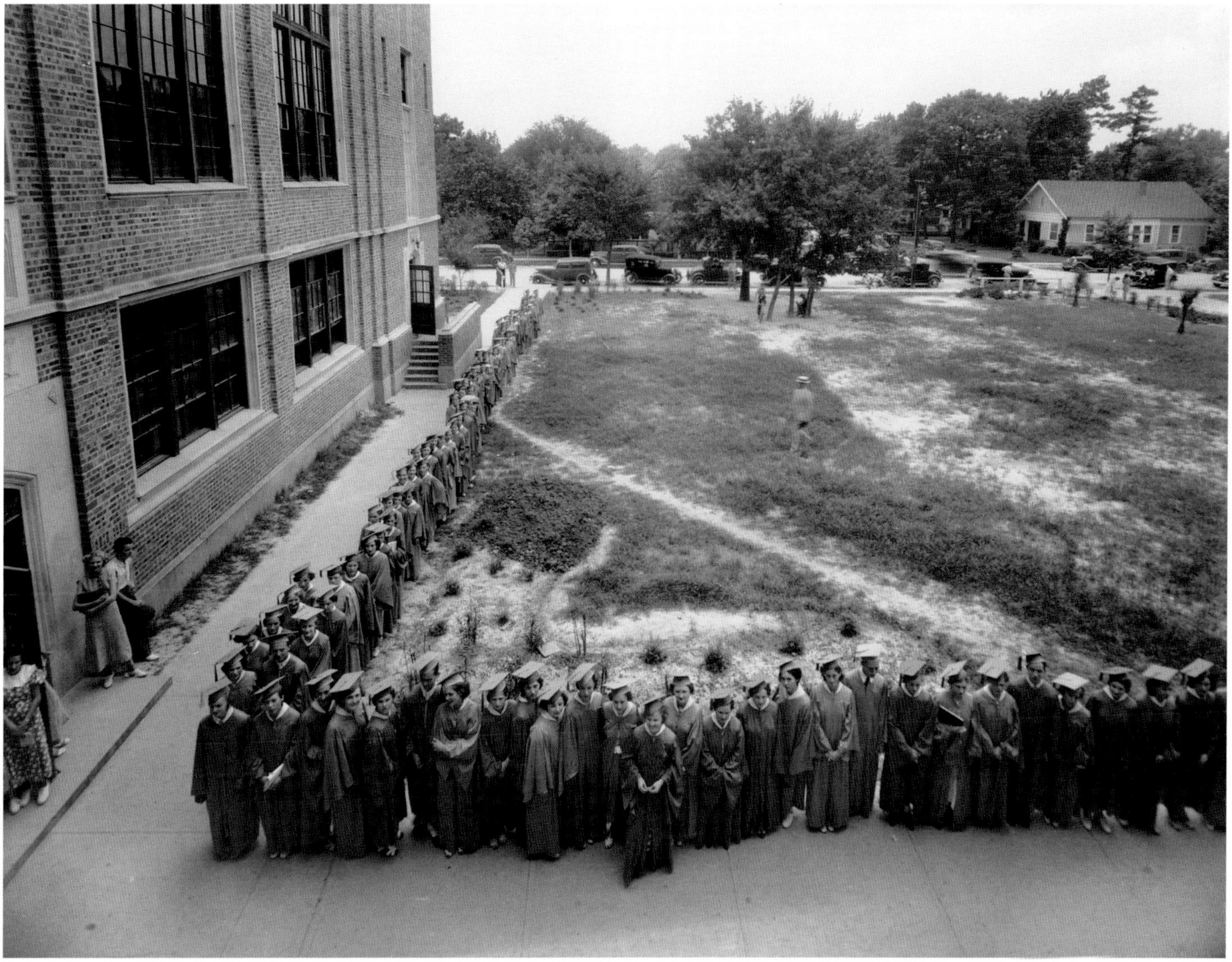

The 1936 graduating class of John H. Reagan Senior High School, which first opened in 1926, stands in line before their graduation ceremony on June 8. At least as early as 1933, Bob Bailey served as the photographer for *The Pennant,* Reagan High's yearbook.

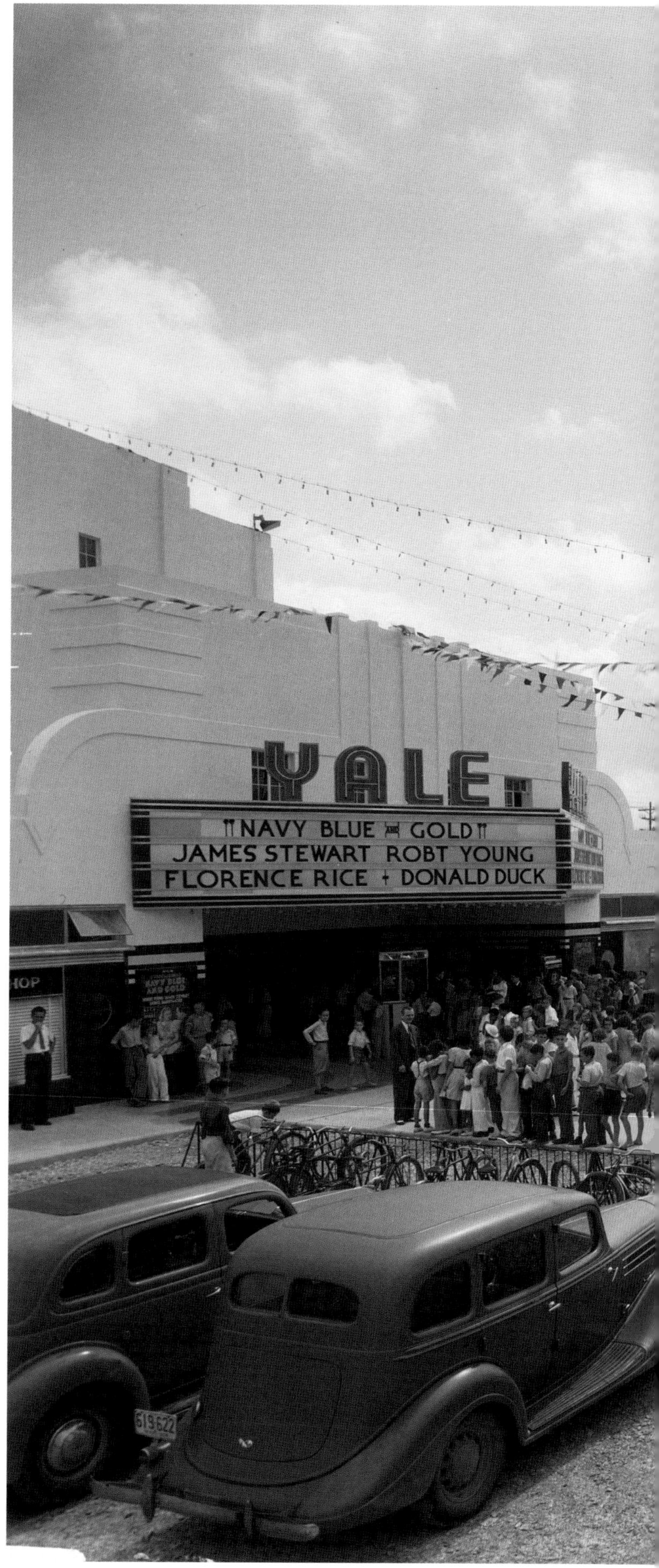

Lines of children waiting to get into Interstate's Yale Theatre on its opening day on May 20, 1938. The children were members of the Popeye Club, which featured Saturday morning films, cartoons, and other entertainment. The Yale was demolished in 1972.

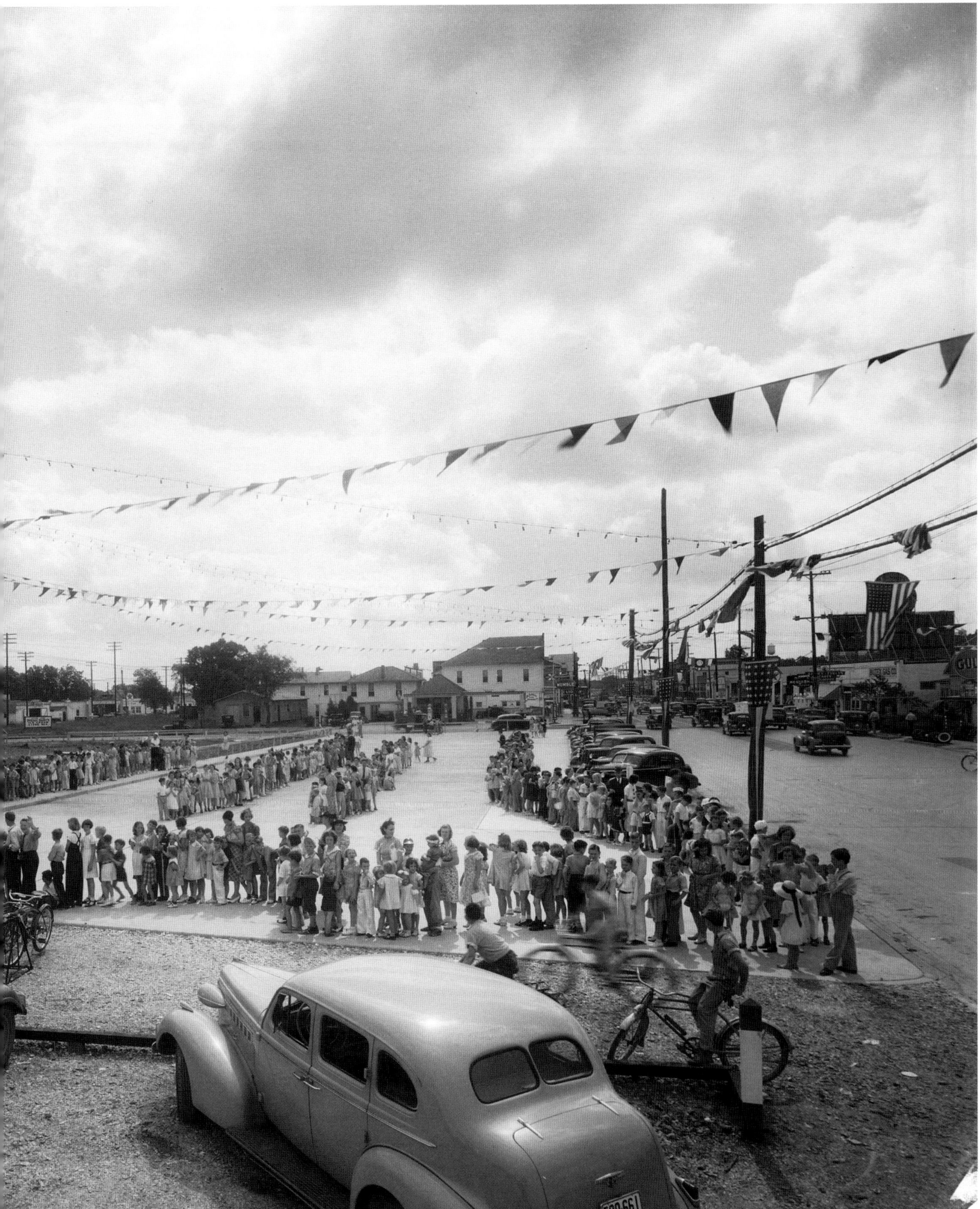
599-661

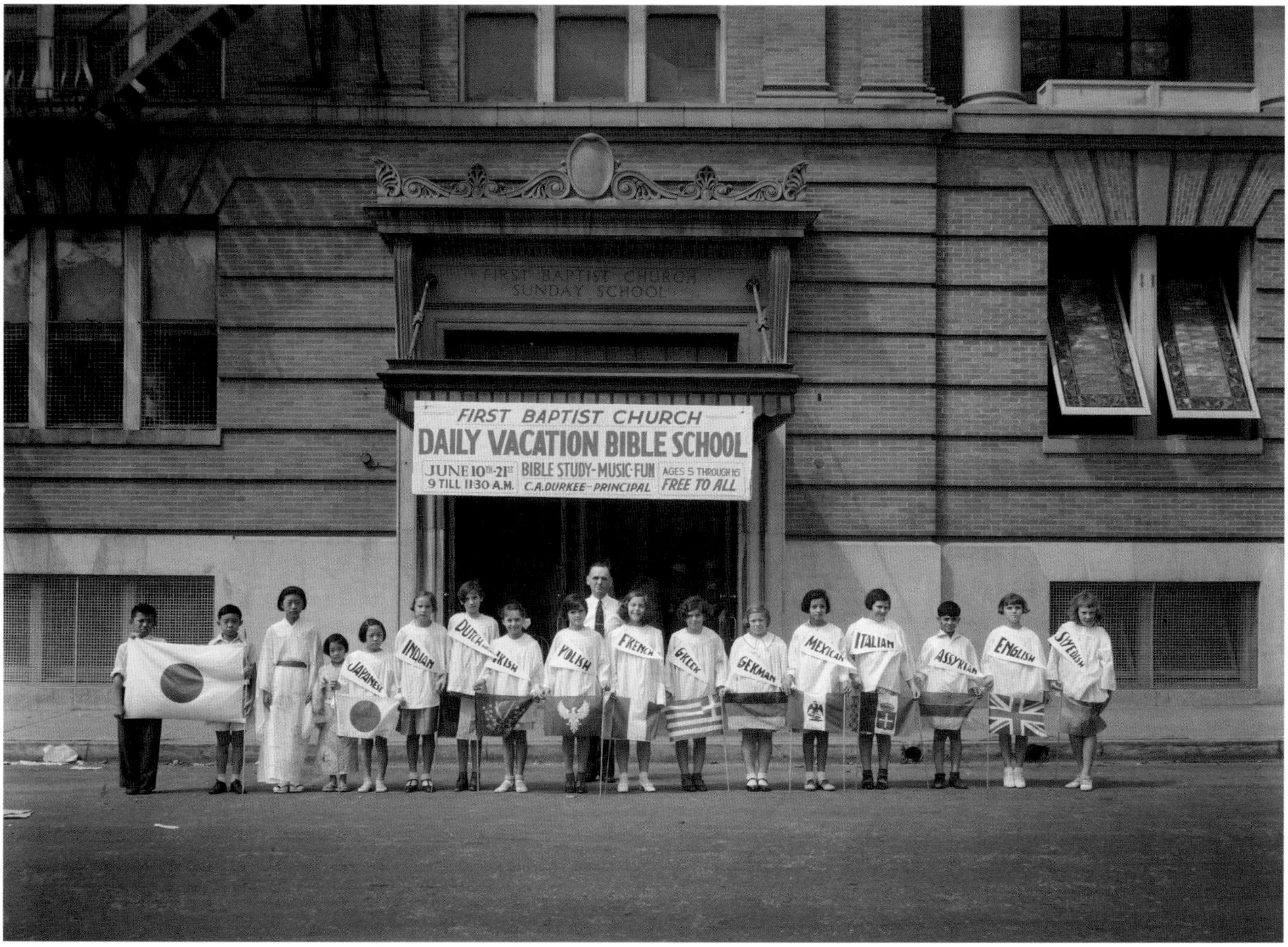

The summer 1938 Vacation Bible School class of the First Baptist Church, then located at 1020 Lamar Avenue. The students, holding flags representing the world's nations, were likely learning geography.

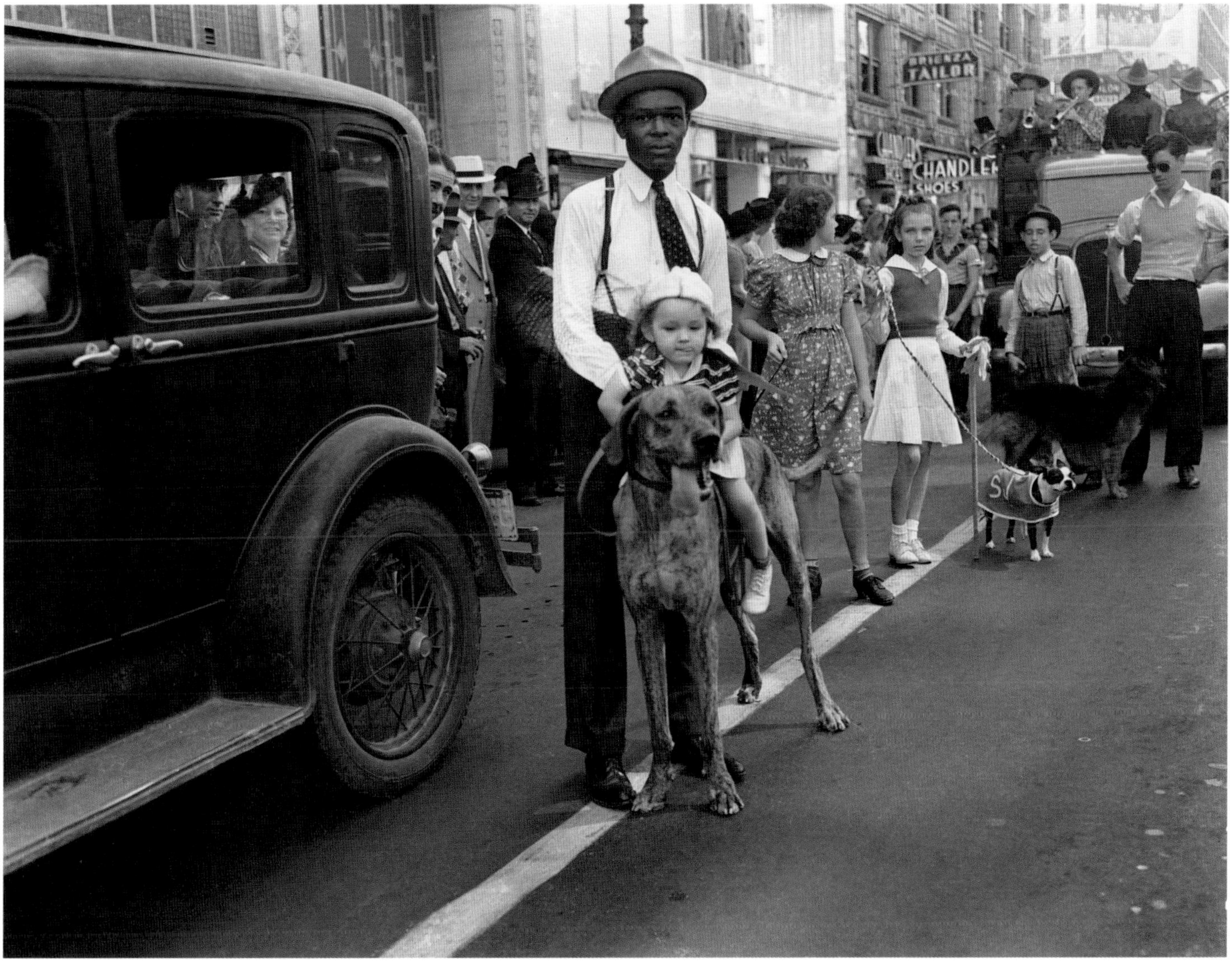

In October 1938, children and their dogs paraded down Houston's Main Street in the aptly named "Mutt Parade."

This scene of a boy fishing in Buffalo Bayou was taken for a 1940 Foley Brothers' back-to-school advertisement. Despite the fact that it was posed, this photo gives a very good idea of the heavy tropical growth that surrounded and wound through Houston at that time, along the city's extensive network of bayous and streams. For Houston's children, the dense foliage often served as a vast playground for fishing, swimming, exploring, or hiking.

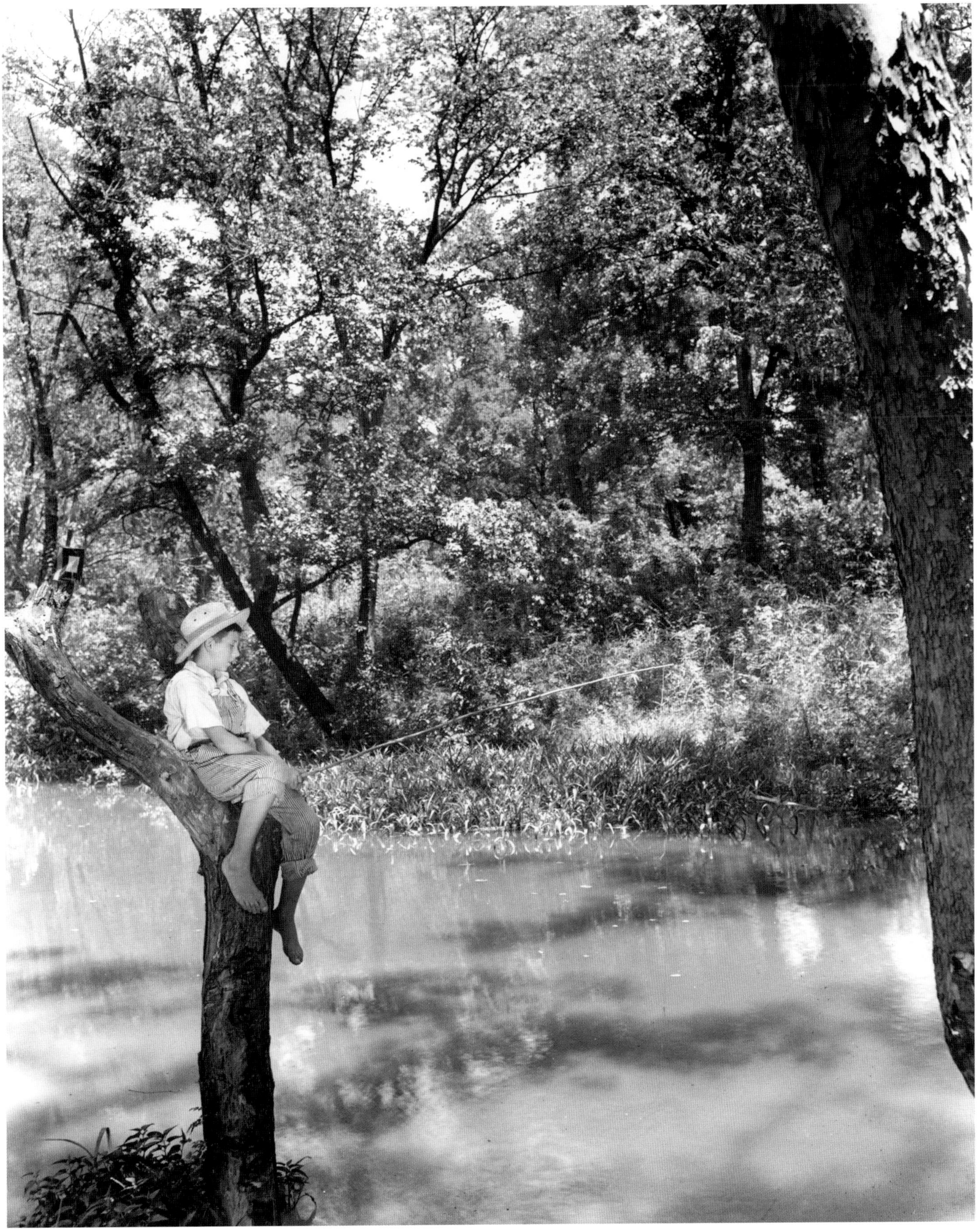

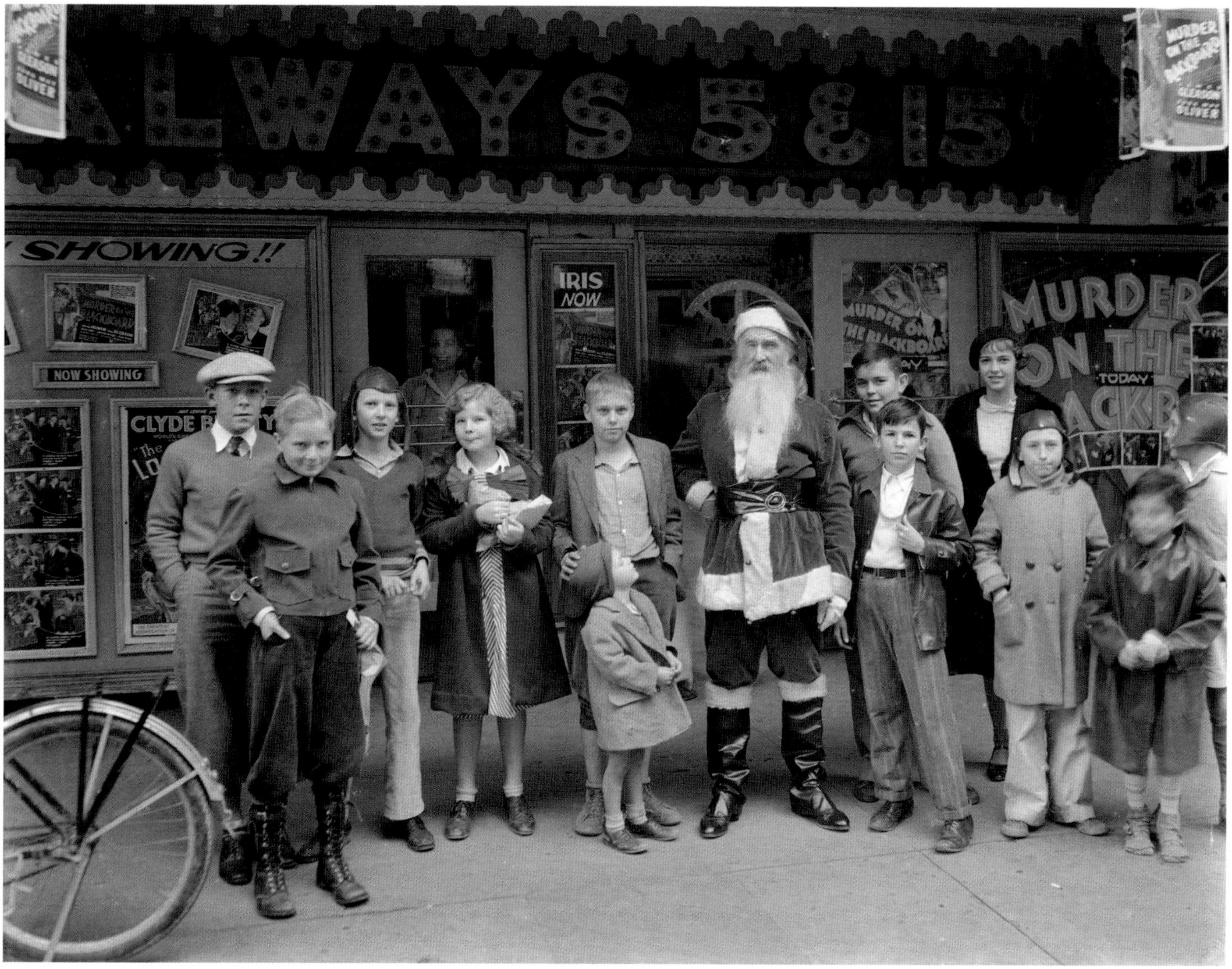

Group of children with Santa Claus at Houston's Iris Theatre, 615 Travis, in December 1934. The Iris was showing the film *Murder on the Blackboard*, starring noted character actress Edna May Oliver as a schoolteacher who teams up with her detective friend to solve a murder mystery. It is unclear what the film had to do, if anything, with either Christmas or children.

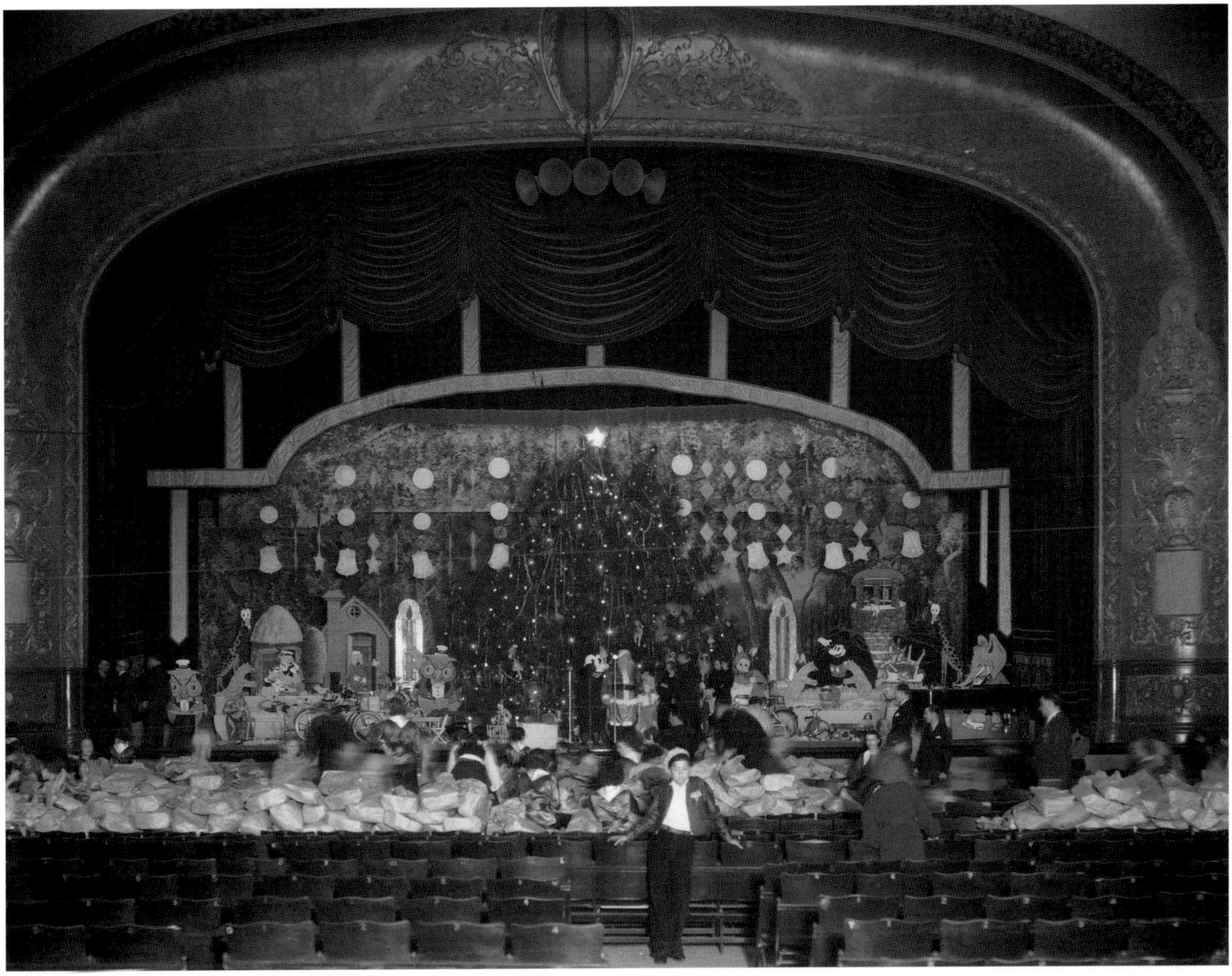

The 1936 Christmas party, held by entrepreneur and philanthropist Will Horwitz in the City Auditorium. Horwitz held annual Christmas parties for Houston's poor children beginning in 1926 and continued them for 20 years. The Christmas parties were first held at the Horwitz-owned Texan Theatre, but the crowds eventually became too large; the parties were later held at the City Auditorium. Under the huge Christmas tree are some of the thousands of gifts that Horwitz gave to the city's children at each Christmas party.

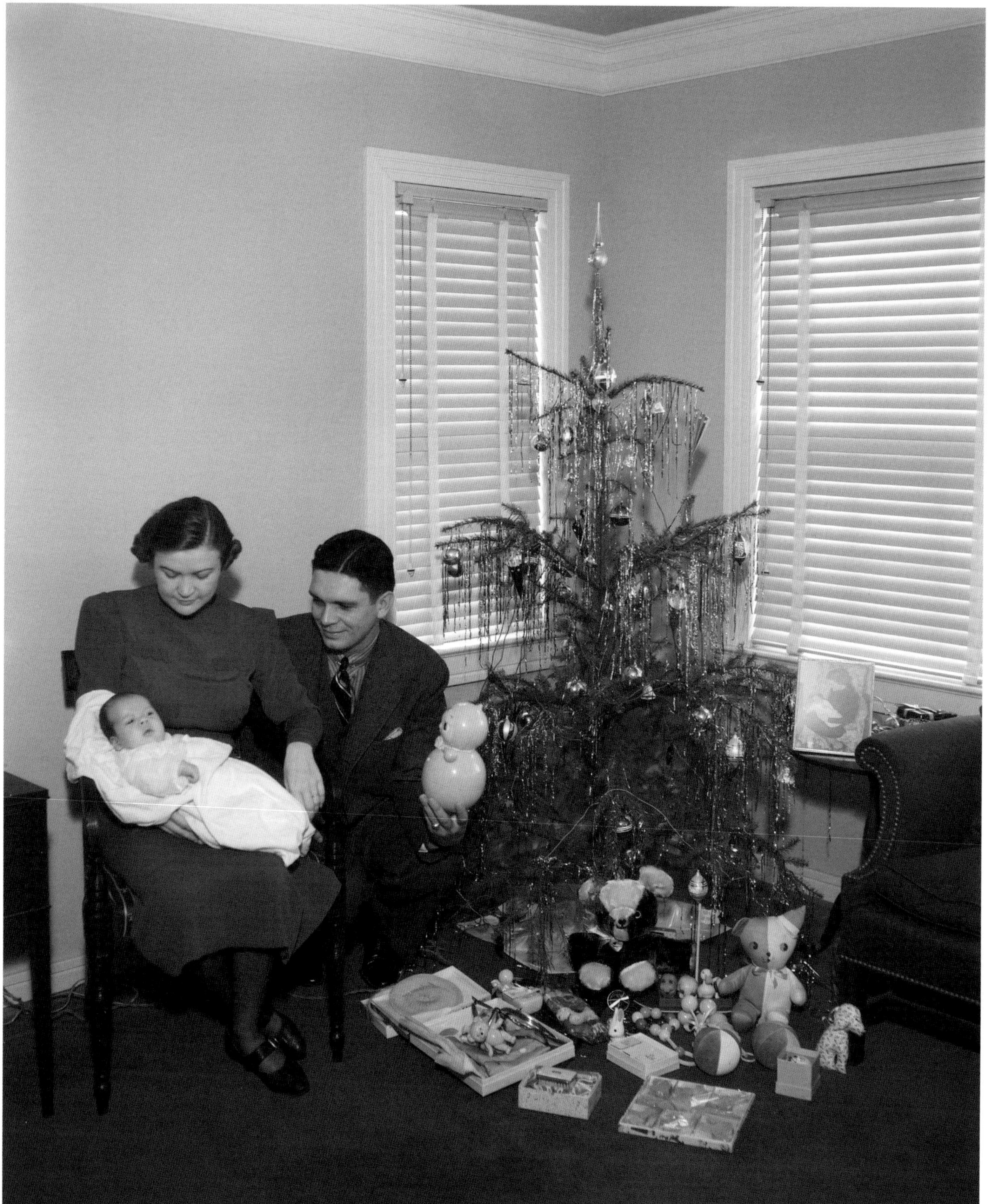

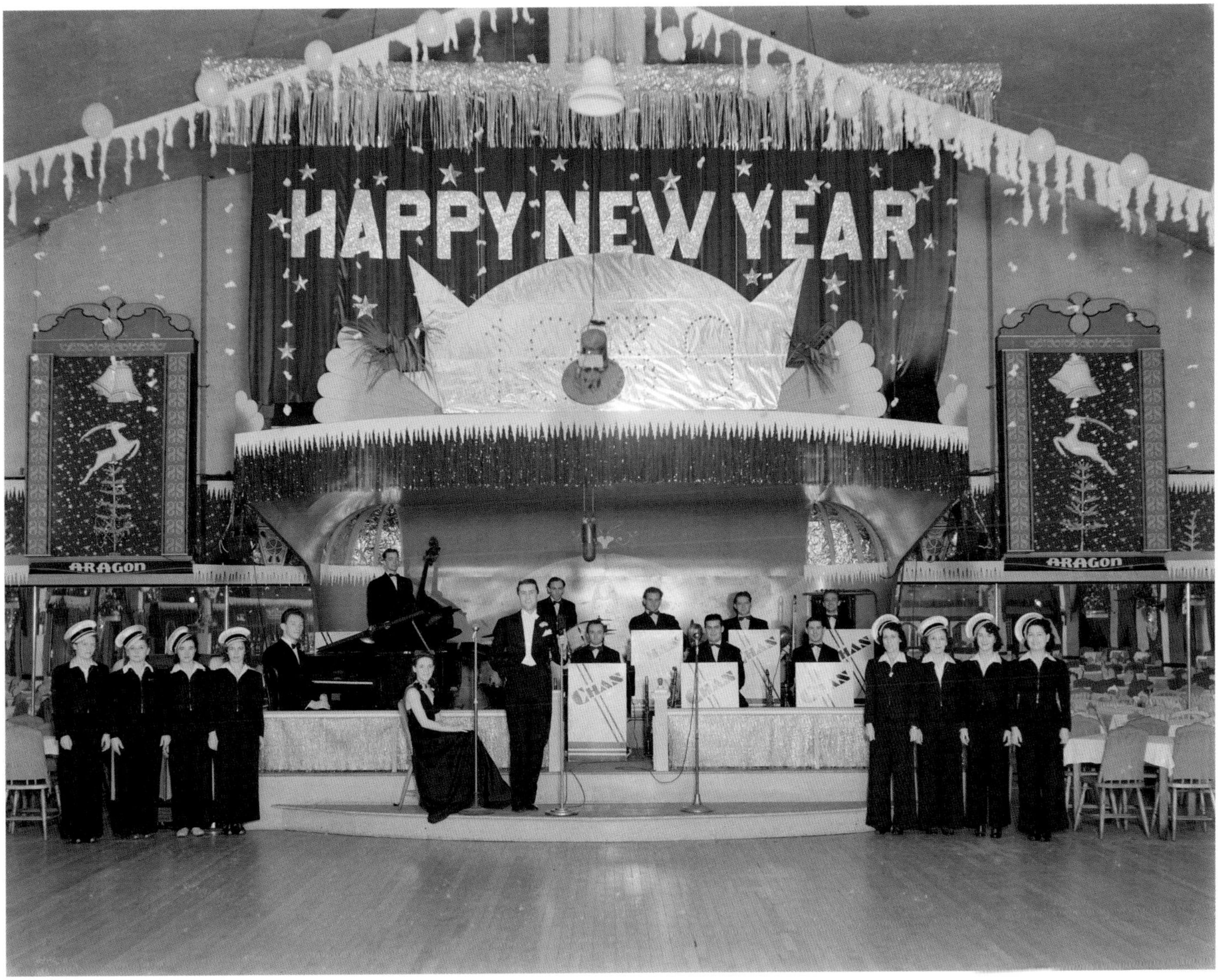

Facing: The Blainey family posed beside their Christmas tree on Christmas Day in 1936. Bailey took a great number of photos over the years in which families posed with their children, Christmas tree, and gifts. As the middle class steadily grew in America, people were anxious to show that they had reached a middle-class level of financial success. A family, a beautifully decorated tree, and Christmas gifts served as proof that the photo's proud subjects had arrived financially.

Above: The popular Aragon Ballroom's orchestra and attendants, ready for New Year's Eve celebrations in 1938. The Aragon was located upstairs at 1010-½ Rusk.

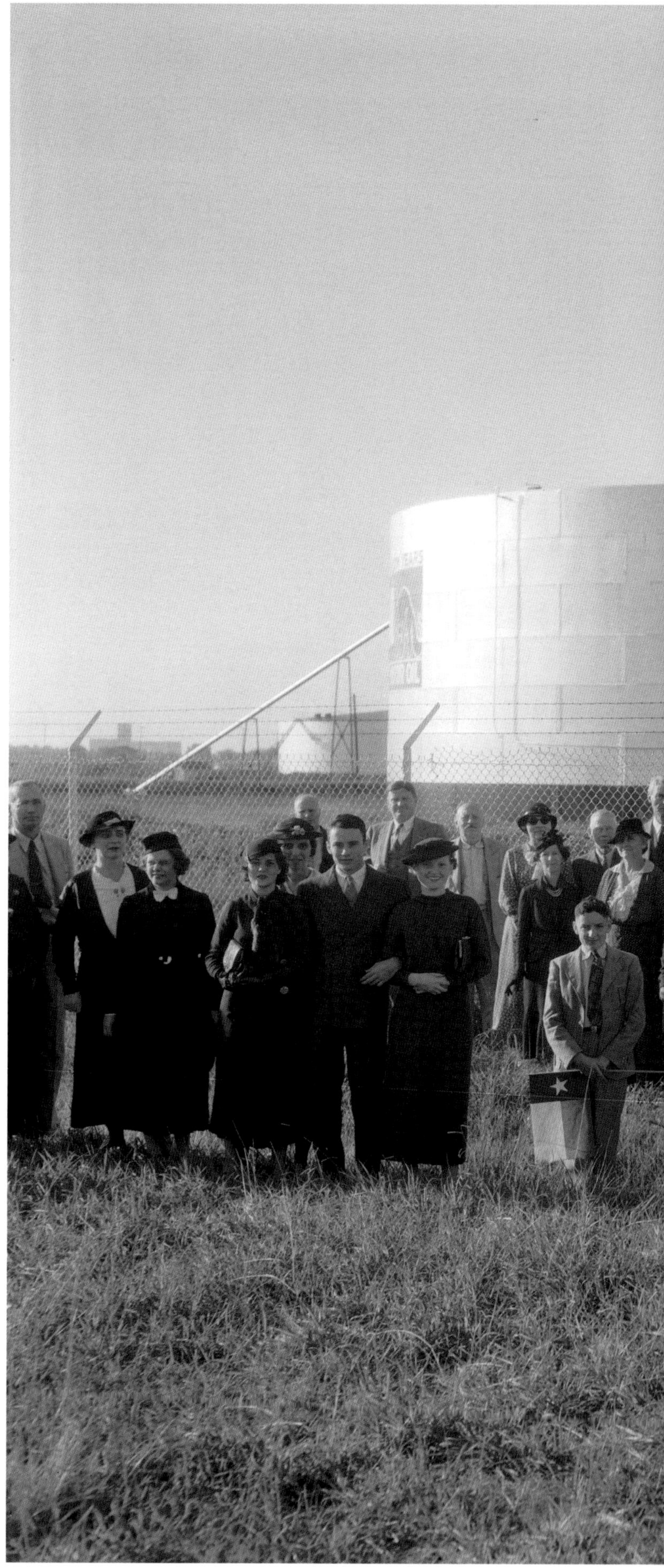

In October 1936, these people posed around a newly unveiled historical marker commemorating the site, three thousand feet to the north, where Sam Houston and the Texas Army crossed Buffalo Bayou on April 19, 1836, just two days before defeating the Mexican Army at the Battle of San Jacinto. The Texas Centennial Commission erected the marker as part of the Centennial observance that year. The army crossed the bayou, using a raft constructed from the flooring of a nearby home, and it took almost an entire day to complete the transport of both men and supplies to the opposite bank. Few photos could better capture the enormous contrast between the vast, almost completely unpopulated coastal prairie that the Texas Army crossed on its route to the San Jacinto battlefield and the Texas of 1936, with oil tanks in the background.

The historical marker is still located at 12000 Lawndale Street in present-day Houston. A refinery operated by the LyondellBasell Company currently occupies the land adjacent to the marker.

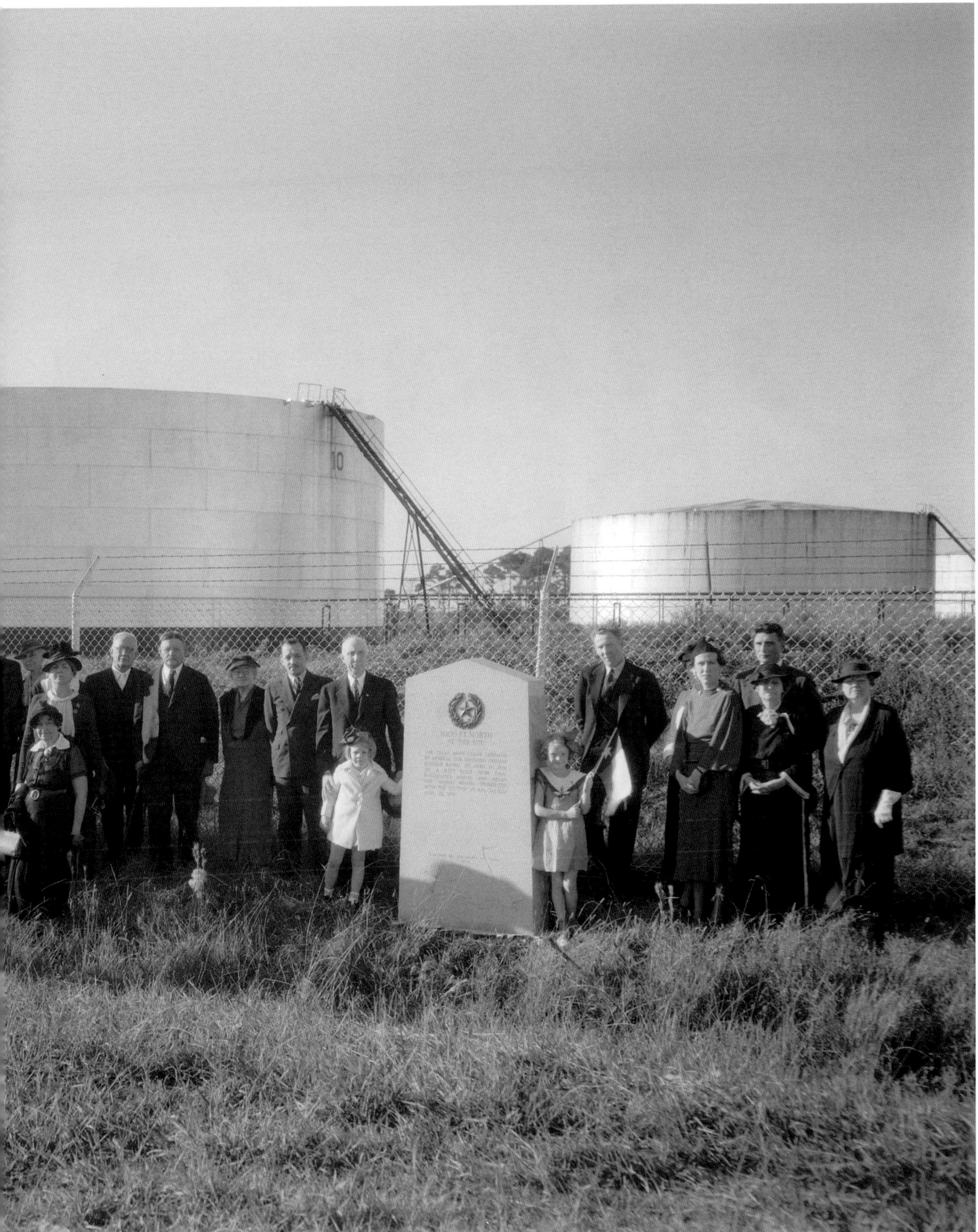
10

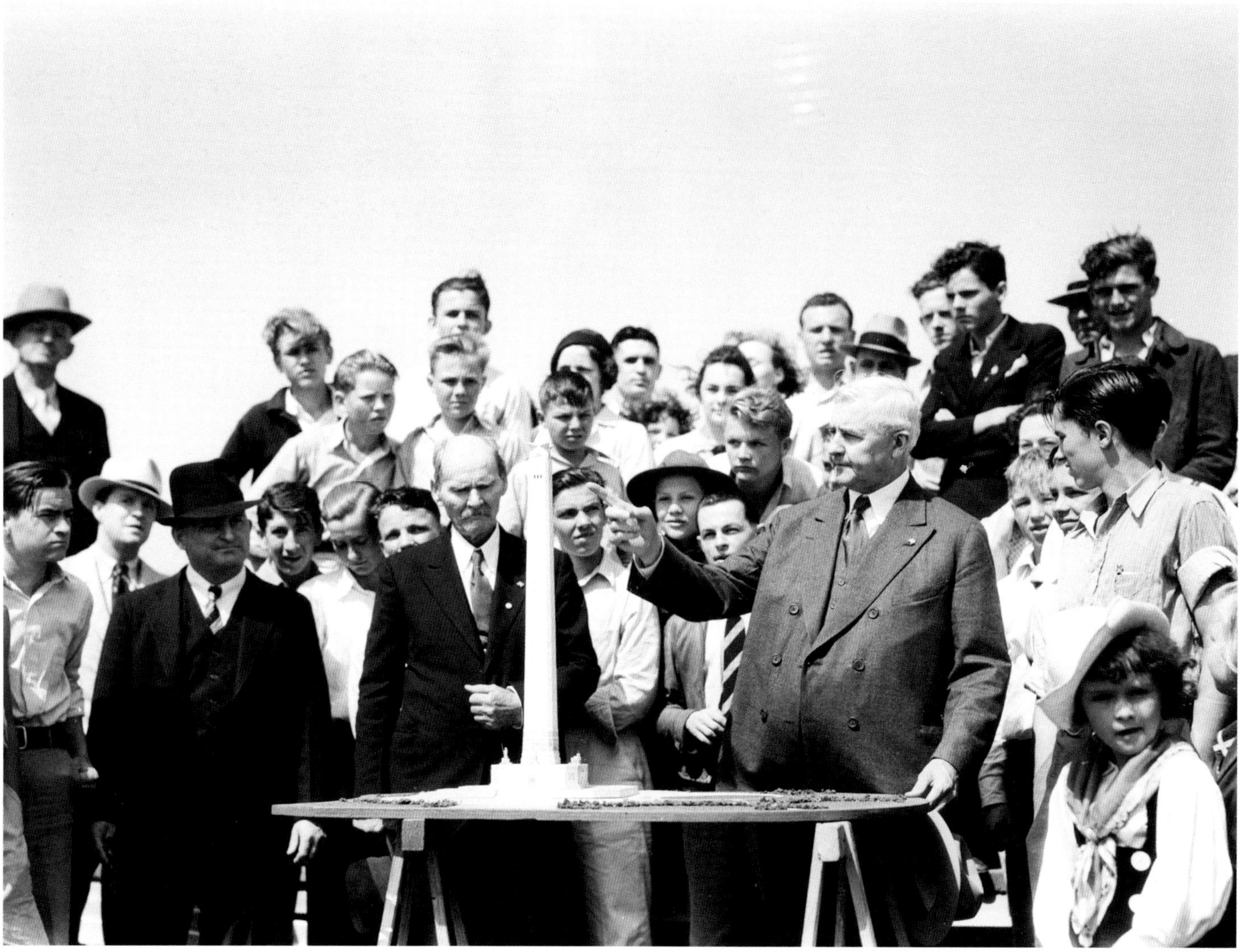

Above: This group gathered for the unveiling of the model of the San Jacinto Monument at its groundbreaking ceremony on March 27, 1936. Houston financier and civic leader Jesse H. Jones points to the model, and at his right stands the sole surviving son of Sam Houston, Andrew Jackson Houston. To Houston's right stands architect Alfred C. Finn. Jones was one of the most powerful men in the nation, due to his role as chairman of the Reconstruction Finance Corporation (RFC), a position he was appointed to by President Franklin Roosevelt in 1933. The RFC was responsible for distributing federal assistance to state and local governments and making loans to banks, private businesses, and railroads.

Facing: The 567-foot San Jacinto Monument under construction in 1938. The monument to the Battle of San Jacinto was completed in 1939 and is located within the 1,200-acre San Jacinto Battleground State Historic Site.

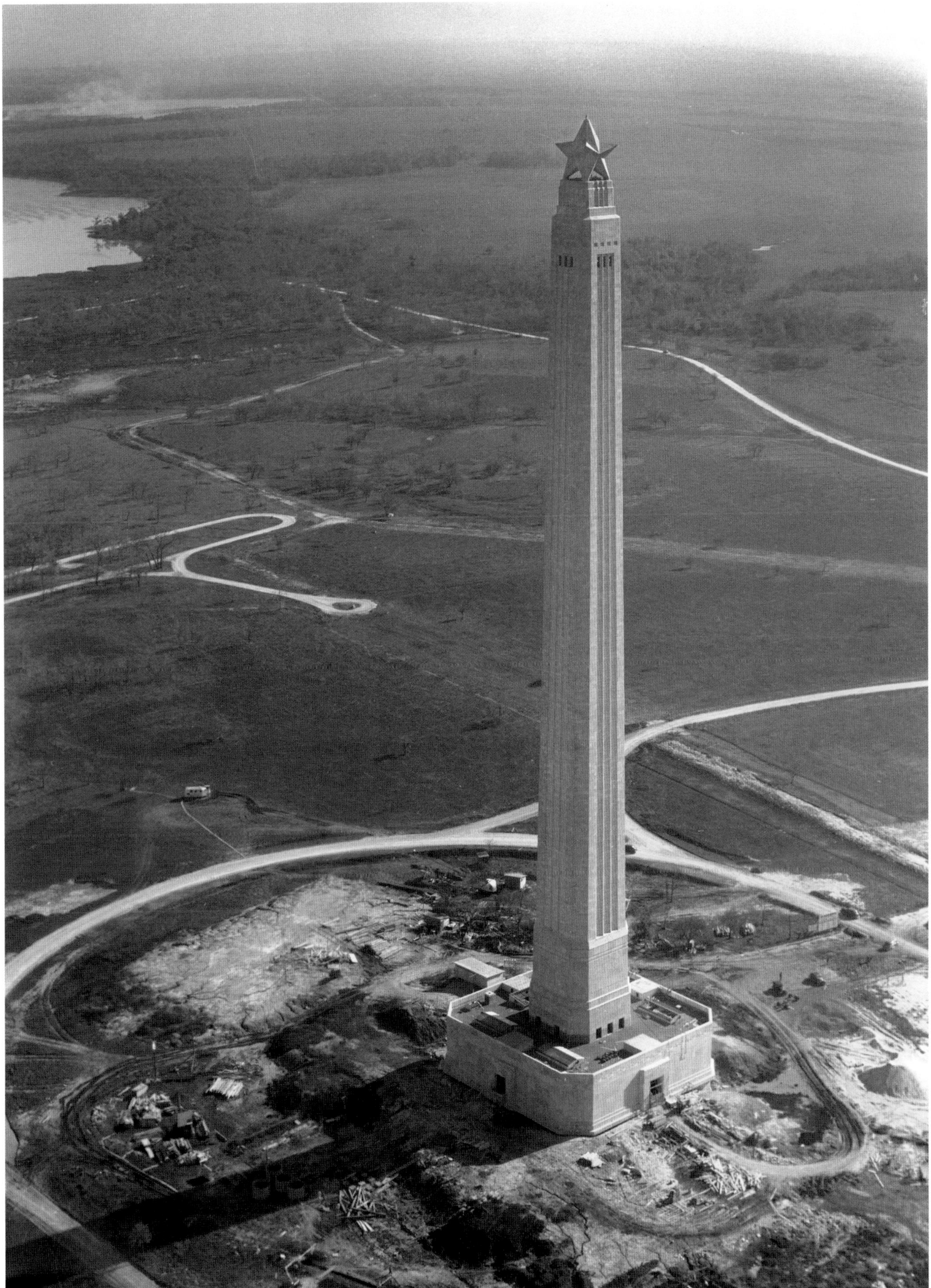

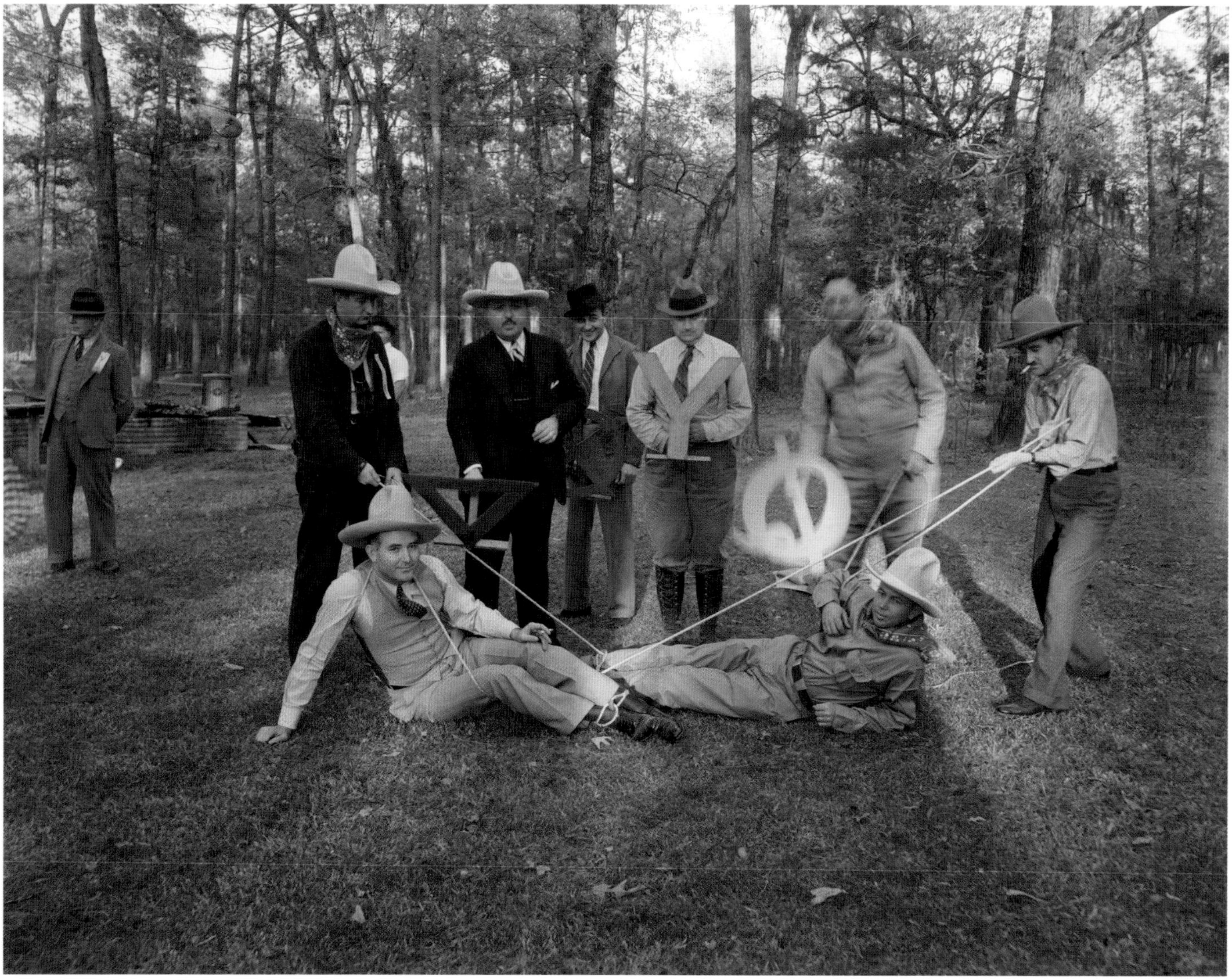

A group of men from Houston's YMCA participated in the celebration of the Texas Centennial in Memorial Park in March 1936. It is unclear why the two men on the ground have been lassoed and are about to be "branded" by their fellow participants.

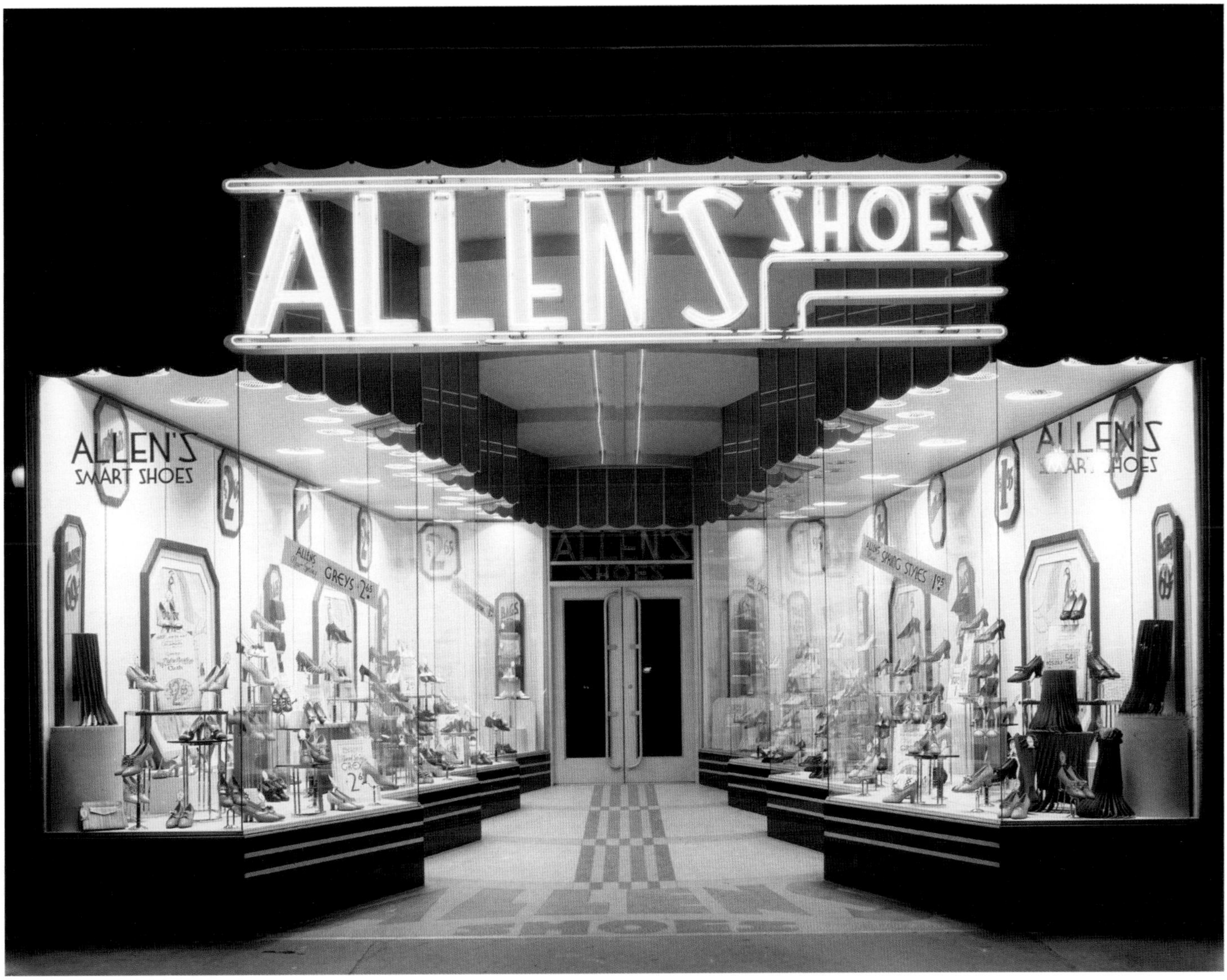

Nighttime shot of Allen's Shoes' entrance, display windows, and neon sign in January 1935. This is a good example of the artistry that Bob Bailey was able to achieve with what could have been, taken by another photographer, a mundane shot.

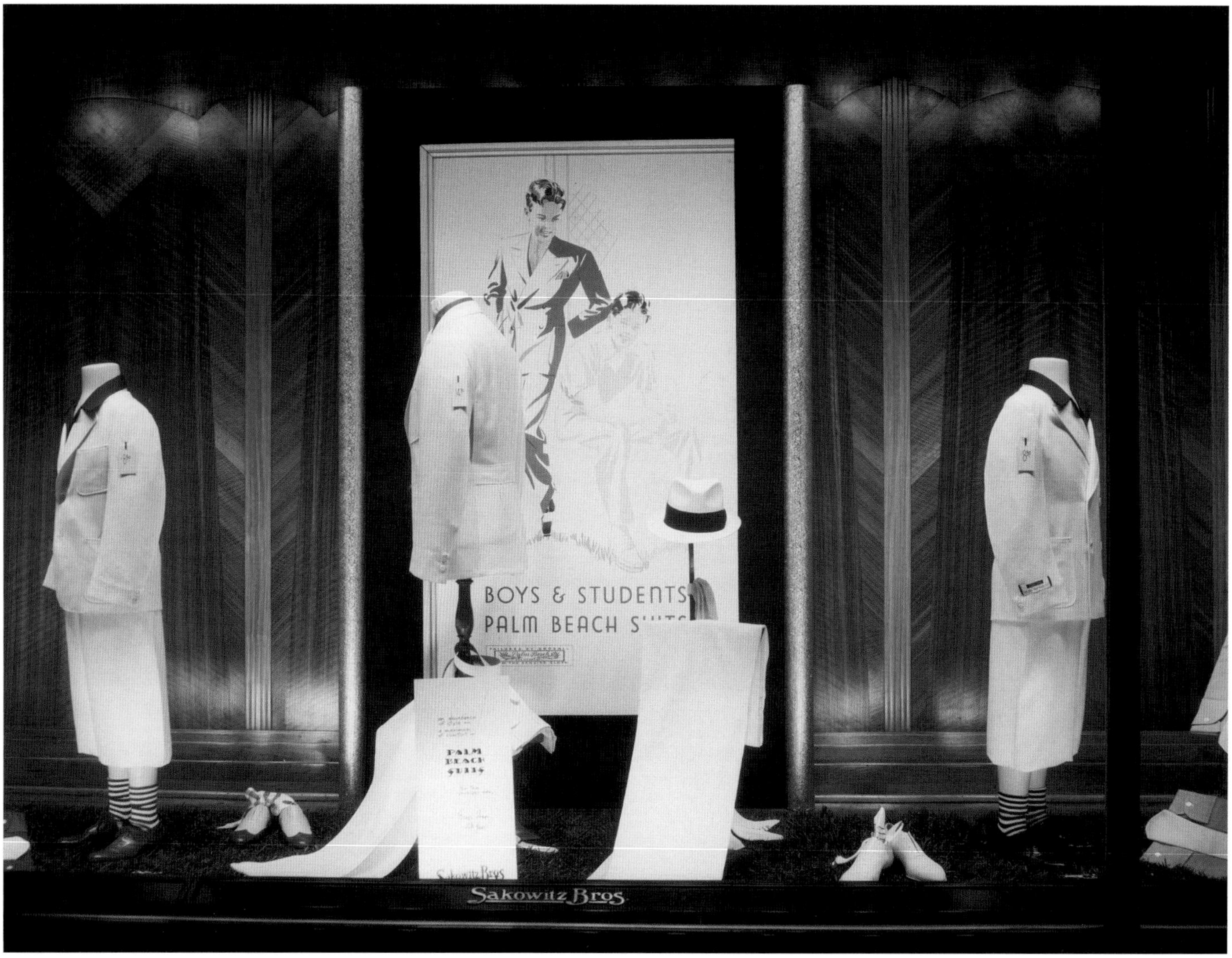

Above: Houston never suffered from the worst effects of the Great Depression, largely due to the quick thinking and planning of its business and civic leaders at the Depression's outset. Upscale department stores like Sakowitz Brothers, at 512 Main, continued to thrive during the 1930s. In 1935, this Sakowitz store window displayed high-end Palm Beach suits for boys. At the time, Sakowitz Brothers occupied the first five floors of the Gulf Building.

Facing: This 1935 Sakowitz Brothers Christmas window epitomized Art Moderne styling with its streamlined reindeer, ultramodern spiral Christmas tree, and mannequin's sleek, draped outfit.

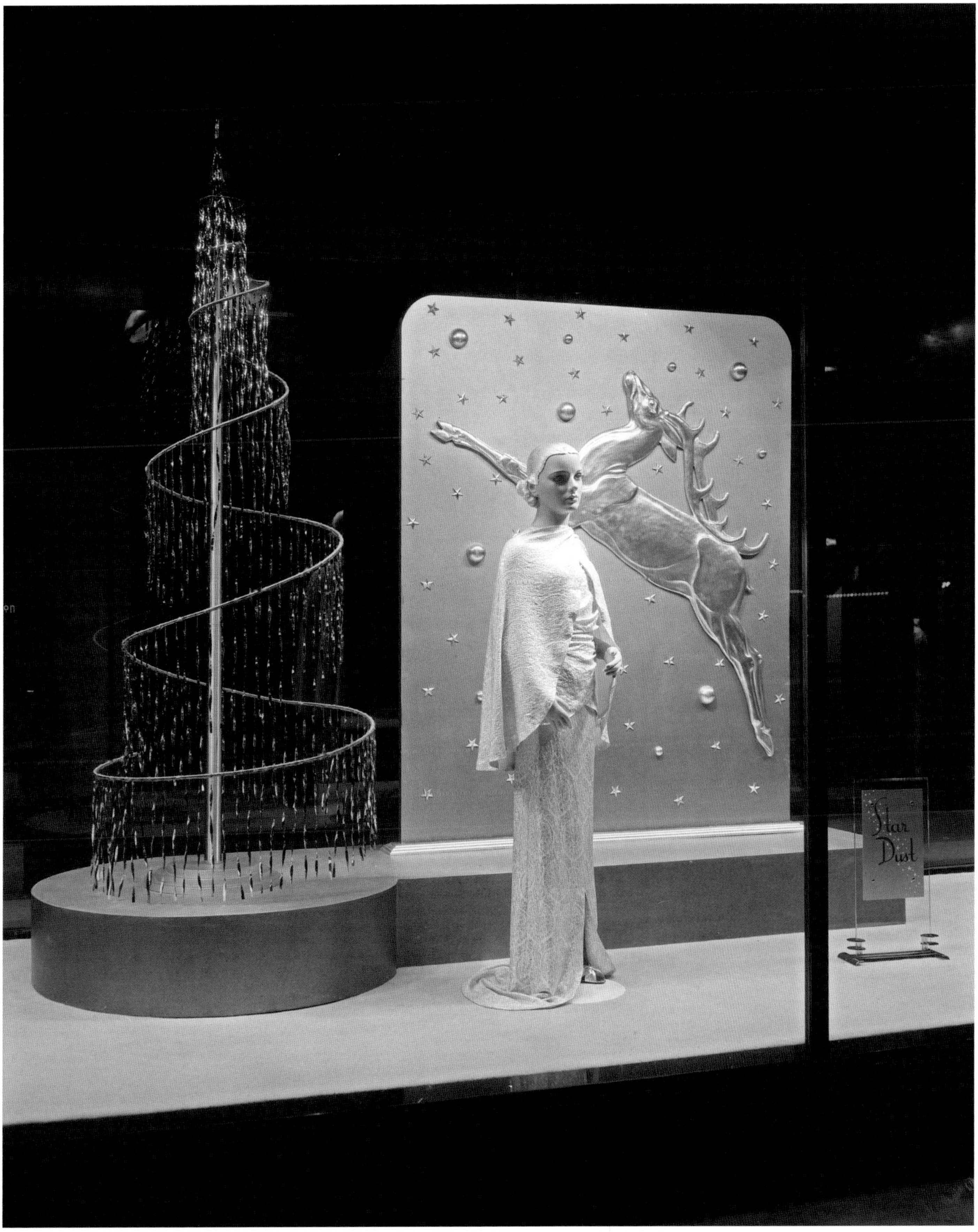
Star
Dust

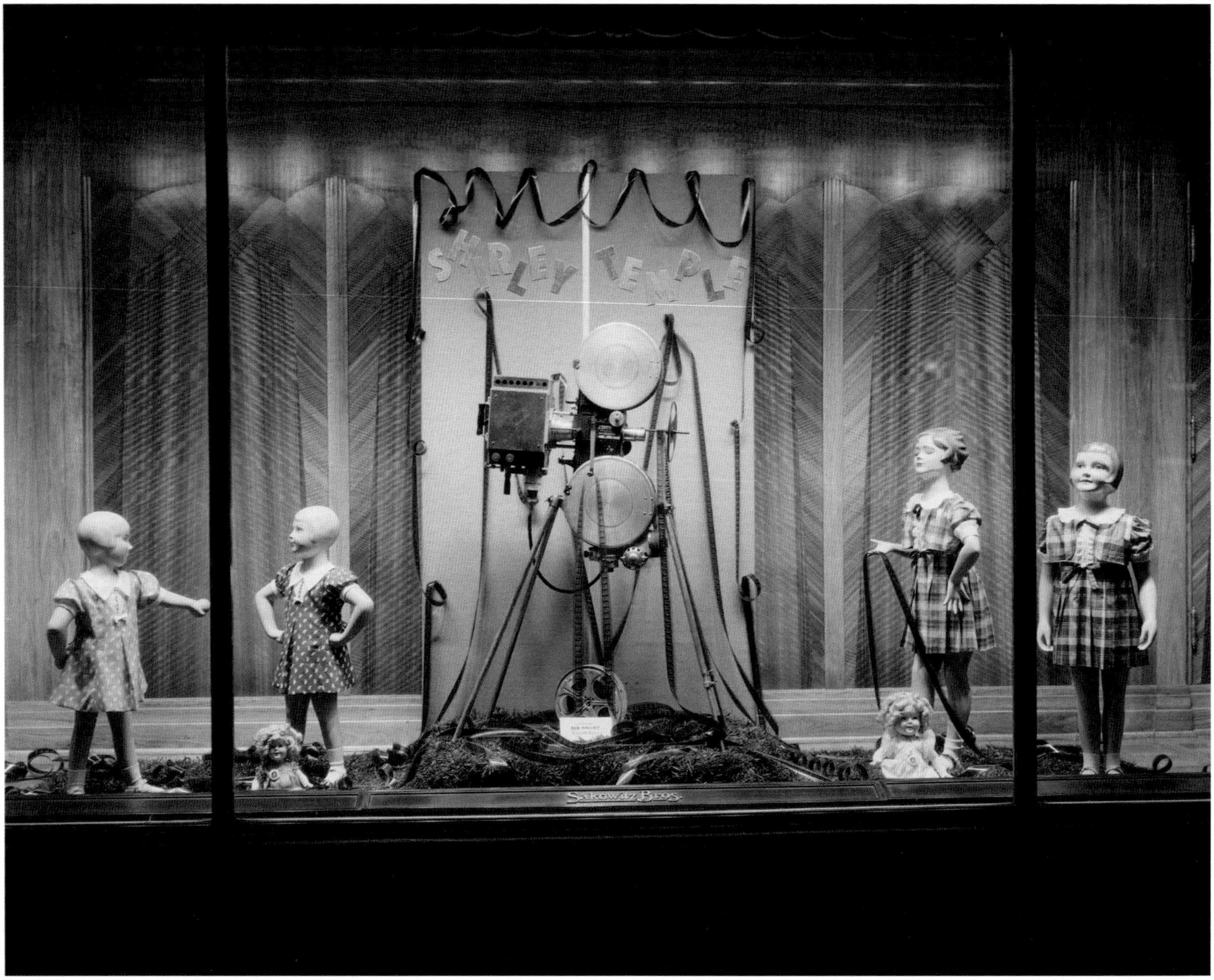

The Shirley Temple window at Sakowitz Brothers Department Store, complete with film canisters and camera. When this picture was taken in 1936, Shirley Temple reigned supreme as America's top movie star, a position she held for four consecutive years beginning in 1935; her image saturated the popular culture. The same year this photo was taken, almost ninety percent of 20th Century-Fox's corporate earnings came from the profits made by Temple's previous four films.

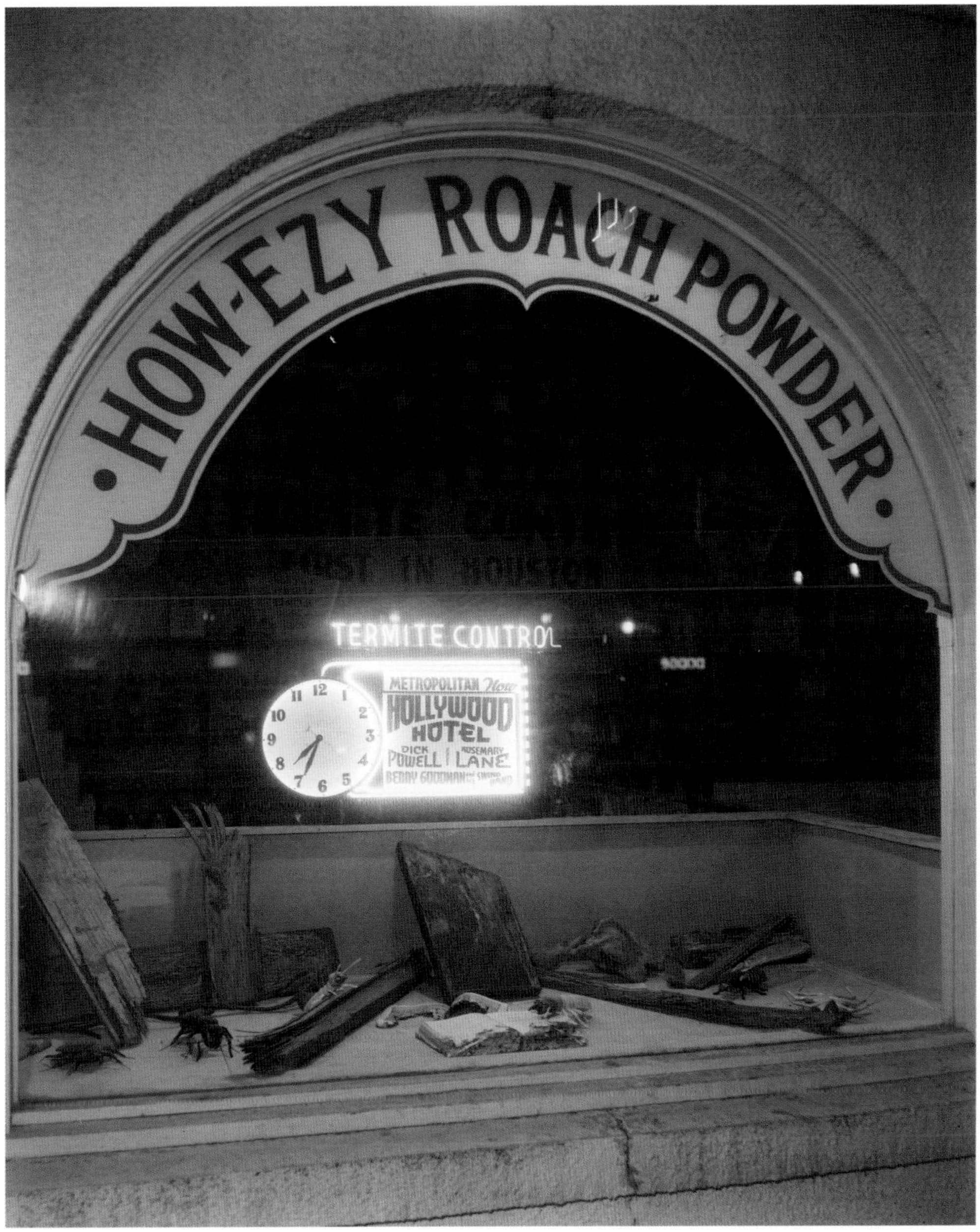

Not all of Houston's display windows imaginatively transported potential customers to exotic locales or turned them into participants in a fantasy world; some were much more utilitarian. How-Ezy Roach Powder advertised the ability of one of its products to control termites by showing the effects of a termite infestation on wood construction in this January 1938 photo. The display came complete with large-scale models of termites (at left) to add to the realism. In the background, the electric Metropolitan Theatre sign advertises the showing of *Hollywood Hotel*, starring Dick Powell and Rosemary Lane. If *Hollywood Hotel* is remembered at all today, it is remembered as the musical in which Hollywood's unofficial anthem, "Hooray for Hollywood," was first introduced.

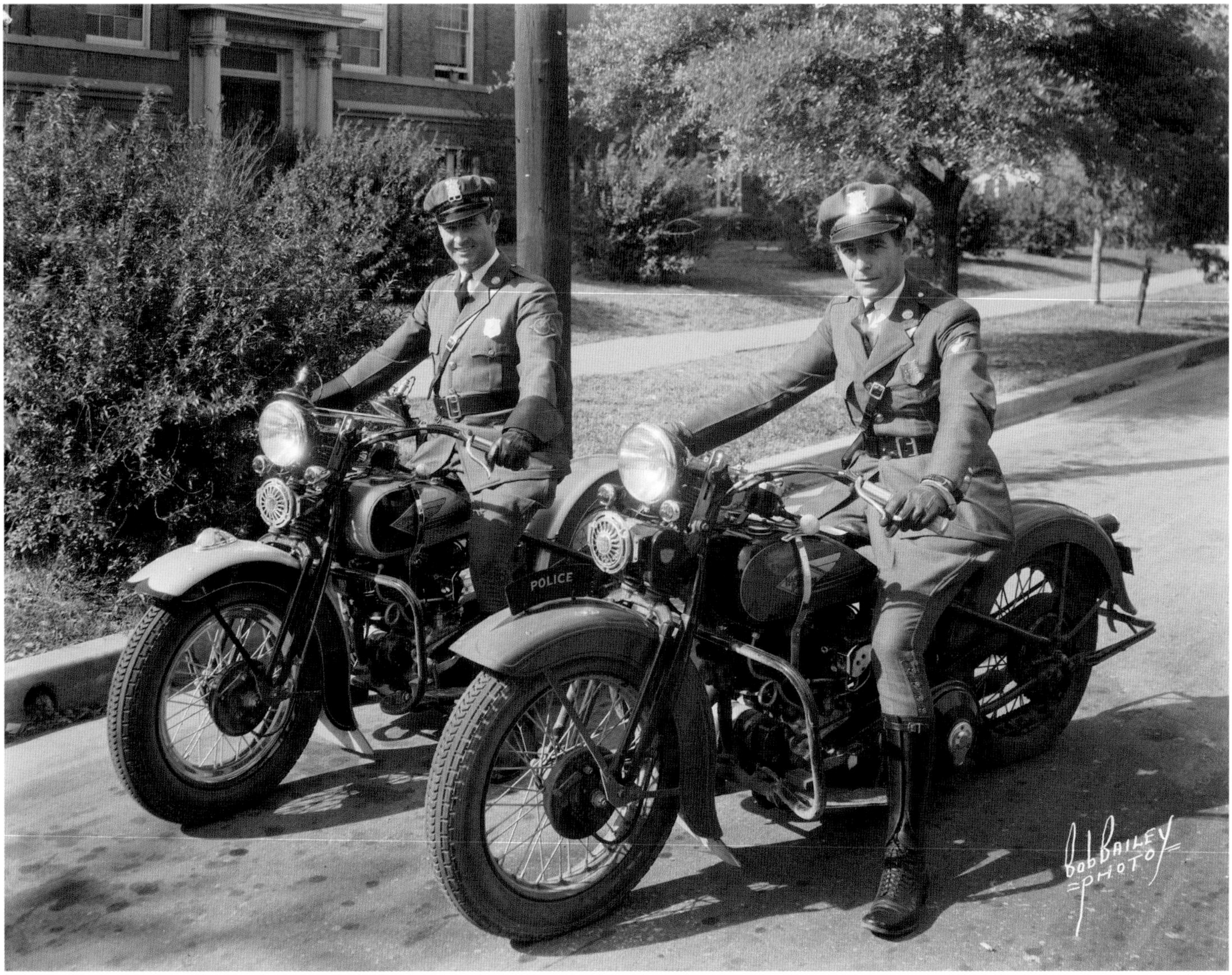

Two Houston motorcycle policemen, March 1935. The Houston Police Department acquired its first motorcycle in 1909. Since that time, motorcycles have become an integral part of the department's daily operations.

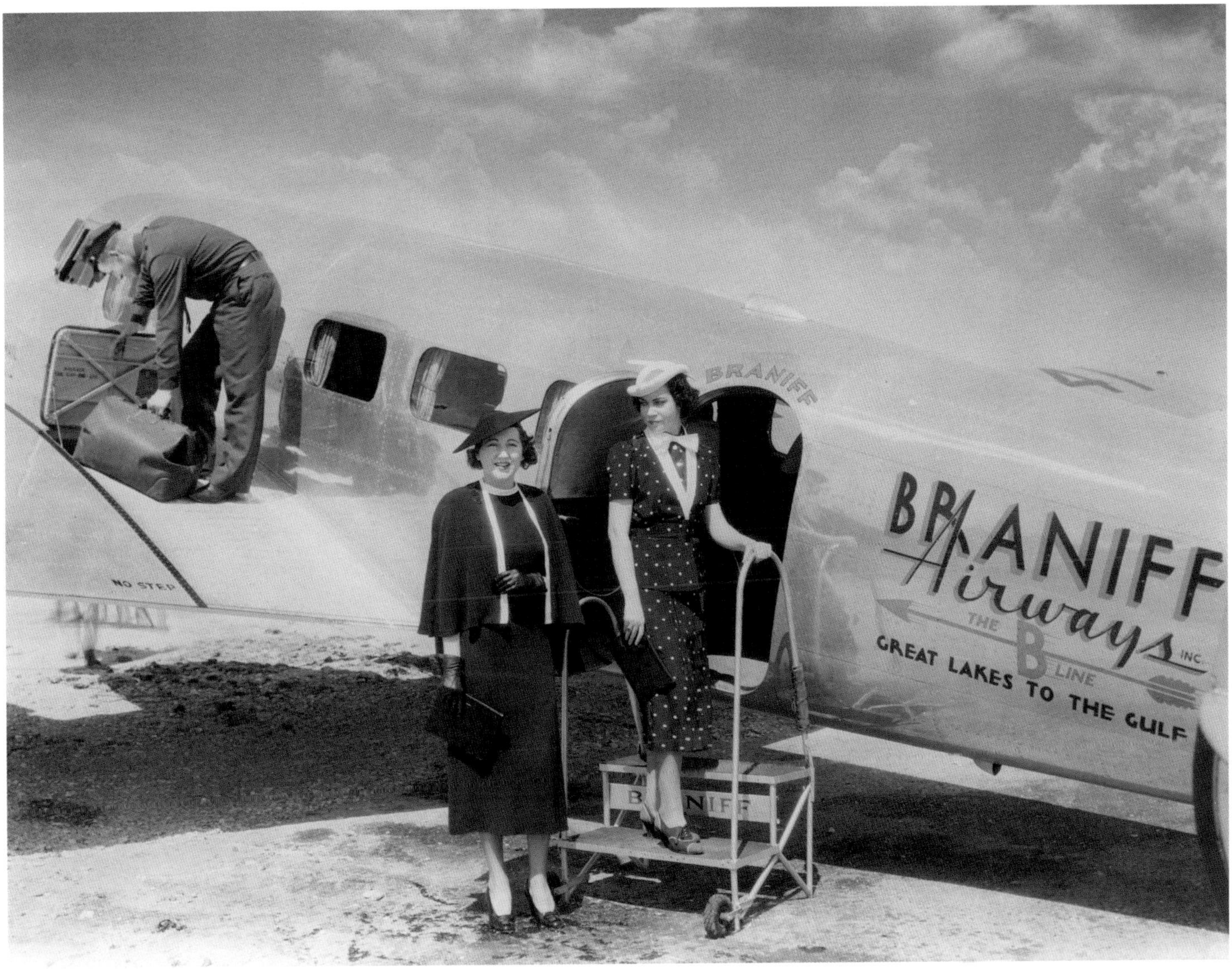

Women boarding a Braniff Airways passenger plane at Houston's Municipal Airport in 1936. Braniff began its operations in 1930, primarily serving the Midwest and southwestern states in its early years. Although the airline thrived for decades, Braniff—later Braniff International Airways—was forced to file for bankruptcy. It halted all flights in 1982, following the deregulation of the airlines in 1978.

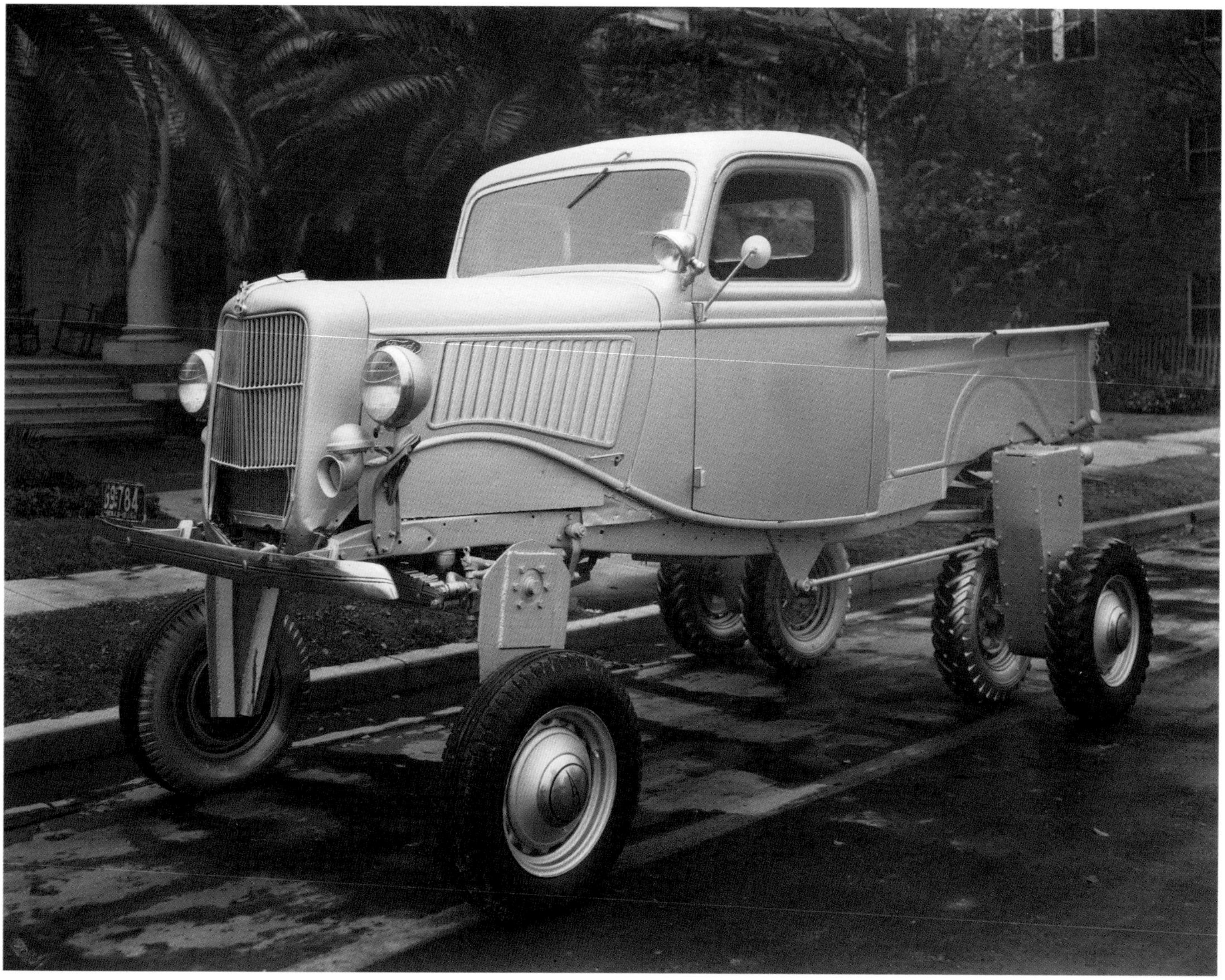

The Humble Oil Company converted this Ford truck into a "swamp buggy" in 1936. Vehicles like this were a vital necessity to local oil companies, since many of their wells and pipelines were located in swampy areas.

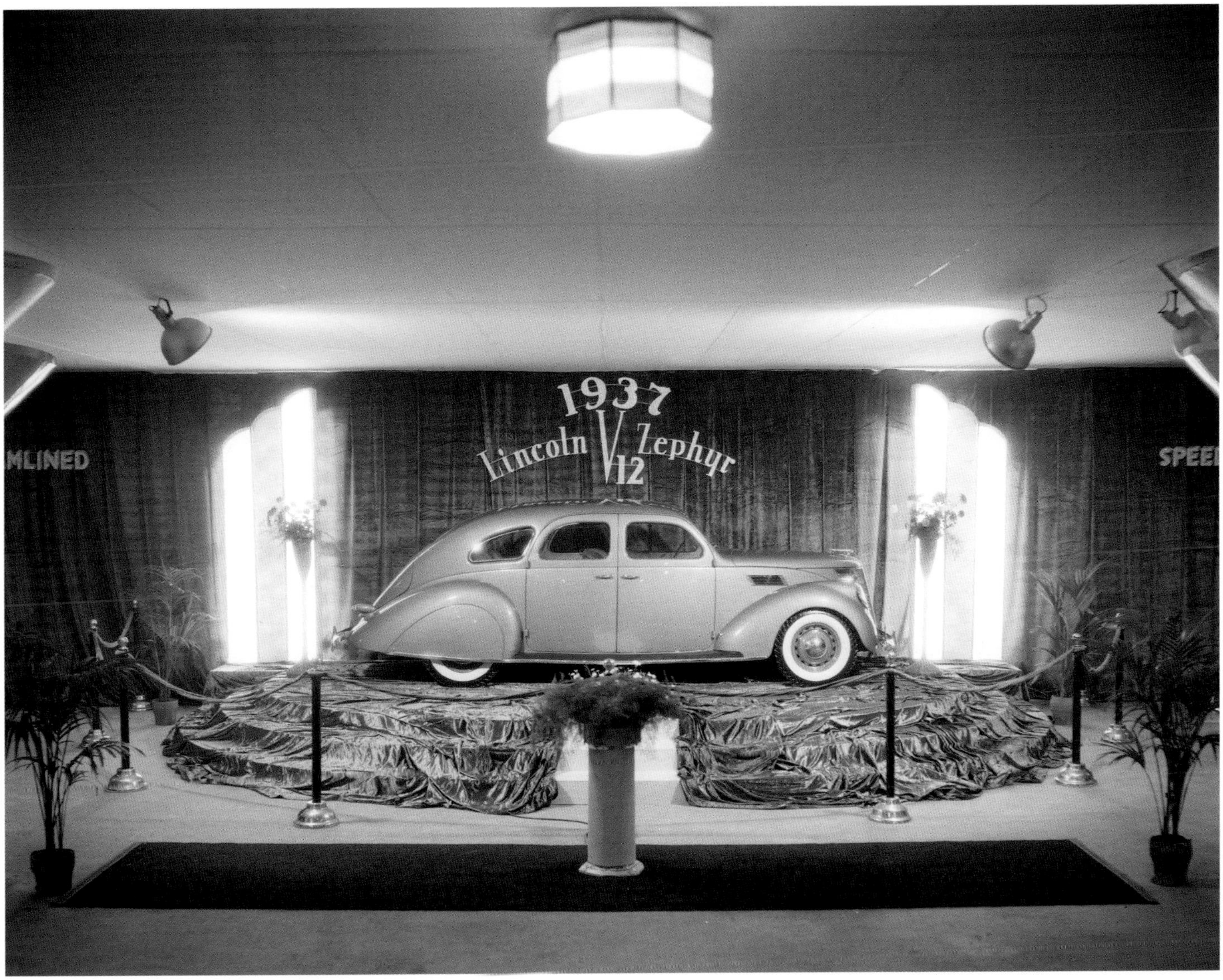

A 1937 V12 Lincoln Zephyr displayed at a Houston automobile show in October 1936. The Zephyr was a very successful model for Lincoln, and much of its appeal came from its aerodynamic look, which was based on streamlined vehicle designs conceived by industrial designer Norman Bel Geddes.

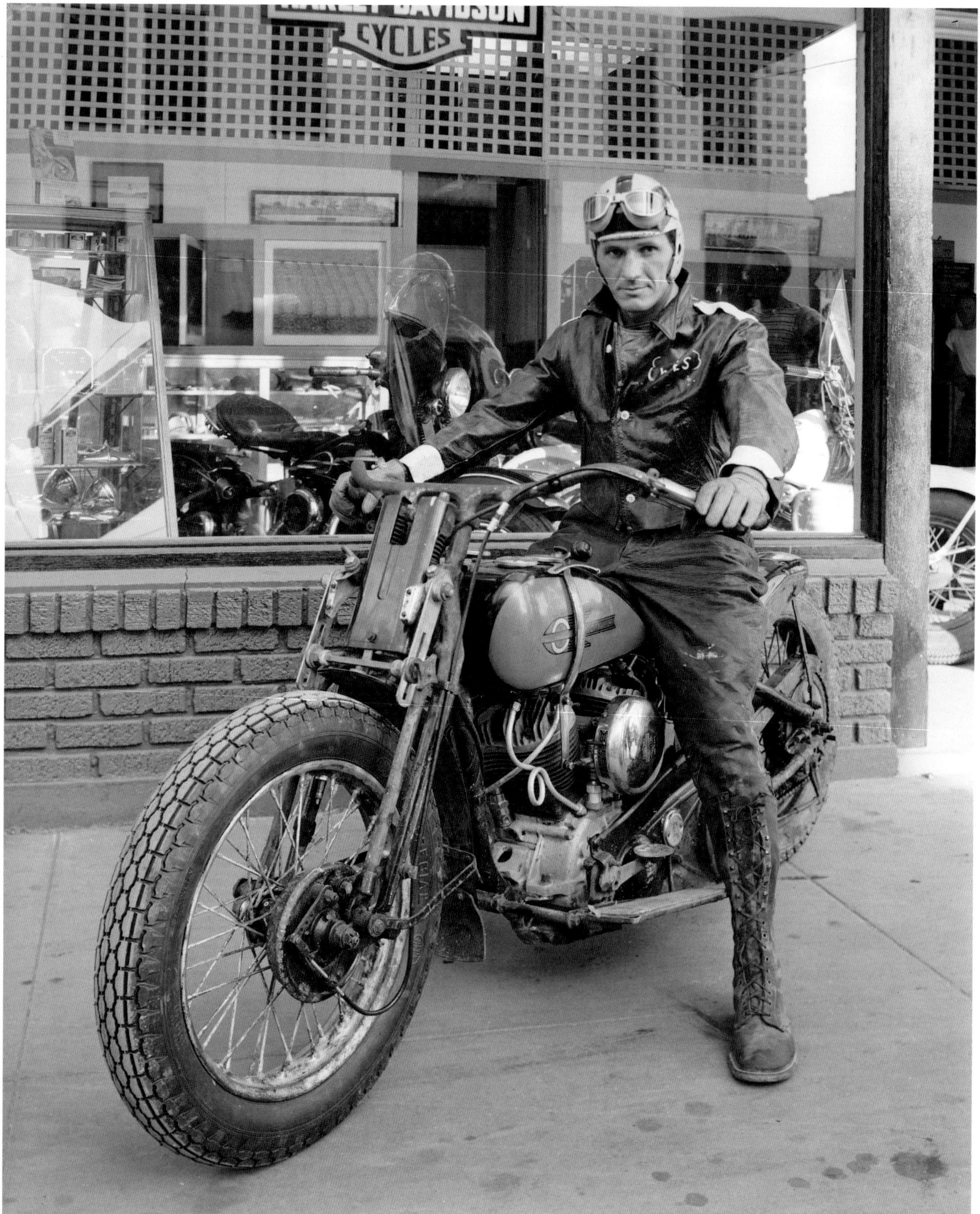
CYCLES

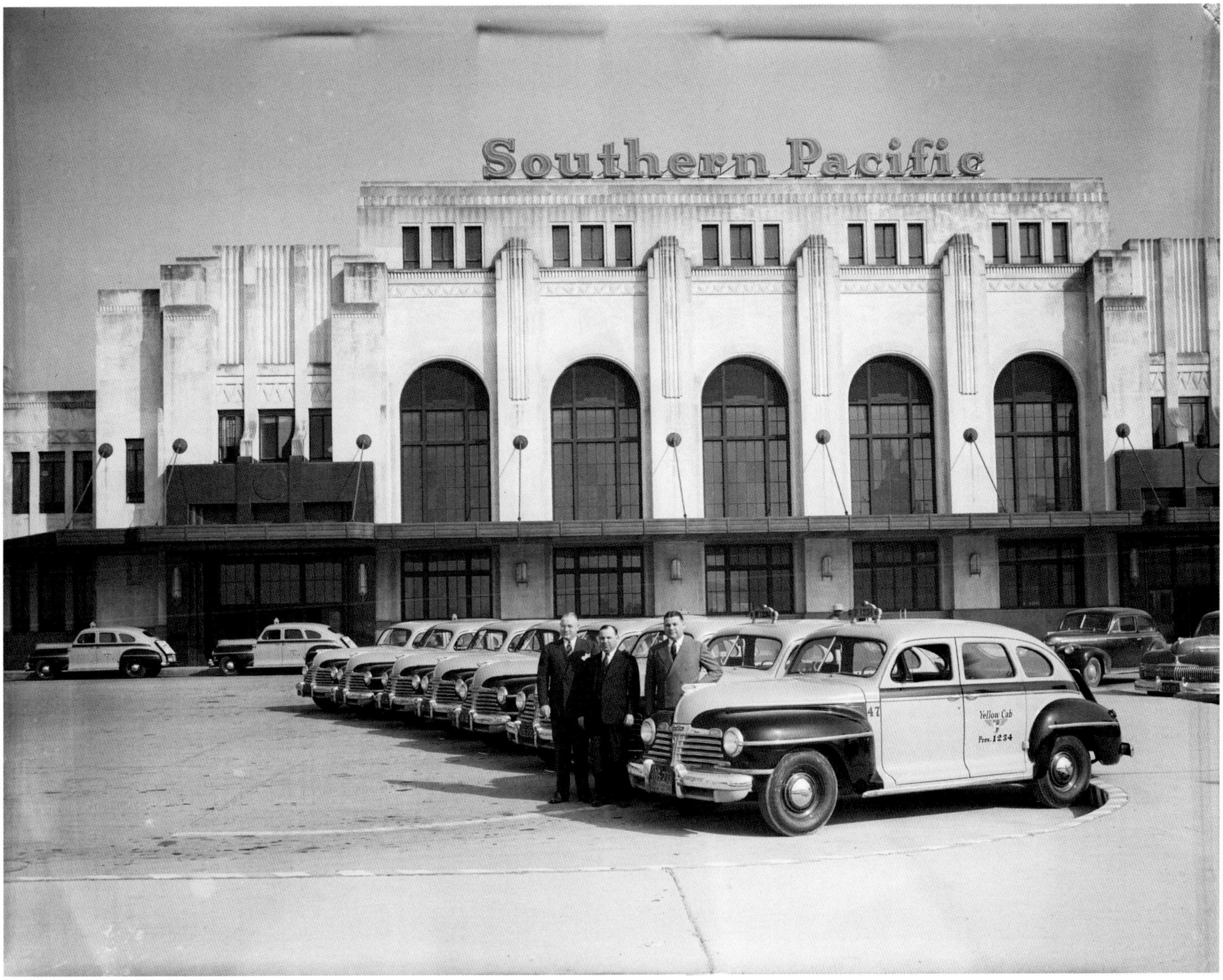

Facing: This man proudly shows off his Harley-Davidson motorcycle, ca. 1938.

Above: Cabs parked outside Houston's Southern Pacific train depot, the Grand Central Railroad Station. The photo was commissioned by the Radcliff Motor Company to show off its latest yellow cab models and was taken in December 1941.

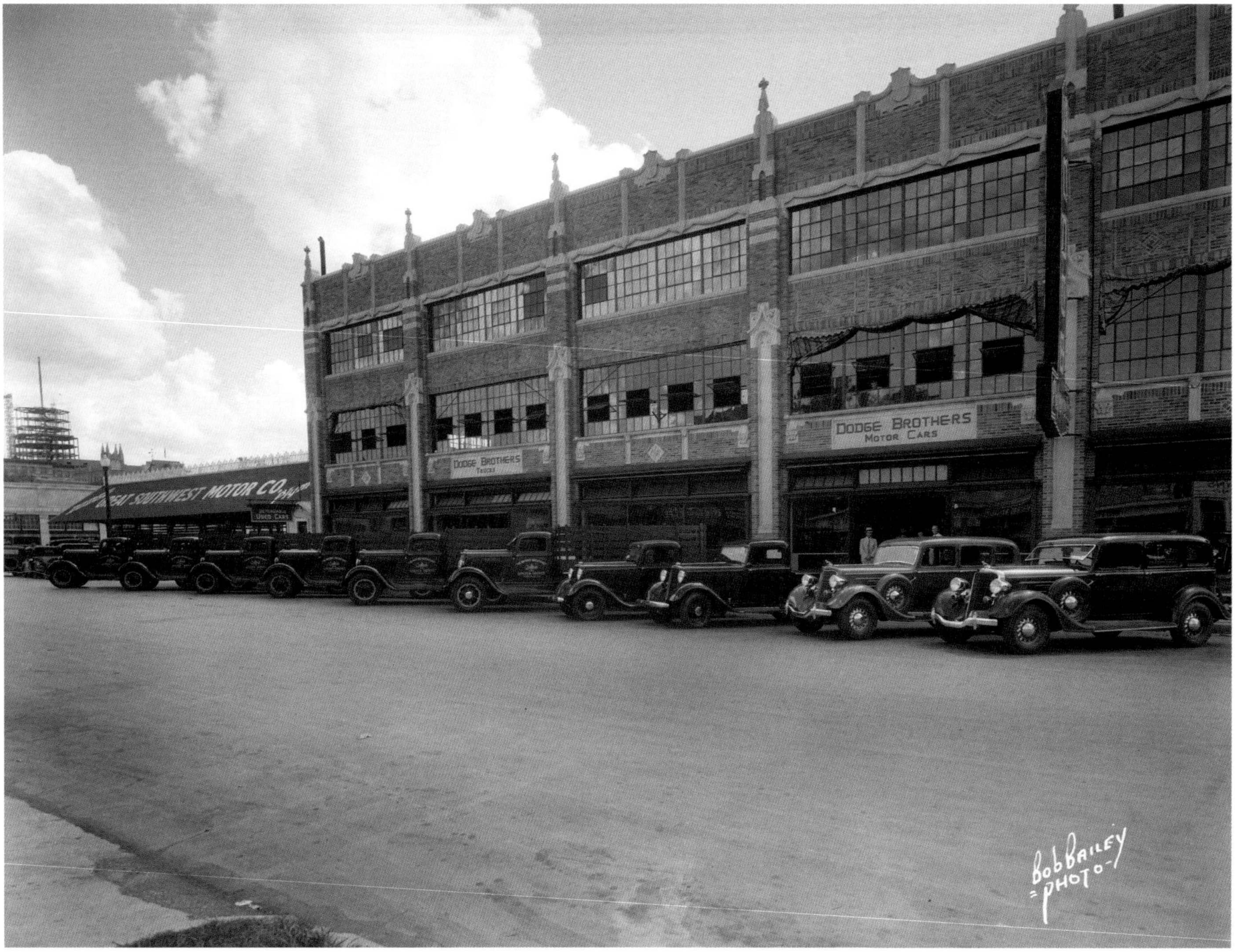

The Great Southwest Motor Company served as a Dodge Brothers dealership when this photo was shot, ca. 1934.

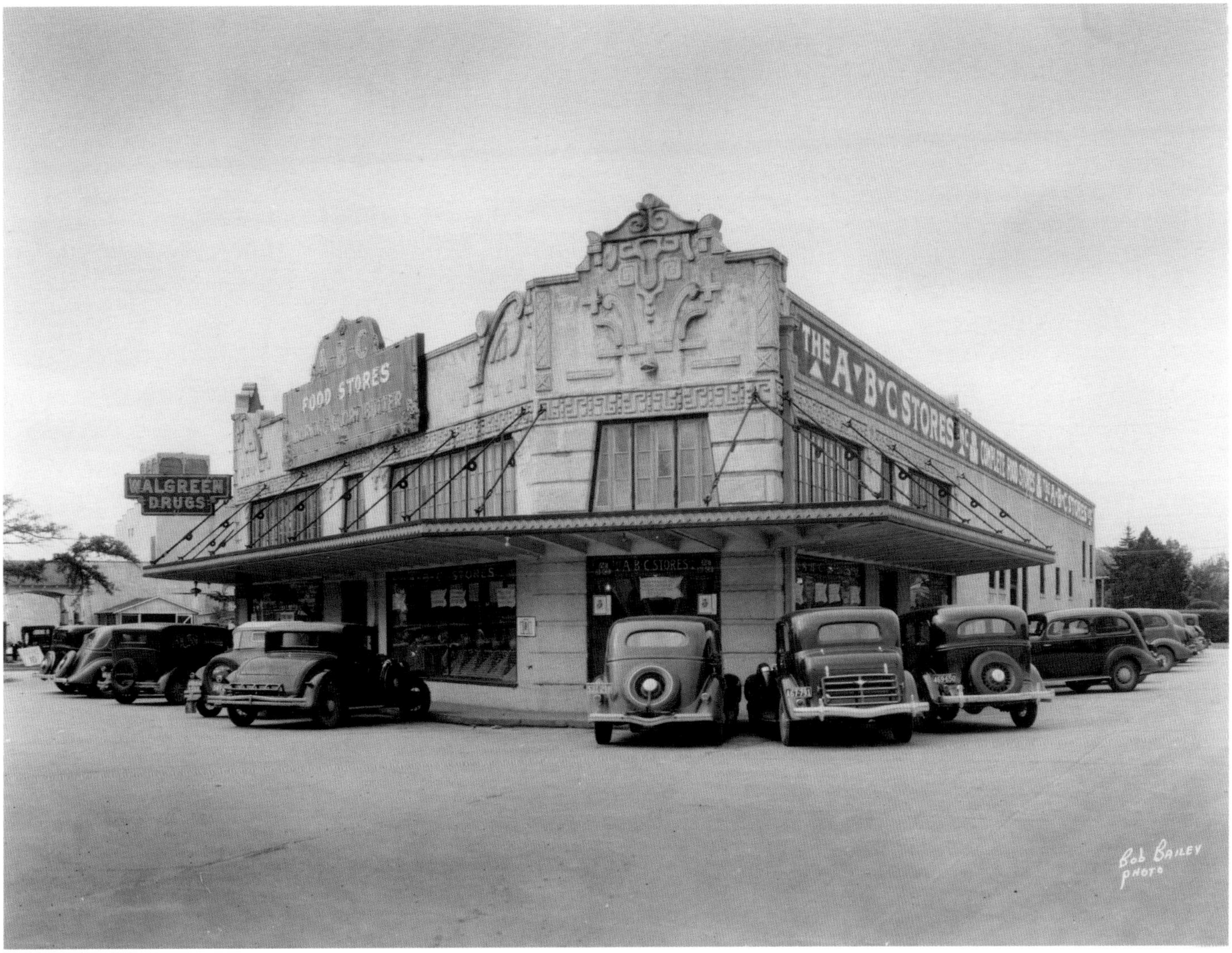

One of the small chain of A.B.C. food stores in 1935 (address unknown). This building may have been only the second instance in Houston of the use of the Mayan revival style of architecture, the other example being the twenty-two-story Petroleum Building.

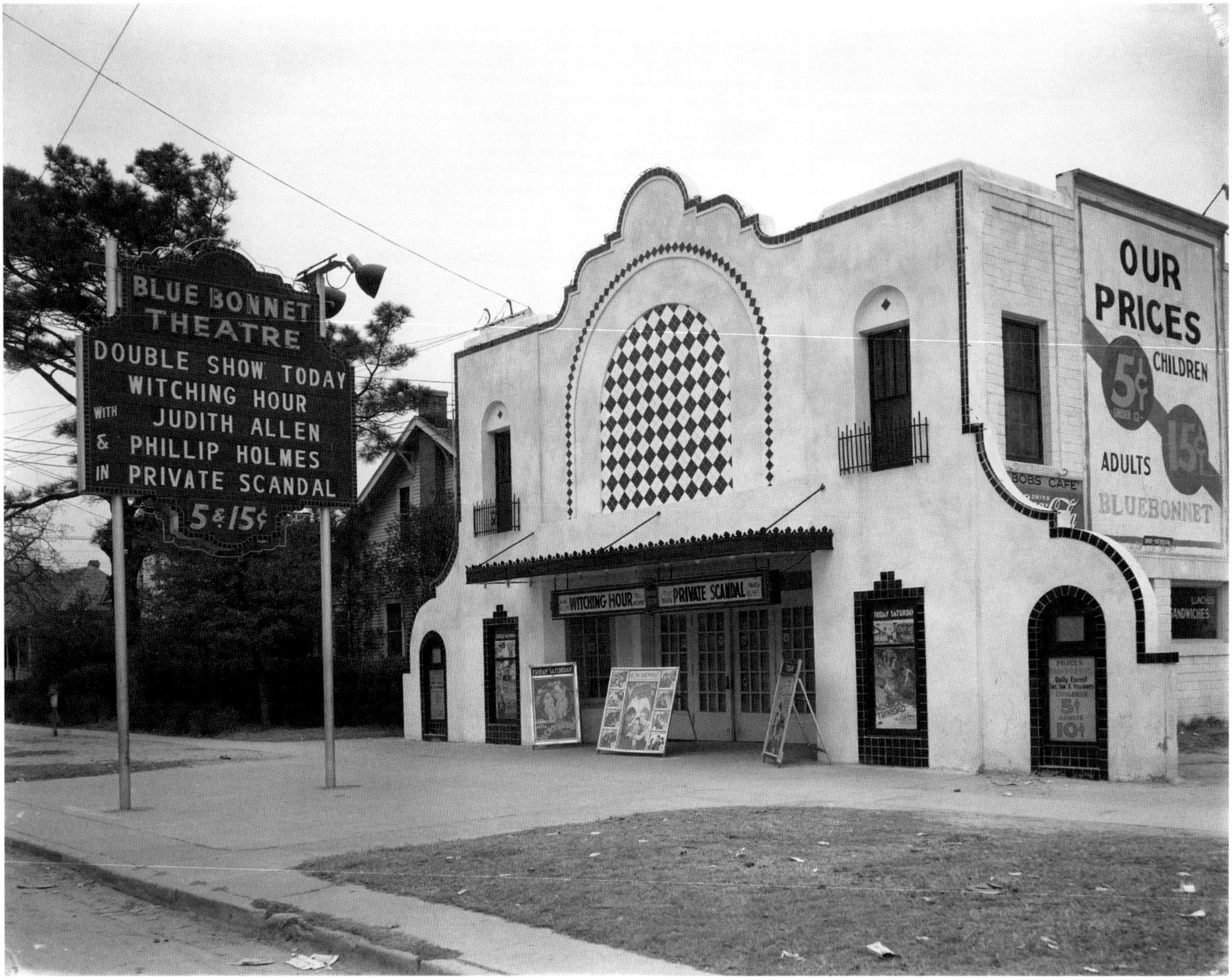

The Bluebonnet Theatre shown in 1935. The theater was built in a mixture of Mission revival and Moorish revival styles, with an Alamo-like parapet and Moorish tiles on the facade. The Bluebonnet was located at 1015 Broadway.

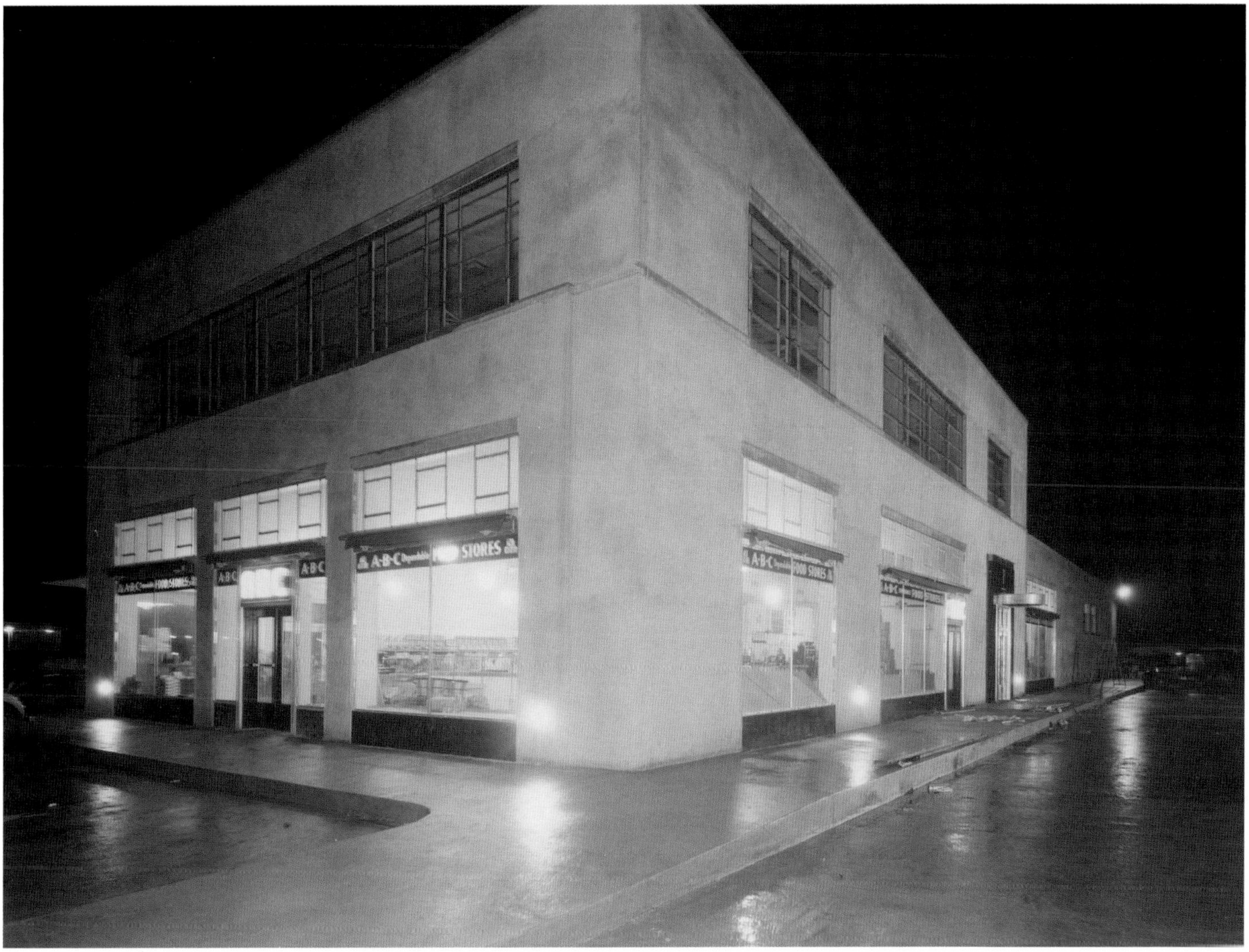

Exterior of a new member of the A.B.C. grocery store chain, designed in the Streamline Moderne style. When this photo was taken in December 1937, the A.B.C. chain had ten stores in Houston.

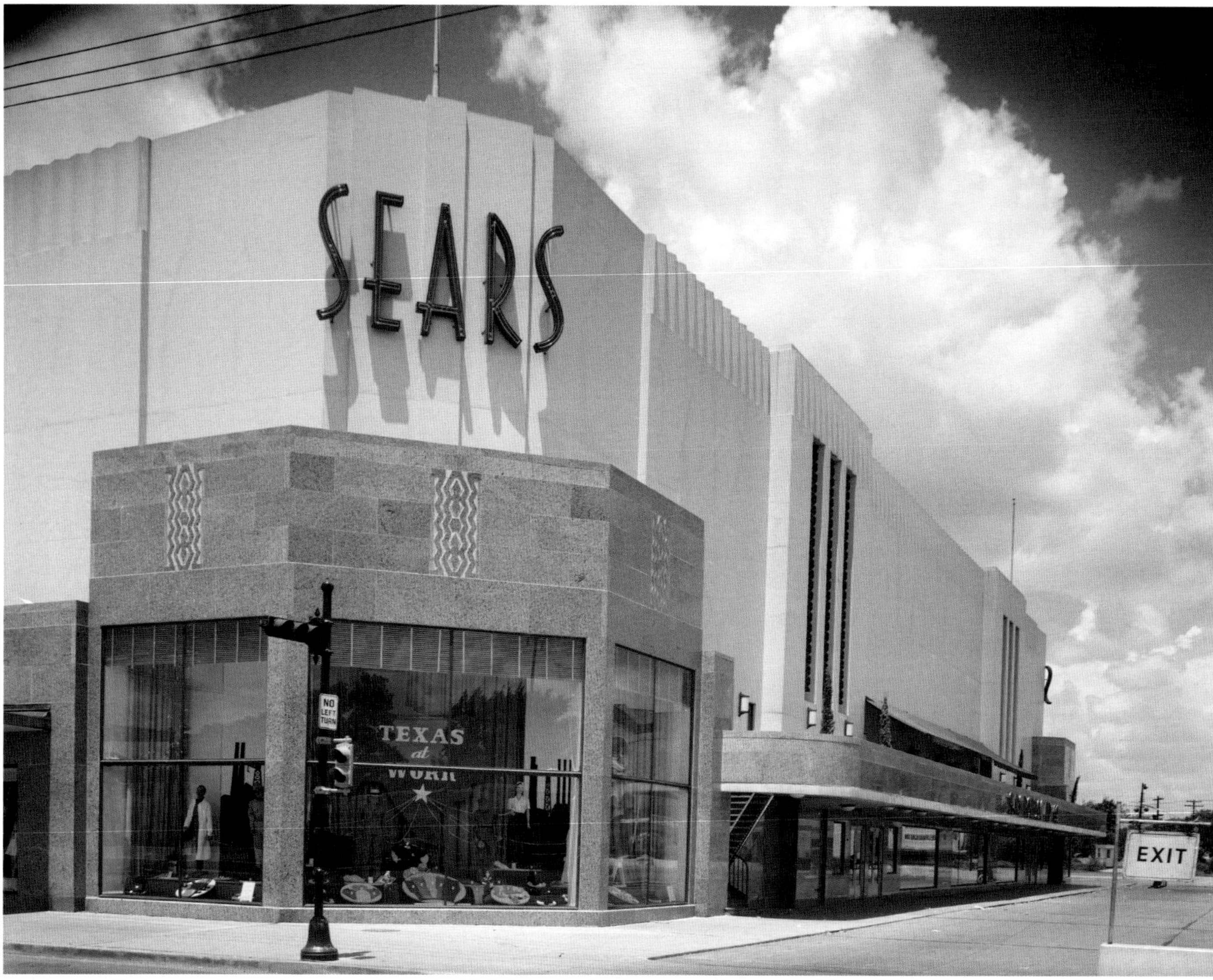

The northwest corner of the Sears store at 4201 South Main Street contained the store's major display window. The theme of the display was "Texas at Work" when this photo was taken in June 1939. The store is still in operation, but the grand display windows that wrapped around much of the building were covered during the 1960s, out of fear that the large expanses of glass would make convenient targets should any political demonstration turn violent.

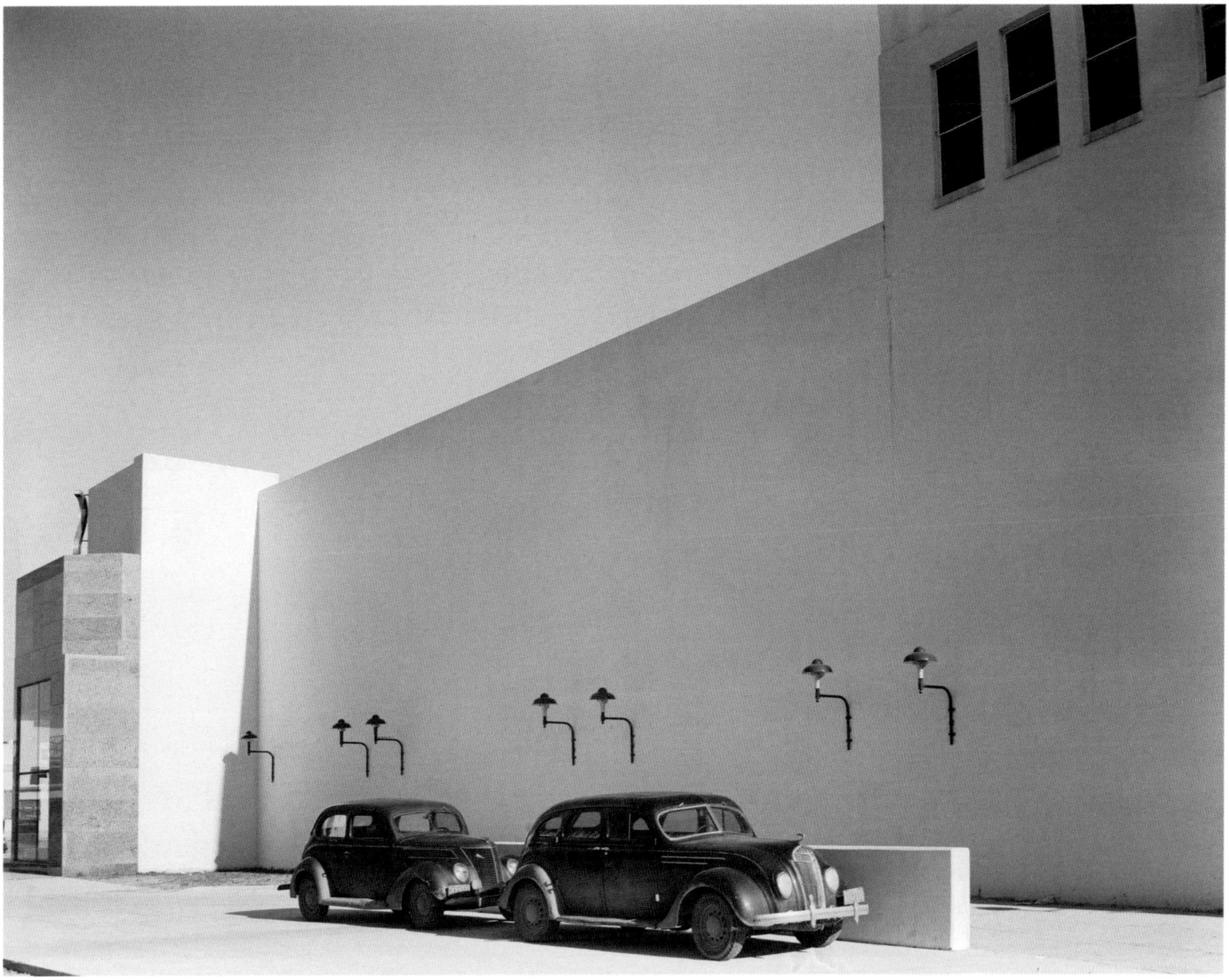

It is not known why Bailey photographed these cars parked alongside the Sears store on South Main in February 1940, but it was probably to show the availability of lighted parking immediately adjacent to the store, which was not available at downtown department stores. Taken on its own merits, the picture's composition is pure industrial and technological photographic artistry. This particular shot resembles photographs of similar subjects taken in the 1920s by the Bauhaus-influenced artist and photographer László Moholy-Nagy.

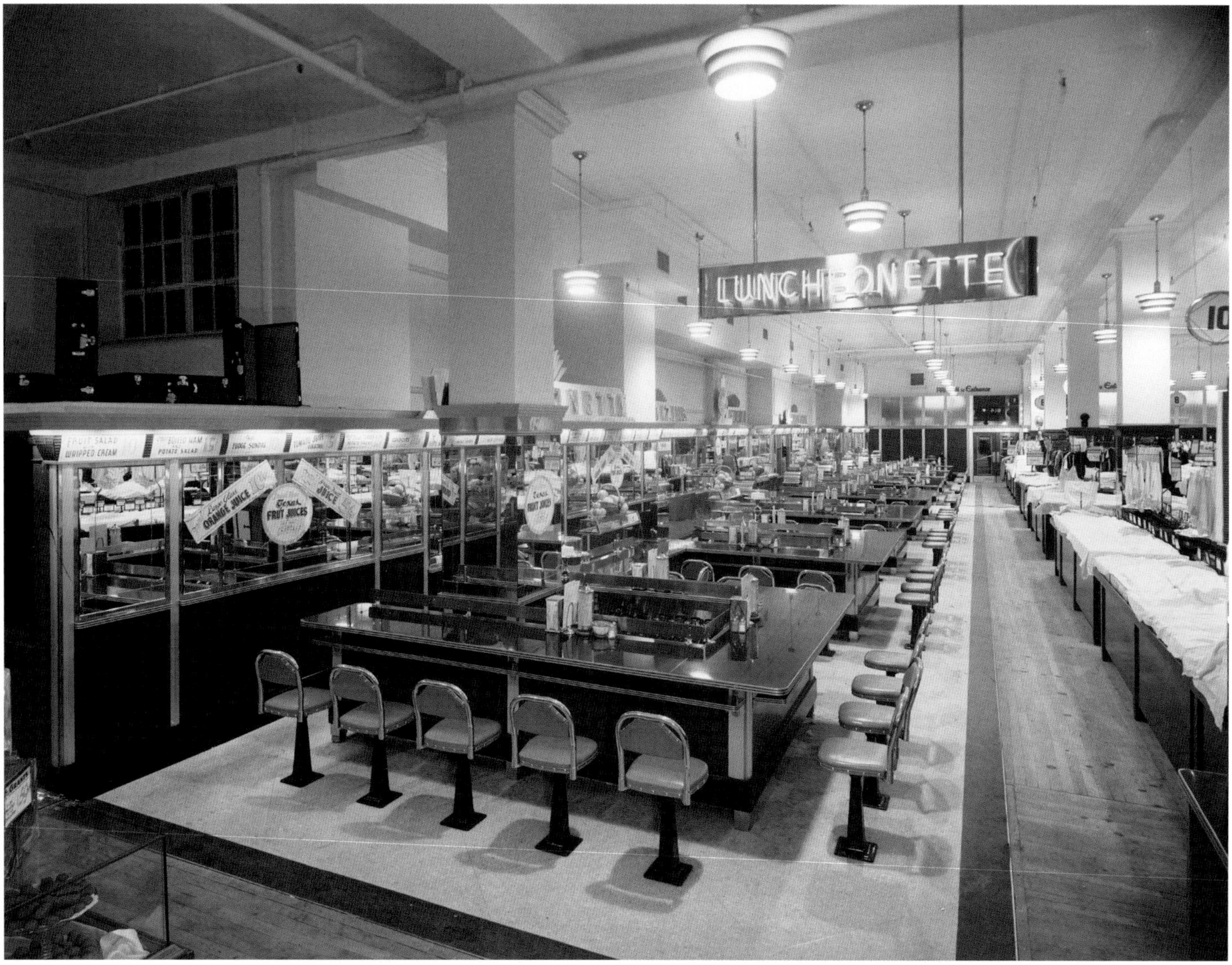

The interior of W. T. Grant Department Store, located at 609–611 Main, showing the store's huge luncheonette in 1939.

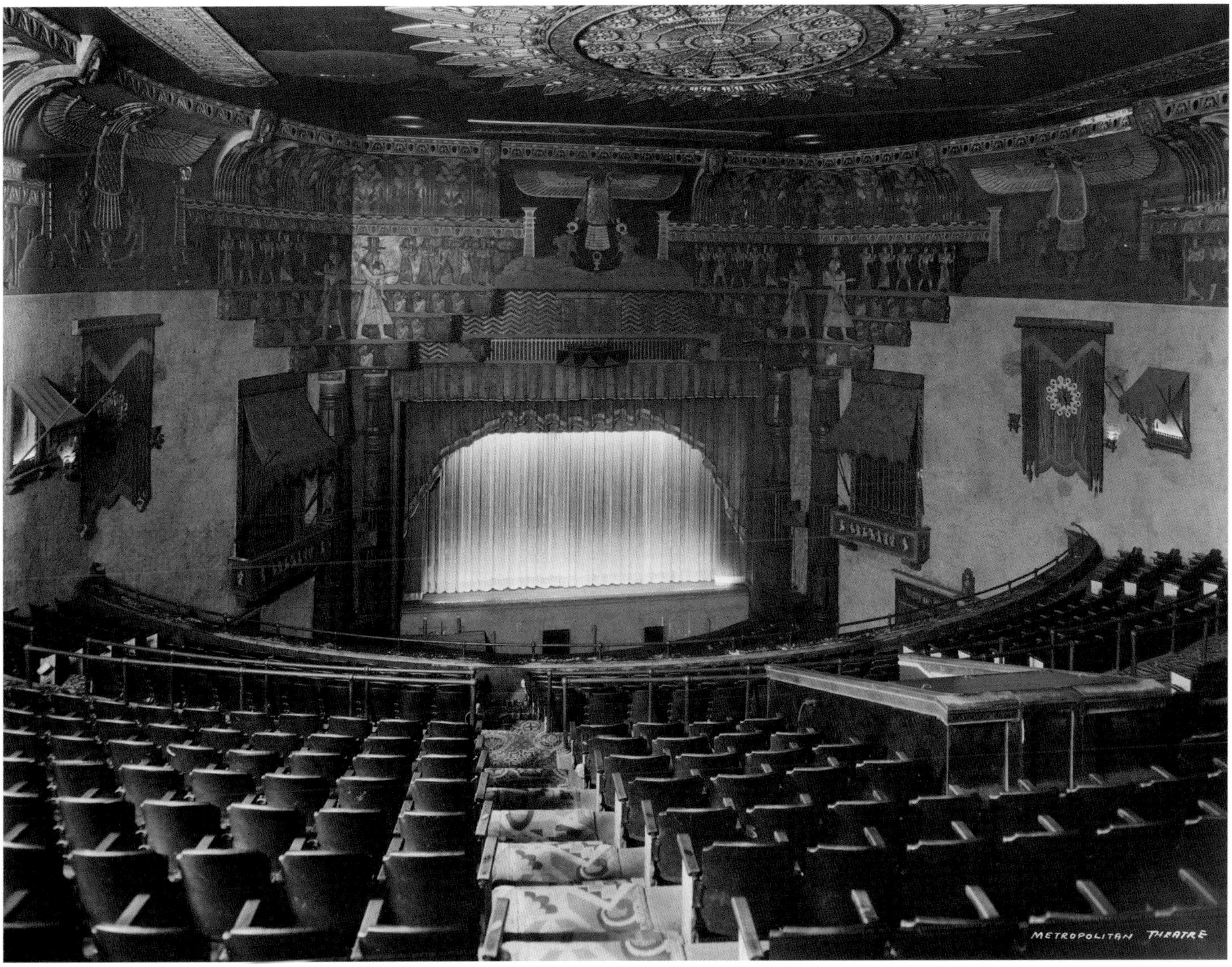

Stage and interior of the Metropolitan Theatre, 1018 Main, photographed from the balcony in August 1937. The Metropolitan was designed in an over-the-top Egyptian revival style by architect Alfred Finn and was completed in 1926. *American Theaters of Today*, published in 1927, named the Metropolitan as one of the nation's outstanding theaters.

Movie theaters and other entertainment venues were among the very first businesses to recognize and successfully exploit the value of electric signage to attract nighttime customers. The Queen Theatre, 613 Main, used a combination of advertising, a mixture of both electric and traditional sign boards and posters, when it showed the "lurid" film *Guilty Parents* in 1934. Note the parked truck at right, which was also driven around Houston to promote the film.

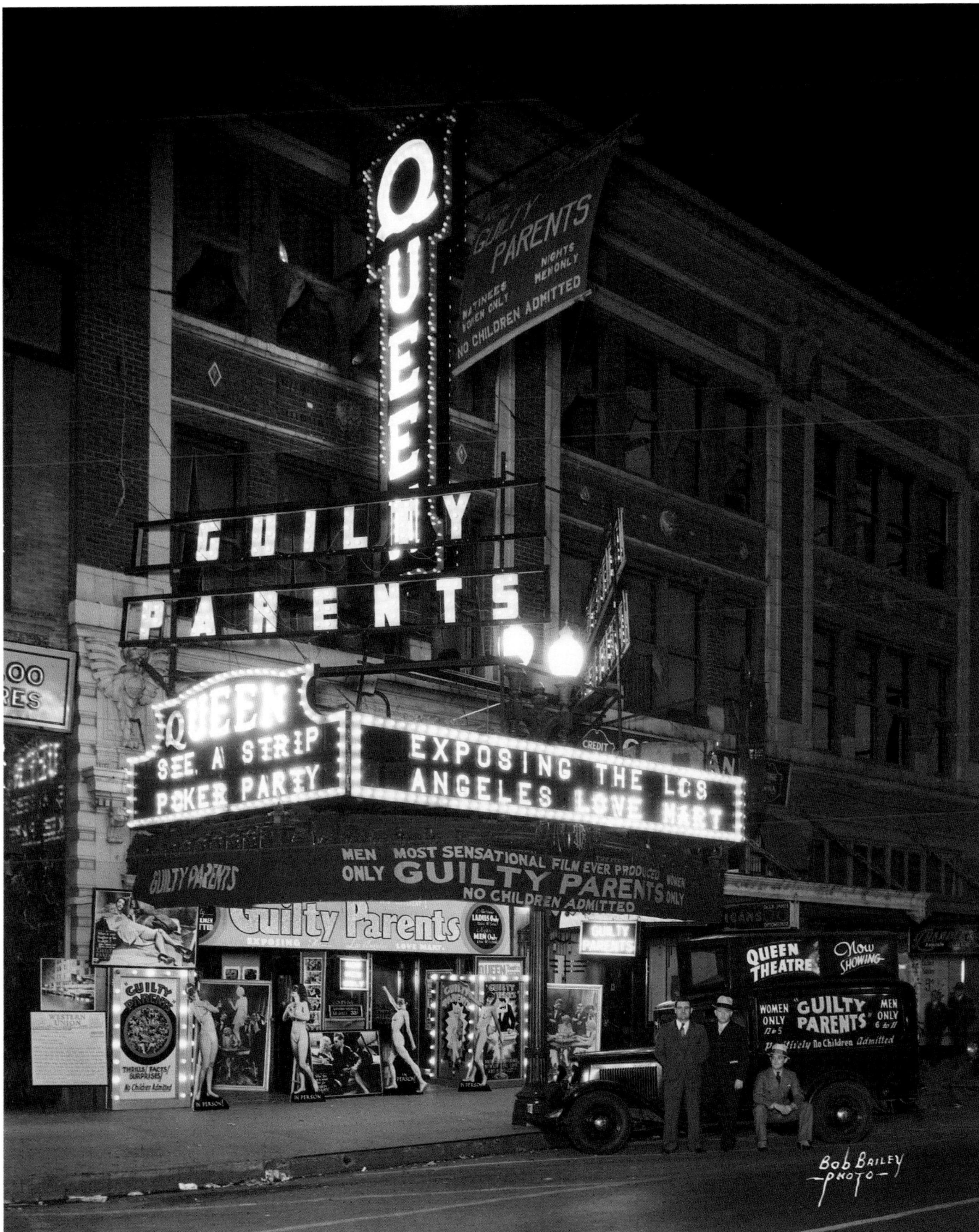
QUEEN
GUILTY PARENTS
NIGHTS MEN ONLY
MATINEES WOMEN ONLY
NO CHILDREN ADMITTED
PARENTS
QUEEN
SEE A STRIP
POKER PARTY
EXPOSING THE LOS
ANGELES LOVE MART
GUILTY PARENTS
MEN ONLY
MOST SENSATIONAL FILM EVER PRODUCED
GUILTY PARENTS
WOMEN ONLY
NO CHILDREN ADMITTED
Guilty Parents
EXPOSING
LOVE MART
GUILTY PARENTS
THRILLS! FACTS! SURPRISES!
No Children Admitted
WESTERN UNION
IN PERSON
QUEEN THEATRE
Now SHOWING
WOMEN ONLY 12 to 5
GUILTY PARENTS
MEN ONLY 6 to 11
Positively No Children Admitted
Bob Bailey
PHOTO

The Pruitt Company, at 1315–17 Polk, indicated its location by utilizing one of the oldest (and simplest) directional devices, a pointing arrow, in combination with the lighted outline of a modern-day traffic policeman. The signage received another twentieth-century twist by using neon lighting, as shown in this 1935 photo. The Pruitt Company was an automotive repair shop and is still in business today.

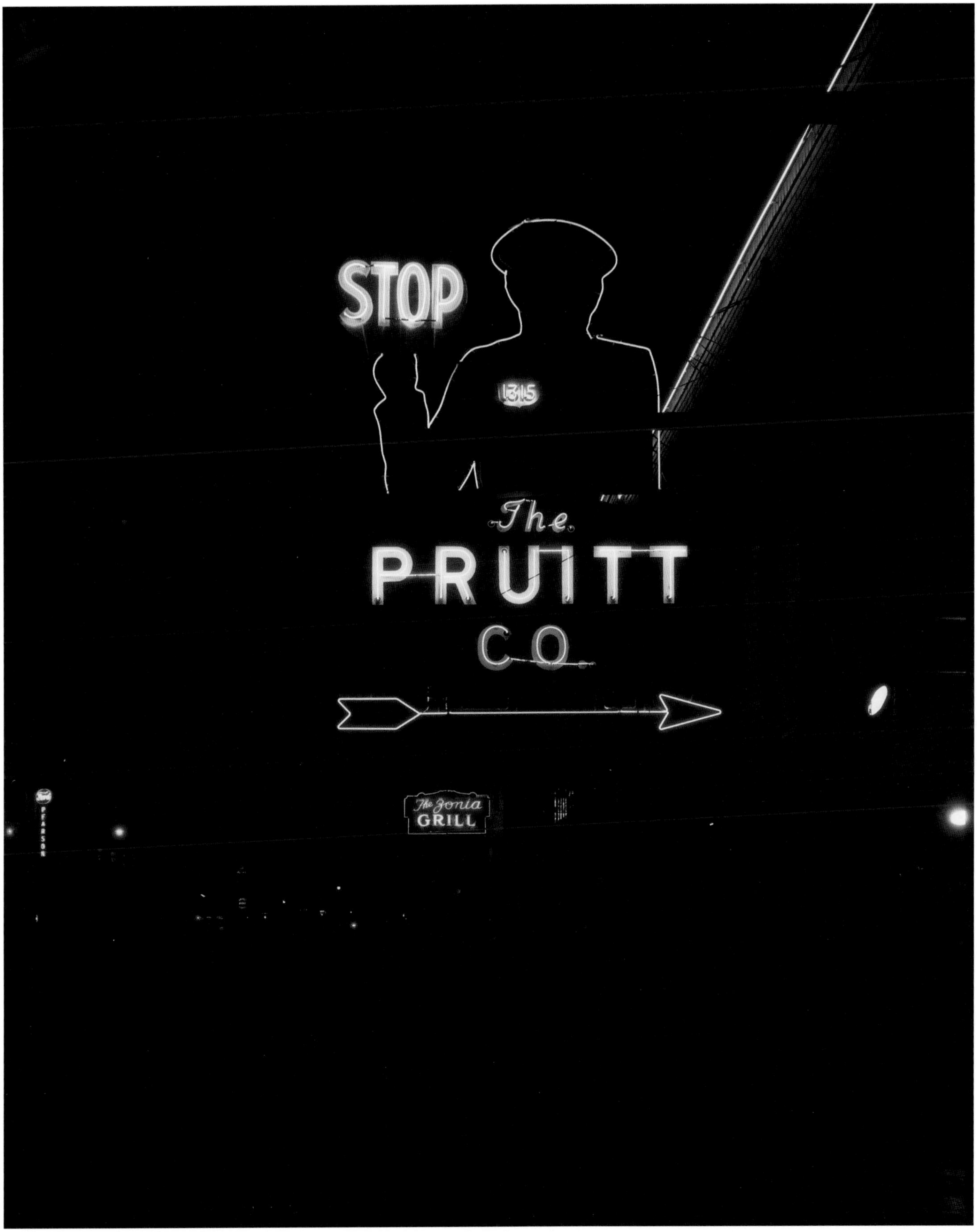
STOP
1315
The
PRUITT
CO.
The Zonia
GRILL

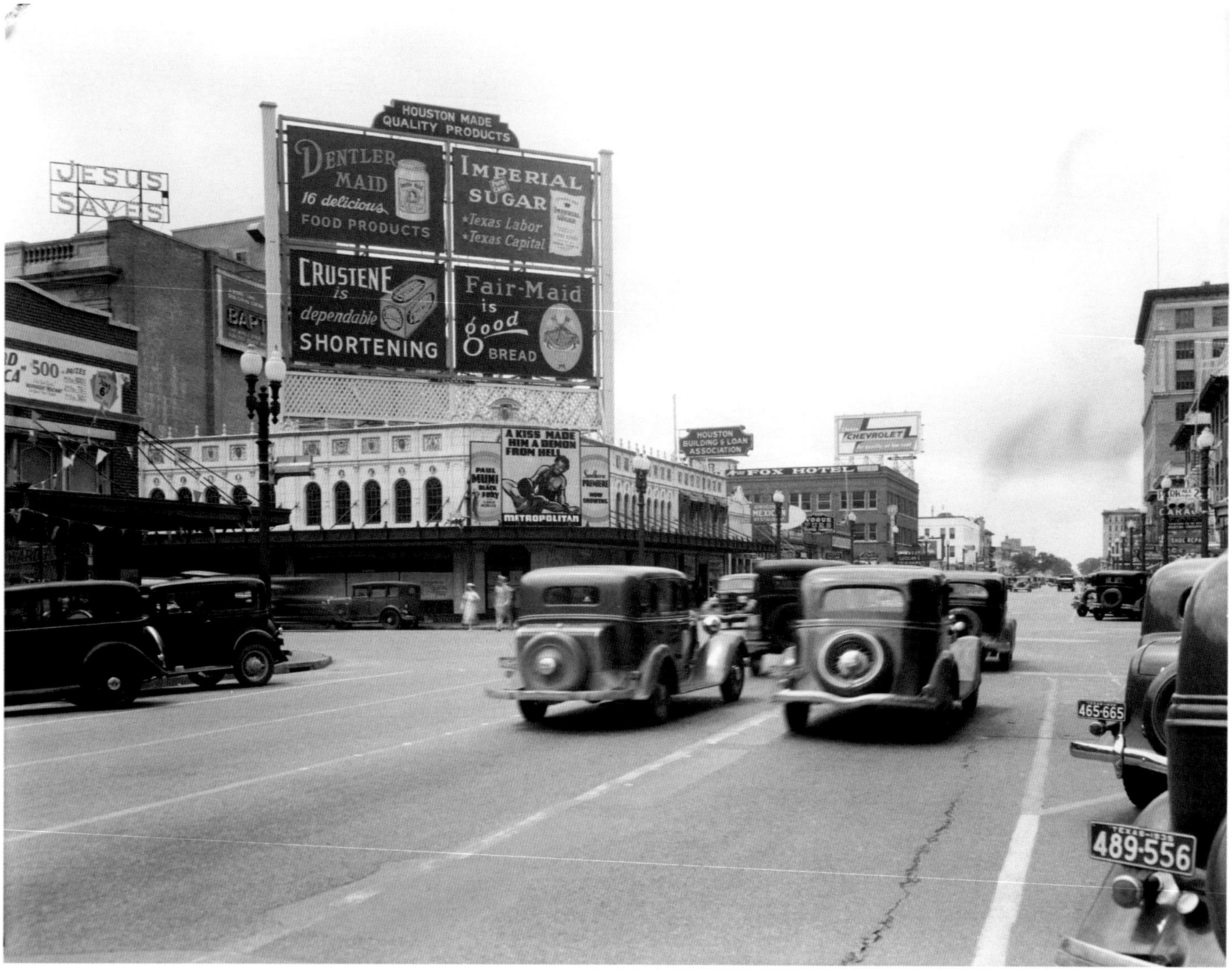

Above: A jumble of food billboards on Main Street in May 1935, with "Jesus Saves" sign in background on the roof of First Baptist Church at Lamar and Fannin. Signage congestion greatly increased along Houston's principal streets in tandem with the city's growth, becoming an eyesore for some, while serving as a useful consumer service for others and a boon for businesses. By 1980, an estimated ten thousand billboards cluttered the Houston landscape, gaining Houston international notoriety and initiating a widespread citizens' movement for their removal. In 2013, less than 1,500 billboards remained.

Facing: As Houston's principal commercial buildings grew in height and crowded into the densely built downtown area, business owners and advertisers began to use increasingly taller vertical advertising and signage to compensate for their lack of horizontal space. This May 1936 shot of the 400 block of Main Street shows the exterior of the original Foley Brothers store with its vertical sign above the building's entrance. Foley Brothers also used its available wall space on the building's side to display a large painted sign, complete with the six flags of Texas, to advertise the store. Main Street was crossed with Texas flag pennants in honor of the Texas Centennial that year.

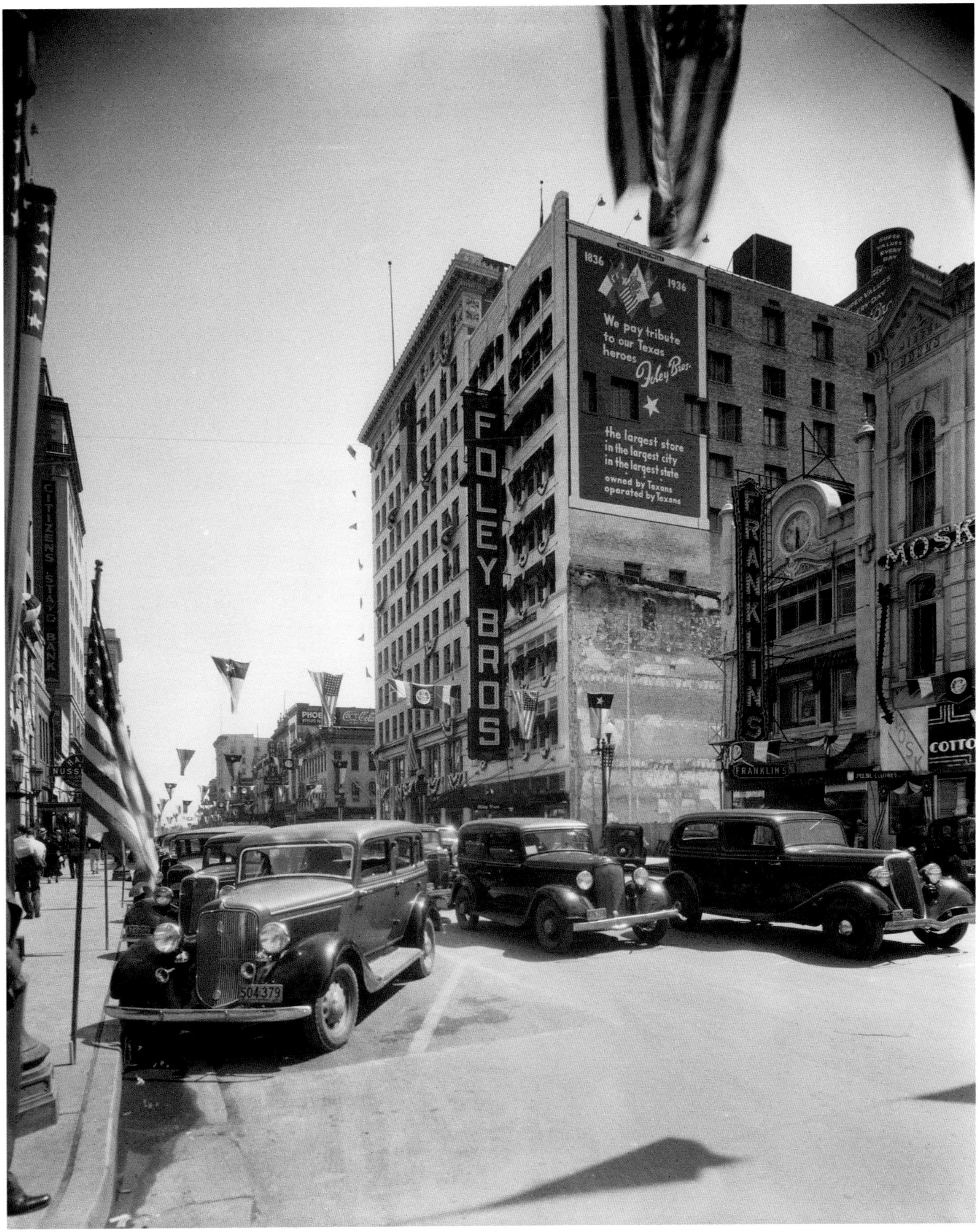
1836
1936
We pay tribute
to our Texas
heroes
Foley Bros.
the largest store
in the largest city
in the largest state
owned by Texans
operated by Texans
FOLEY BROS
FRANKLINS
MOSK
CITIZENS STATE BANK
504 379

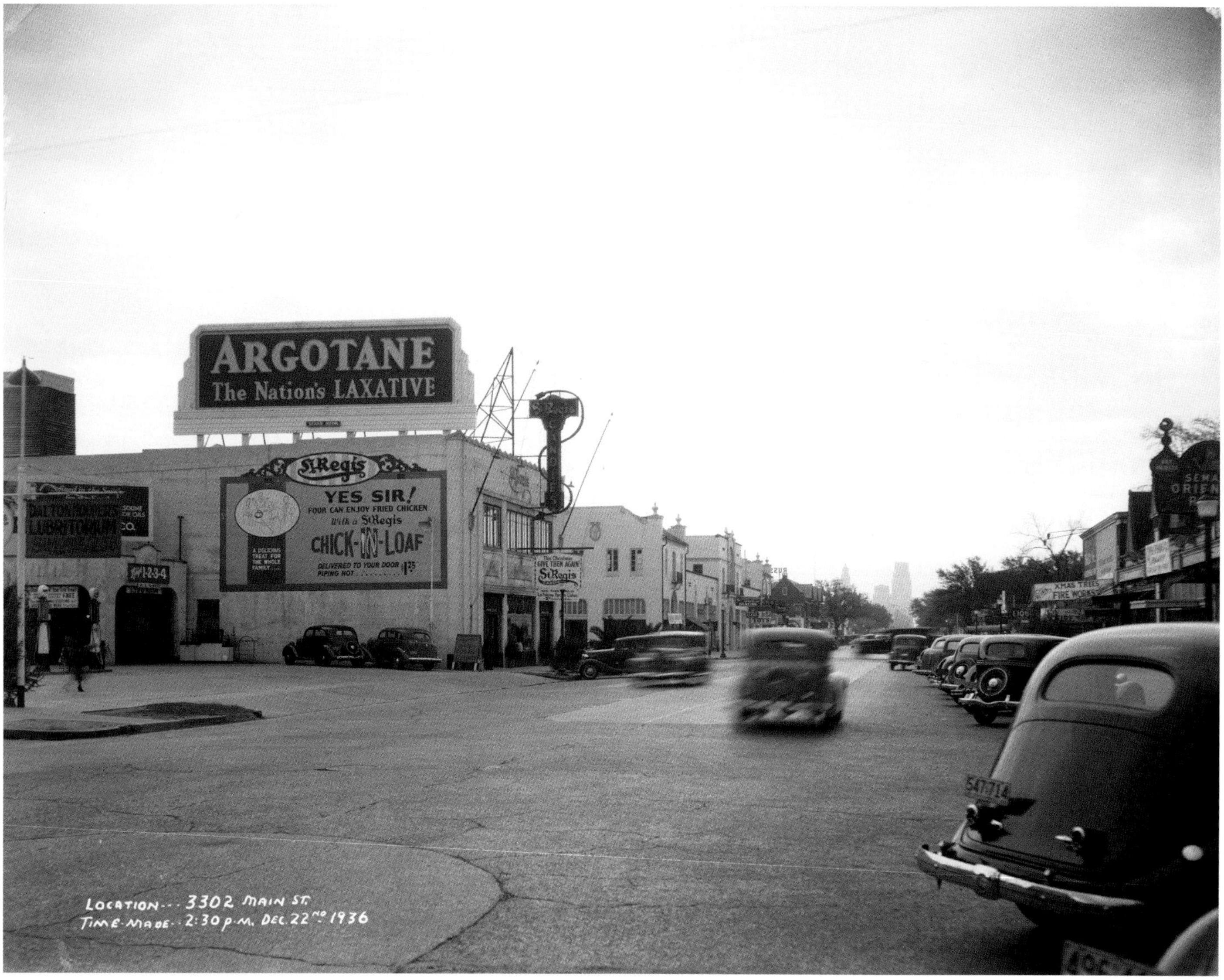

Although the southern Bible Belt, of which Texas was considered by many to be the "buckle," was generally thought to be more puritanical than much of the country, there was nothing prudish about the placement of this Argotane Laxative billboard, photographed in December 1936. The view looks north from 3302 Main Street toward downtown, which can be seen in the distance.

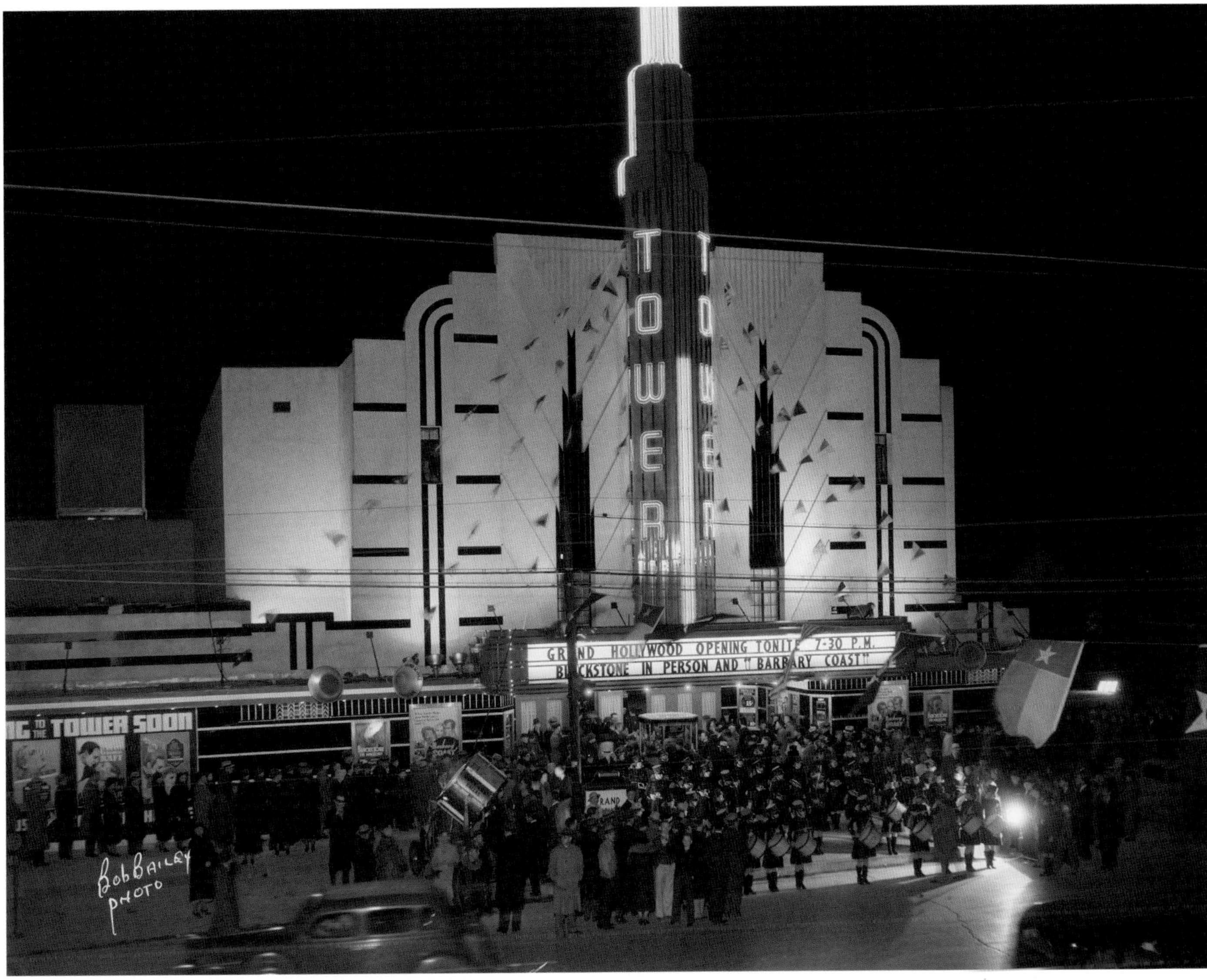

Tower Theatre, Westheimer at Waugh Drive, on its opening night, February 14, 1936. Klieg lights lit the sky, and various forms of entertainment, both inside the theater and outside, were provided for the opening-night audience by Interstate Theatres.

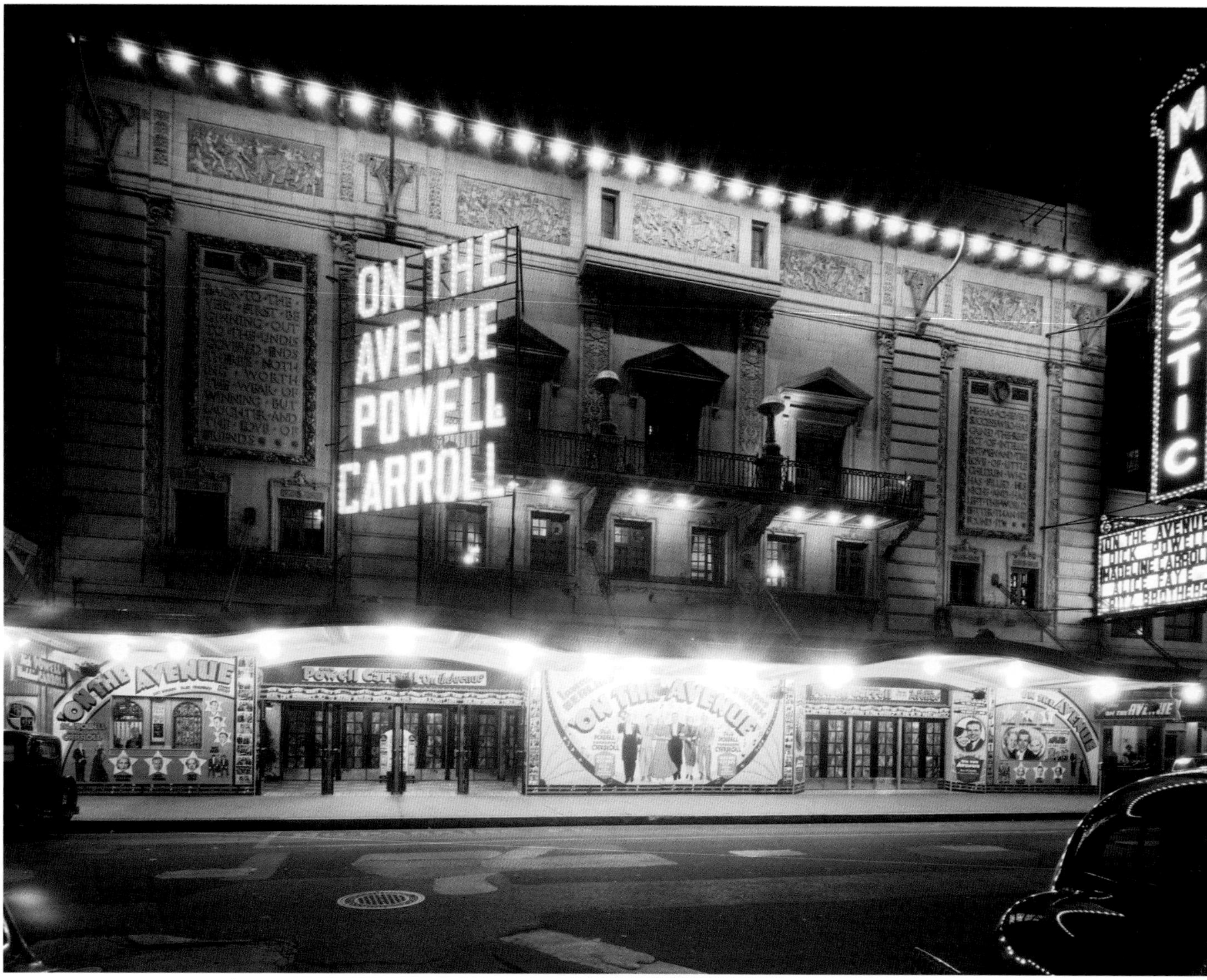

Above: The brilliantly illuminated marquee and facade of the Majestic Theatre promoted the theater's showing of the film *On the Avenue,* starring Dick Powell and Madeleine Carroll, in February 1937.

Facing: As a promotional technique, the Metro-Goldwyn-Mayer film company provided false plantation-like, portico exteriors to the major theaters in the Loew's State chain for the local premieres of *Gone With the Wind.* Loew's State Theatre was the venue for the film's Houston showing in February 1940.

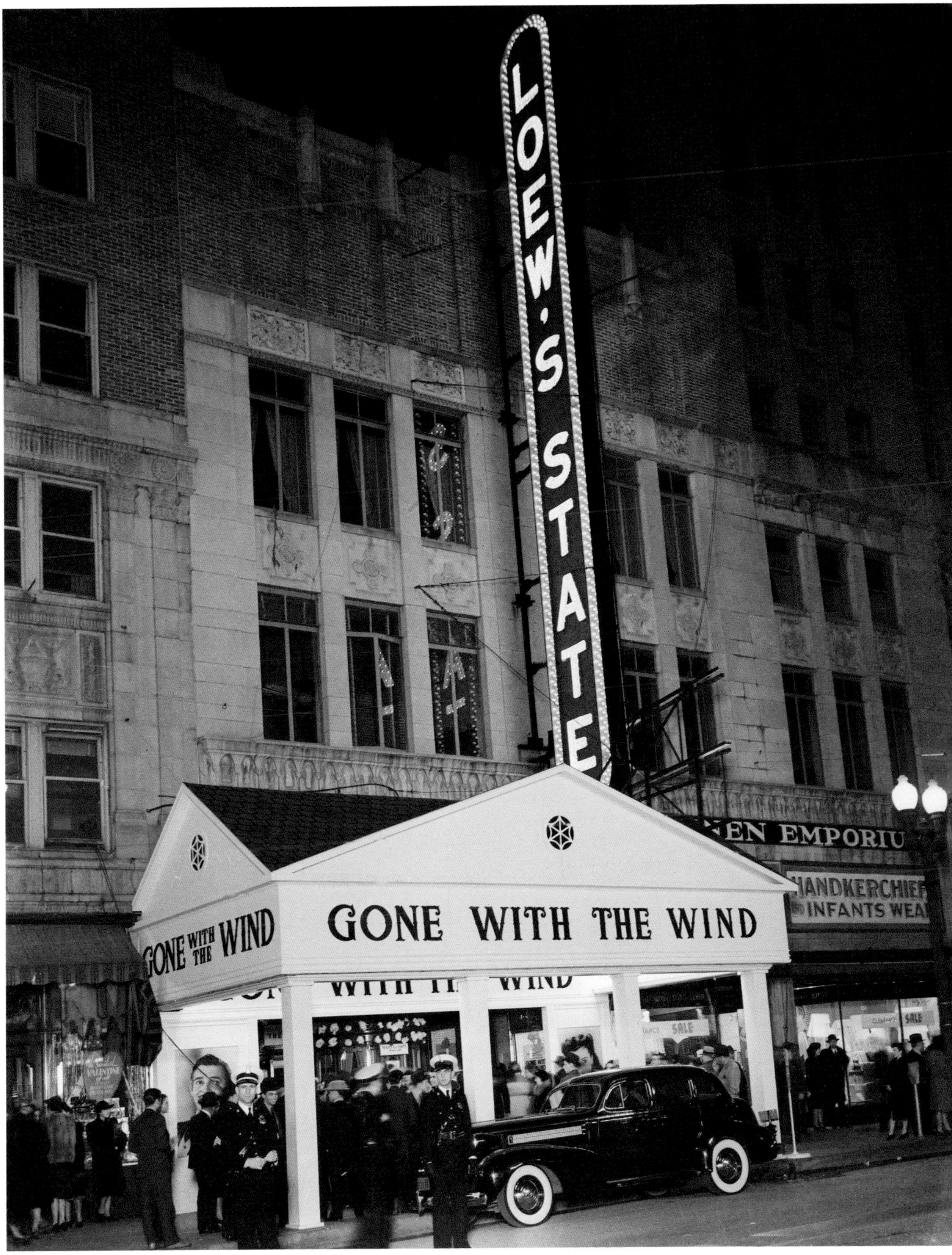
LOEW'S STATE
GONE WITH THE WIND
GONE WITH THE WIND

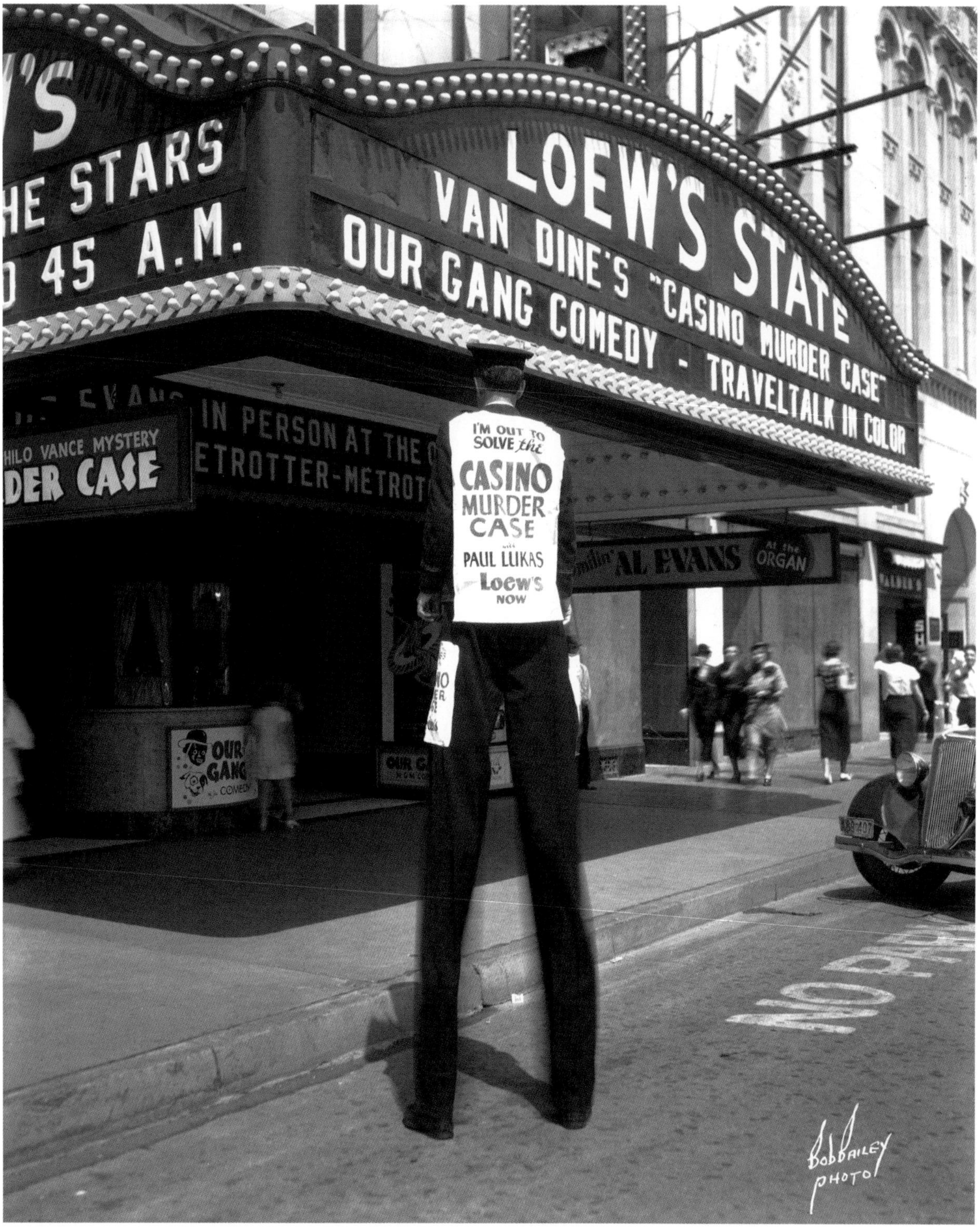

A stilt walker was employed by Loew's State Theatre in 1935 to advertise the film *Casino Murder Case*, starring Paul Lukas. Stilt walkers were often employed by businesses in pre–World War II American cities. On crowded city sidewalks, this early form of vertical advertising was sure to draw attention.

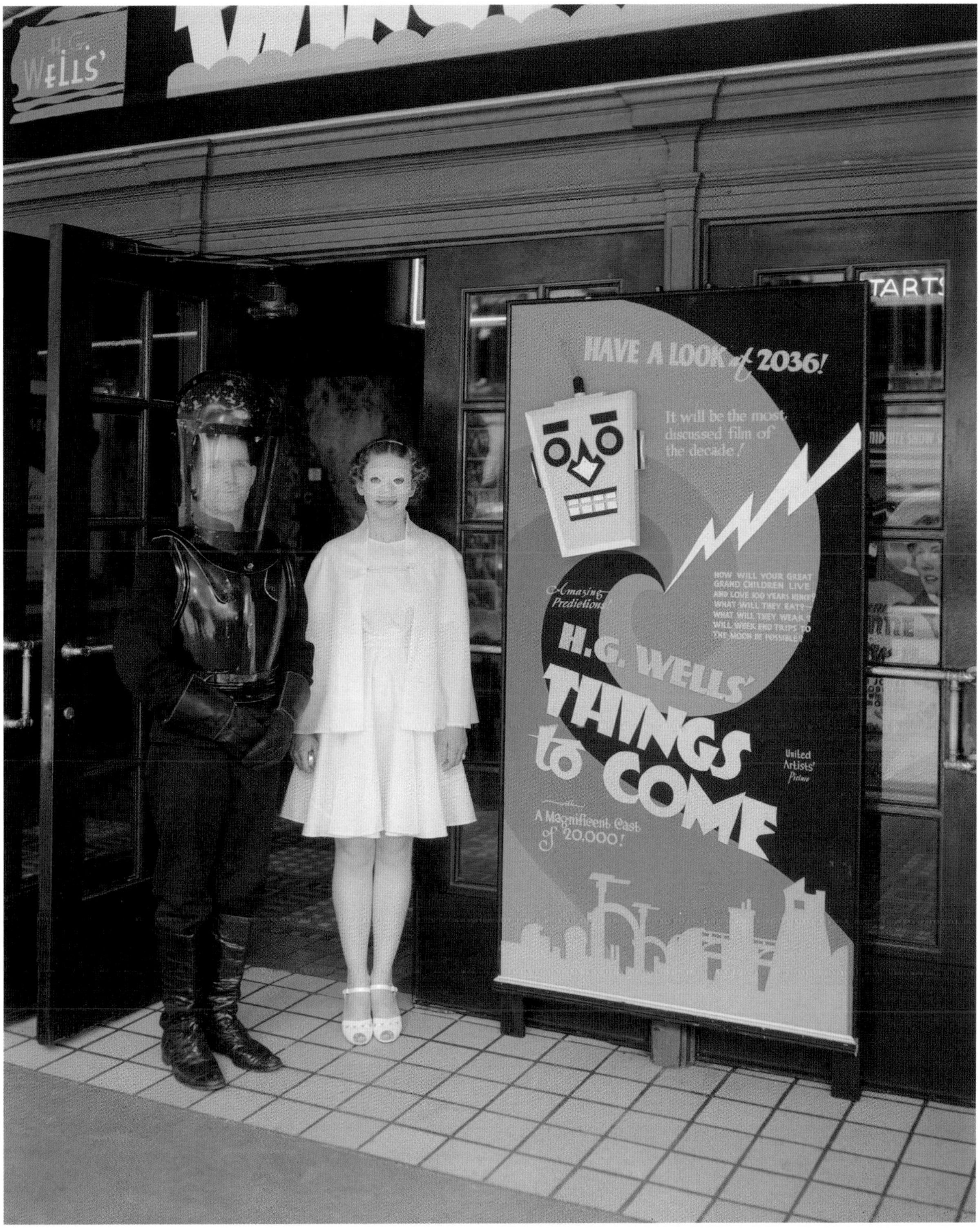

The Metropolitan Theatre's promotion for the 1936 film version of H. G. Wells's novel *Things to Come*, which was set a century in the future in the year 2036. In addition to the modernistic styling of the signboard, complete with a robot's head, the Metropolitan utilized two employees dressed in "futuristic" costumes to draw attention to the film.

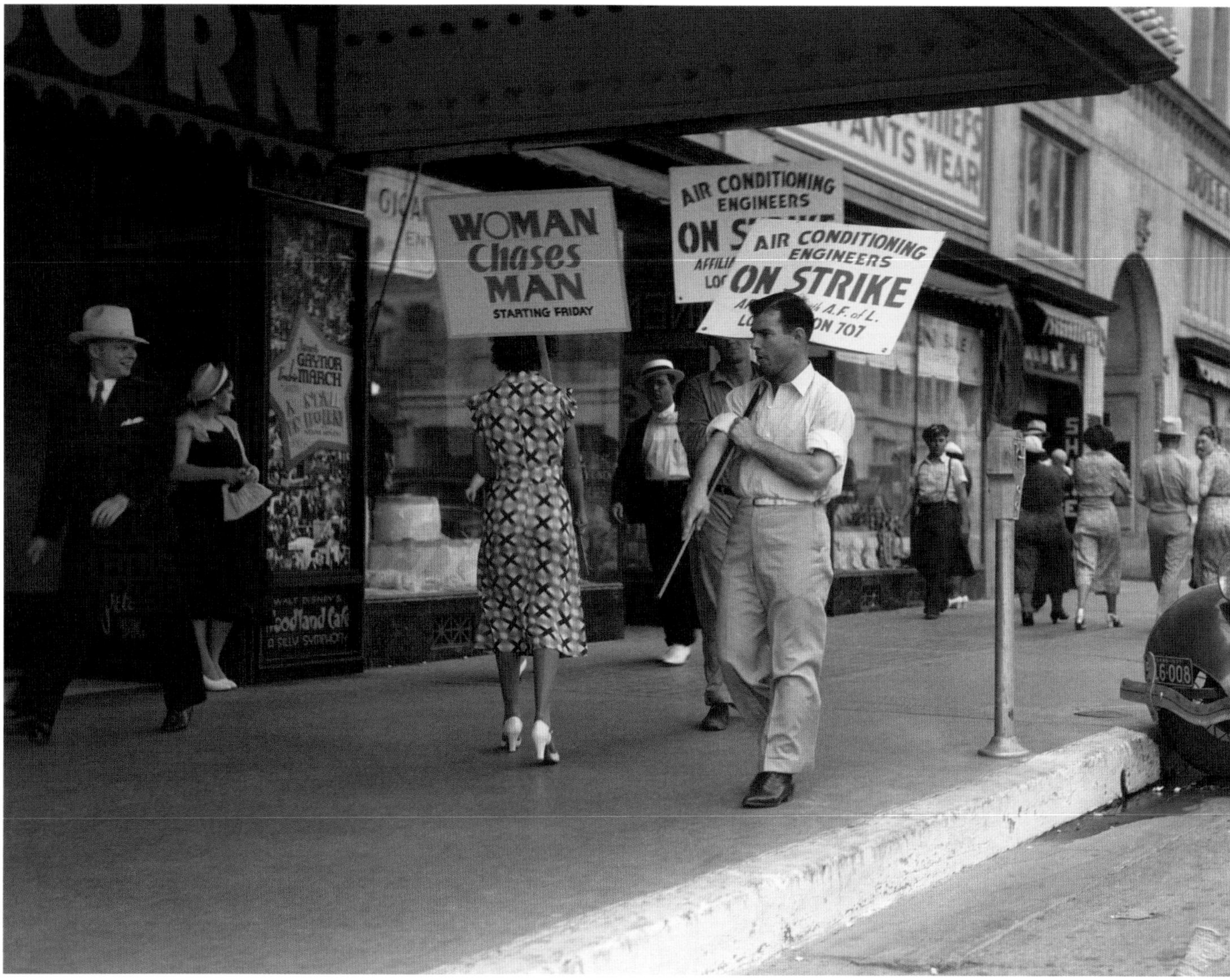

Above: This is one of the many photographs taken by the Bailey Studios that reveal multiple layers of Houston's history to twenty-first century viewers. In the midst of a picket line, conducted by striking air conditioning engineers, a Loew's State Theatre employee has taken advantage of the situation and carries her own picket sign. The passerby at the left is enjoying her sign, which promotes the upcoming film *Woman Chases Man.* The strike was presumably against Loew's, since movie theaters were among the few buildings that had air conditioning when this picture was taken in 1937. The strength that organized labor once enjoyed in Houston as well as the humorous advertising achieved by the Loew's employee are both evident in the image.

Facing: As advertising of all types increased tremendously in the twentieth century, government agencies also learned the value of good promotional signage. This 1938 display, placed by the Houston Police Department's homicide squad, was probably on view in the Iris Theatre, located at 614 Travis.

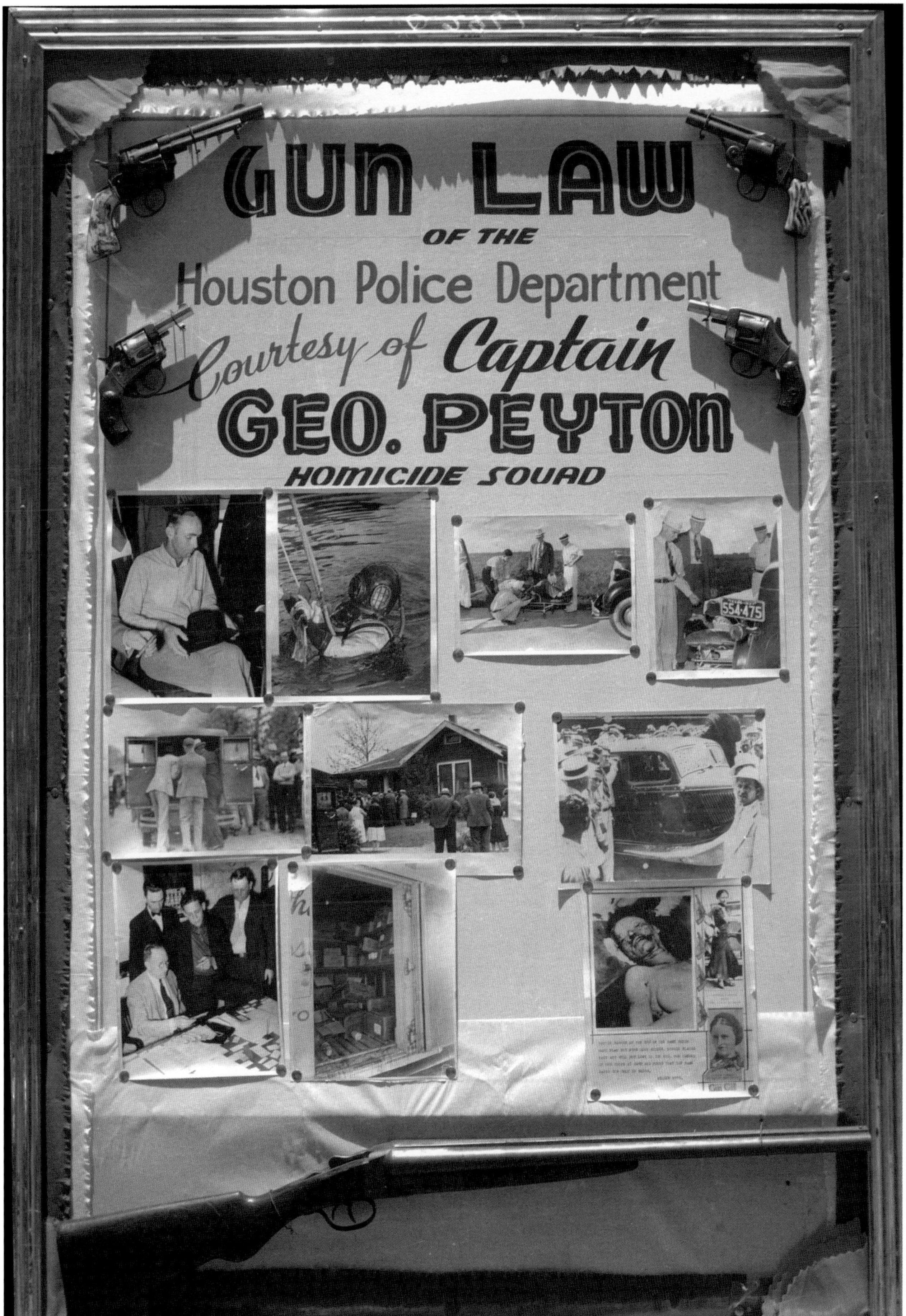
GUN LAW
OF THE
Houston Police Department
Courtesy of Captain
GEO. PEYTON
HOMICIDE SQUAD

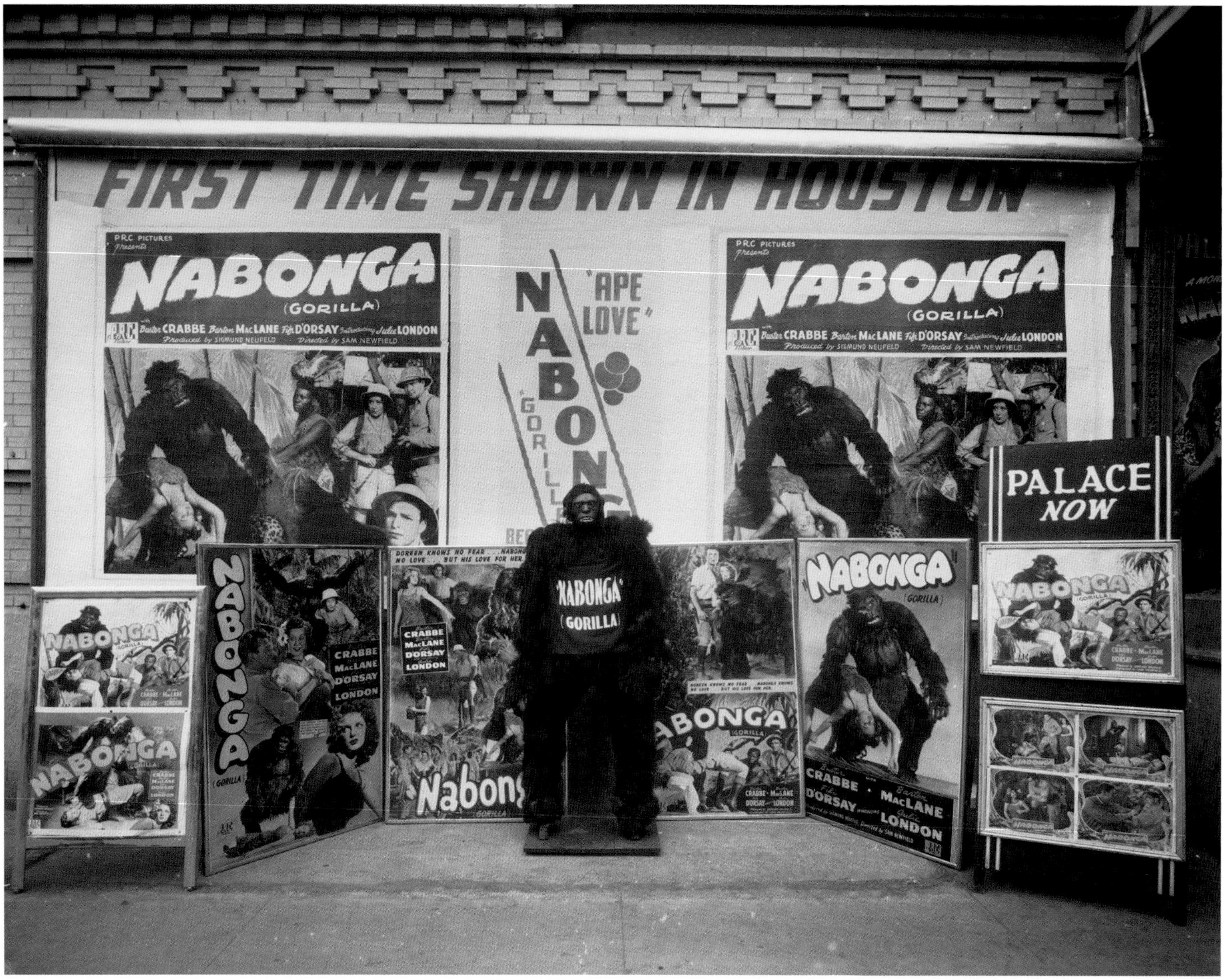

The Palace Theatre (807-811 Texas Avenue) took a no-holds-barred approach with its advertising for the film *Nabonga,* which was released in 1944. Although the gorilla mannequin looks pretty cheesy by today's standards, it most likely scared many children at the time, while enticing many others to see perennial adventurer Buster Crabbe, a former Tarzan, battle with the giant ape Nabonga.

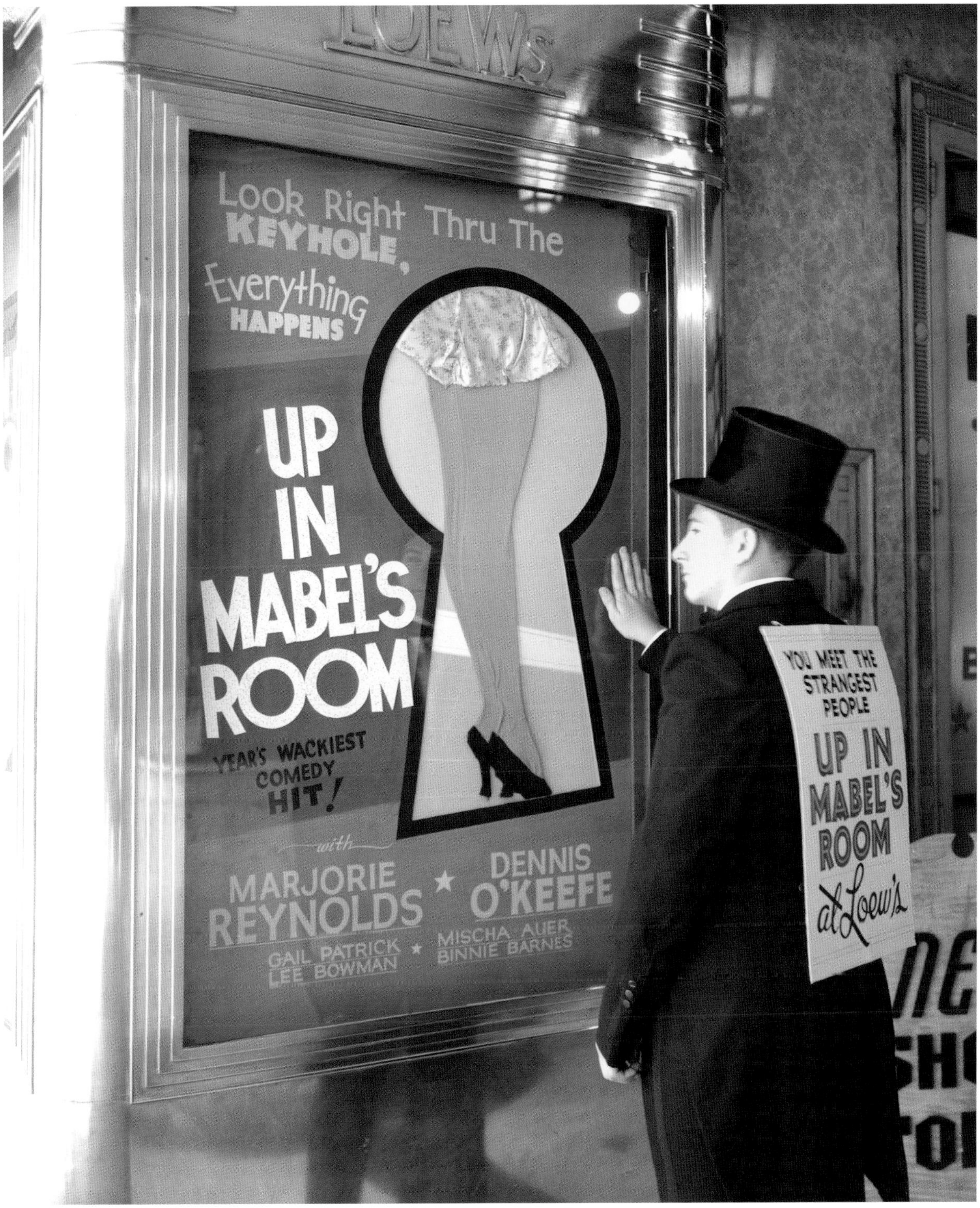

One of the many forms of advertising along streets in cities in the early-twentieth century was the sandwich board. In this instance, Loew's State Theatre employed this man to advertise the film *Up in Mabel's Room* (1944) by taping a sign on his back in a manner similar to sandwich boards. Here he poses next to a poster for the film at Loew's Theatre. In an era thought of today as prudish, sex is used in the poster as the primary draw.

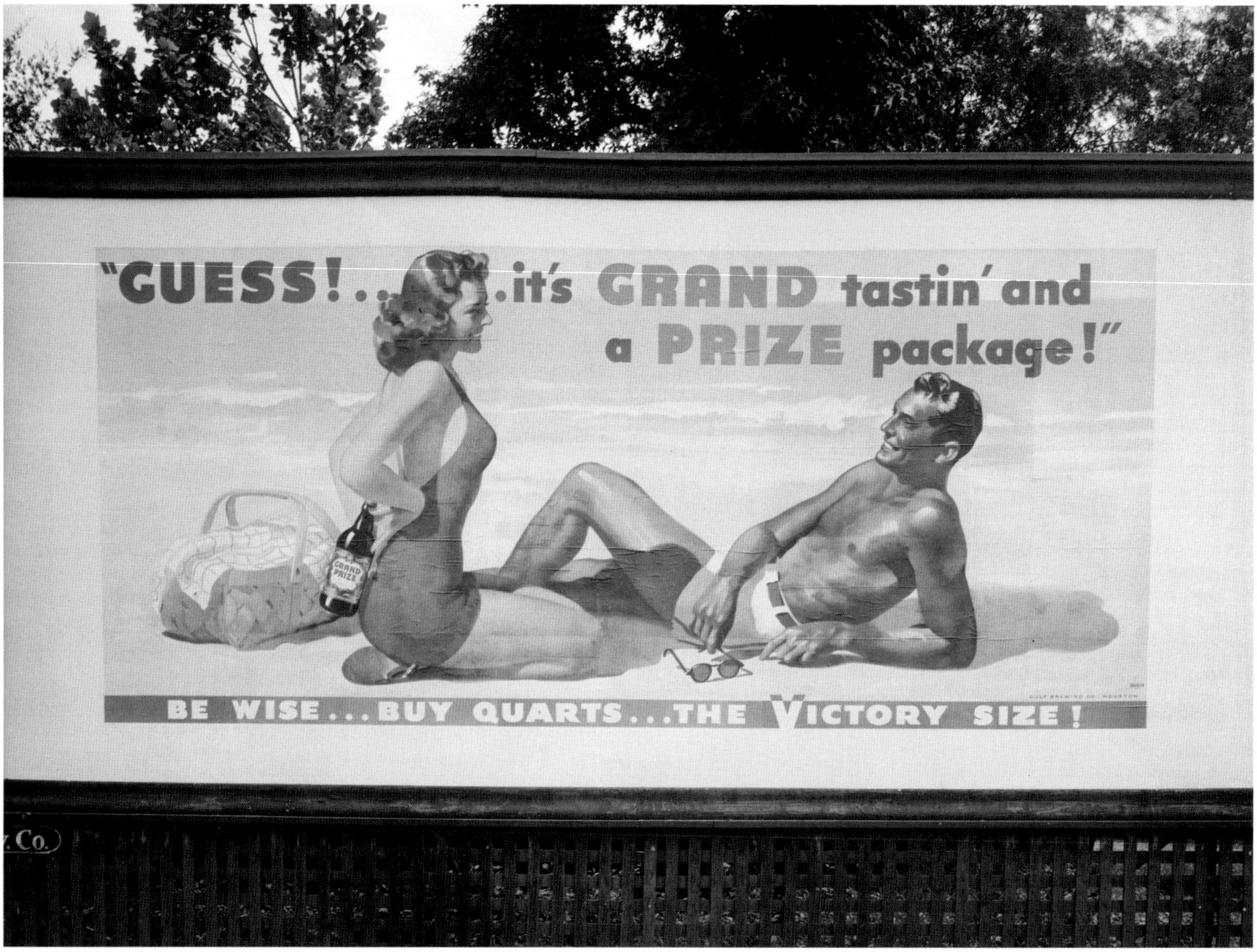

Grand Prize Beer had a winner in 1941 with this outdoor billboard utilizing sex appeal, with its swimsuit-clad beauty, Freudian innuendo, and appeal to patriotism, urging buyers to purchase "victory size" quarts. Grand Prize Beer was brewed by the Houston Brewing Company, which was owned by Howard Hughes.

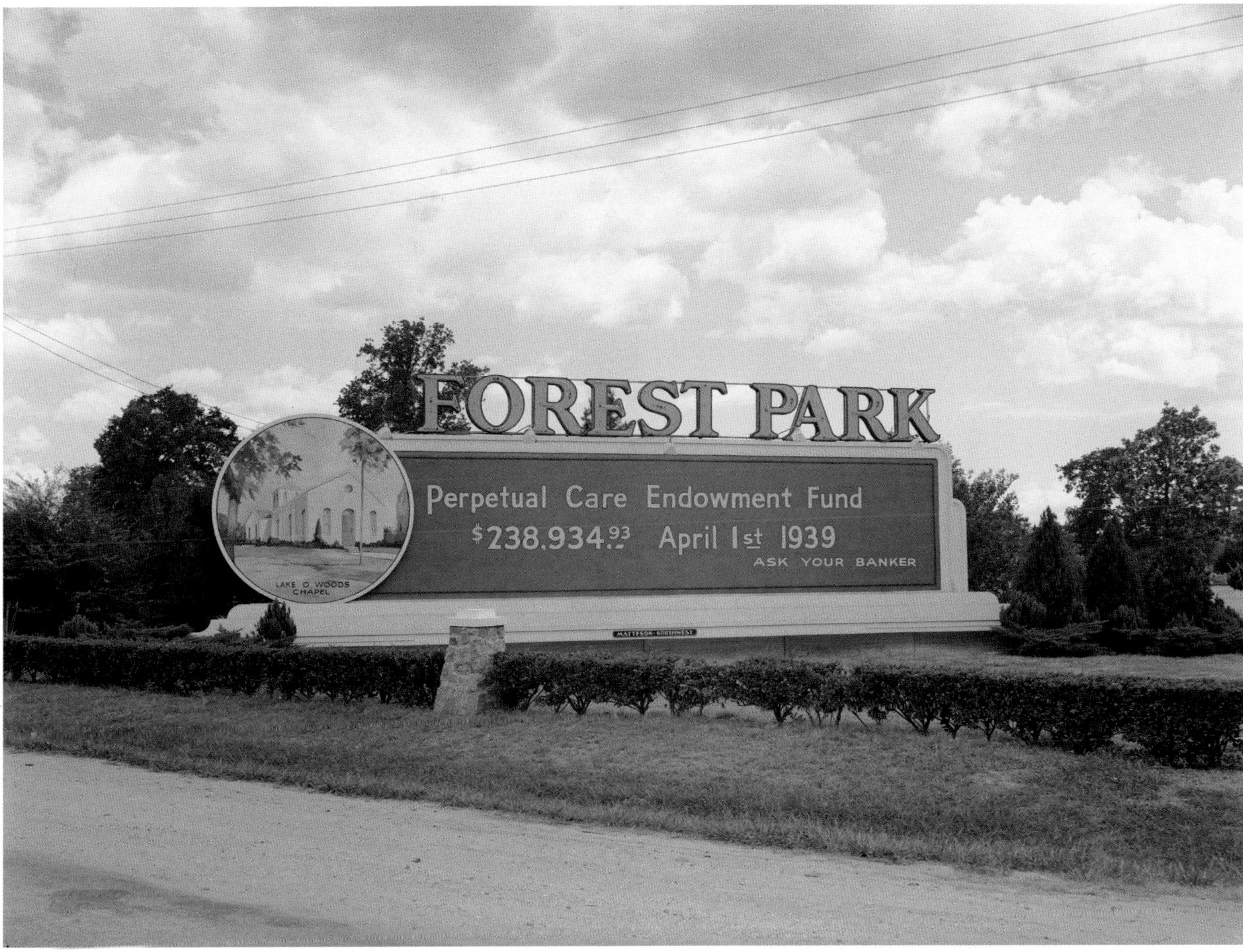

Billboard for Forest Park Cemetery, located at 6900 Lawndale Street. The concept of "perpetual care" for cemeteries was relatively new when this photo was taken in 1939. The trend-setting Forest Lawn Cemetery in Glendale, California, was the first cemetery to feature perpetual care, and like so many other of Forest Lawn's innovations, the concept became a prototype for other large urban cemeteries across the country.

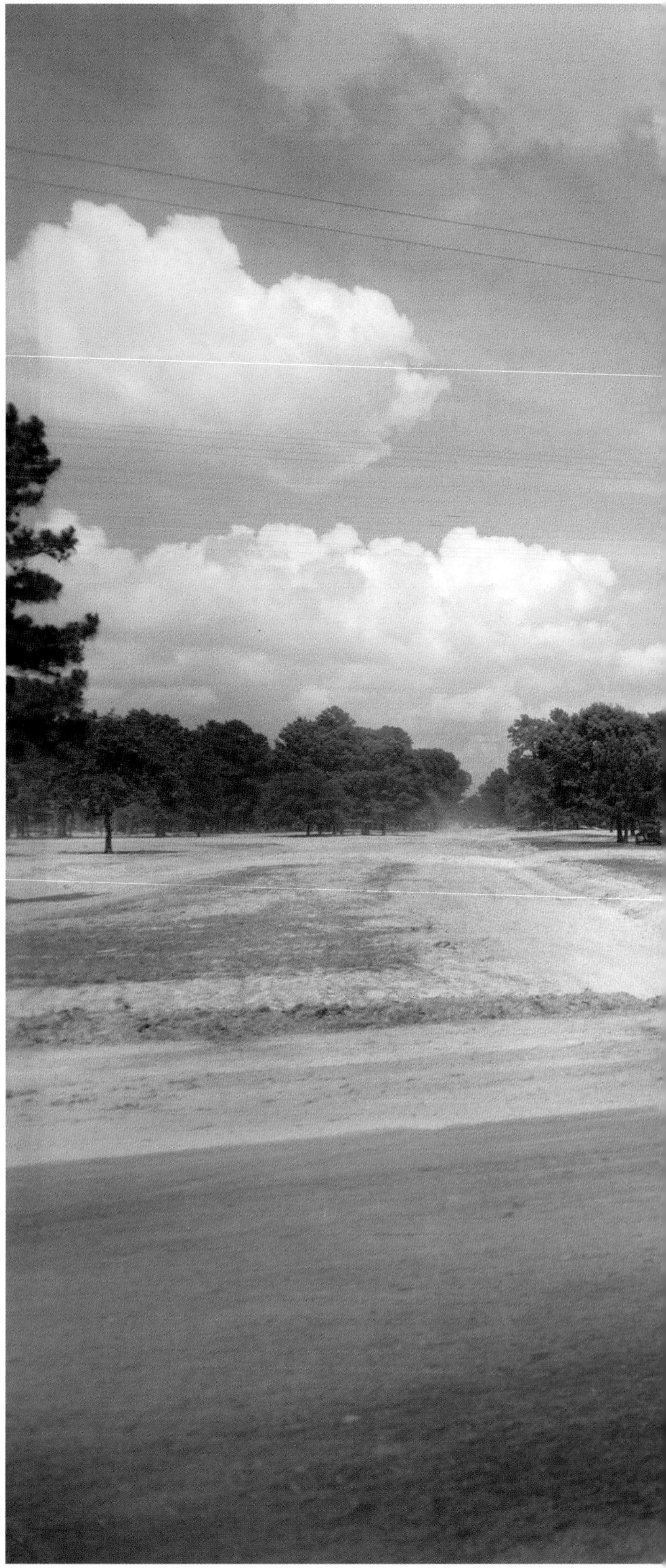

The Garden Oaks subdivision entrance as it appeared in 1937, shortly after its opening. The sign reads: "Garden Oaks, among the trees, beautiful but not expensive."

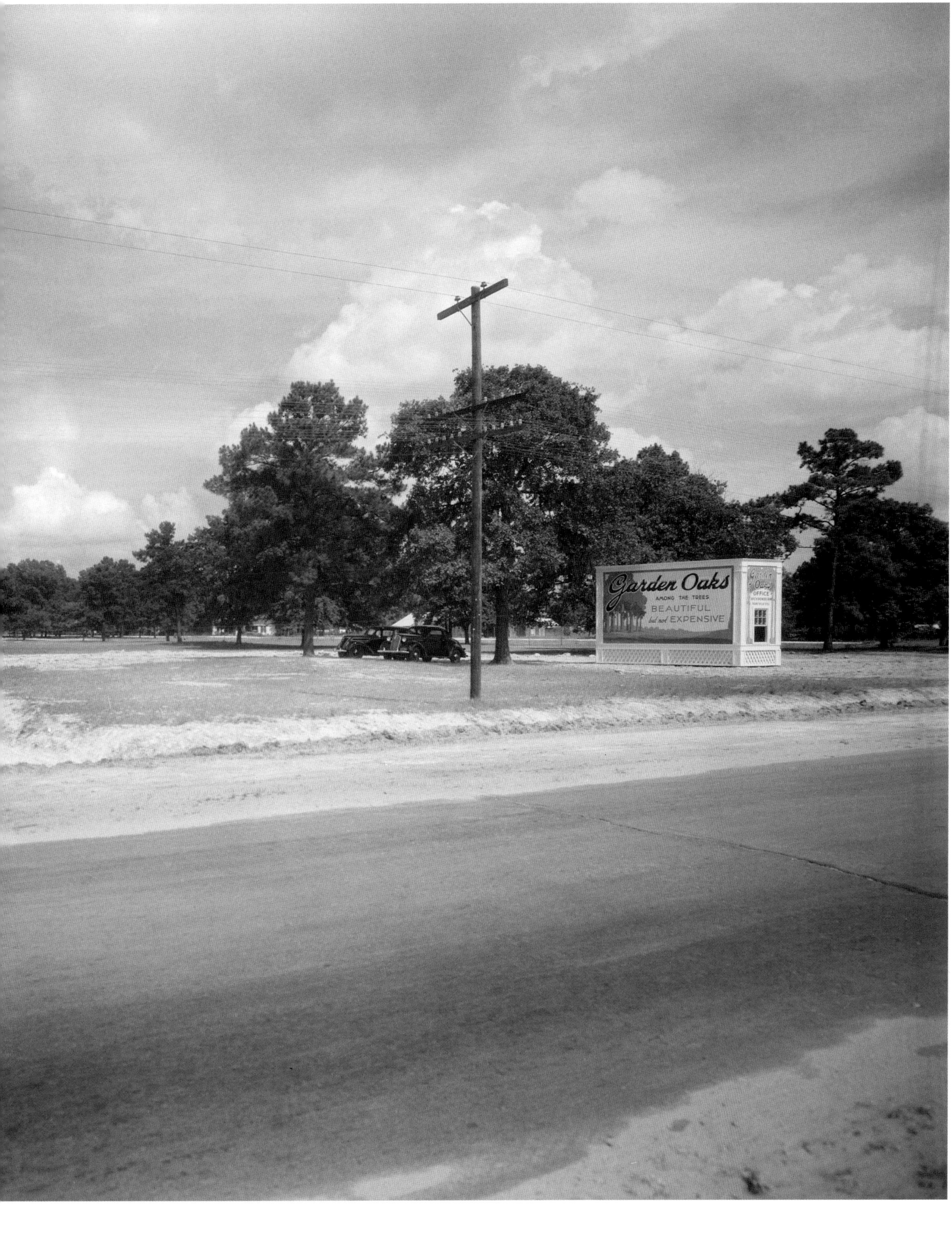
Garden Oaks
AMONG THE TREES
BEAUTIFUL
but not EXPENSIVE
OFFICE

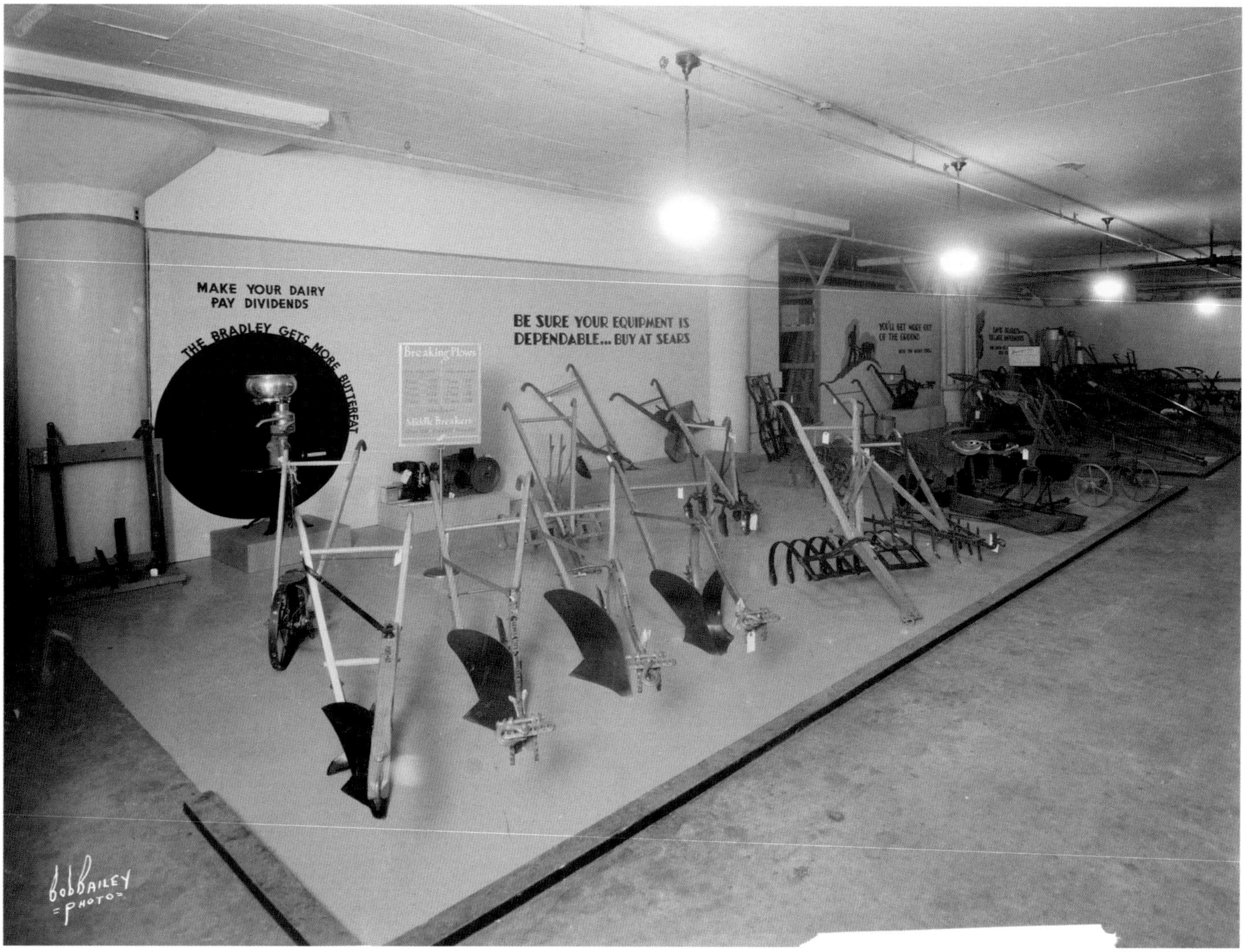

Farm tool display at the original "suburban" Sears store located at Waugh and Buffalo Drive (now Allen Parkway) in 1935. Many Houston department store branches provided farm implements and supplies for the largely agricultural areas that surrounded the city well into the 1970s. For decades, all three of the local Houston commercial television stations broadcast their own agriculture-oriented programming, geared specifically to nearby farmers and ranchers.

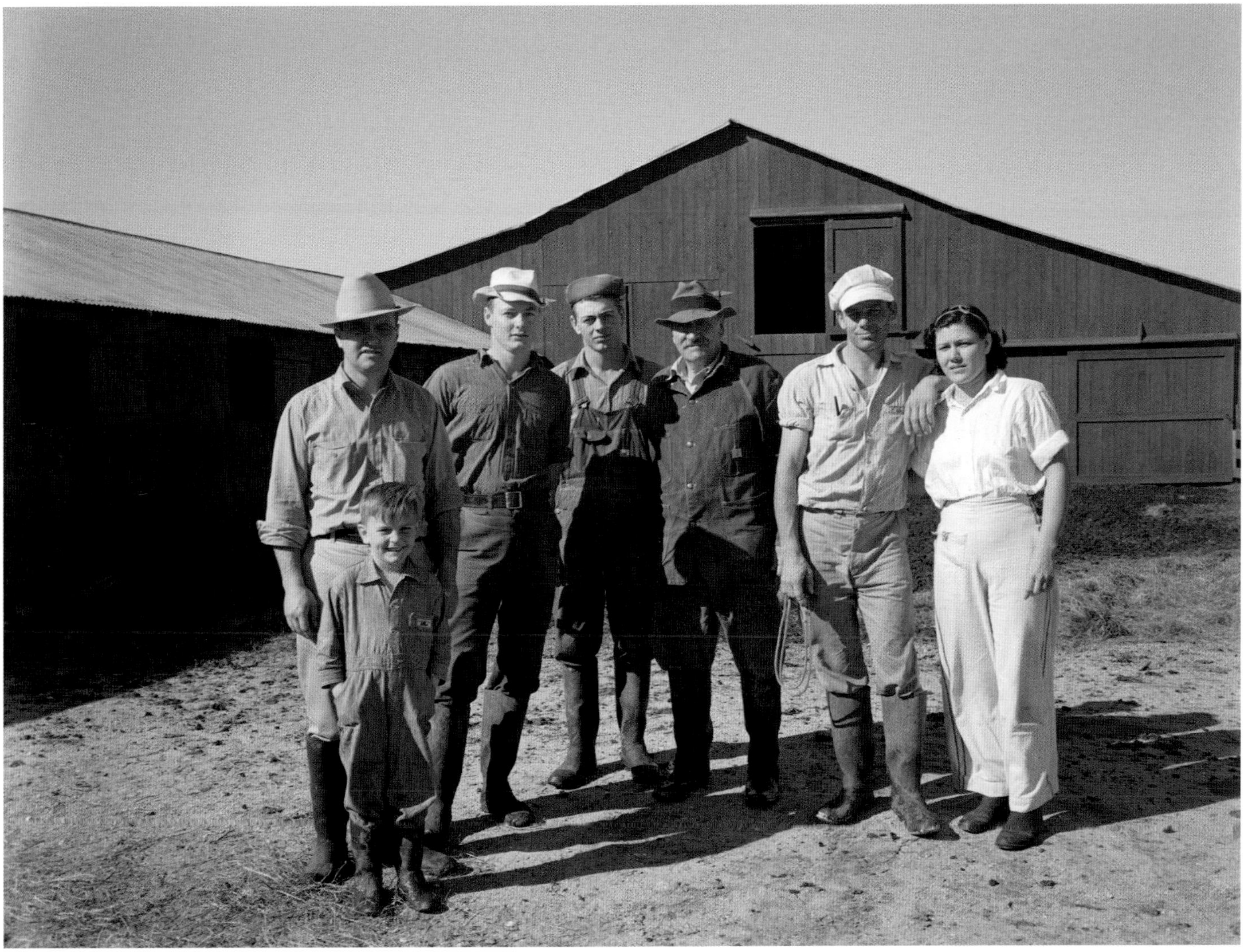

Unidentified people pose at a ranch near Alvin, Texas, in February 1939. The ranch was likely a family enterprise, given the presence of a woman and small boy in the photo. Bob Bailey's photos of some of the lifestyles of the rural communities surrounding Houston became a visual record of a bygone way of life in only a few decades, as suburbanization rapidly spread to the nearby countryside.

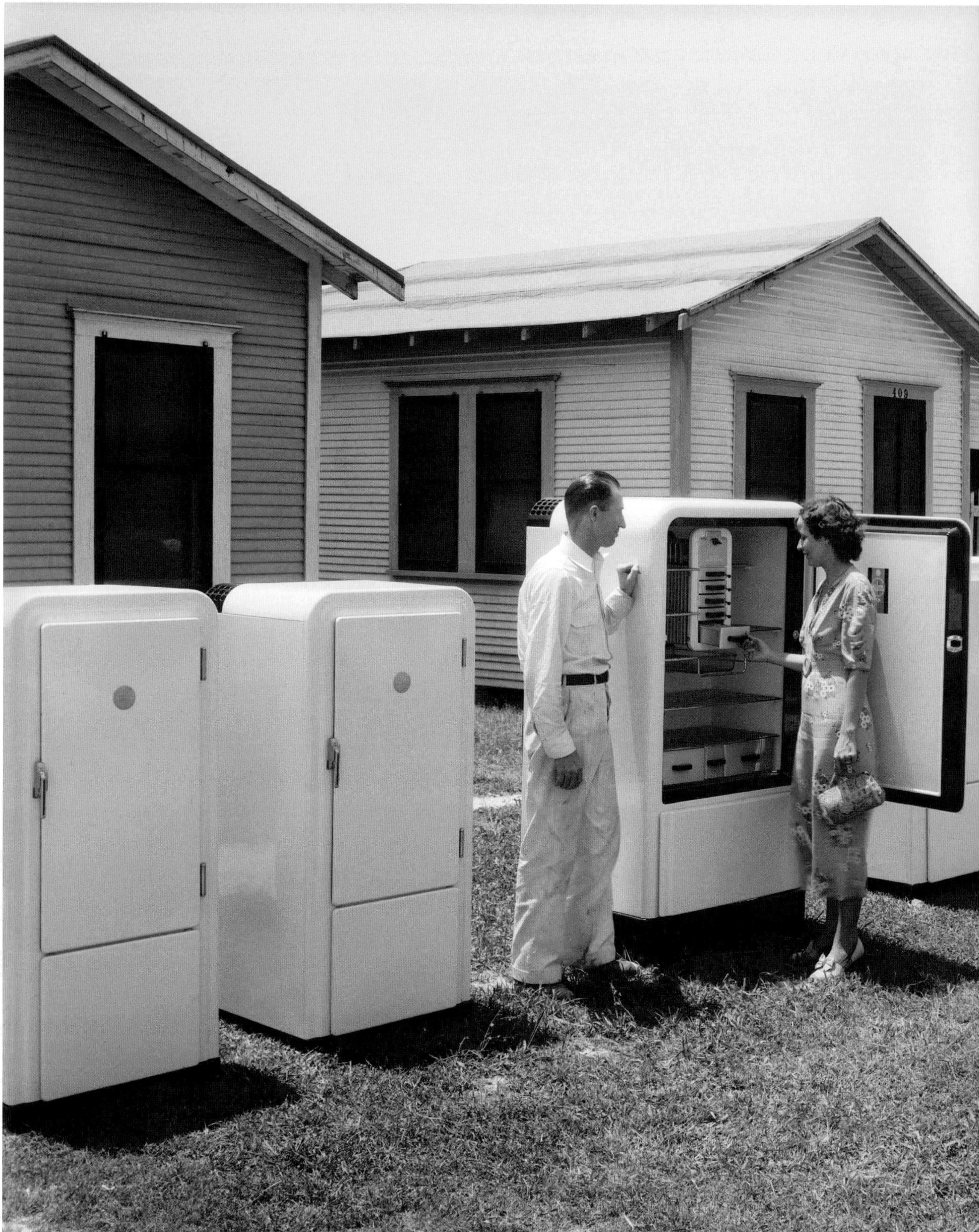
409

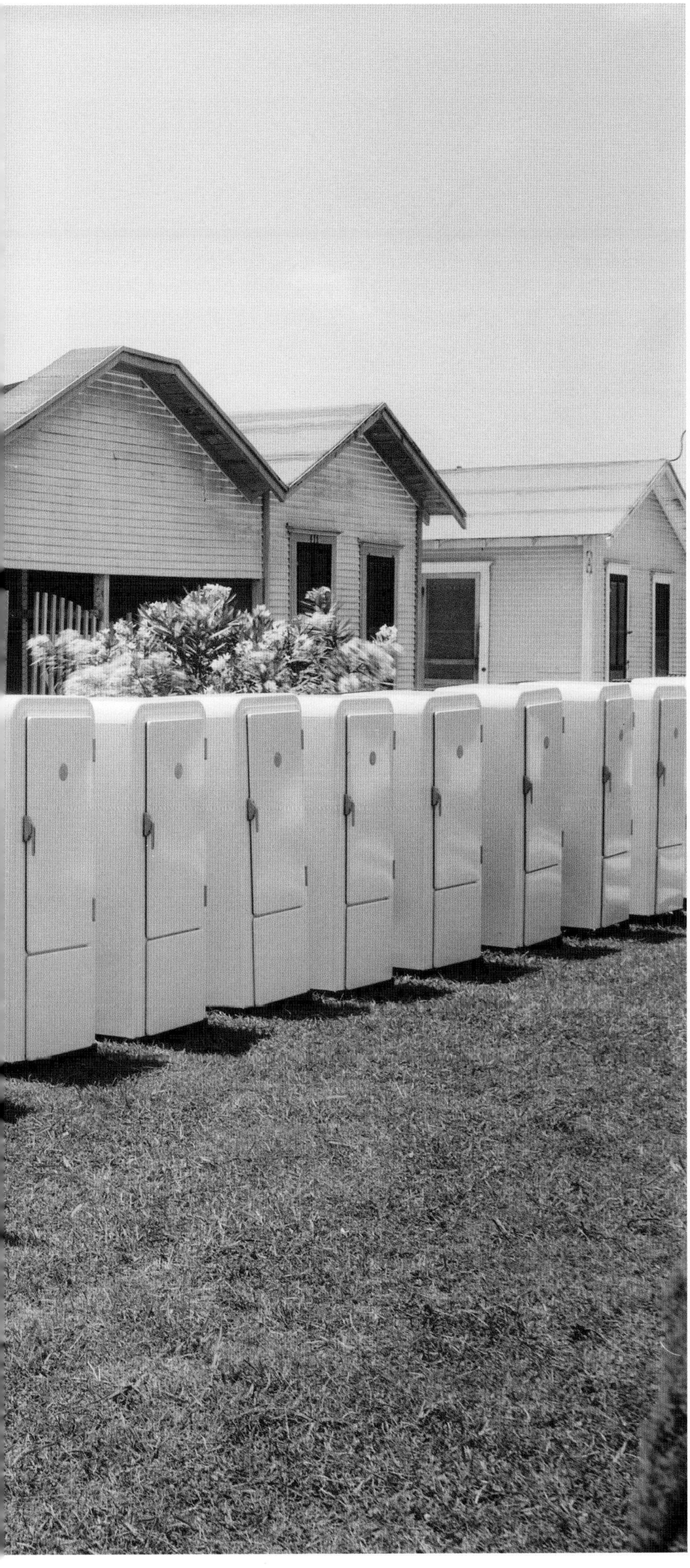

Two unidentified people inspect one of a line of Electrolux refrigerators standing before a row of shotgun houses, ca. 1935. It is unclear whether Electrolux, another private donor, or even one of the New Deal programs supplied the refrigerators to the residents of the shotgun houses, as most of these residents could not have afforded refrigerators at the time. The image, however, is a good representation of what was occurring within the wider world of American consumerism. Despite the hardships caused for so many by the Great Depression, an emerging view was developing during the 1930s among sociologists and economists that consumers strengthened the nation by expending their purchasing power, rather than always saving. In the past, most working people almost always paid for their goods with cash. The new viewpoint that advocated spending, even if buyers had to pay with credit or use installment plans, made New Deal policymakers eager to promote consumerism among all income levels. The Electrolux Company that manufactured these refrigerators is almost certainly the same Electrolux that remains in operation today and still produces household appliances.

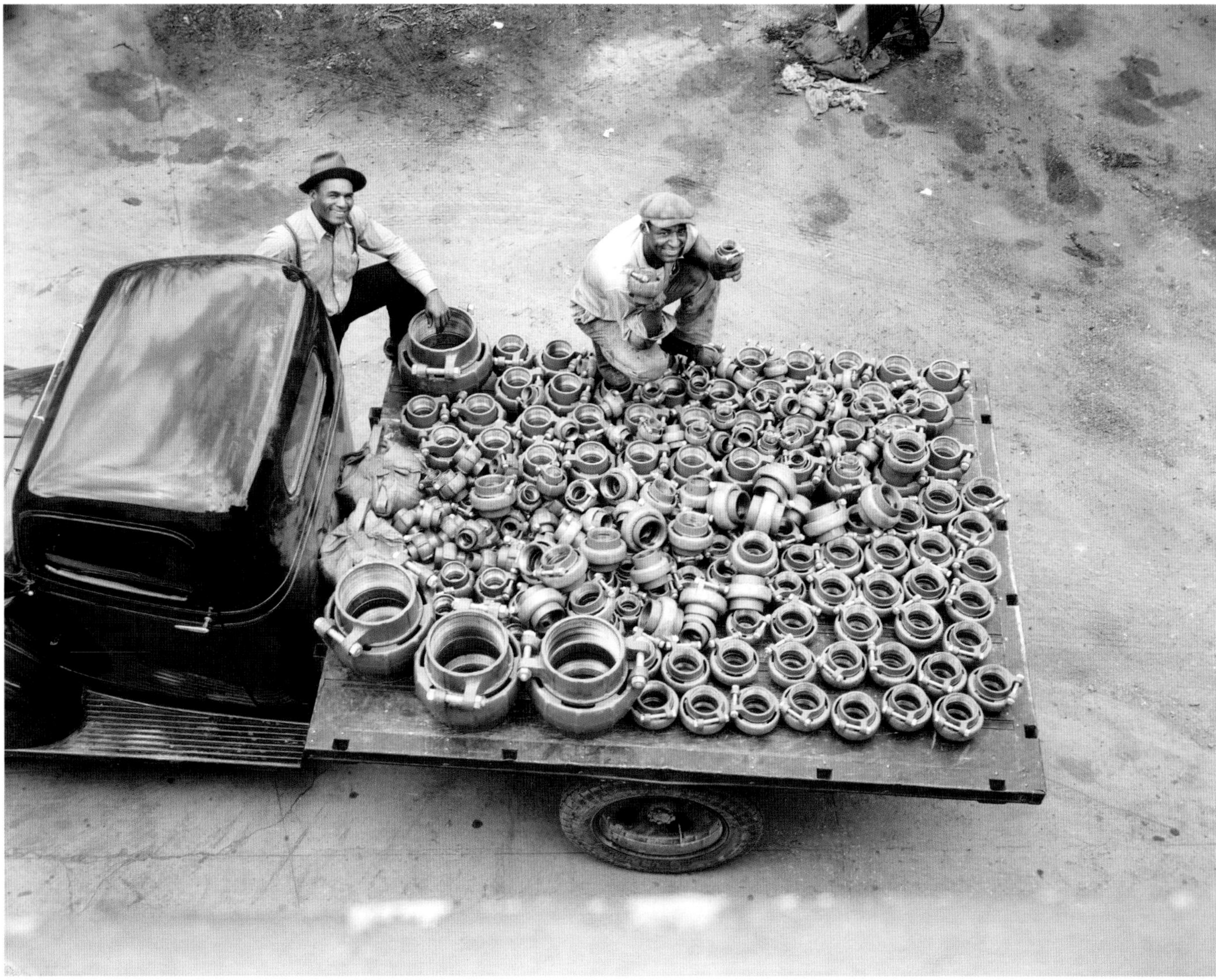

Always creative, Bob Bailey shot this photo of a load of pipe fittings from above for the Thornhill-Craven Company, ca. 1936. By using an unusual angle and including the truck and two workers within the frame, Bailey gives style to what could have been a mundane industrial photograph. Images of industrial parts made up a substantial portion of Bailey's commissions.

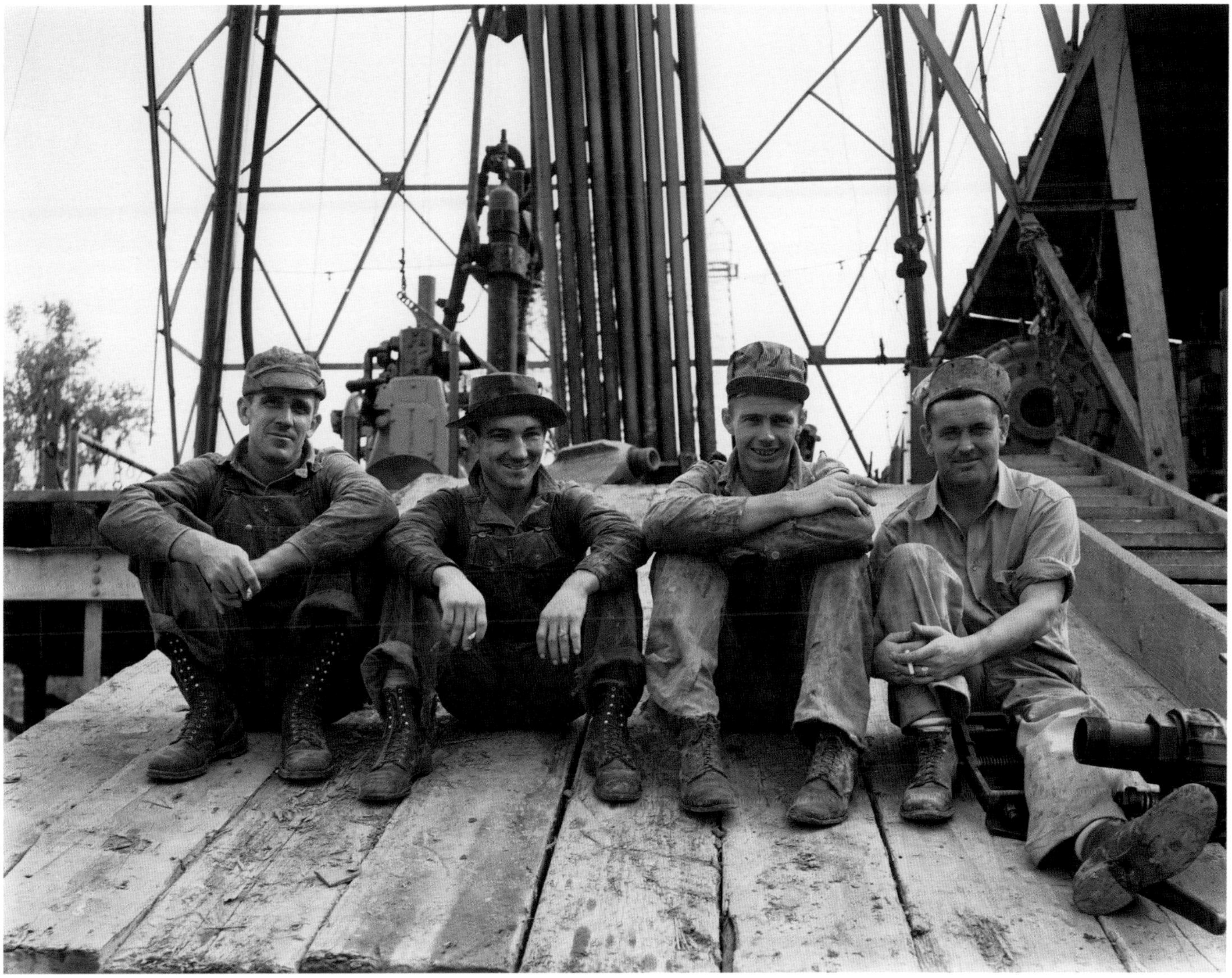

Group of workers and an oil rig in the Houston Heights in March 1939. The drilling rig was operating in an oil field that was located between 11th and 18th Streets in the Heights. In the minds of many Americans, no other business was so closely associated with Houston as was the oil industry.

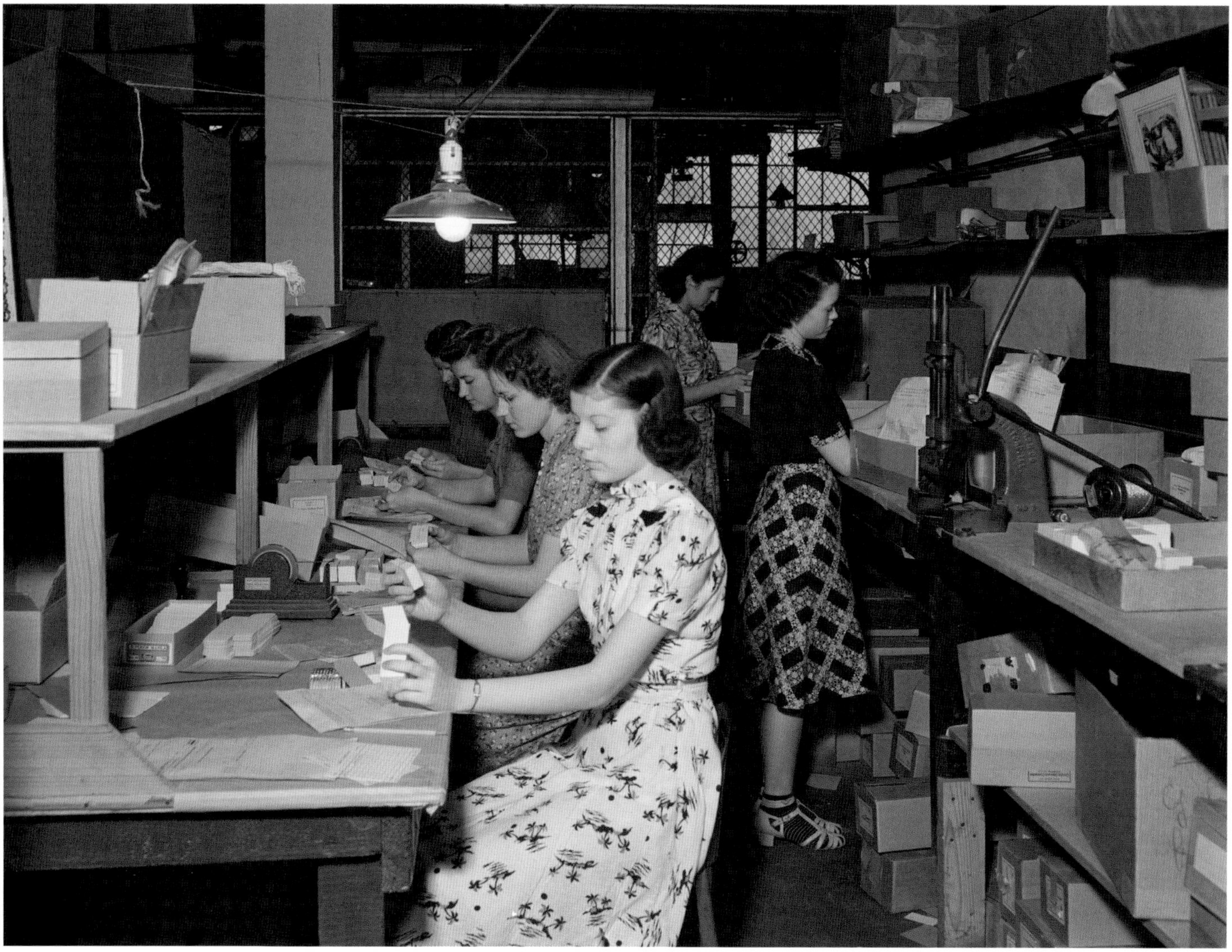

Employees at work for the Star Engraving Company in 1939. The Star Engraving Building was constructed in 1930 at 3201 Buffalo Drive (now Allen Parkway). The building still exists. It is now owned by Stages Repertory Theatre and currently serves as a cultural center.

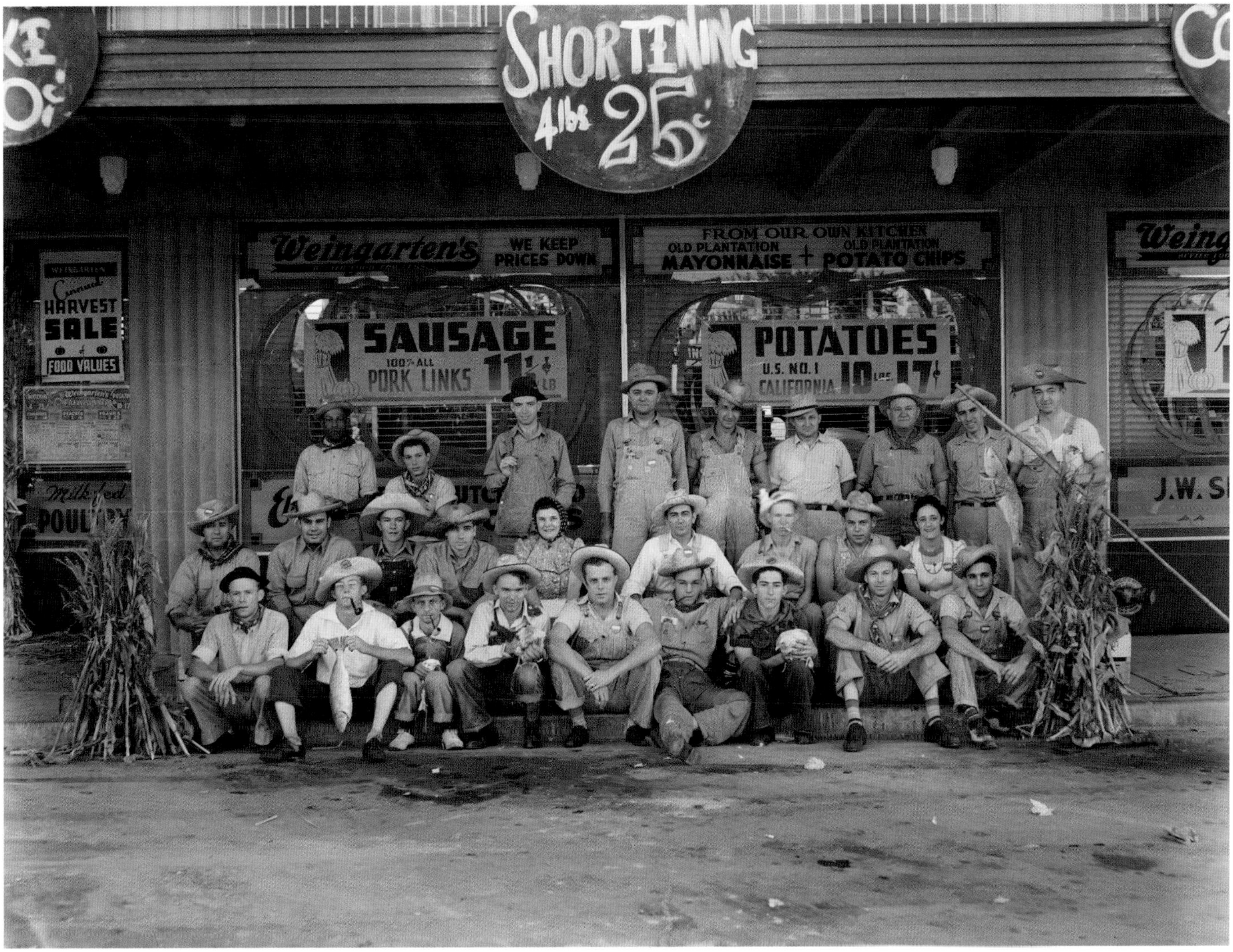

In October 1940, this group of Weingarten's grocery store employees wore farm clothes to mark the store's fall harvest sale.

A creatively composed shot of a women's hairstyle model, commissioned by Foley Brothers Department Store's beauty salon in 1940.

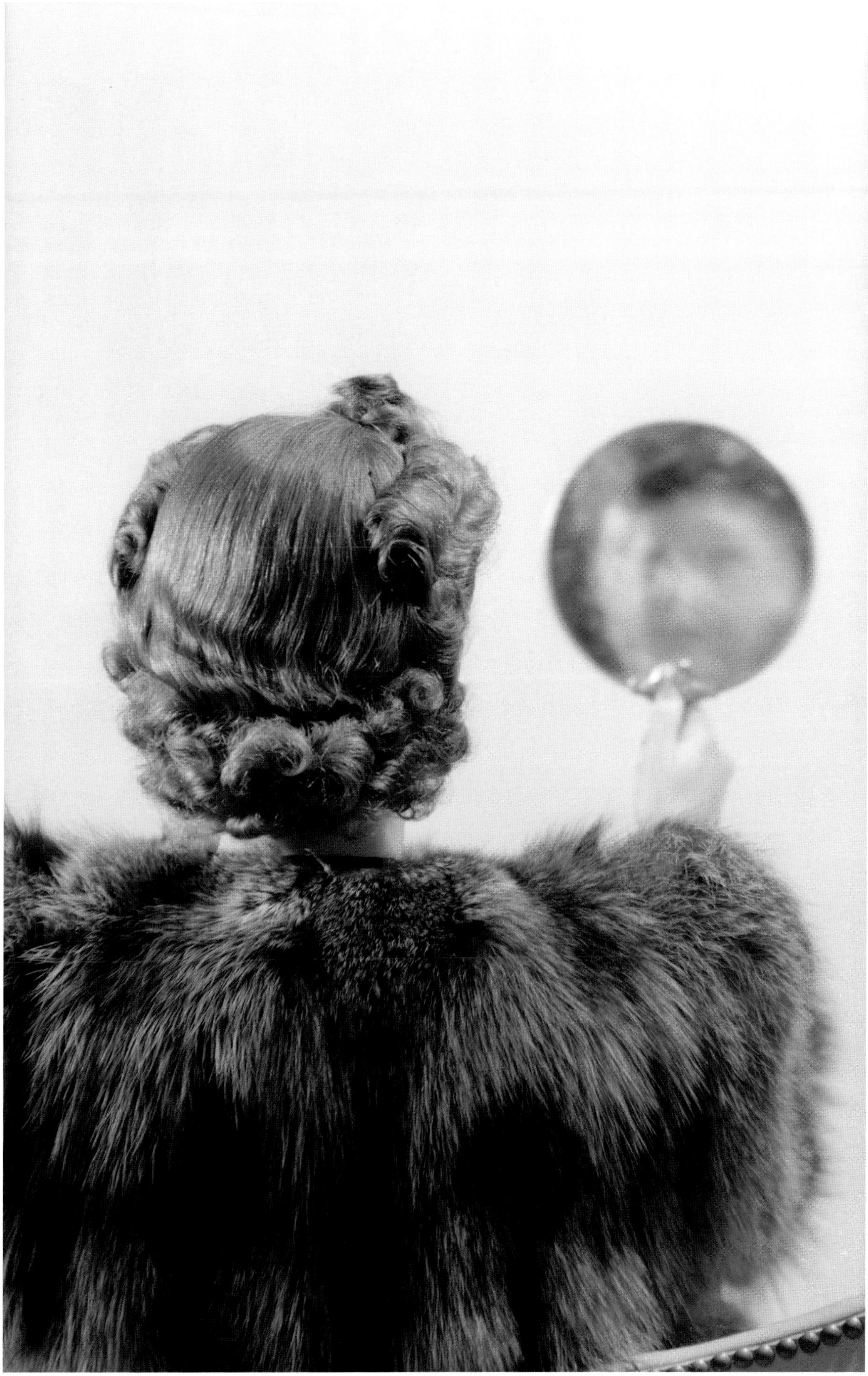

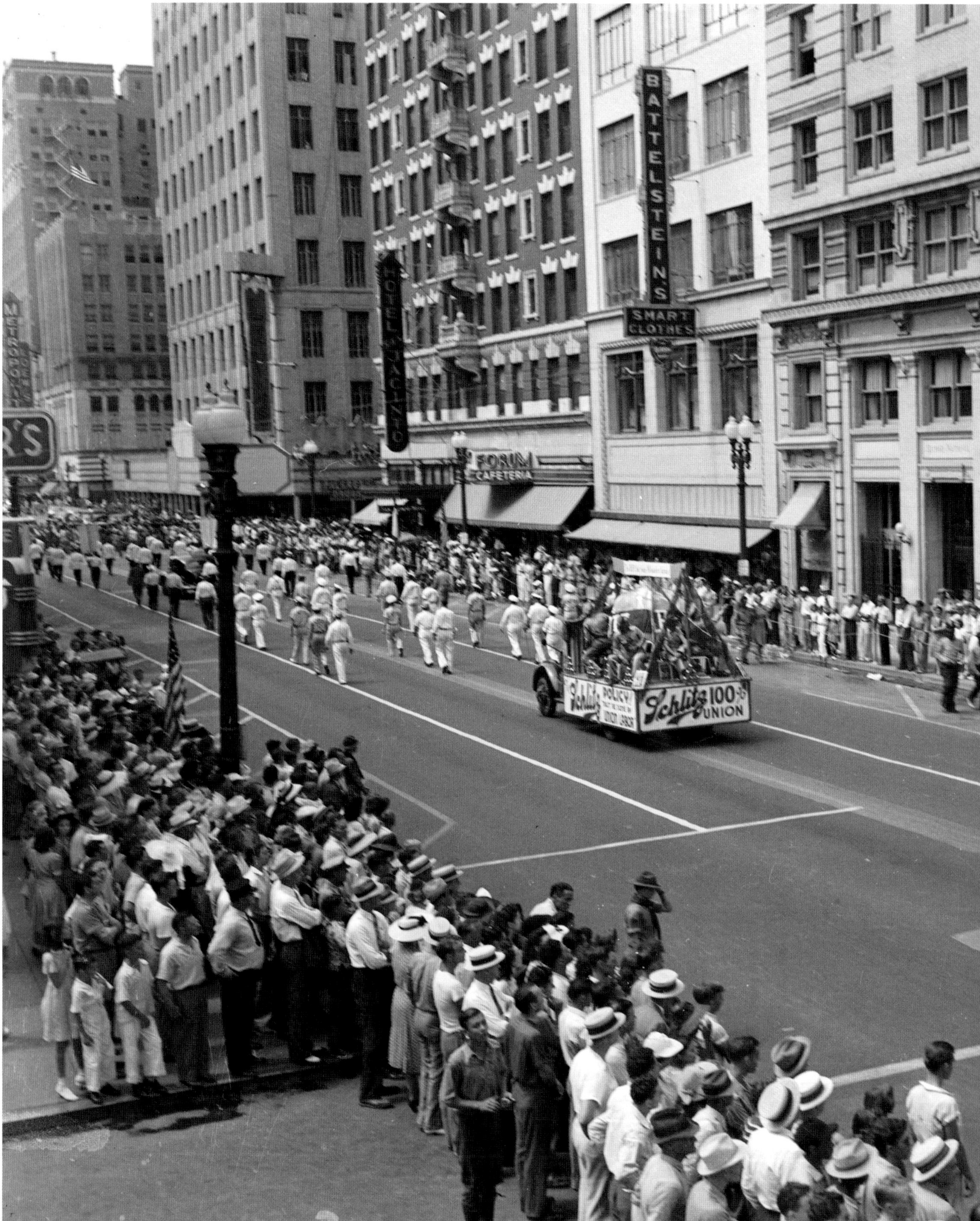
BATTELSTEINS
SMART CLOTHES
FORUM
CAFETERIA
Schlitz
POLICY
Schlitz 100%
UNION

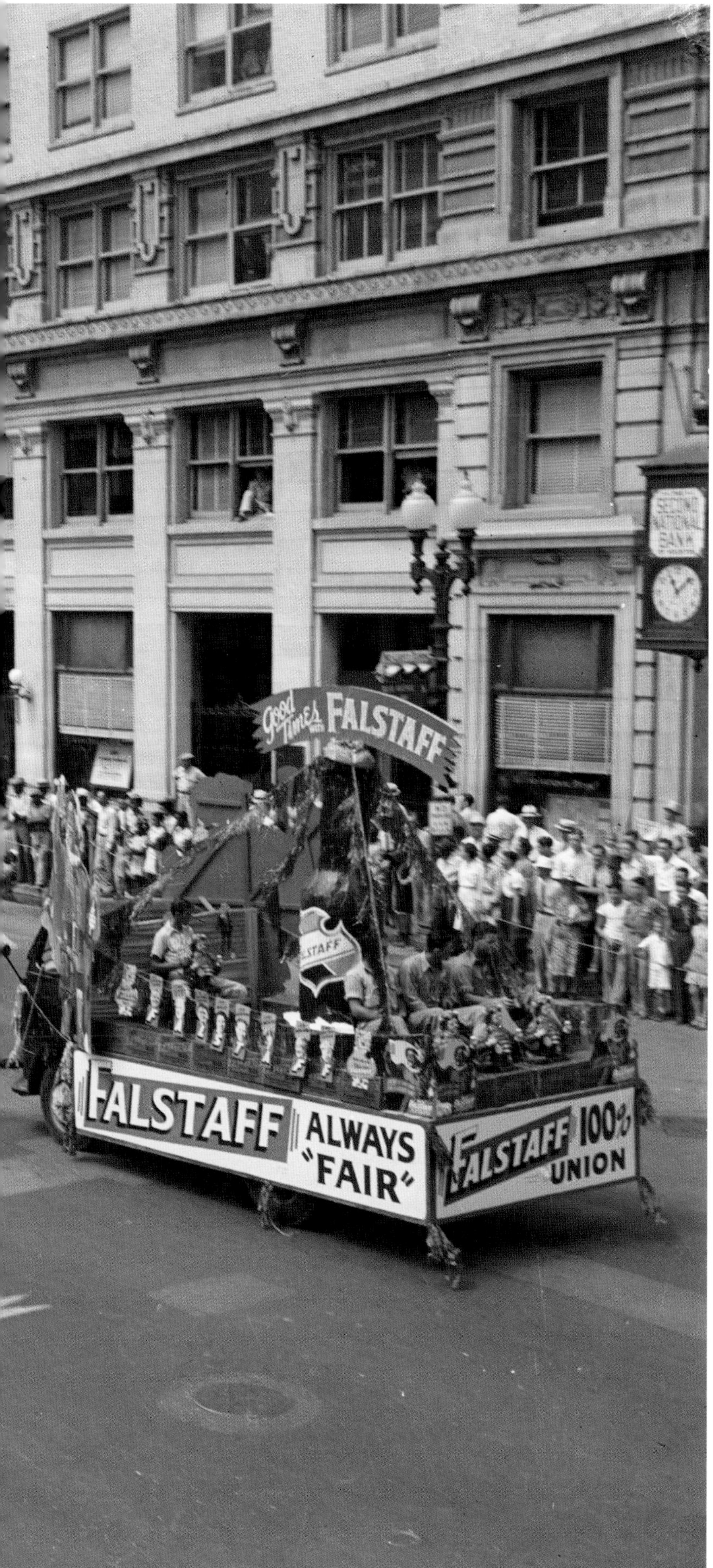

Floats for the 1939 Labor Day parade. The Falstaff beer float in the right foreground was immediately preceded by the Schlitz beer float as the parade proceeded down Main Street. As another sign of a long-vanished Houston, both floats proclaim that the companies are "100% Union," while a sign on the side of the Schlitz float maintained that it was company policy to only employ "union labor."

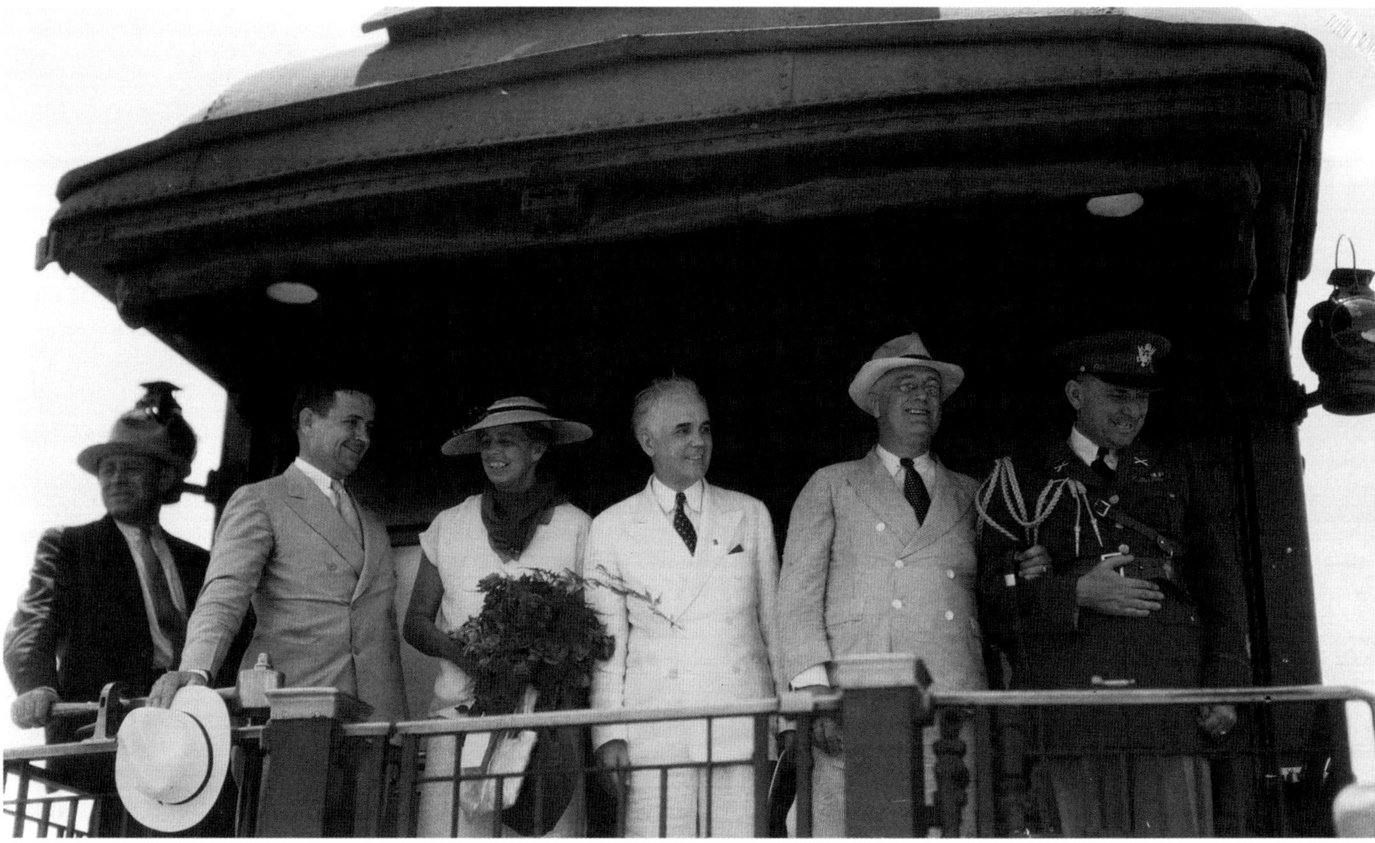

President Franklin Roosevelt (second from right) made a Houston appearance by train in 1936 as part of his first reelection campaign. First Lady Eleanor Roosevelt (third from left) appeared with him, as did Governor James V. Allred, second from the left with the Panama hat. Between the president and the first lady is serial Houston mayor Oscar Holcombe, who seems to have always been ready for a personal appearance.

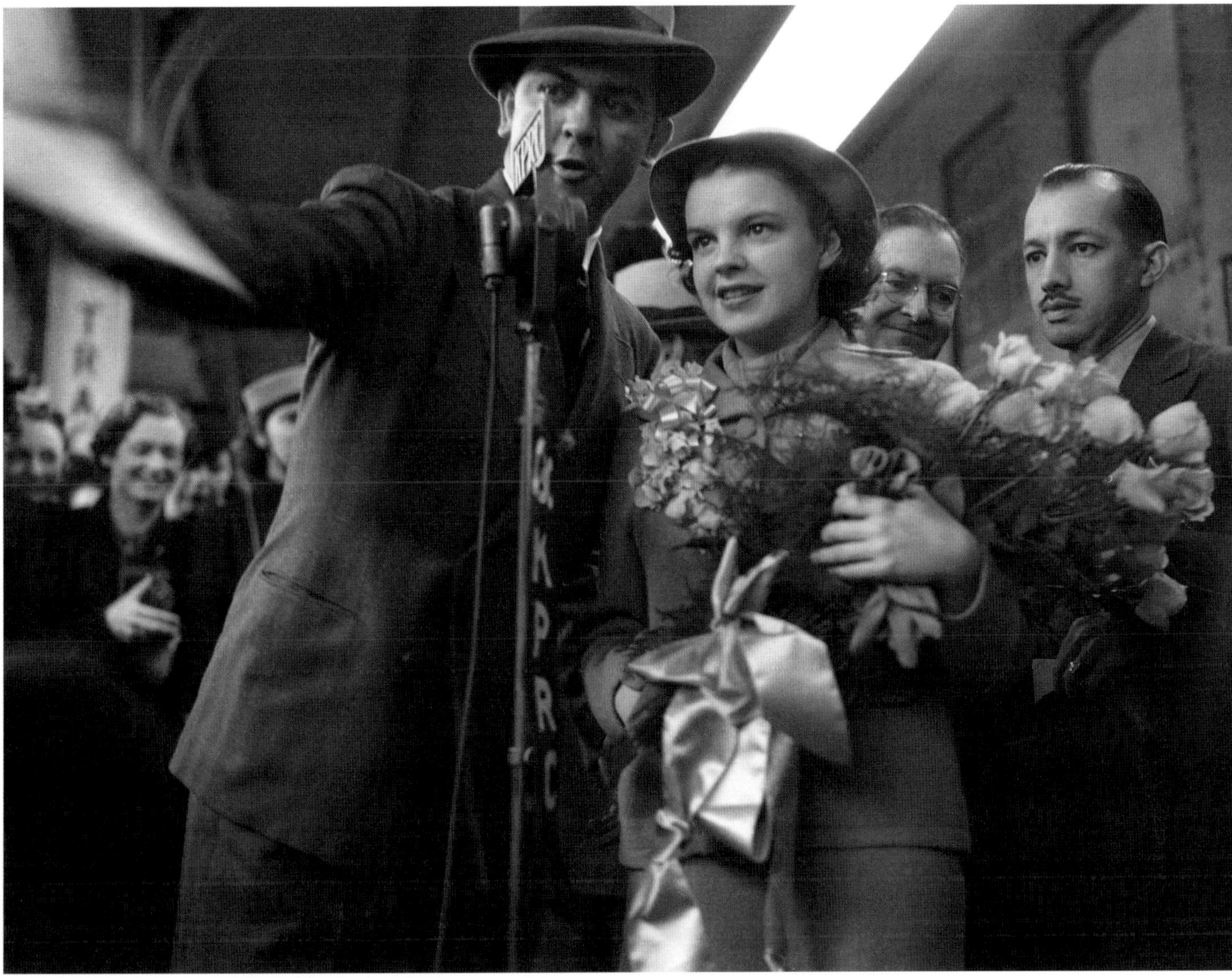

Judy Garland arriving at a Houston train station in January 1938. Like the arrival of other "A-list" stars at the time, hers was broadcast by local radio stations, in this instance by KPRC. Garland may have been in town to promote her most recent film, *Thoroughbreds Don't Cry*, which was released on December 3, 1937. Along with local broadcasters and reporters, Bob Bailey was also a fixture at celebrity arrivals.

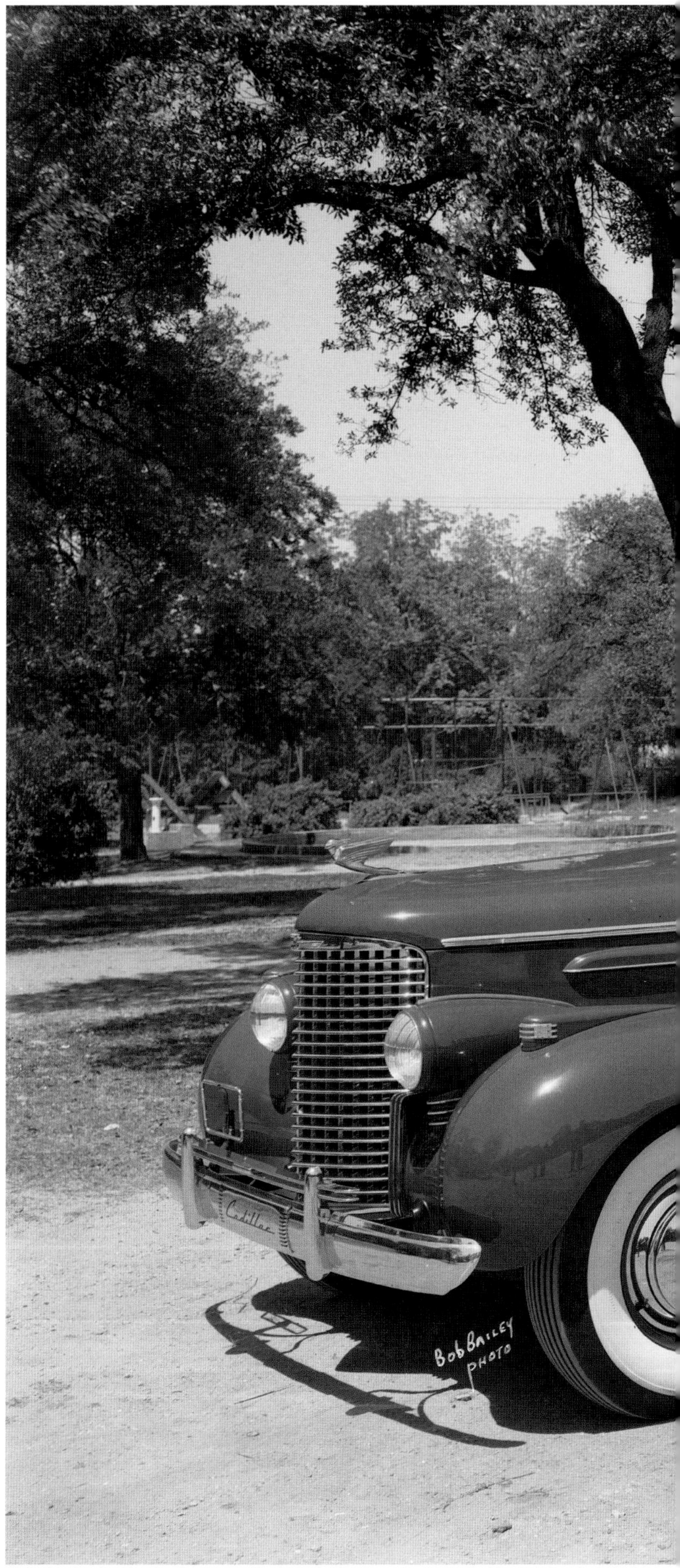

Actress Mae West is seen here posing with her V–16 Cadillac limousine and chauffeur in Hermann Park when she visited Houston in 1939. West was in town to present her one-woman show at the Metropolitan Theatre.

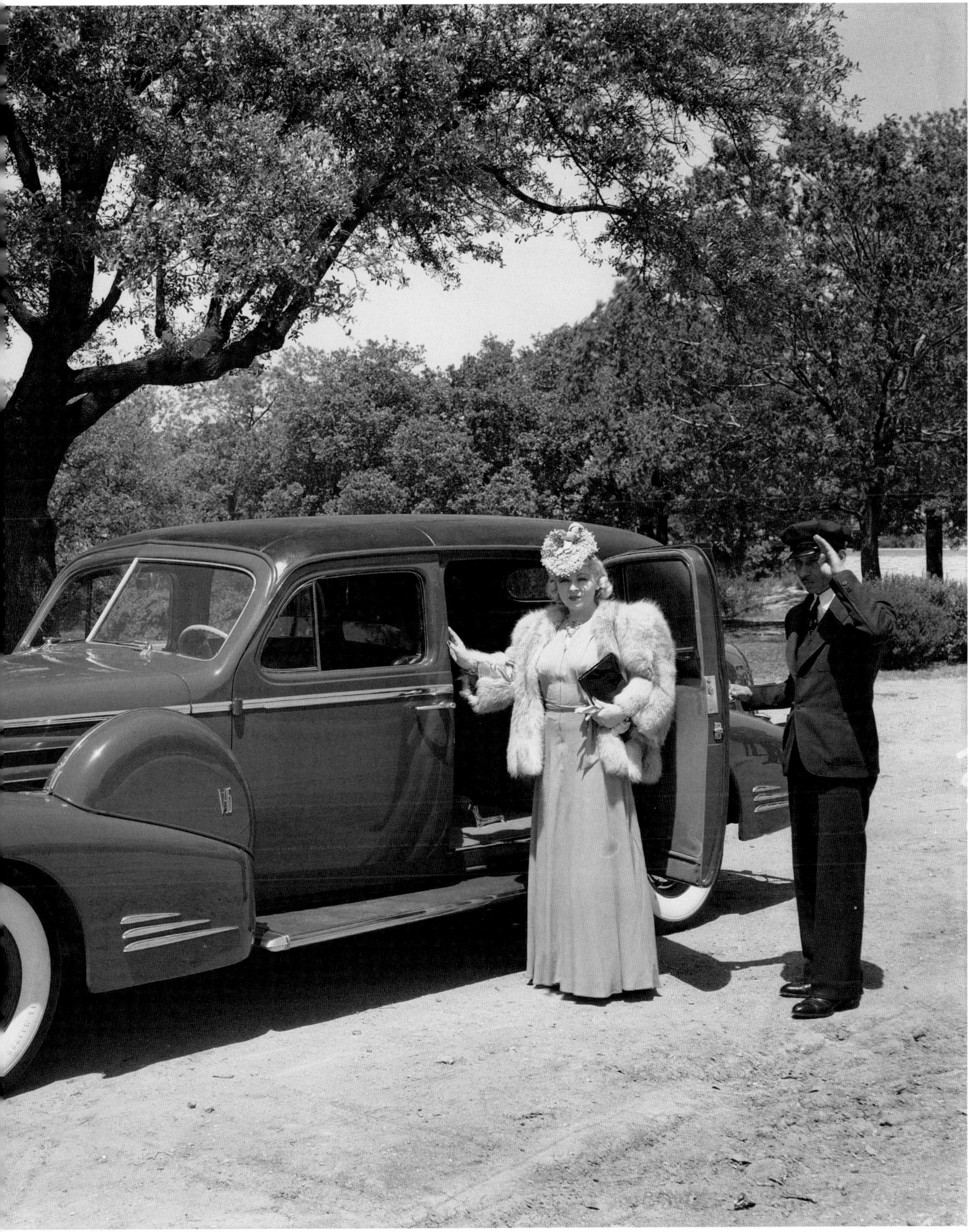

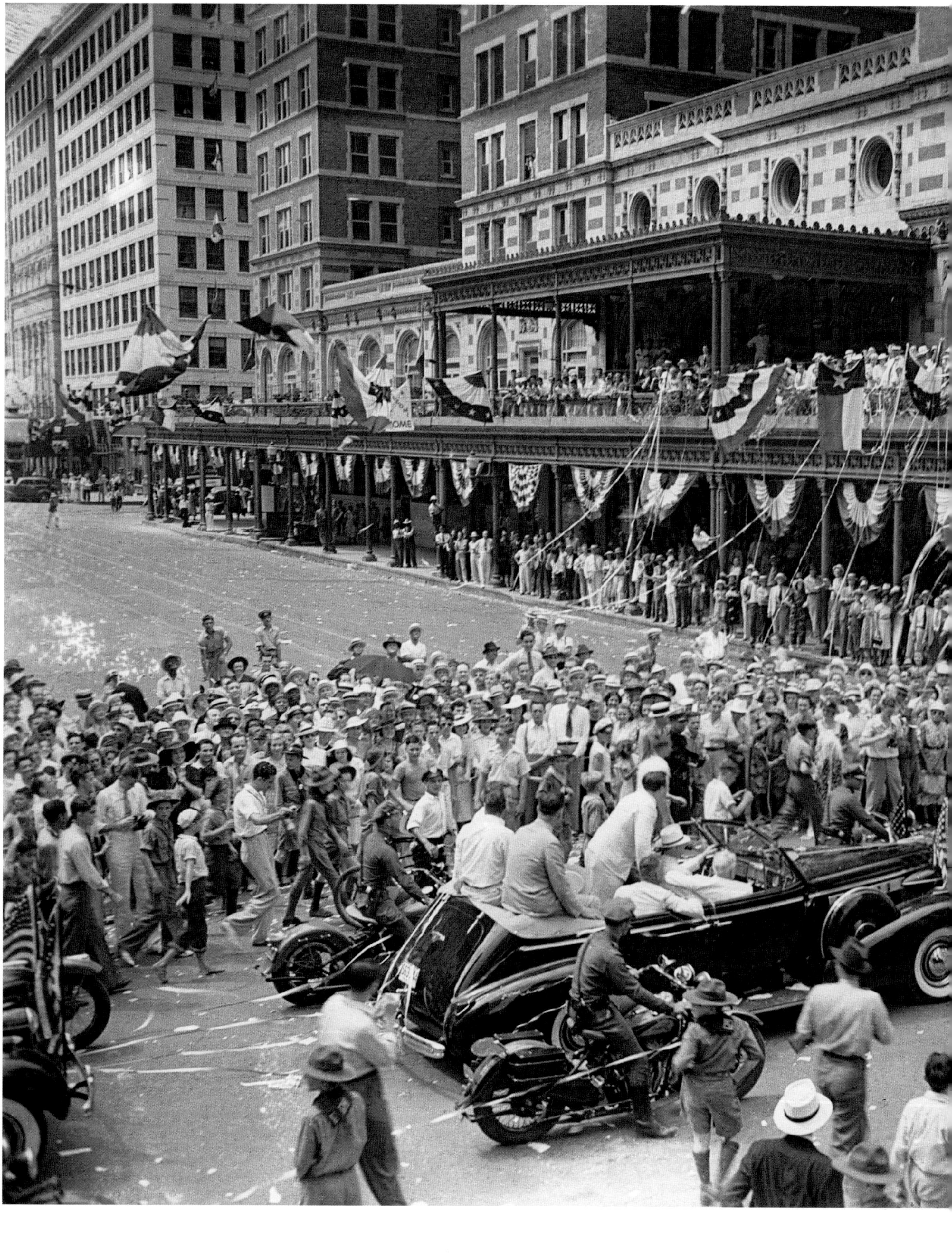

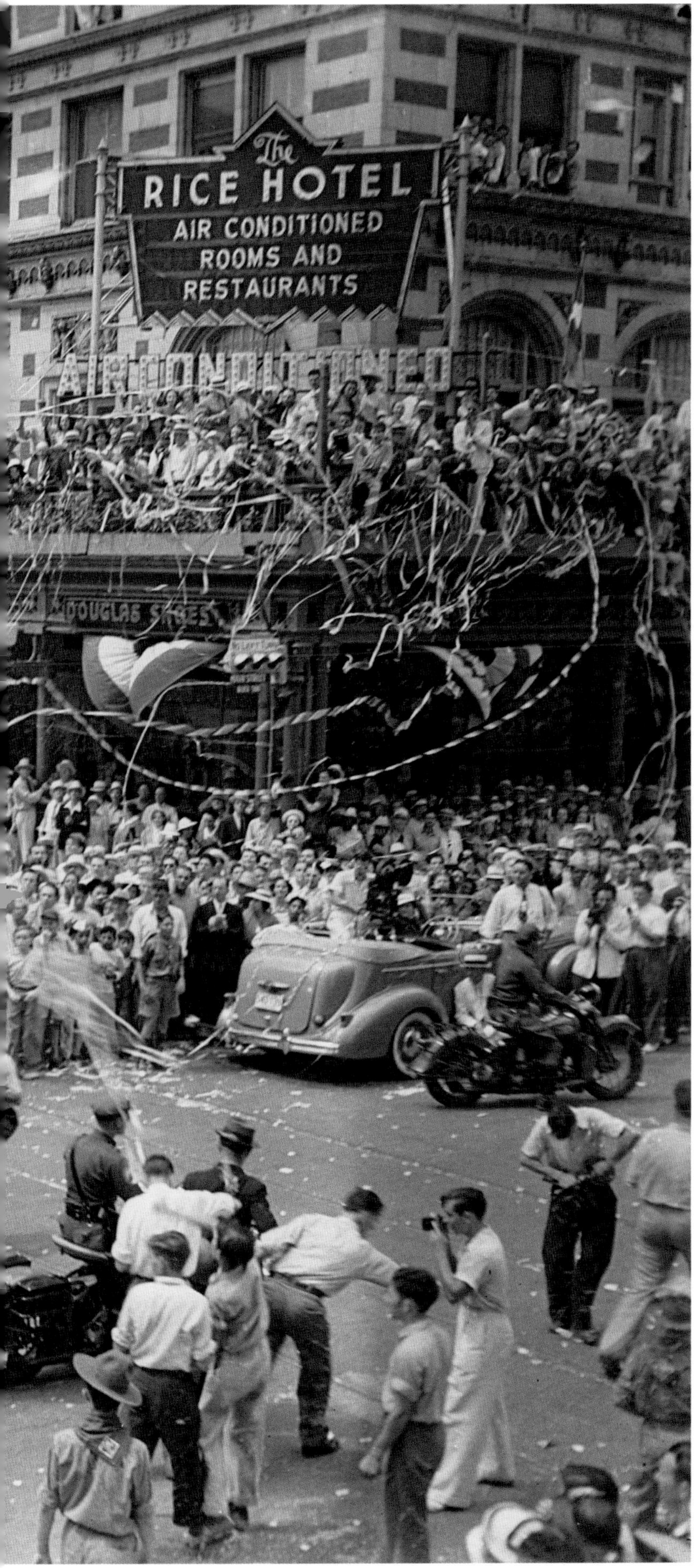

On July 30, 1938, Houston held a ticker-tape parade for its native son Howard Hughes, who had just set the speed record for flying around the world. Here his motorcade passes near the Rice Hotel, where a reception was held for him. This was Hughes's first visit to Houston since he moved to Los Angeles in 1924, and he would never again return to the city of his birth. The future recluse and germophobe was reputedly warned by his mother when he was a child that Houston had an unhealthy climate. Ironically, Hughes died in 1976 at the age of seventy as he was flying to a Houston hospital for treatment and was then buried in Houston's Glenwood Cemetery.

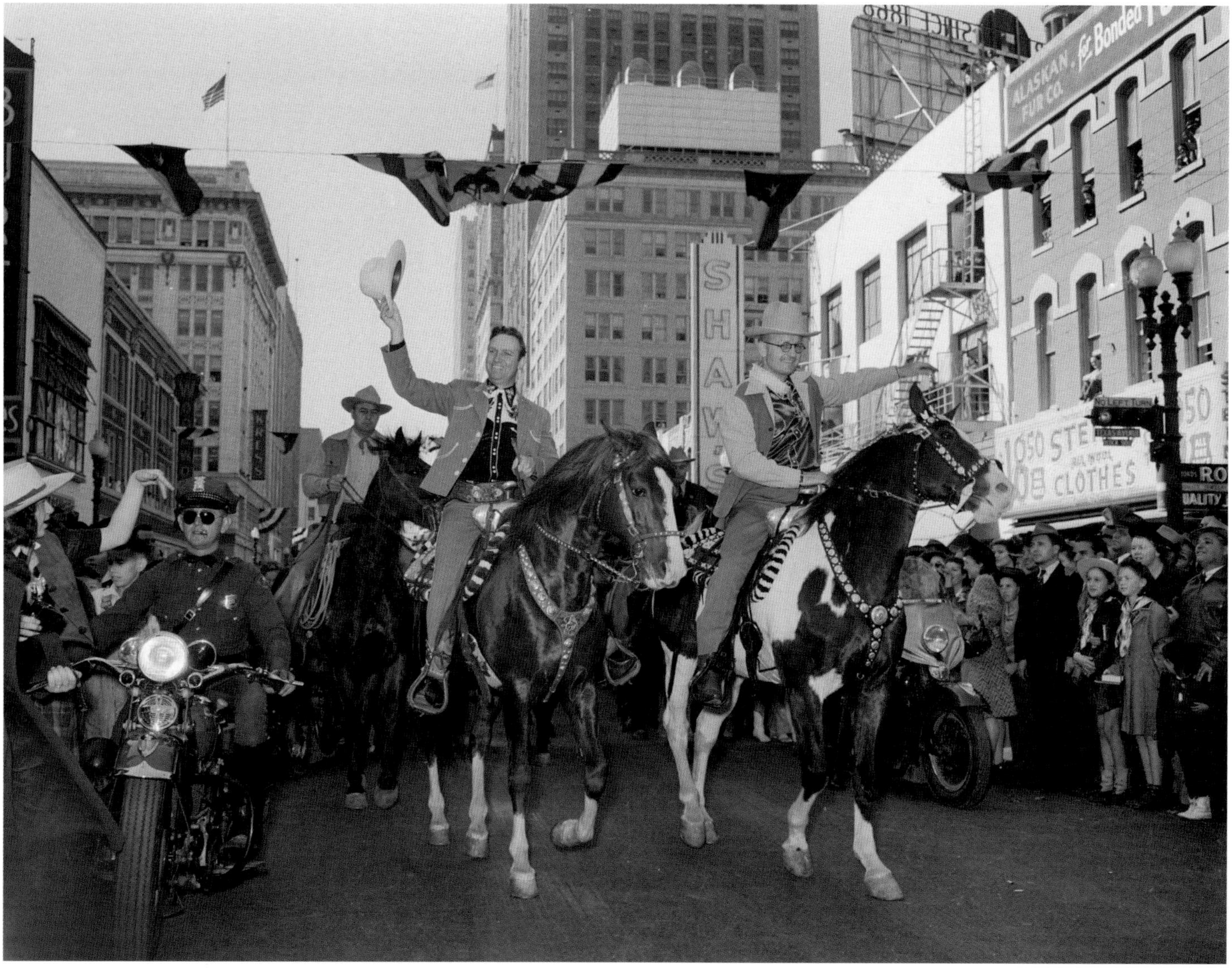

Cowboy star Gene Autry rides in the 1942 Houston Fat Stock Show's parade. Autry was the first star performer to entertain at the rodeo. The Houston Fat Stock Show and Livestock Exhibit was founded in 1931 and is known today as the Houston Livestock Show and Rodeo.

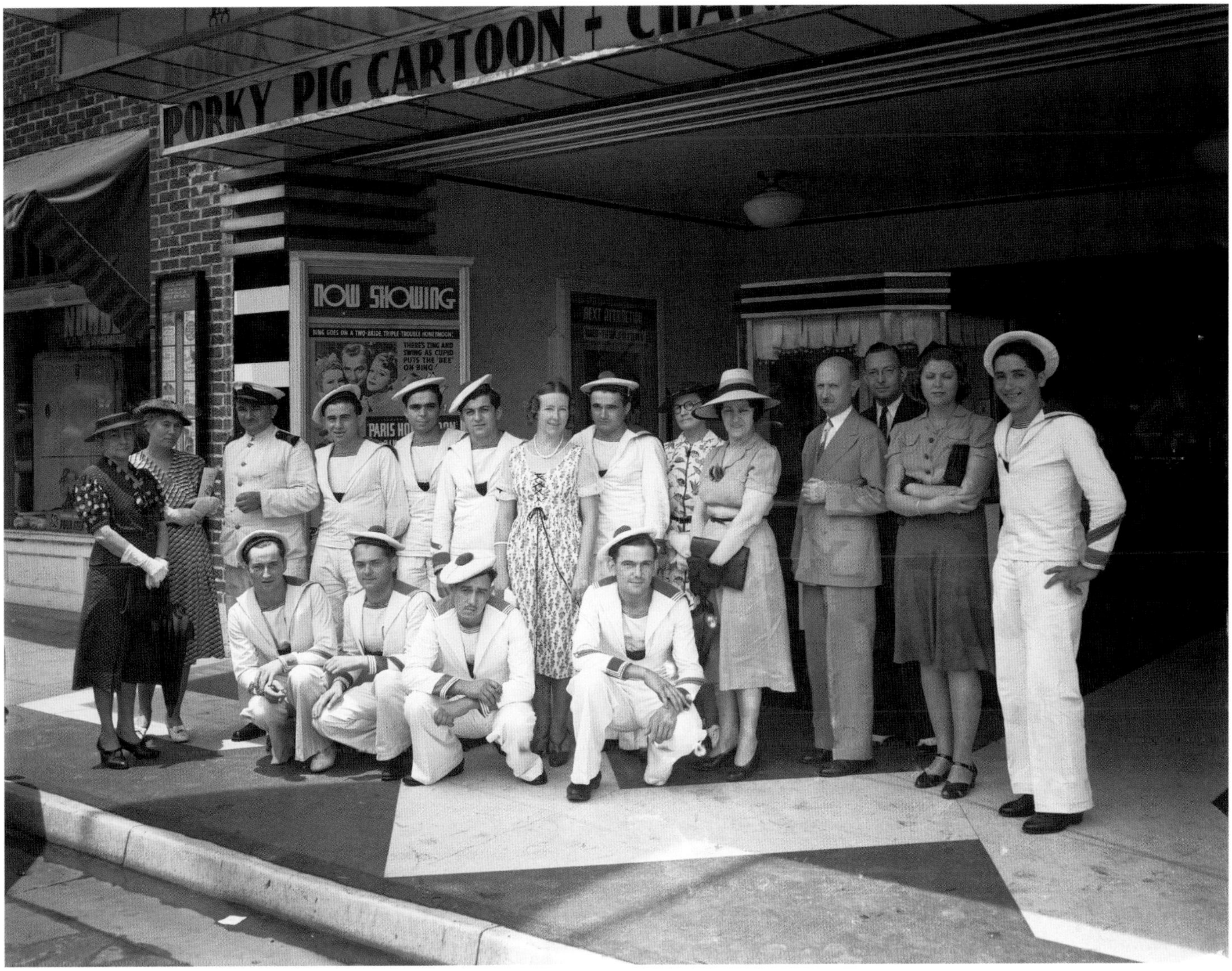

A group of French sailors on leave visiting the Delman Theatre in May 1939, just before the start of World War II.

A soldier, at left, crossing the street in front of Sakowitz Brothers at 712 Main Street in a rare color view of downtown Houston, ca. 1942. This image is a still taken from a brief color film that Bailey shot of Main Street's crowds, giving us a unique opportunity to see a past that we envision as being largely black and white. Bailey may have shot the sequence to experiment with color film.

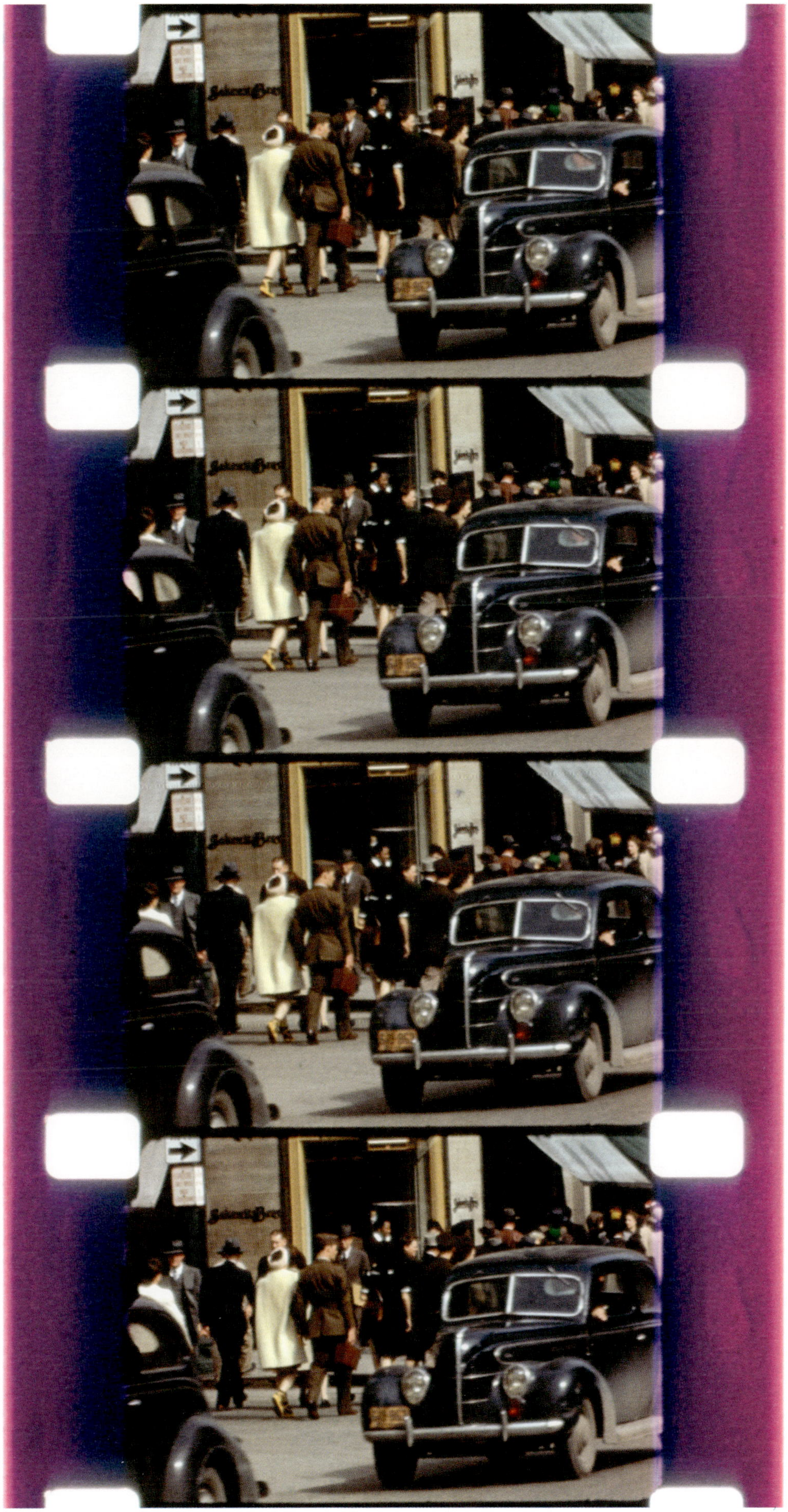

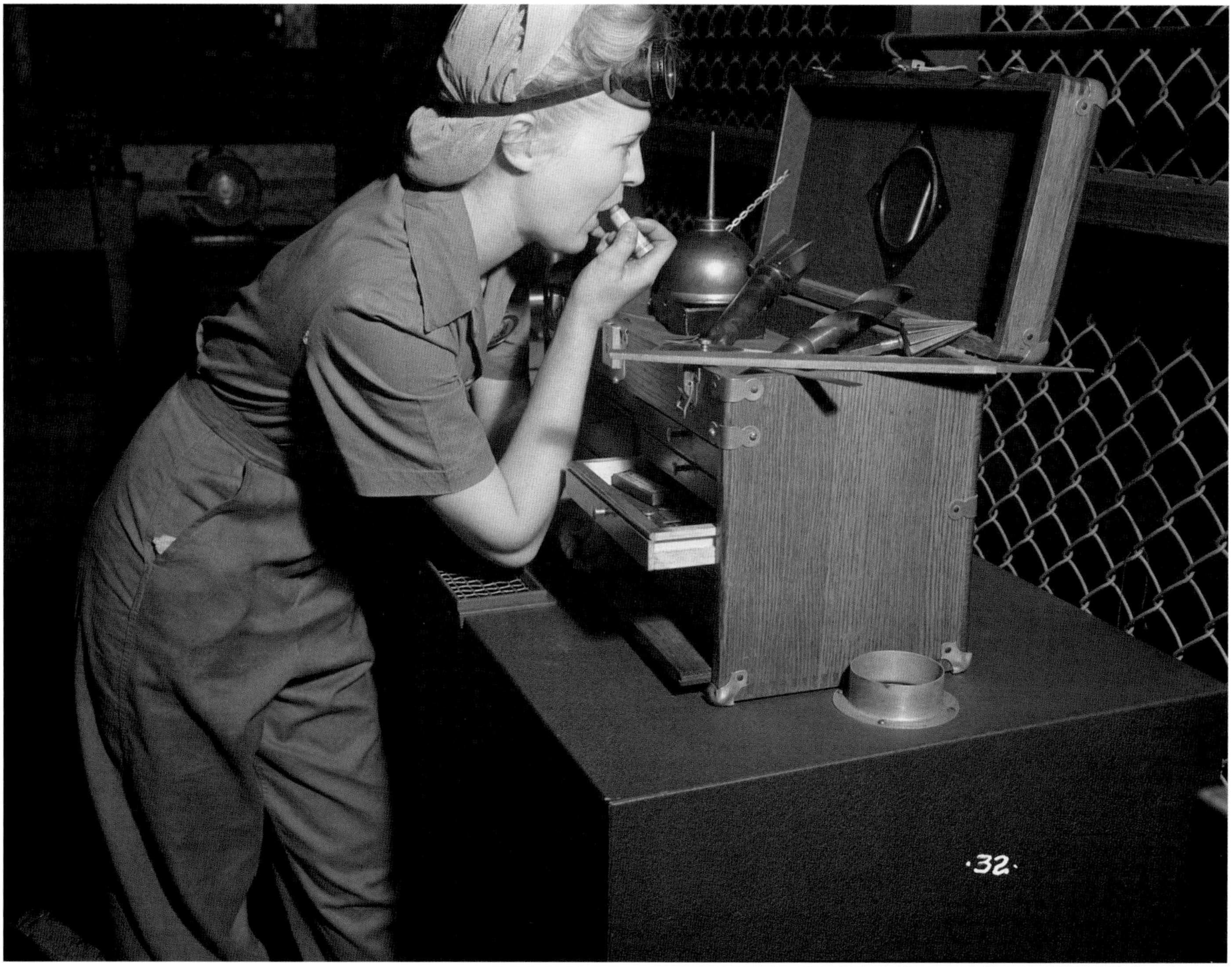

A female employee at the Dickson Gun plant takes a moment to apply her lipstick. The 124-acre facility opened in 1942 and was operated by the Hughes Tool Company. The Dickson plant, which manufactured centrifugally cast gun tubes, remained in operation until August 1945, when the chief of artillery for the US Army ordered a halt to production. This is a wonderful example of "Rosie the Riveter" type photos taken during World War II, showing both how quickly women were integrated into the workforce and how rapidly they adjusted to balancing their personal lives with their new found employment.

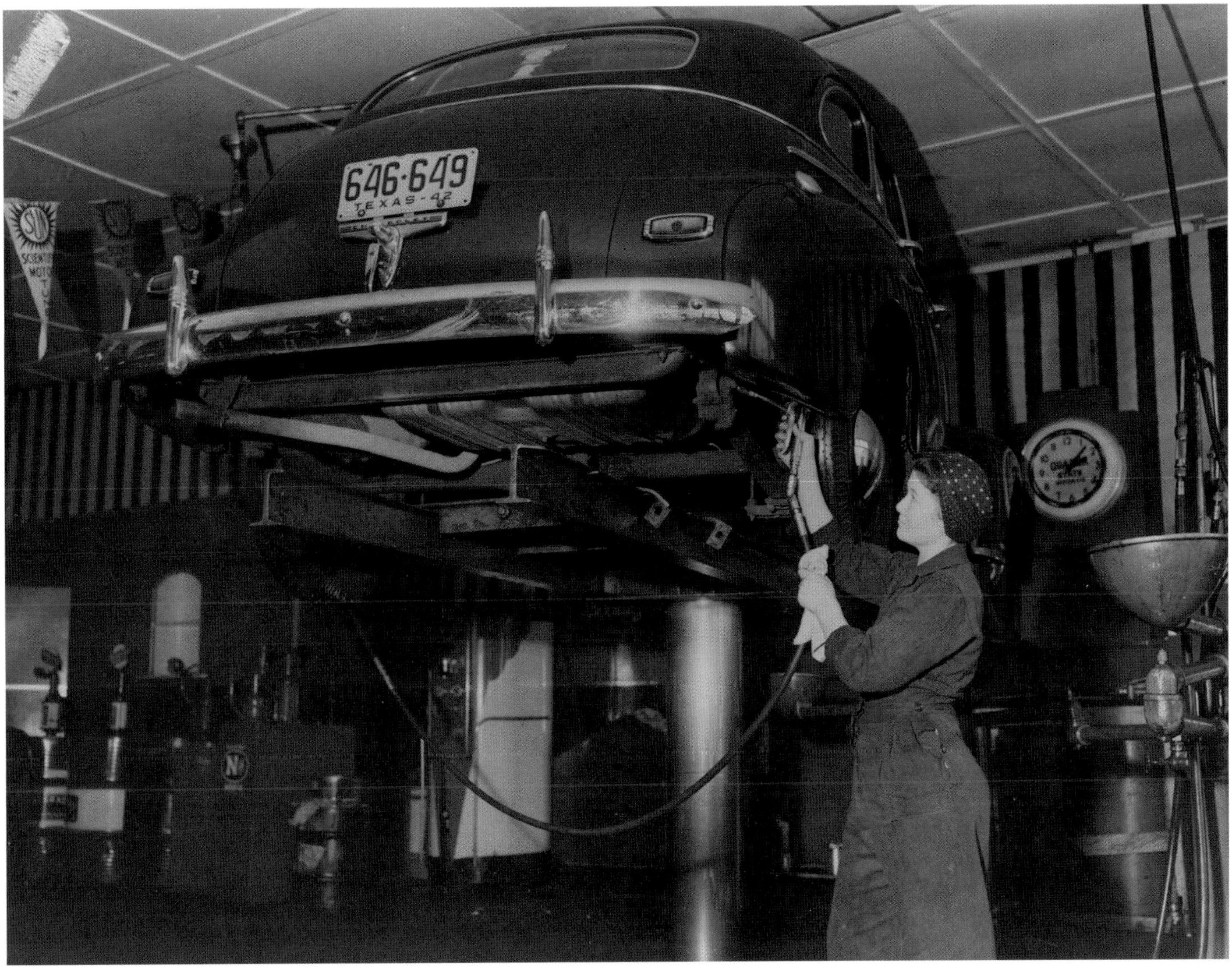

Woman working in a car garage, ca. 1942. With so many men away serving in the armed forces, women in Houston and around the country were allowed to fill many formerly male-only jobs for the duration of World War II.

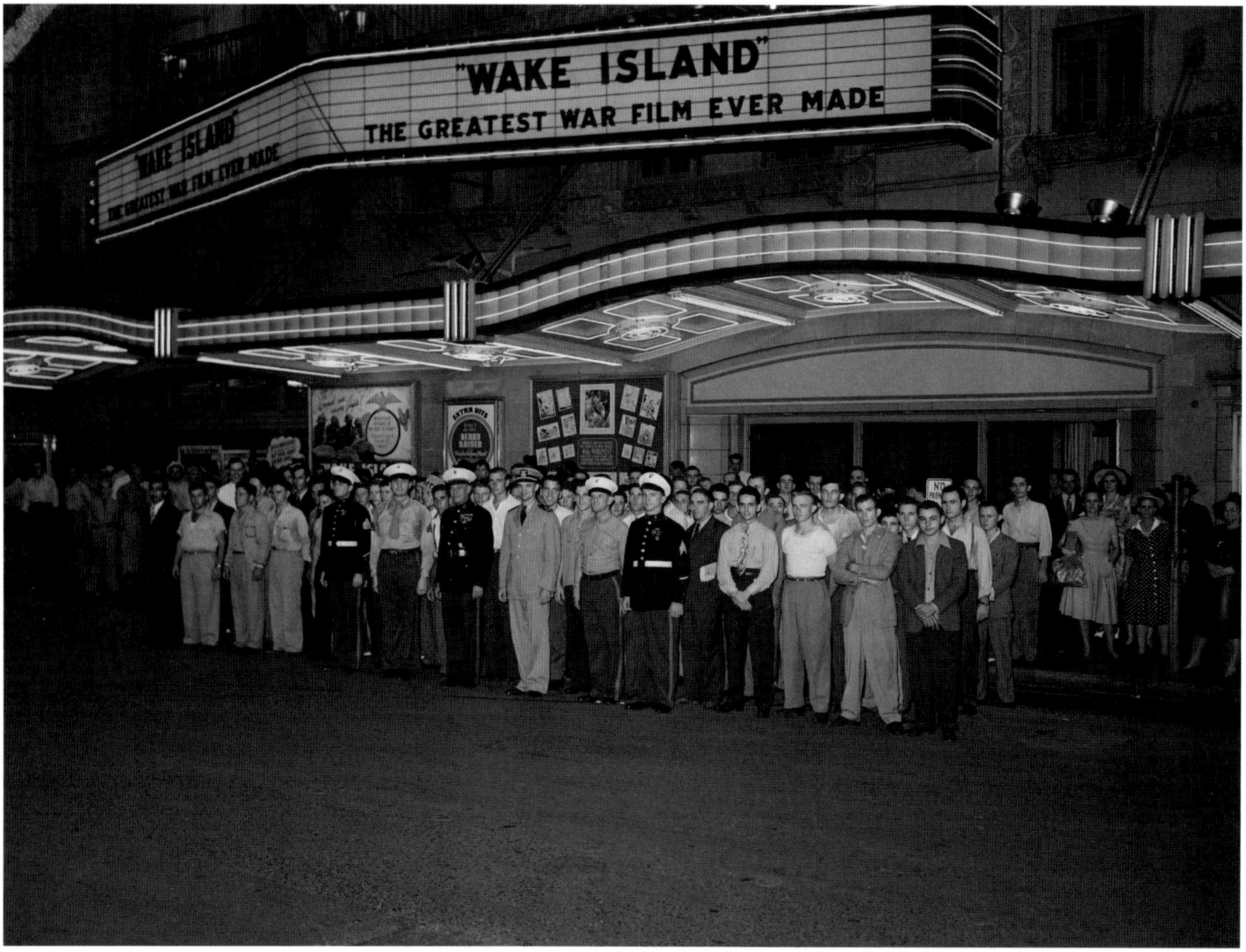

Above: Representatives from the US Navy and Marines made a promotional appearance at a war bond sale at an Interstate Theatre's showing of *Wake Island* in October 1942. The two branches of the armed forces had valiantly, but unsuccessfully, attempted to defend Wake Island from a Japanese invasion in December 1941. It was this battle that inspired the film version of *Wake Island*, which was released in the United States in August 1942, only eight months after the garrison's surrender to the Japanese.

Facing: Even children were involved with the civilian effort to help win World War II. This boy buys a war bond at the Village Theatre during the nation's fifth war bond drive. The poster urges Americans to buy war bonds to "Invest in Invasion." This picture was taken in June 1944, the very month that Allied forces first breached Hitler's "Fortress Europe" by successfully invading France.

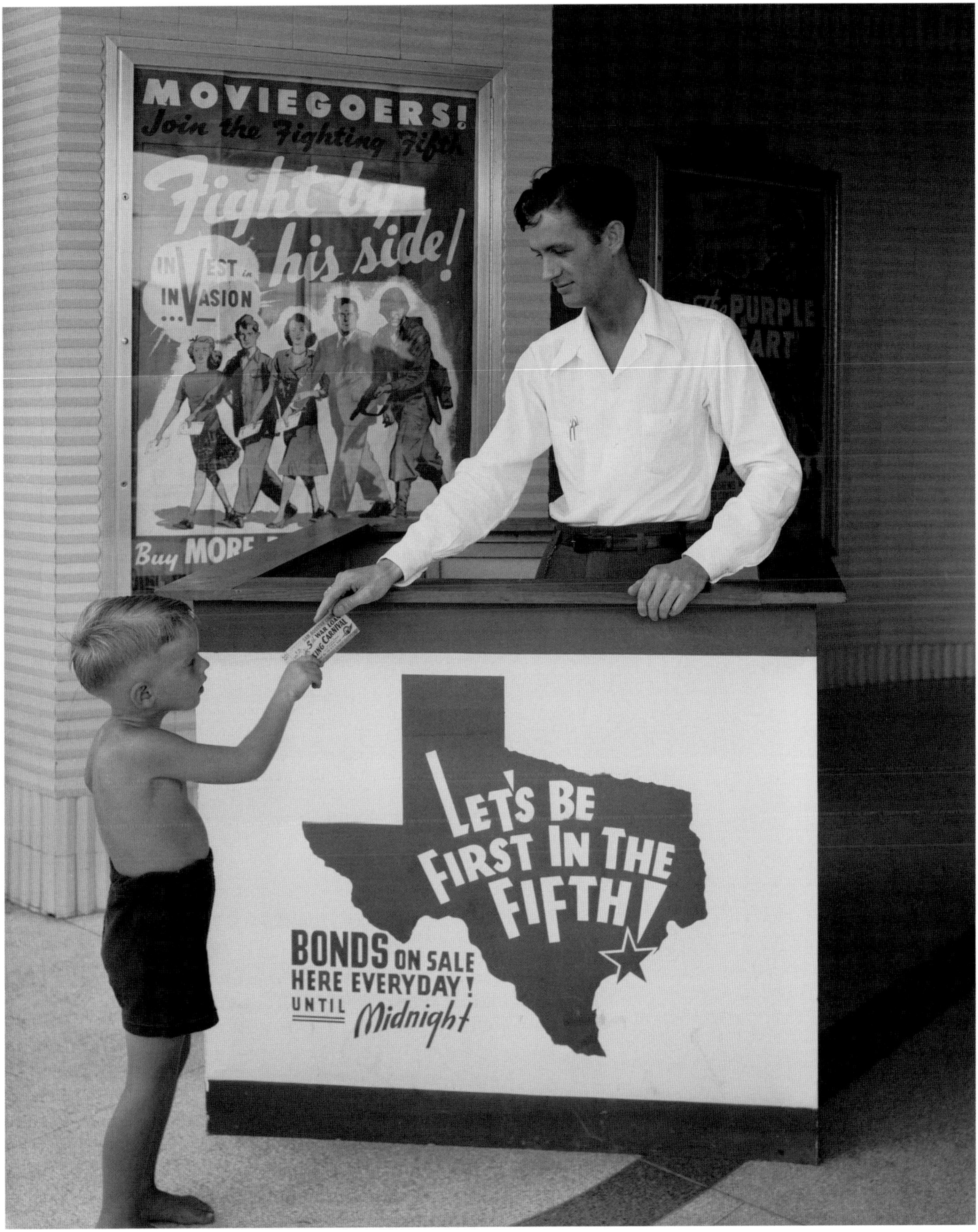
MOVIEGOERS!
Join the Fighting Fifth
Fight by his side!
INVEST in INVASION
Buy MORE
LET'S BE FIRST IN THE FIFTH!
BONDS ON SALE HERE EVERYDAY! UNTIL Midnight

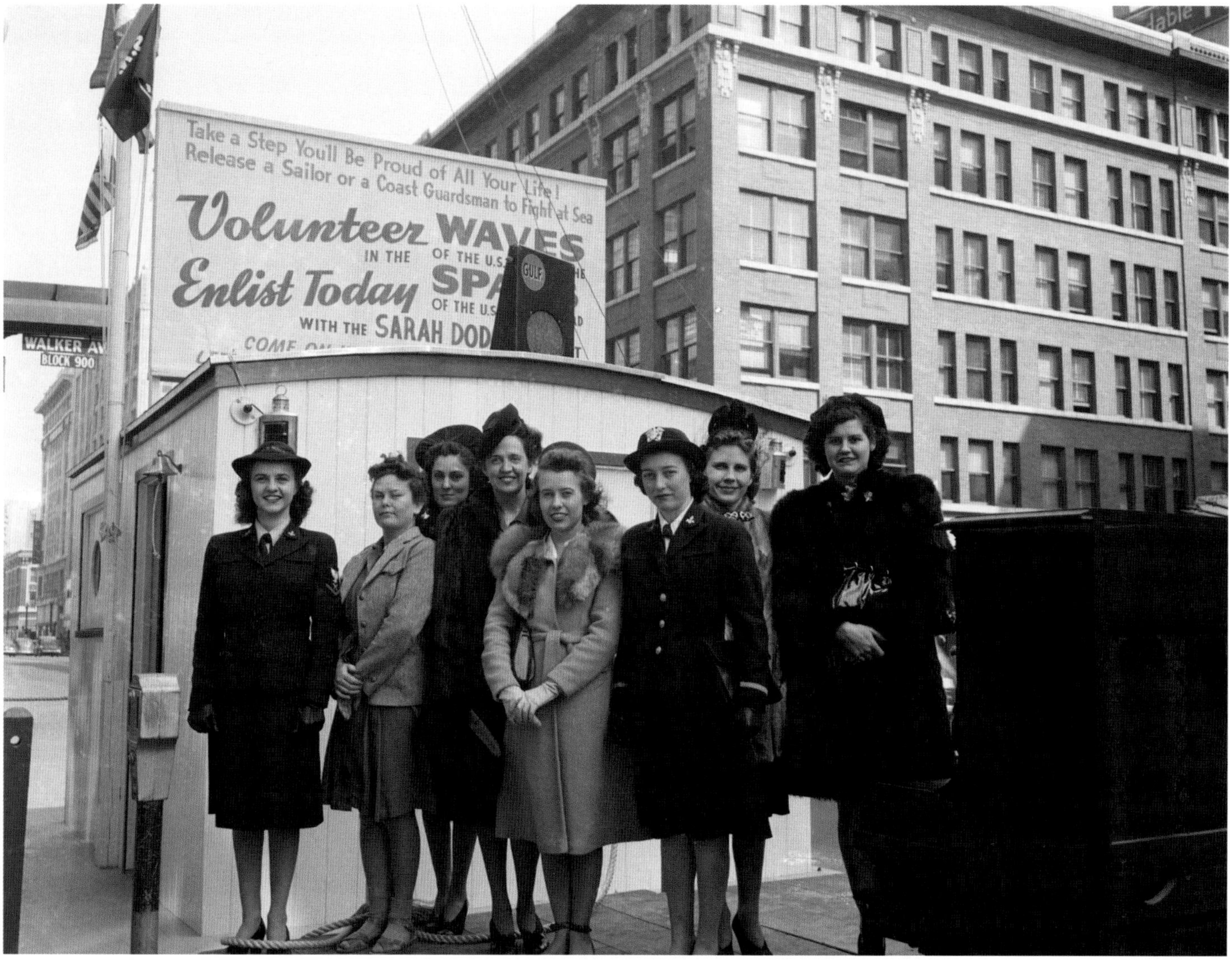

Above: These WAVES, or Women Accepted for Voluntary Emergency Service, staffed a recruitment booth that was erected downtown in 1943. A division of the US Navy, the WAVES had been established only the year before and primarily served on duty within the continental United States.

Facing: A film still from color footage, shot ca. 1942 by Bob Bailey, showing downtown crowds on Main Street during wartime. The promotional sign for the fourth national war bond drive shown in the following photo can be seen in the right background.

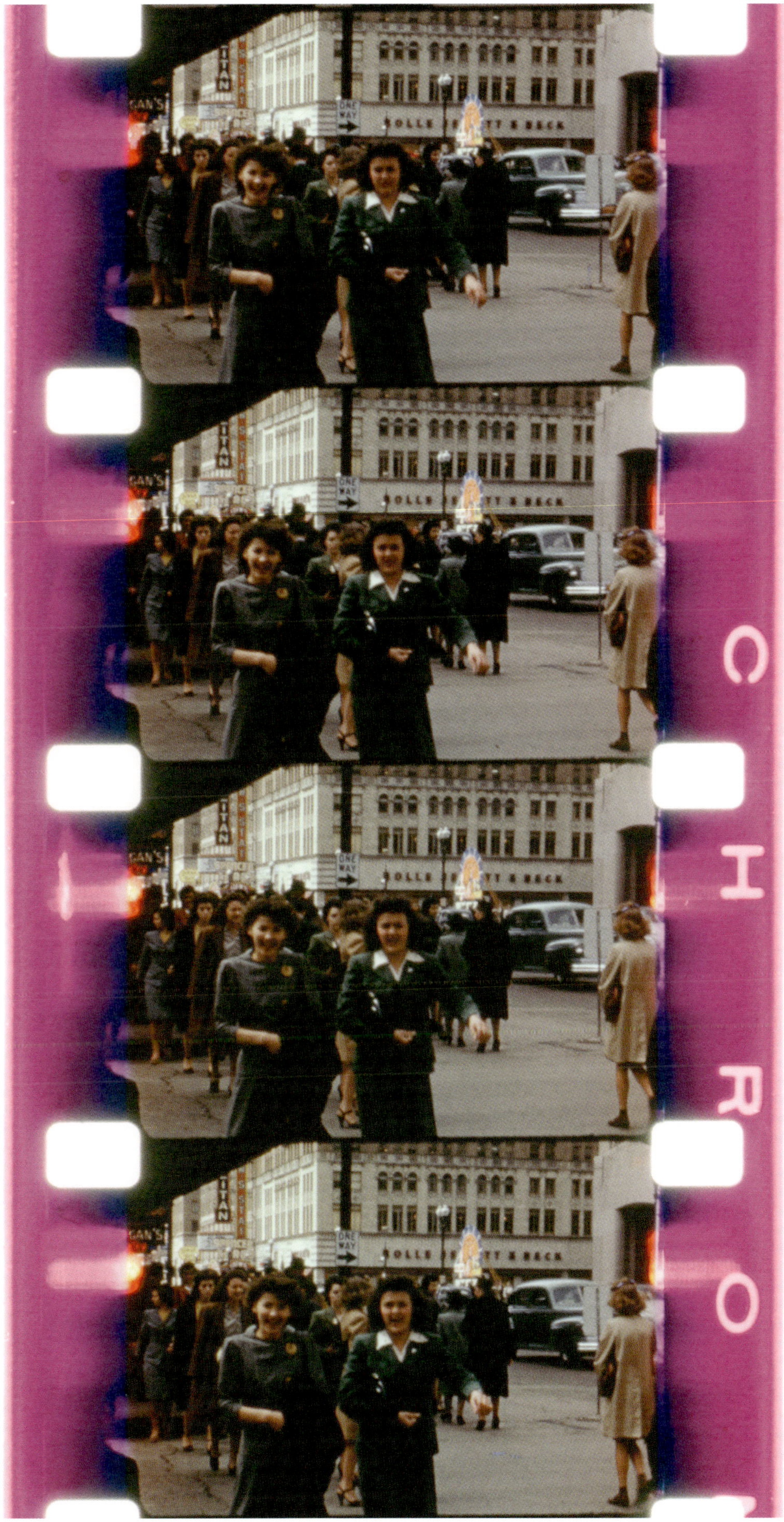
ONE WAY

Promotional sign provided for the fourth national war bond drive showing Uncle Sam preparing to let Adolf Hitler and General Hideki Tojo "have it." The photo was taken in January 1944 and commissioned by the War Advertising Committee. It appears, from some of Bailey's photographs, that there were either multiple copies of this sign or that a single sign was moved around town to different locations. In this scene, the sign was displayed next door to the former First Presbyterian Church at Main and McKinney.

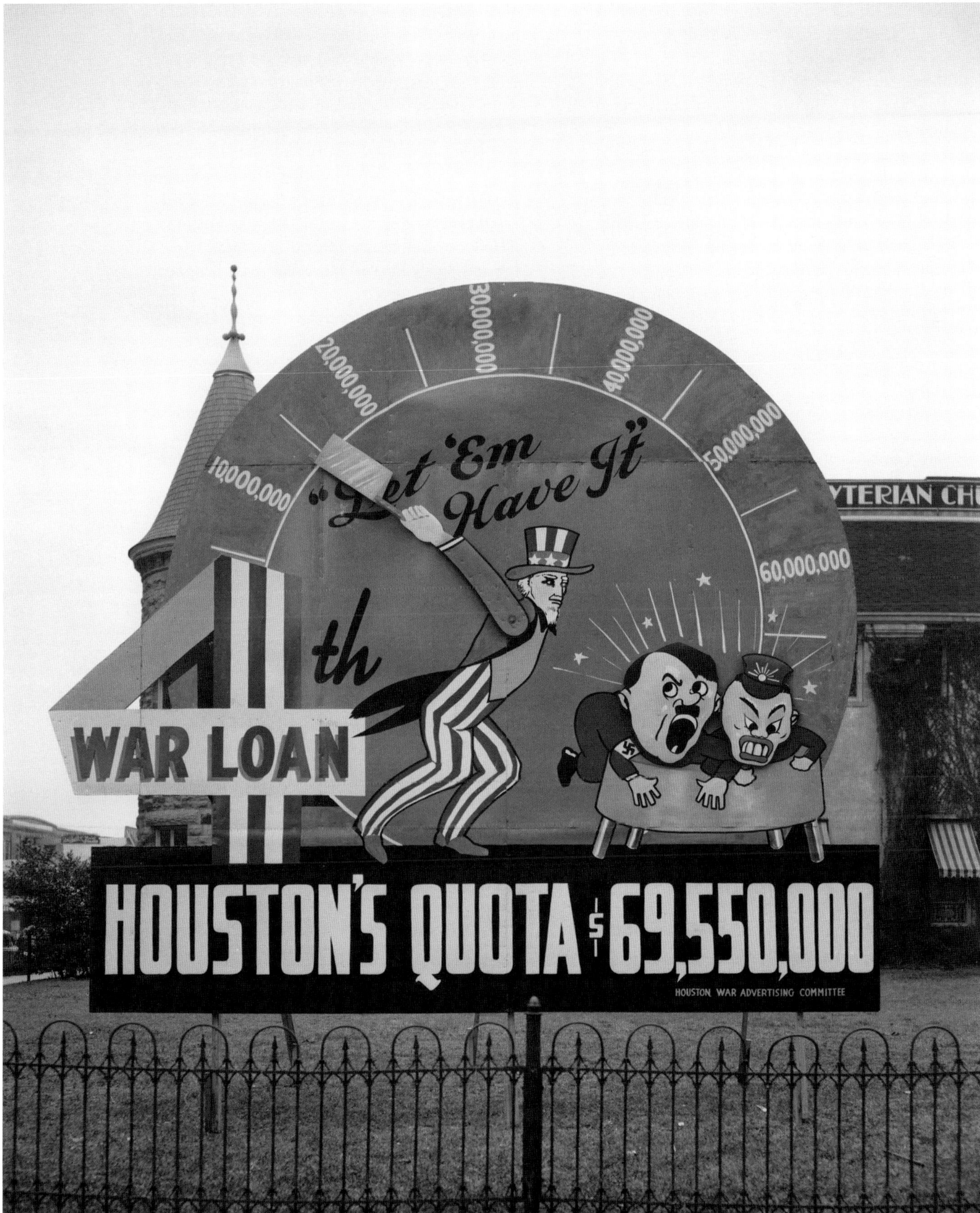
10,000,000
20,000,000
30,000,000
40,000,000
50,000,000
60,000,000
"Let 'Em Have It"
th
WAR LOAN
HOUSTON'S QUOTA $69,550,000
HOUSTON WAR ADVERTISING COMMITTEE

23 *900 block of Rusk Street*: "History: Police Department," City of Houston, accessed July 6, 2015, http://www.houstontx.gov/police/history/

26 *View of Main Street with San Jacinto Hotel*: *San Jacinto Hotel Vertical File*, Houston Metropolitan Research Center.

36 *The Sunset Royals performing at the Harlem Grill*: Strom, *Houston Lost and Unbuilt*, 18–24.

40 *Rice Institute's 1935 football team*: "Rice Institute Football Player, Bill Wallace," Rice Digital Scholarship Archive, accessed July 1, 2015, http://scholarship.rice.edu/handle/1911/64544

42 *Lines of children waiting to get into Interstate Yale Theatre*: *Yale Theatre Vertical File*, Houston Metropolitan Research Center.

46 *boy fishing in Buffalo Bayou*: Hanson, "Remember When," 8–11.

48 *Group of children with Santa Claus*: "Murder on the Blackboard," Internet Movie Database, accessed July 7, 2015.

49 *The 1936 Christmas party*: *Will Horwitz Vertical File* and *Houston City Auditorium Vertical File*, Houston Metropolitan Research Center.

52 *Where Sam Houston and the Texas Army crossed Buffalo Bayou on April 19, 1836*: Harris County Historical Markers, accessed October 4, 2015, http://harriscountyhistoricalmarkers.com/HistoricalSites/CurrentMarkers.aspx?udt_1462_param_detail=1111; "Camp near Vince's Bayou," Early Texas History, accessed October 4, 2015, http://www.earlytexashistory.com/Tx1836/camp20.html; Stephen Kirby, "Texas Army's Route from Cypress to San Jacinto, April 17–April 21, 1836," *Meander and Gander* (blog), accessed October 4, 2015, http://www.meanderandgander.com/2013/10/texas-army-route-from-cypress-to-san.html.

54 *unveiling of the model of the San Jacinto Monument*: "The San Jacinto Centennial Association and the Houston Observances during the Texas Centennial of 1936," TexasEscapes.com, accessed July 1, 2015.

54 *San Jacinto Monument under construction*: *San Jacinto Monument Vertical File*, Houston Metropolitan Research Center.

60 *The Shirley Temple window at Sakowitz Brothers Department Store*: "Shirley Temple Dead: Legendary Child Star Dies at 85," *Hollywood Reporter*, accessed September 12, 2015, http://www.hollywoodreporter.com/news/shirley-temple-dead-legendary-child-677643; Zoe Jacobson, "Shirley Temple—The Little Girl That Saved 20th Century Fox," Bidness Etc, accessed October 5, 2015, http://www.bidnessetc.com/business/shirley-temple-the-little-girl-that-saved-20-th-century-fox/

61 *If* Hollywood Hotel *is remembered at all today*: "Hollywood Hotel," Internet Movie Database, accessed September 12, 2015.

62 *Two Houston motorcycle policemen*: "History: Police Department," City of Houston, accessed July 8, 2015, http://www.houstontx.gov/police/history/.

63 *Women boarding a Braniff Airways passenger plane*: Brooke Watts, The Braniff Pages, accessed September 28, 2015; "Braniff International Airways: The History of an Amazing Airline," accessed September 29, 2015, Fly Away, https://flyawaysimulation.com/news/4683/.

65 *A 1937 V12 Lincoln Zephyr*: "Futurama," *Paris Review*, Accessed October 3, 2015, http://www.theparisreview.org/blog/tag/norman-bel-geddes/.

72 *Sears store at 4201 South Main Street*: *Sears Department Store Vertical File*, Houston Metropolitan Research Center.

73 *cars parked alongside the Sears store*: For examples of Moholy-Nagy's photographs, see Ingrid Pfeiffer and Max Hollein, *László Moholy-Nagy* (New York: Prestel, 2009).

75 *Stage and interior of the Metropolitan Theatre*: *Metropolitan Theatre Vertical File*, Houston Metropolitan Research Center.

78 *The Pruitt Company*: The Pruitt Company, accessed July 2, 2015, http://www.thepruittcompany.com.

80 *A jumble of food billboards on Main Street*: "Scenic Houston: History," Scenic Houston, accessed June 23, 2015, http://www.scenichouston.org/what-we-do/history/.

90 *The Palace Theatre*: "Nabonga," Internet Movie Database, accessed November 4, 2015.

91 *Grand Prize Beer*: Bryan Carey, "Gulf Brewing: Howard Hughes' Brewery Makes a Comeback," Examiner.com, accessed October 30, 2015, http://www.examiner.com/article/gulf-brewing-howard-hughes-brewery-makes-a-comeback.

93 *Billboard for Forest Park Cemetery*: W. N. Rudd, "Perpetual Care: Its Establishment and Regulation by the State," International Cemetery, Cremation, and Funeral Association, accessed July 2, 2015, http://www.iccfa.com/reading/1920-1939/perpetual-care-its-establishment-and-regulation-state.

99 *a line of Electrolux refrigerators*: Cohen, *A Consumer's Republic*, 18–34.

102 *Employees at work for the Star Engraving Company*: Stages Repertory Theatre, accessed October 11, 2015, http://stagestheatre.com/seating.

113 *ticker-tape parade for its native son Howard Hughes*: "Photograph of Howard Hughes in a parade, Houston, Texas, July 30, 1938," University of Nevada, Las Vegas Digital Collections, accessed July 27, 2015.

114 *Cowboy star Gene Autry*: "History," Houston Livestock Show and Rodeo, accessed July 30, 2015, http://www.rodeohouston.com/AboutUs/WhoWeAre/History.aspx.

118 *A female employee at the Dickson Gun plant*: "Dickson Gun Plant," *Handbook of Texas Online*, Texas State Historical Association, accessed June 20, 2015, http://www.tshaonline.org/handbook/online/articles/dmd01.

120 *Representatives from the US Navy and Marines*: "Wake Island," Internet Movie Database, accessed July 5, 2015.

122 *These WAVES, or Women Accepted for Voluntary Emergency Service*: Jessica Myers, "The Navy's History of Making WAVES," America's Navy, accessed July 15, 2015, http://www.navy.mil/submit/display.asp?story_id=75662; "WWII and WAVES," Armed Forces History Museum, accessed October 9, 2015, http://armedforcesmuseum.com/wwii-and-waves-women-accepted-for-volunteer-emergency-service/.

1945 TO 1960

POSTWAR SUBURBANIZATION AND EXPANSION

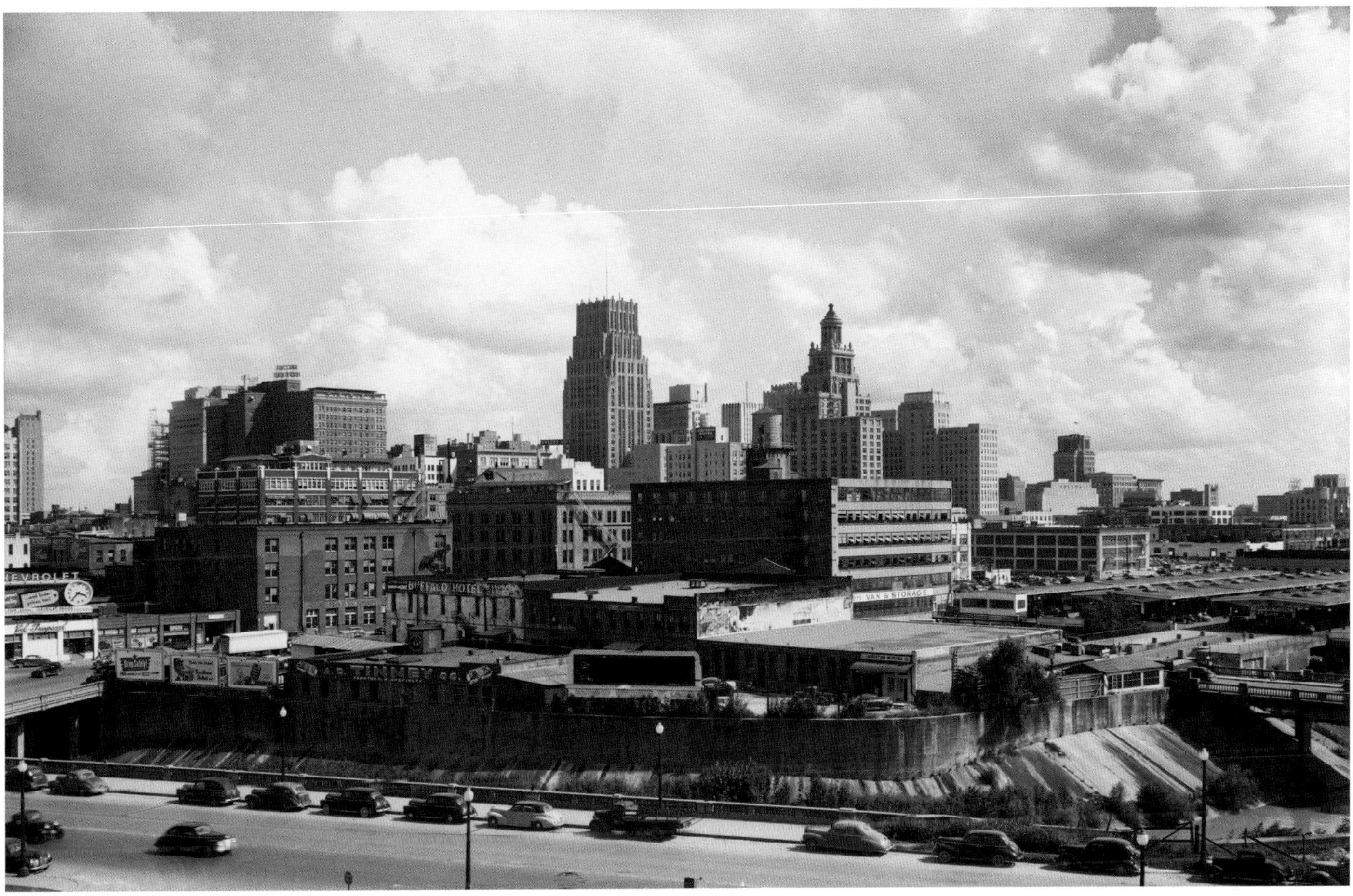

This scene of downtown Houston was taken in 1949 for decorative use in the coffee shop of the Rice Hotel. Houston had thrived during World War II and the immediate postwar period and was on the cusp of a major expansion and boom in the 1950s.

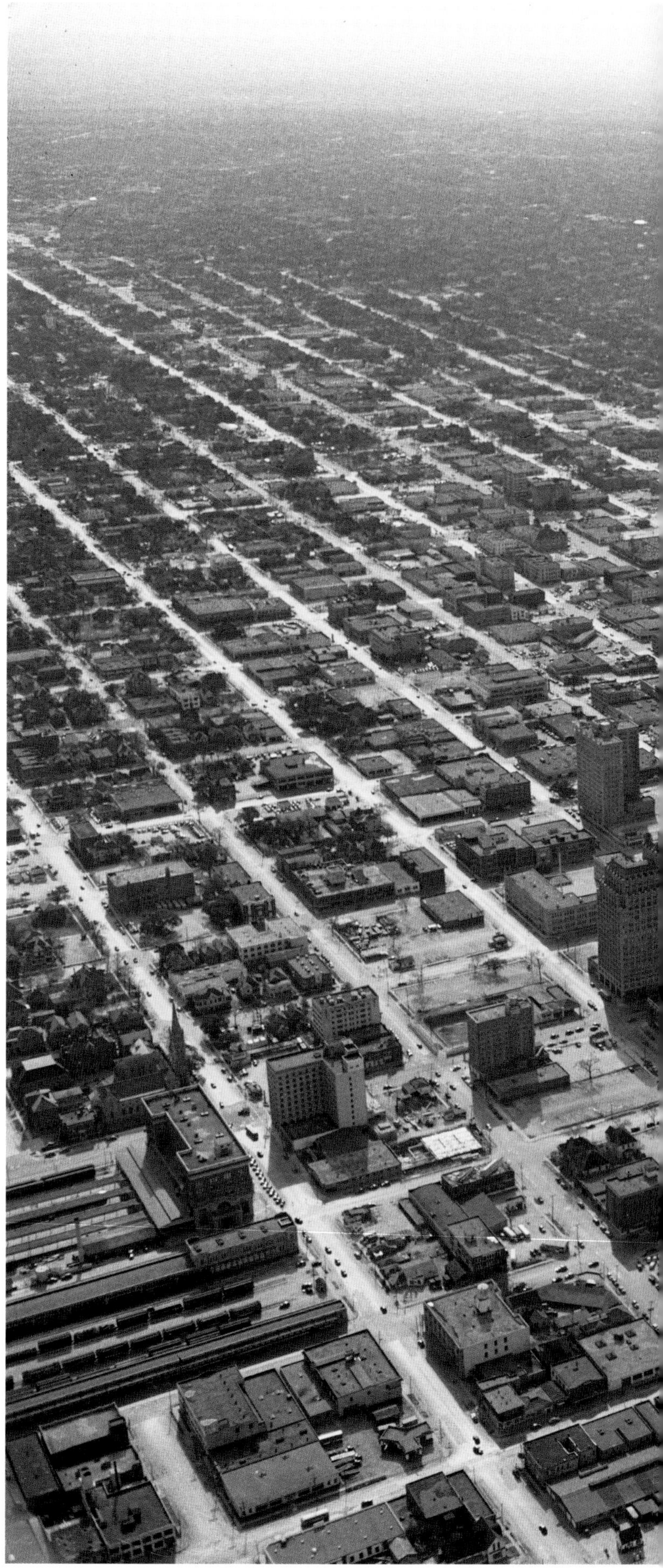

Aerial view of Houston, taken on March 2, 1947. During the following decades, the undeveloped blocks branching out from the downtown area would undergo a startling amount of commercial development.

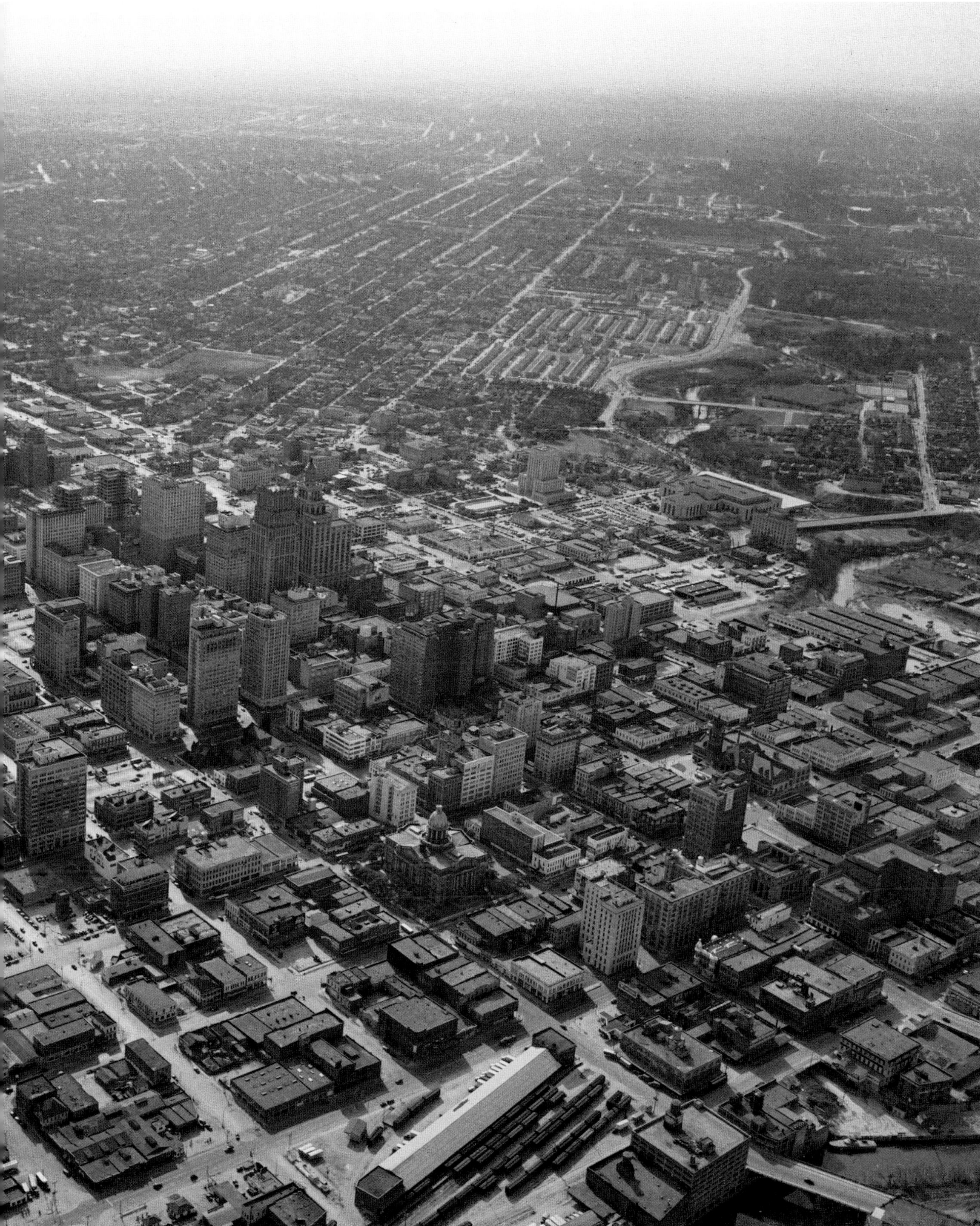

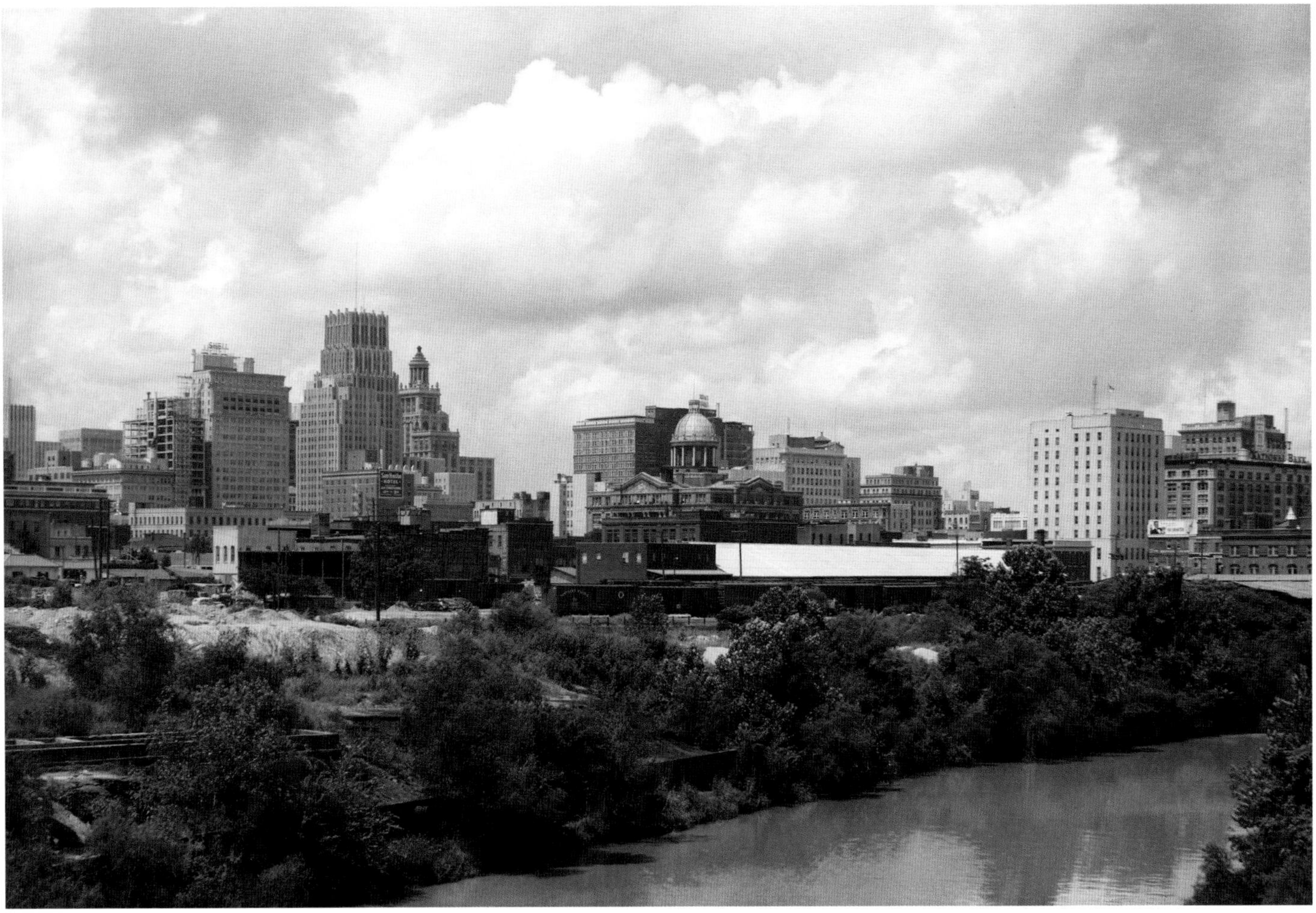

Houston's skyline looking across Buffalo Bayou, with the Harris County Courthouse at its center, ca. 1950. This photograph was taken not far downstream from Allen's Landing, the birthplace of the city, near the confluence of Buffalo and White Oak Bayous. Buffalo Bayou played an enormous and integral role in Houston's growth and expansion from the city's founding, when the Allen brothers promoted Houston as being at the "head of navigation" for the (barely) navigable bayou. From Houston's earliest days, the city's business interests and boosters had determined that only by dredging and widening Buffalo Bayou would Houston ever be able to compete successfully with the Port of Galveston for the Gulf Coast's commercial shipping.

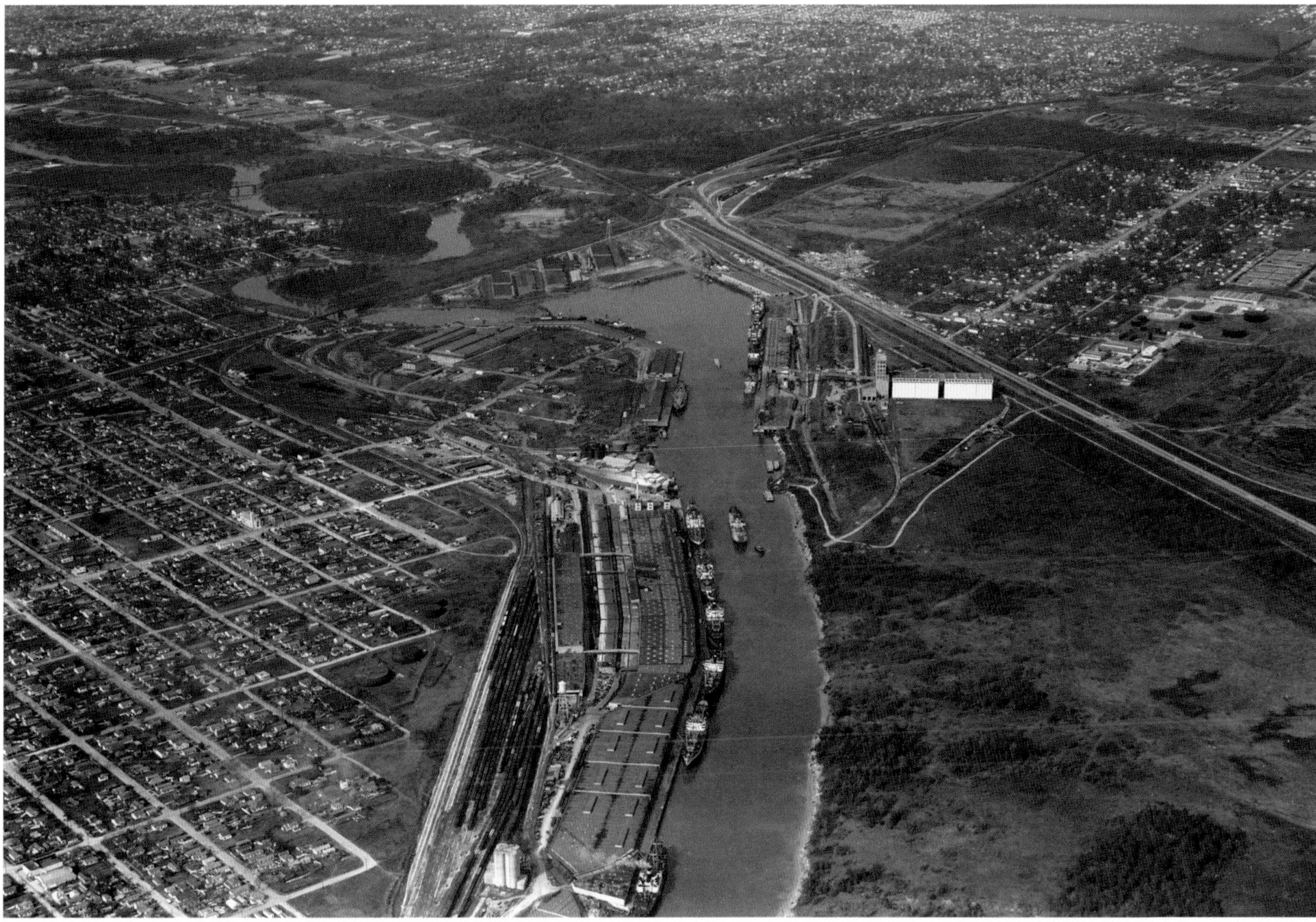

Aerial view of the Houston Ship Channel's Turning Basin, showing vessels docking, loading, and unloading their cargoes, December 28, 1949. The importance of the Ship Channel to Houston's growth cannot be overstated, especially for a city founded along a bayou that initially could only accommodate shallow-draft vessels. Houston's commercial and civic leaders waged a ceaseless campaign for the development of a channel deep enough to handle deep water vessels. Although sporadic attempts were made over the years to dredge Buffalo Bayou, the construction of the present-day channel, with the lower part of the bayou dredged to an initial depth of twenty-five feet, began in June 1912. It was completed in September 1914 and formally dedicated on November 10 of the same year.

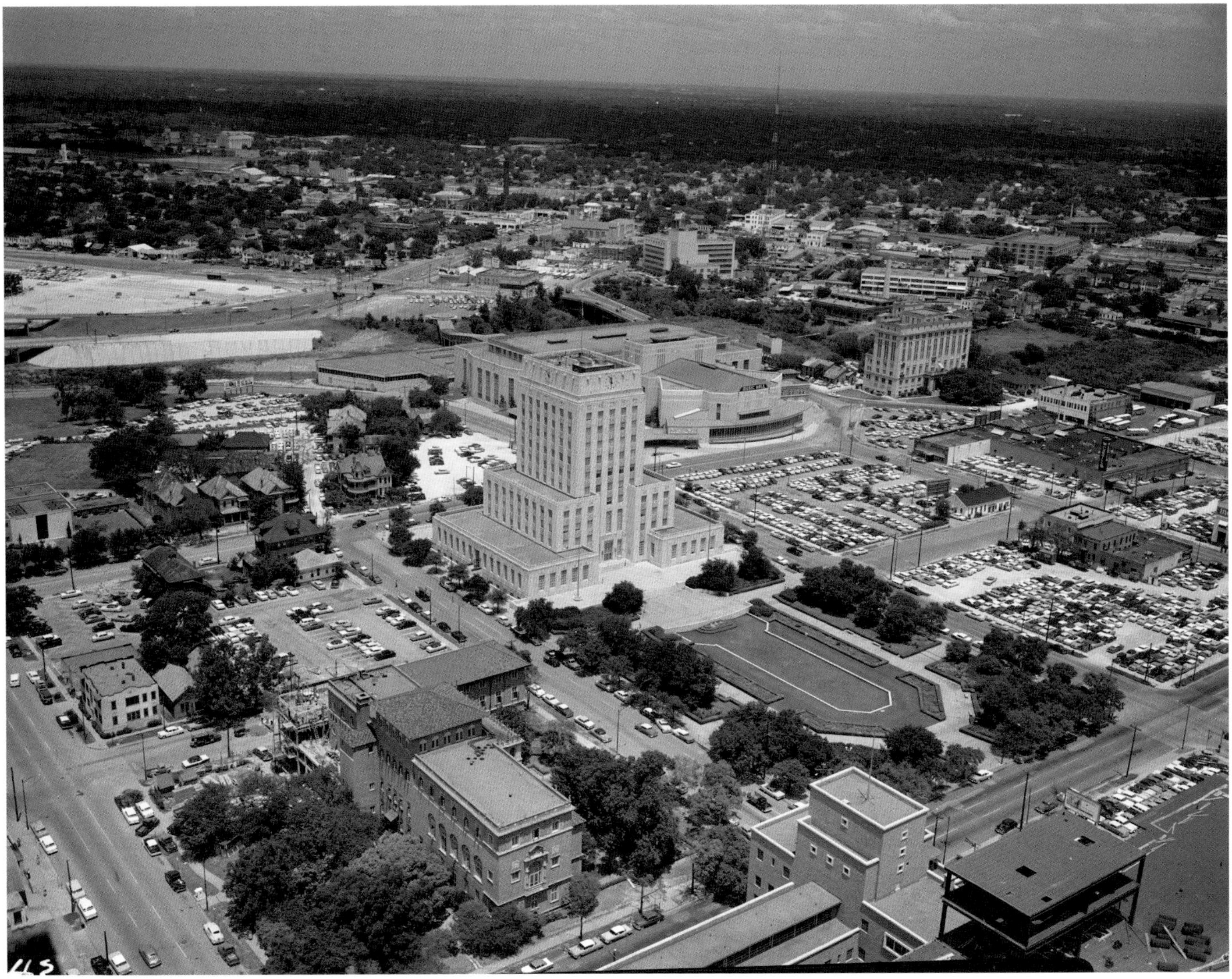

Above: Aerial view of Houston City Hall and the adjacent Civic Center, August 1957. The Julia Ideson Building is at the lower left of the photograph.

Facing: View of the newly constructed Texas National Bank Building, located at 921 Main and McKinney, designed by Kenneth Franzheim, and completed in 1955. The addition of this building to the skyline, along with the Bank of the Southwest (1956) and Alfred Finn's City National Bank Building (1947), seen at the right, helped to solidify Houston's image as a major banking center. The "weather ball" atop the sign signaled changing weather by turning red, green, or white.

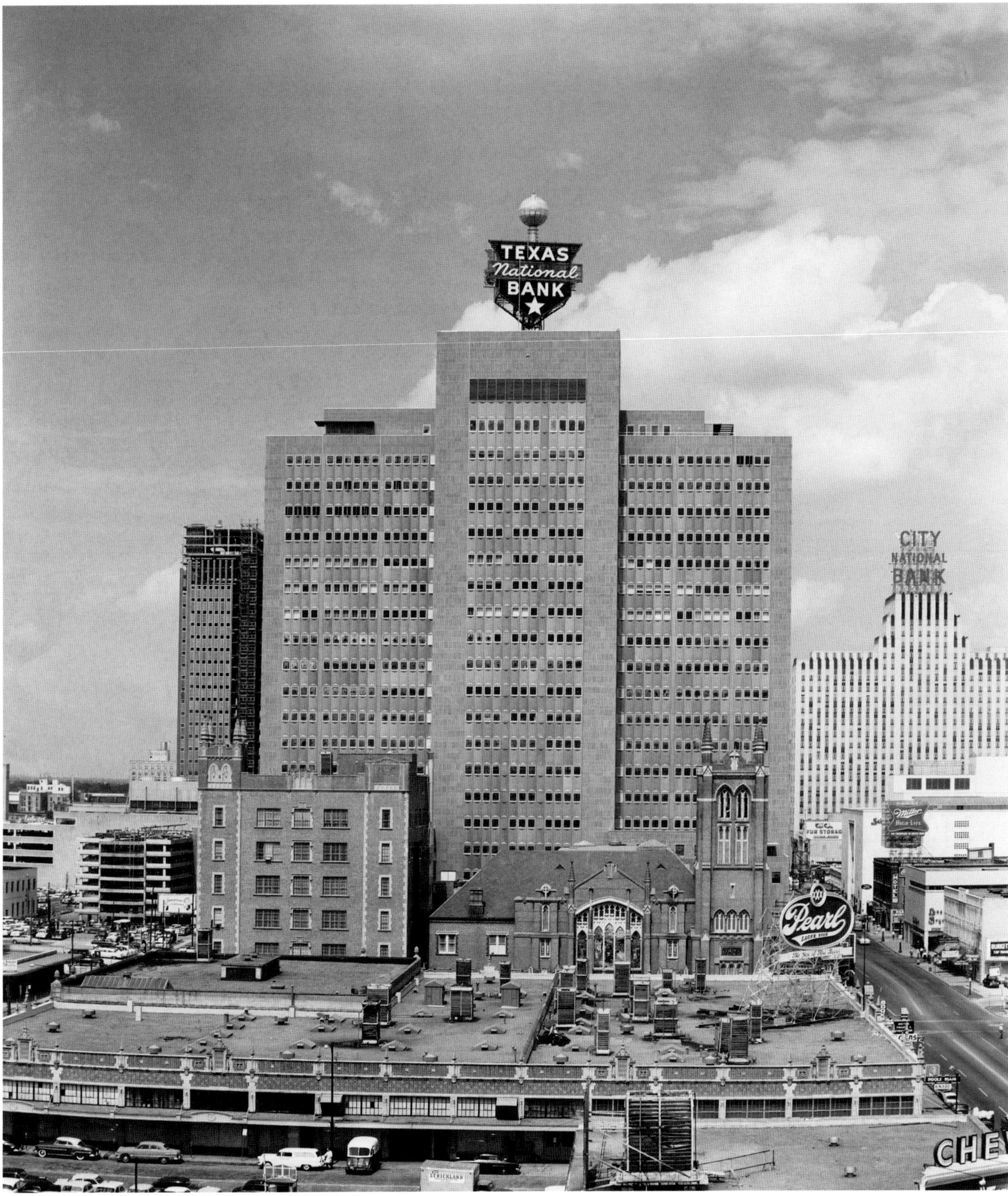
TEXAS
National
BANK
CITY
NATIONAL
BANK
Pearl

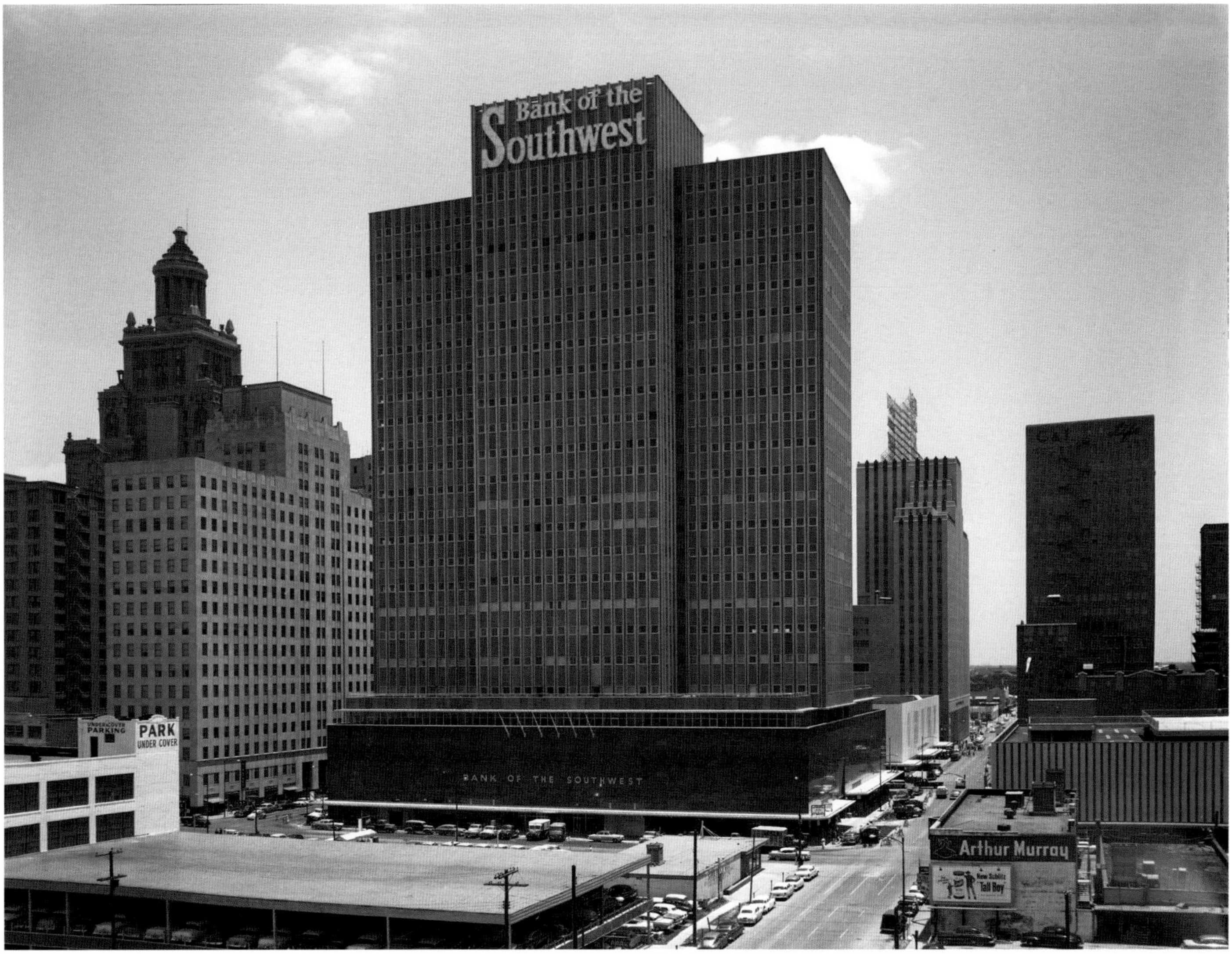

Above: The twenty-four-story Bank of the Southwest Building shortly after its completion in 1956. This building was one of the most significant additions to Houston's skyline during the 1950s. It is known today as 919 Milam and contains leased office space.

Facing: The Gulf Building at night. Although this photo could be dated ca. 1956 by its entry in the Bailey collection's logbook, judging from the cars parked in the street, it appears to be a reproduction of a photo that was probably taken not long after the building's completion in 1929. The thirty-six-story Art Deco masterpiece remained the tallest building in the Houston skyline until the completion of the Humble (now ExxonMobil) Building in 1963. Fortunately, the Gulf Building has been preserved and restored and still graces the city's skyline today as the 712 Main Building.

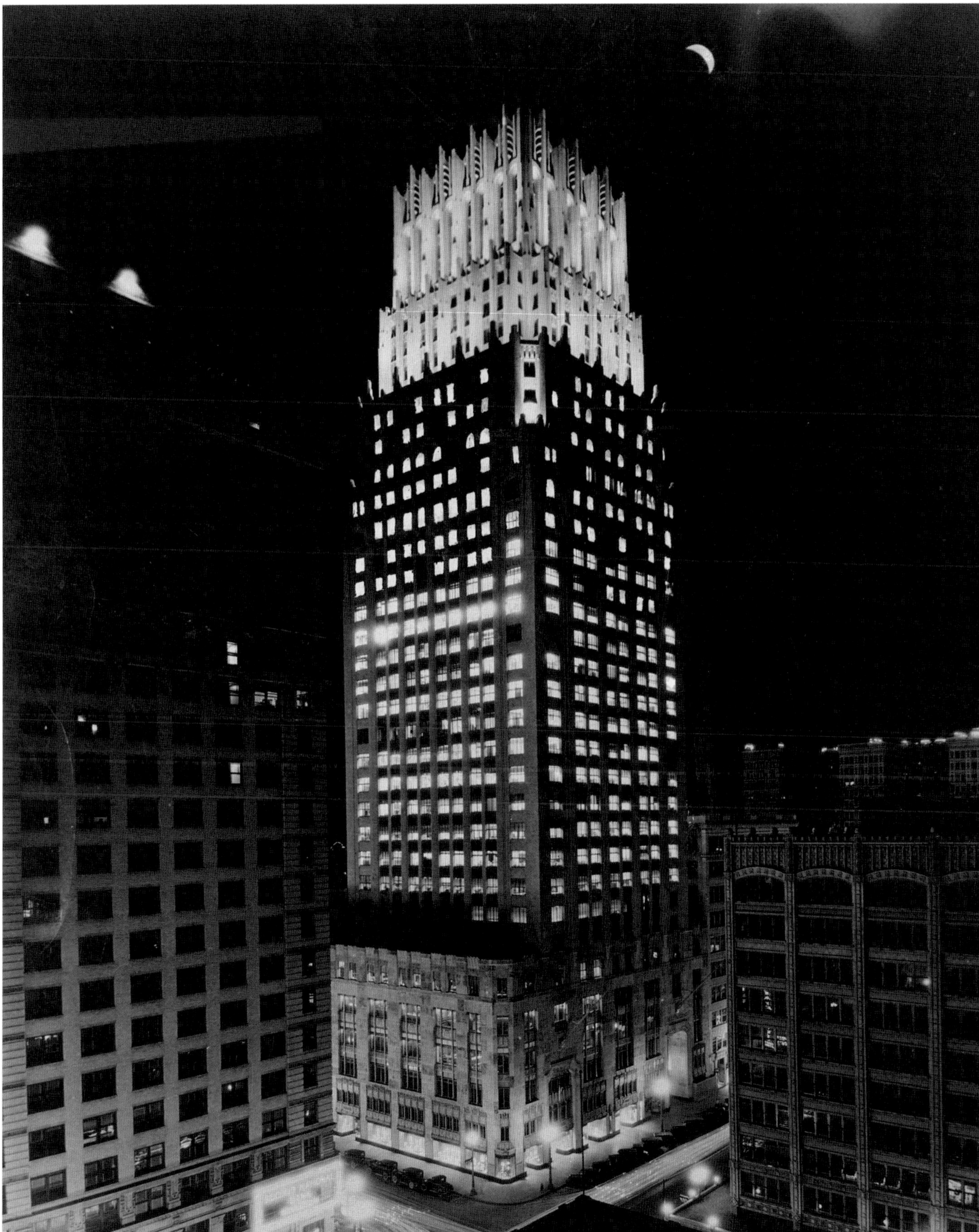

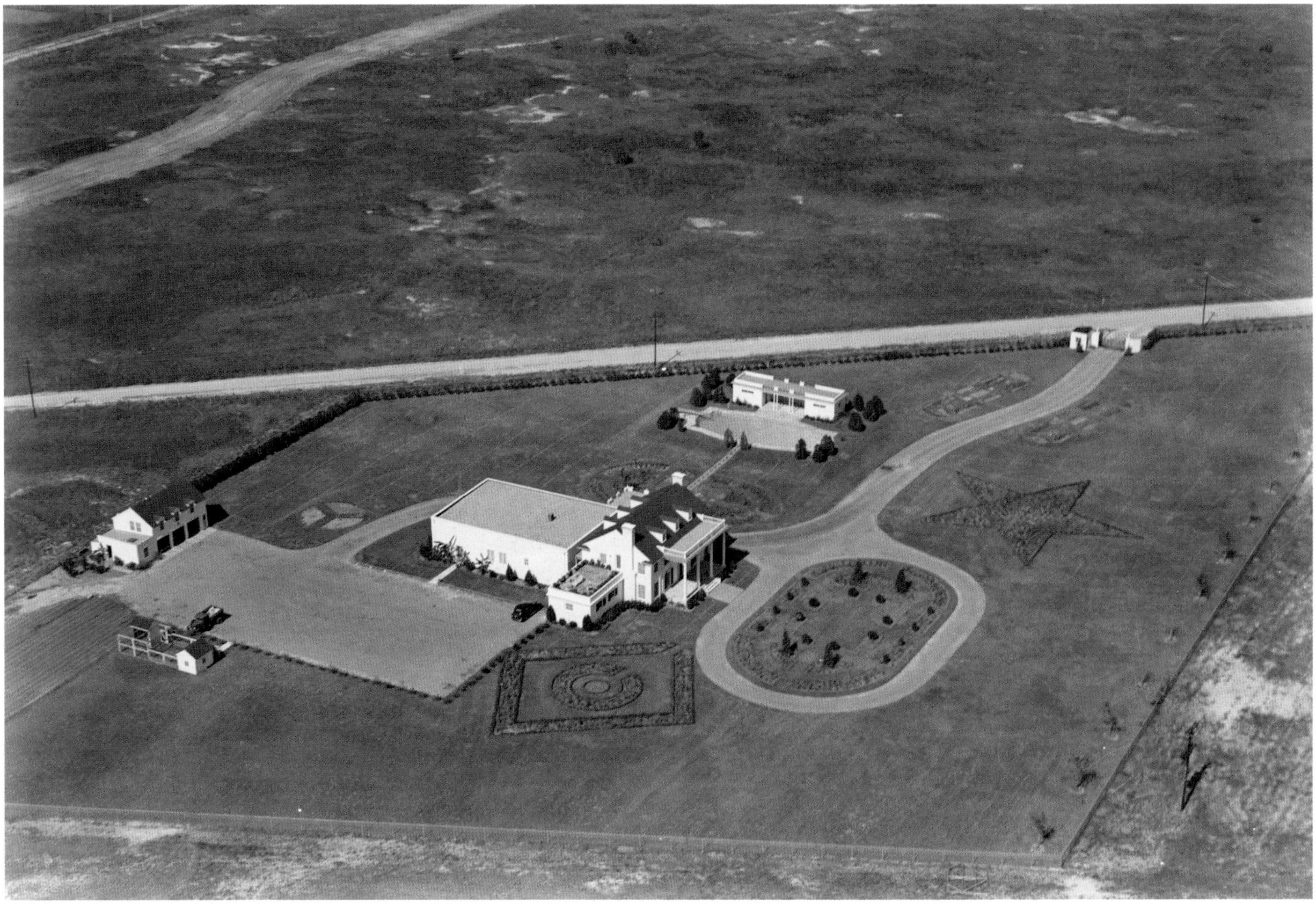

Aerial view of Friedman's Gambling Casino, otherwise known as the Domain Privée, ca. 1950. The casino, which according to some sources also contained a brothel, was owned and operated by Houston gambler Jakie Friedman and was located past the end of South Main. The club allowed only wealthy patrons admission past the guards at the entrance gate and was very popular with Houstonians according to many accounts. By the mid-1950s, however, Texas law enforcement was pushing for stricter adherence to the state's anti-gambling laws, and Friedman closed the Domain Privée and moved to gambling-friendly Las Vegas. There he opened the Sands Hotel and Casino, which became one of the most famous Vegas landmarks.

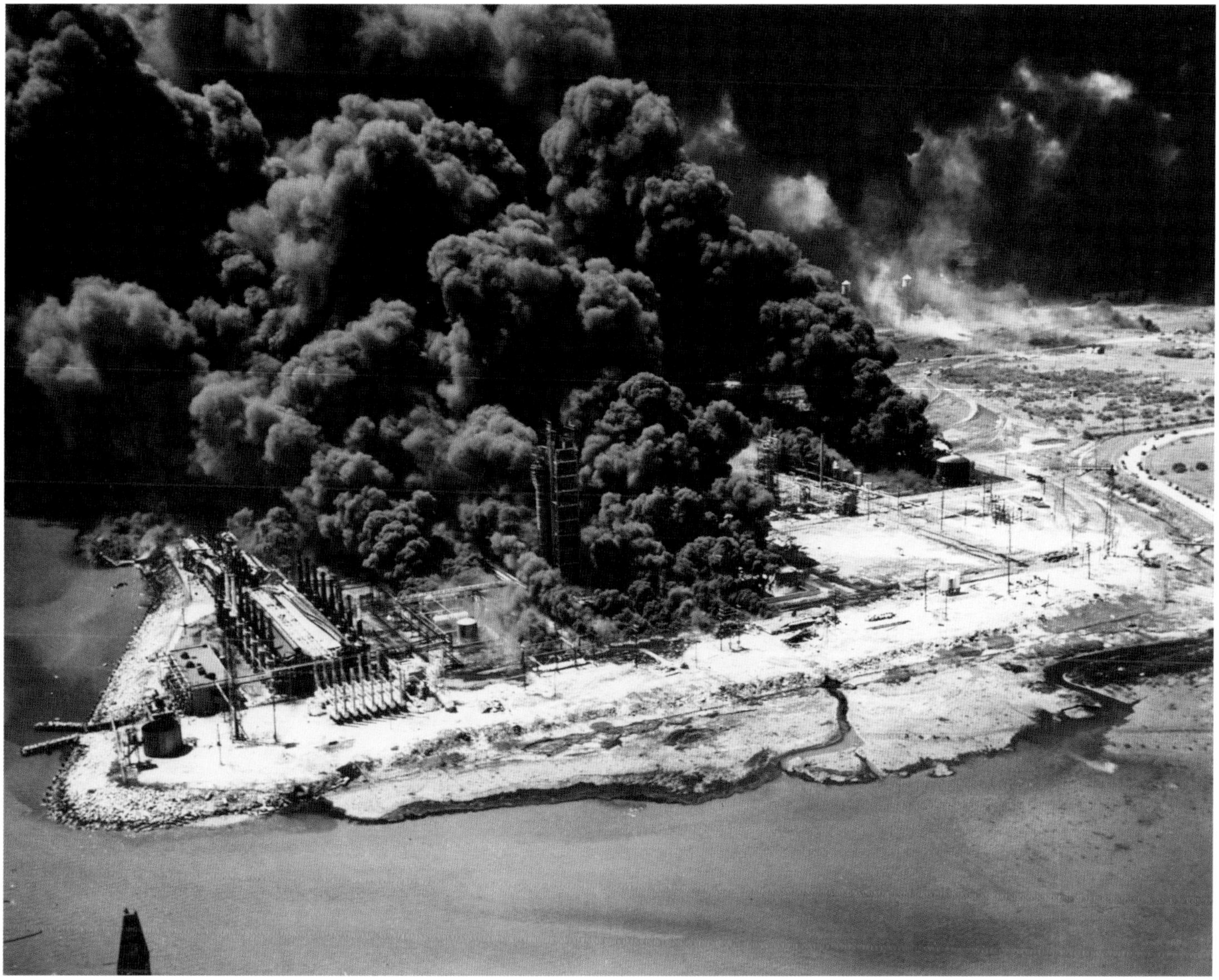

The Texas City Disaster of April 16, 1947, still remains the greatest industrial accident in American history. The explosion occurred when the ammonium nitrate fertilizer cargo being loaded onto the ship *Grandcamp* exploded along one of the docks located near the Monsanto chemical plant. The massive explosion started a chain reaction of explosions on nearby ships, causing expanding fires. To put the disaster in perspective, the explosion of the *Grandcamp* is estimated to be one of the largest non-nuclear explosions ever recorded.

This aerial shot shows the enormous extent of the fire that spread easily through the Monsanto chemical plant's facilities and the adjacent industrial complex. Smoke plumes from the initial explosion reached an estimated two thousand feet.

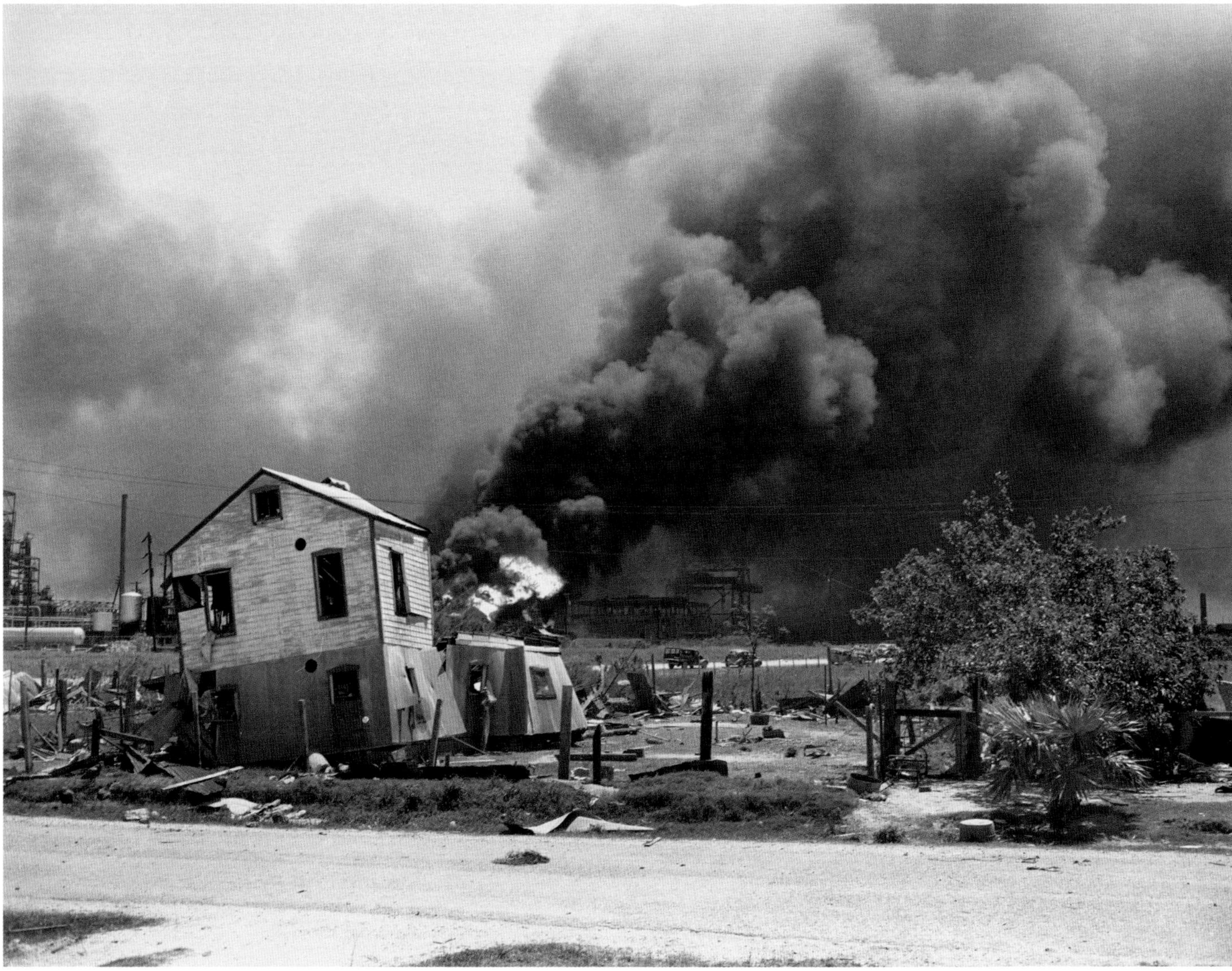

Texas City homes and other structures within roughly a two-mile radius of the explosion were destroyed or damaged by the blast, many of them beyond repair. An estimated ninety percent of the homes and buildings in the town had structural damage following the disaster.

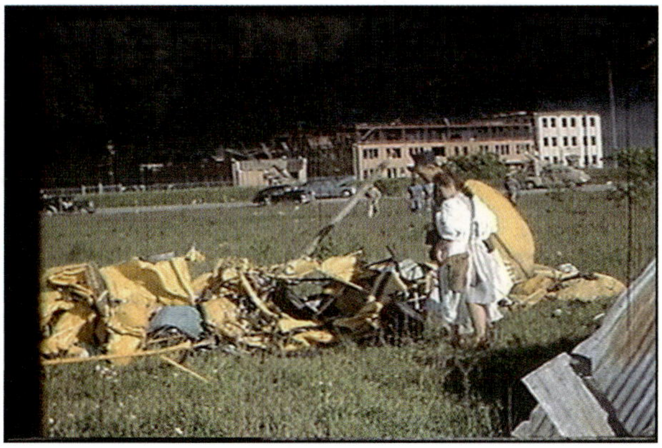

Film still from Bailey's color footage of the Texas City Disaster, showing two people inspecting the wreckage of a plane. Several light aircraft were blown out of the sky when the force of the explosion blew their wings off as they flew overhead. There were no survivors from any of the plane crashes.

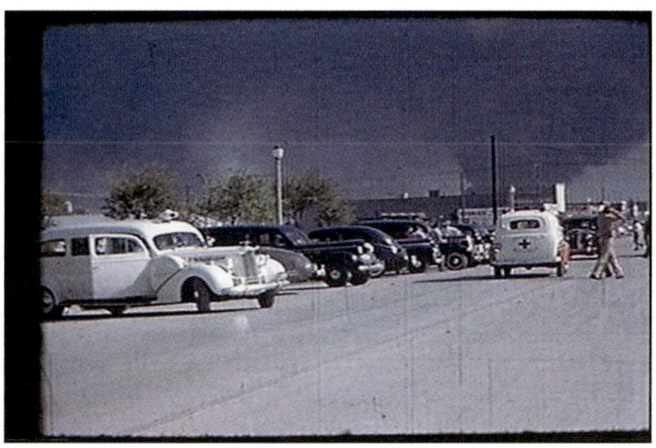

Ambulances, cars, trucks, and even hearses from the surrounding area were pressed into service on the day of the explosion. A few hours after the disaster, the roads leading into Texas City were jammed with vehicles driven by relief volunteers from nearby towns.

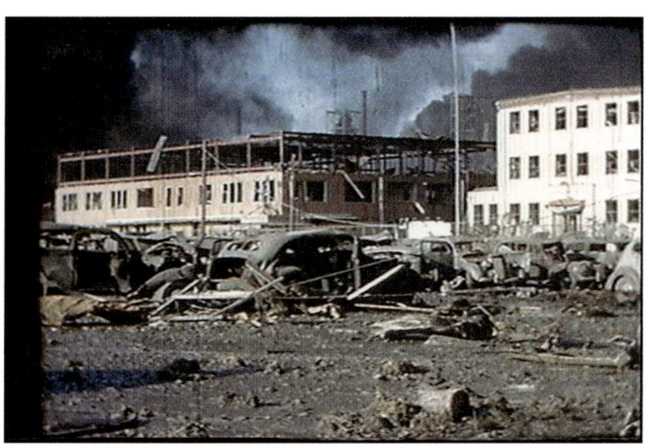

The wreckage of buildings and completely burned-out cars clearly convey the destruction caused by the powerful combination of the ship explosions and the fires that spread through Monsanto's plant and neighboring facilities.

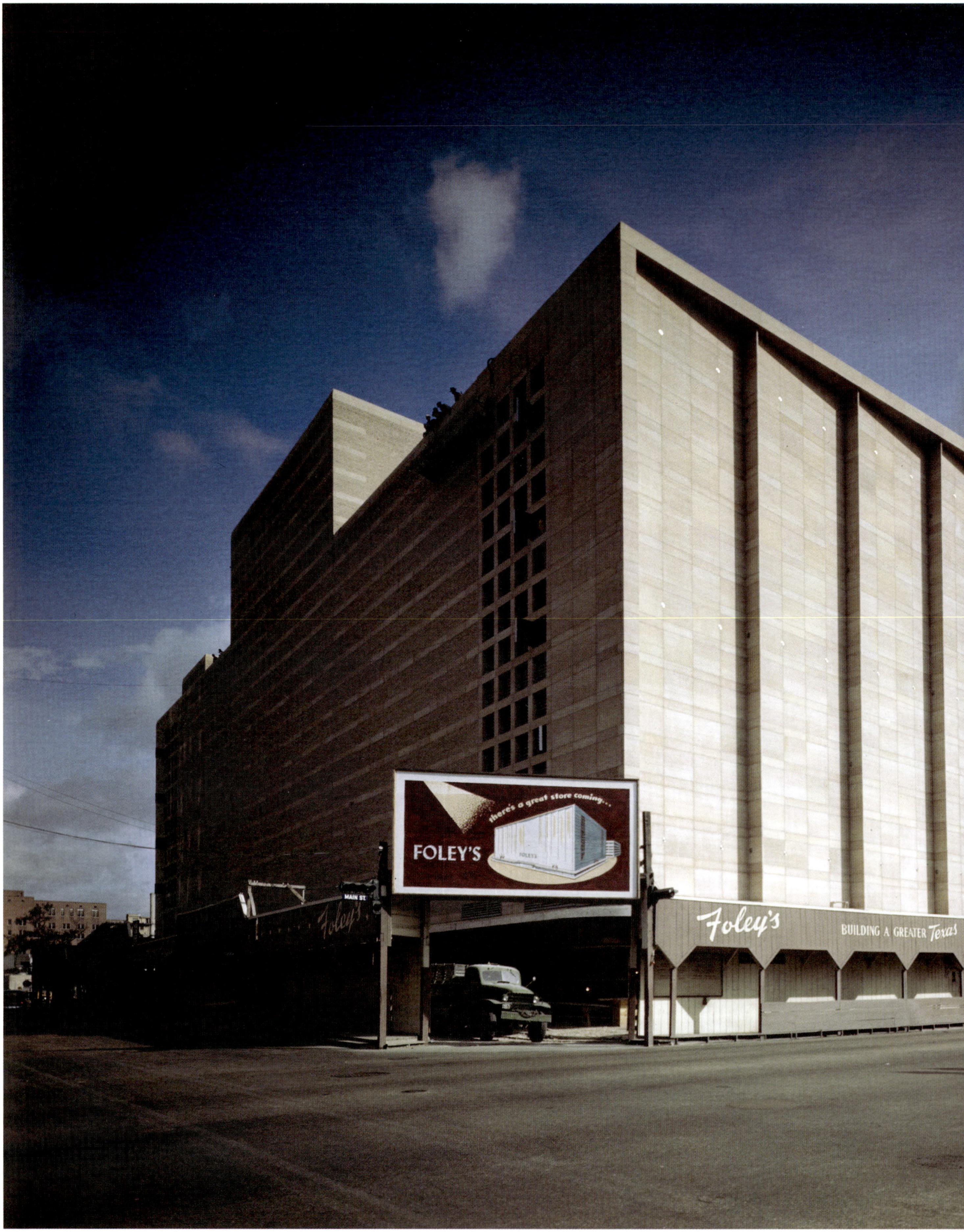
there's a great store coming...
FOLEY'S
MAIN ST.
Foley's
BUILDING A GREATER Texas

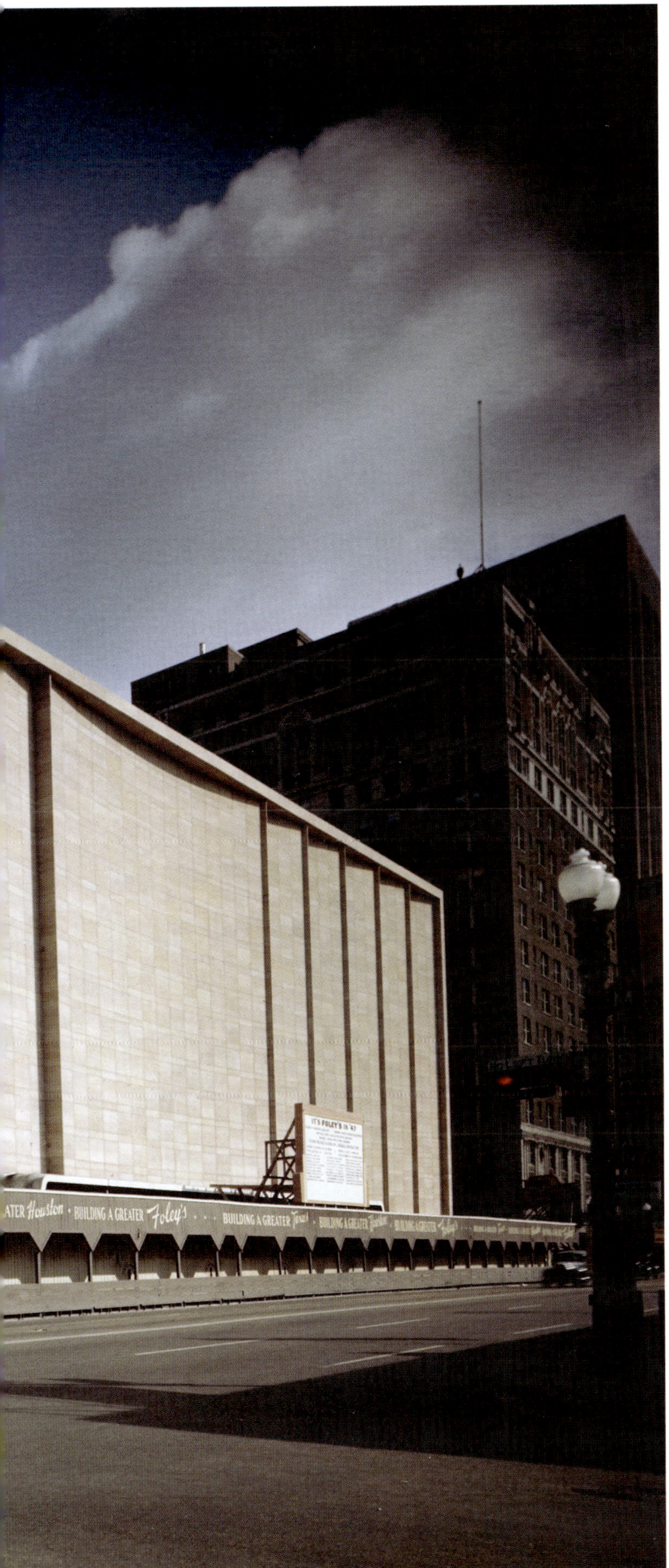

An exterior shot of the nearly completed Foley's Department Store taken shortly before its opening on October 20, 1947. As with other demolished Houston landmarks, the Bailey collection has the most publicly available documentation of this Foley's. Bailey recorded almost every aspect of the store's construction: the hoopla surrounding its opening day, the Foley's-sponsored events, such as parades and exhibits, the window displays, and Foley's well-known Christmas decorations.

The building was sold to Federated Department Stores in 1997 and became a Macy's store in 2005. The store officially closed on March 9, 2013, and the building was demolished on September 22, 2013.

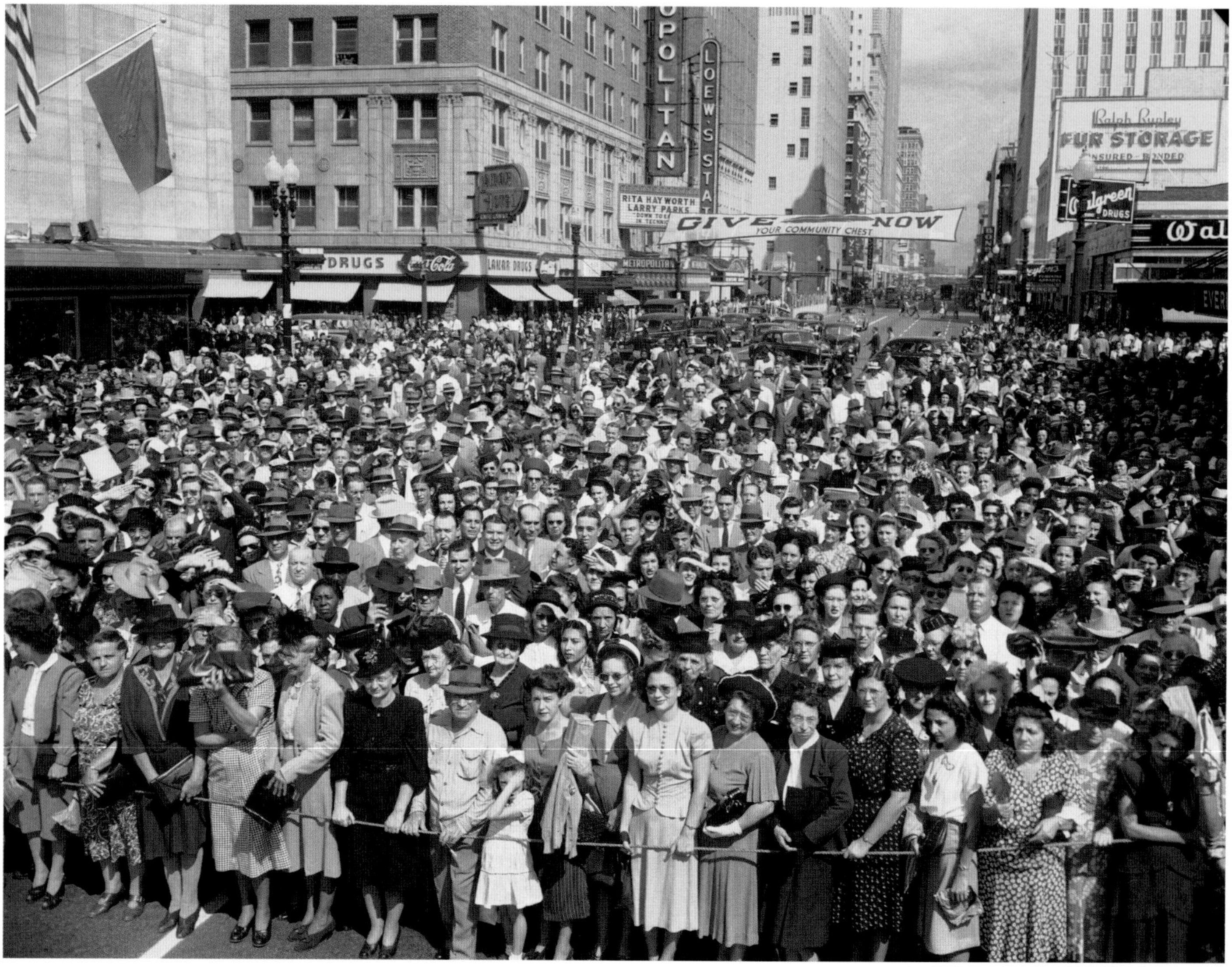

Following months of pre-opening publicity and a huge volume of advertising, this enormous crowd gathered on Main Street for the debut of Foley's Department Store on October 20, 1947. The streets surrounding Foley's were roped off, and forty policemen were assigned to contain the anxious crowds until the store opened.

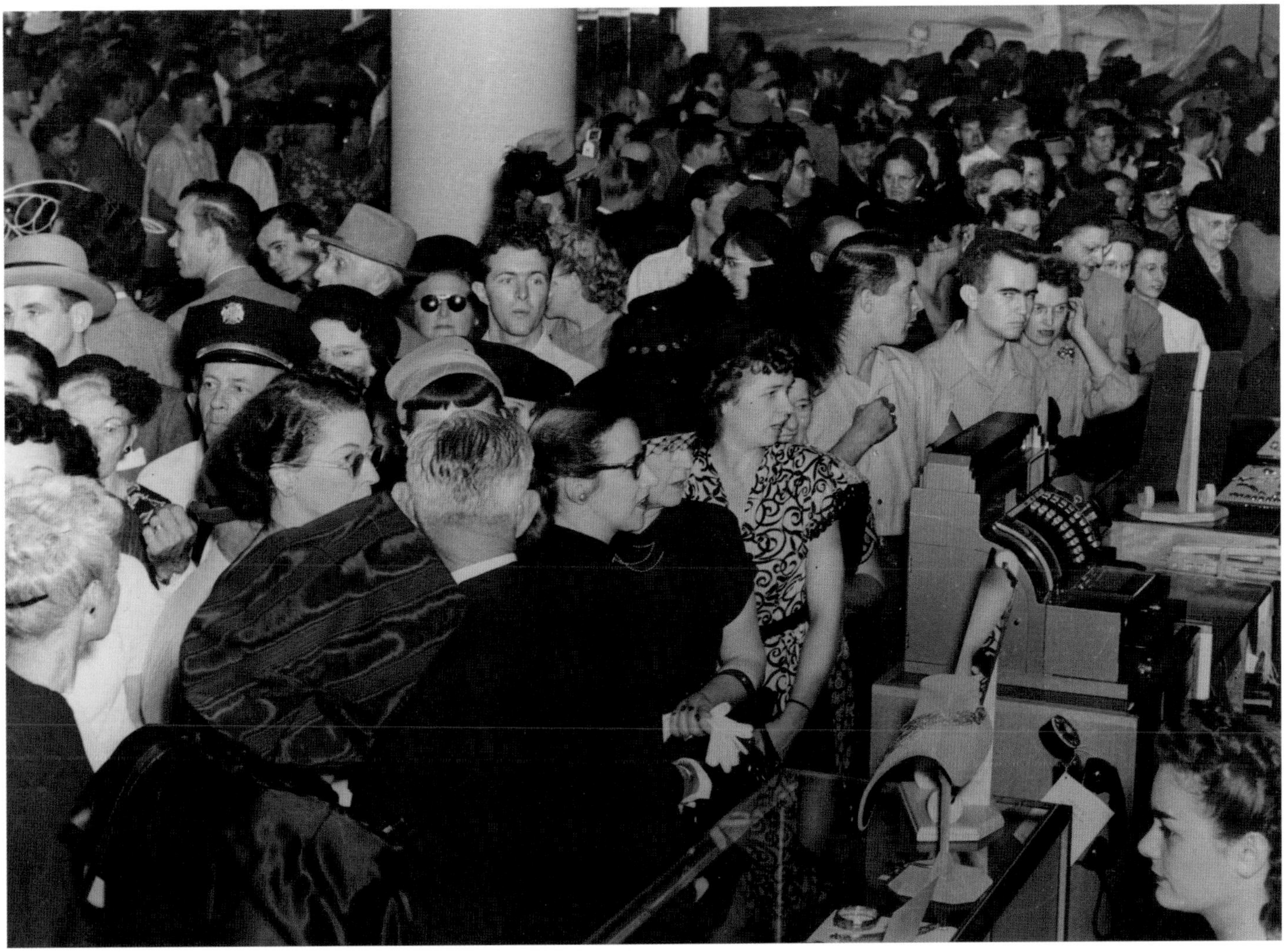

A small portion of the massive crowds that jammed the interior of Foley's Department Store on opening day, October 20, 1947. An estimated eight thousand people per hour poured into the store that day. On hand to greet them were the store's nearly two thousand employees.

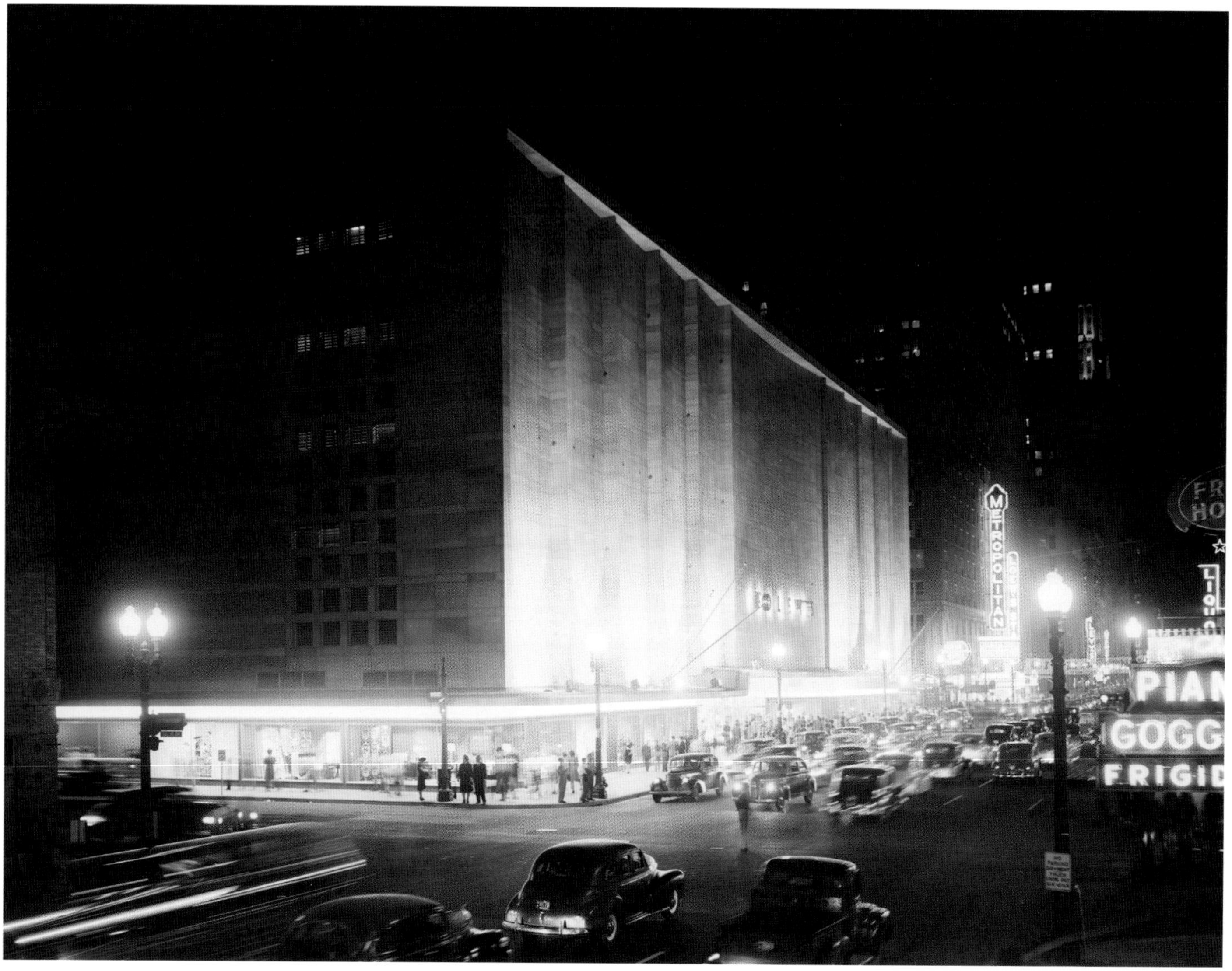

A nighttime view of Foley's 1100 Main Street façade, taken not long after the store's opening in 1947. The glow of the store's extensive lighting, which Bailey utilized so well in his composition, provided a luminous, atmospheric quality to this photograph that accurately reproduced the department store, while simultaneously adding a sense of dreaminess to the image.

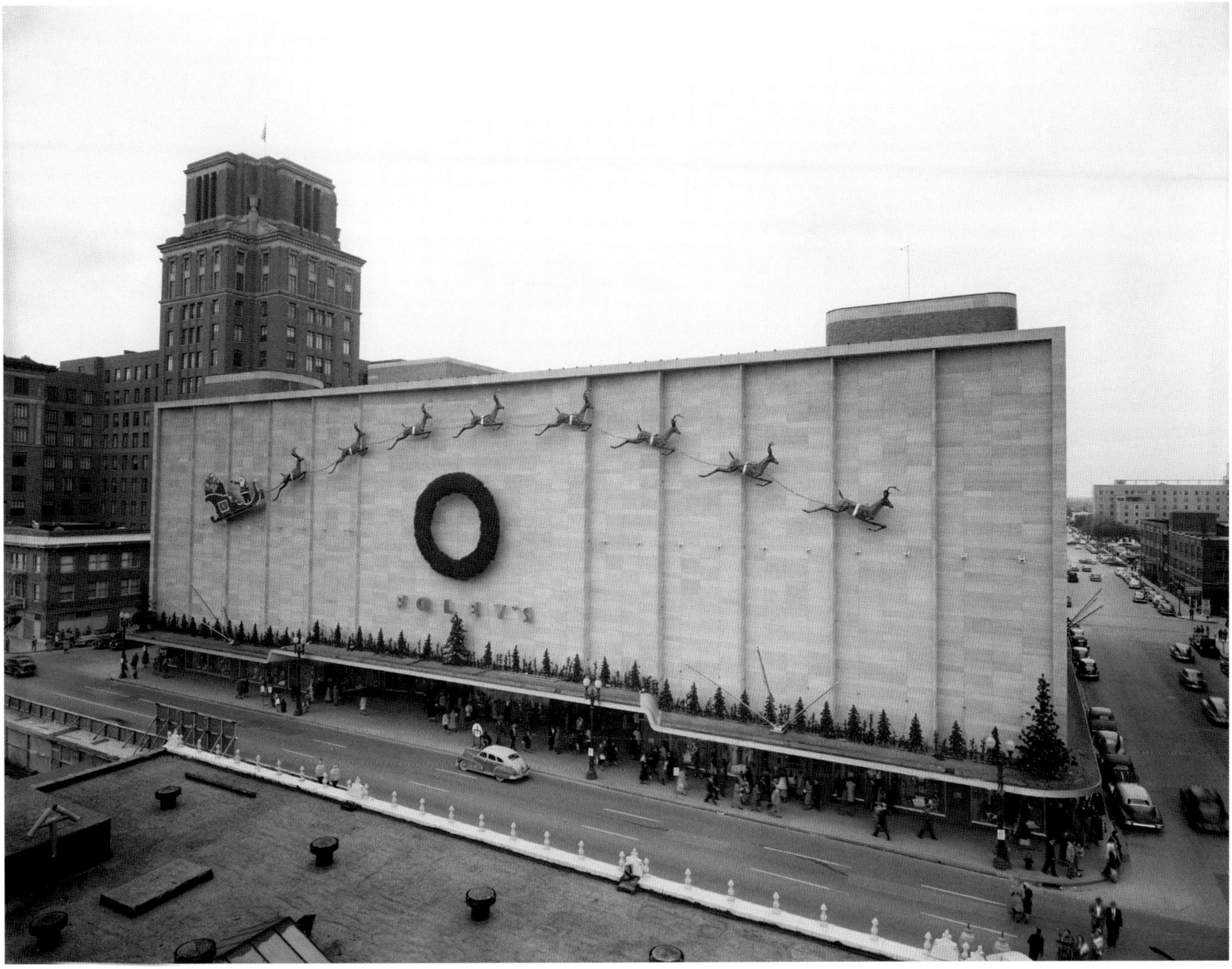

Foley's was locally famous for its elaborate Christmas displays. By shooting the 1949 Christmas display from an adjacent rooftop, Bailey captured the enormous Santa and reindeer display that extended across the length of the store's massive façade.

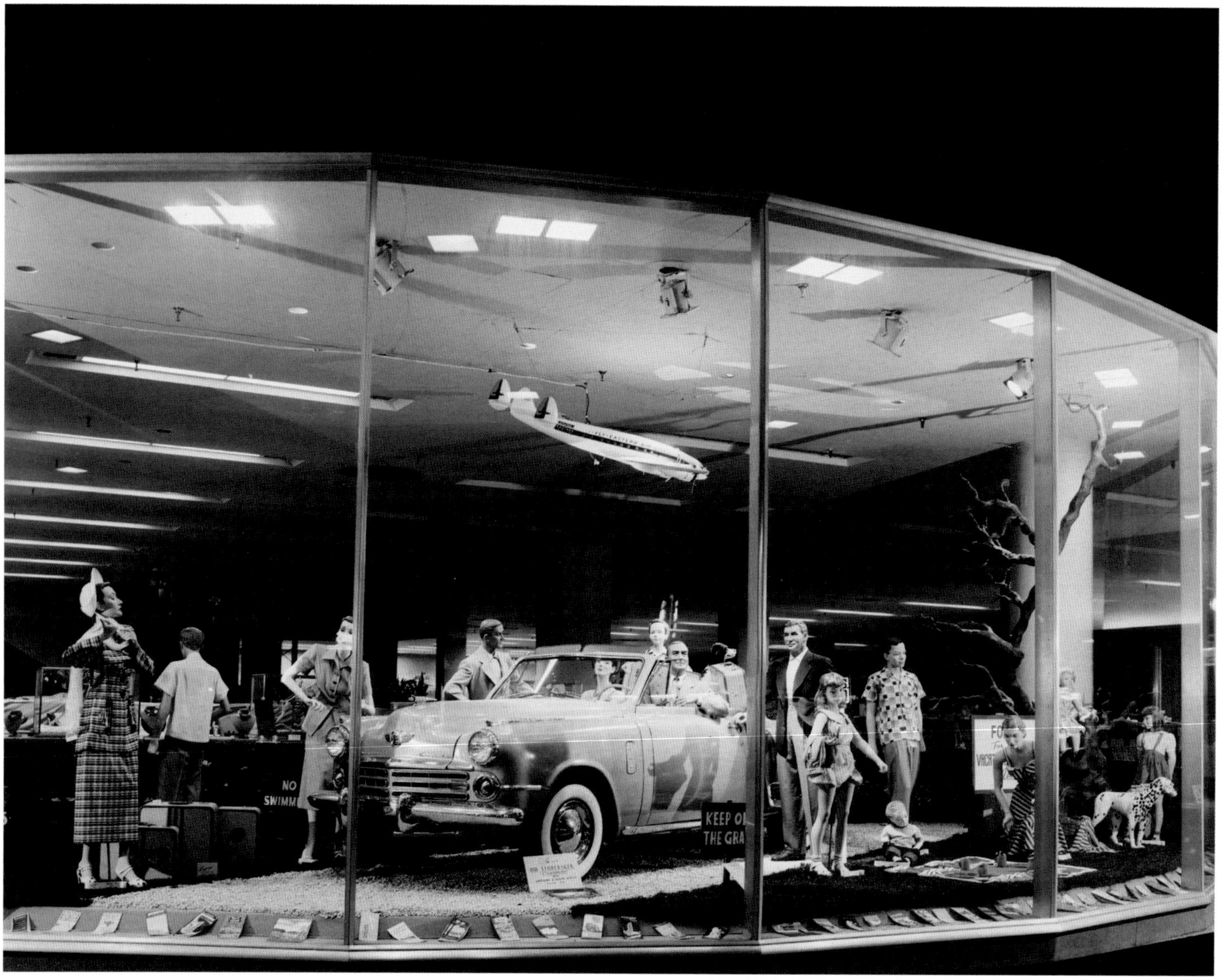

Foley's enormous, 105-foot-wide Vista Window, which fronted Main Street, displayed this scene of American family life and leisure in 1948. It pictures a postwar nation on the move by car and plane, with smiling, small, nuclear families enjoying their leisure time by traveling, socializing, and having an idyllic family picnic. After many years of living ascetic lives due to the Great Depression, followed by the rationing of the lean war years, postwar Americans reasserted their right to conspicuous consumption. Buying consumer goods came to be associated in many people's minds with patriotism; every item purchased could be seen as a blow against communism because it strengthened America's economic might and simultaneously enshrined freedom of choice. Spending for household furnishings and appliances rose an astonishing 240 percent in the postwar years of 1946–1951.

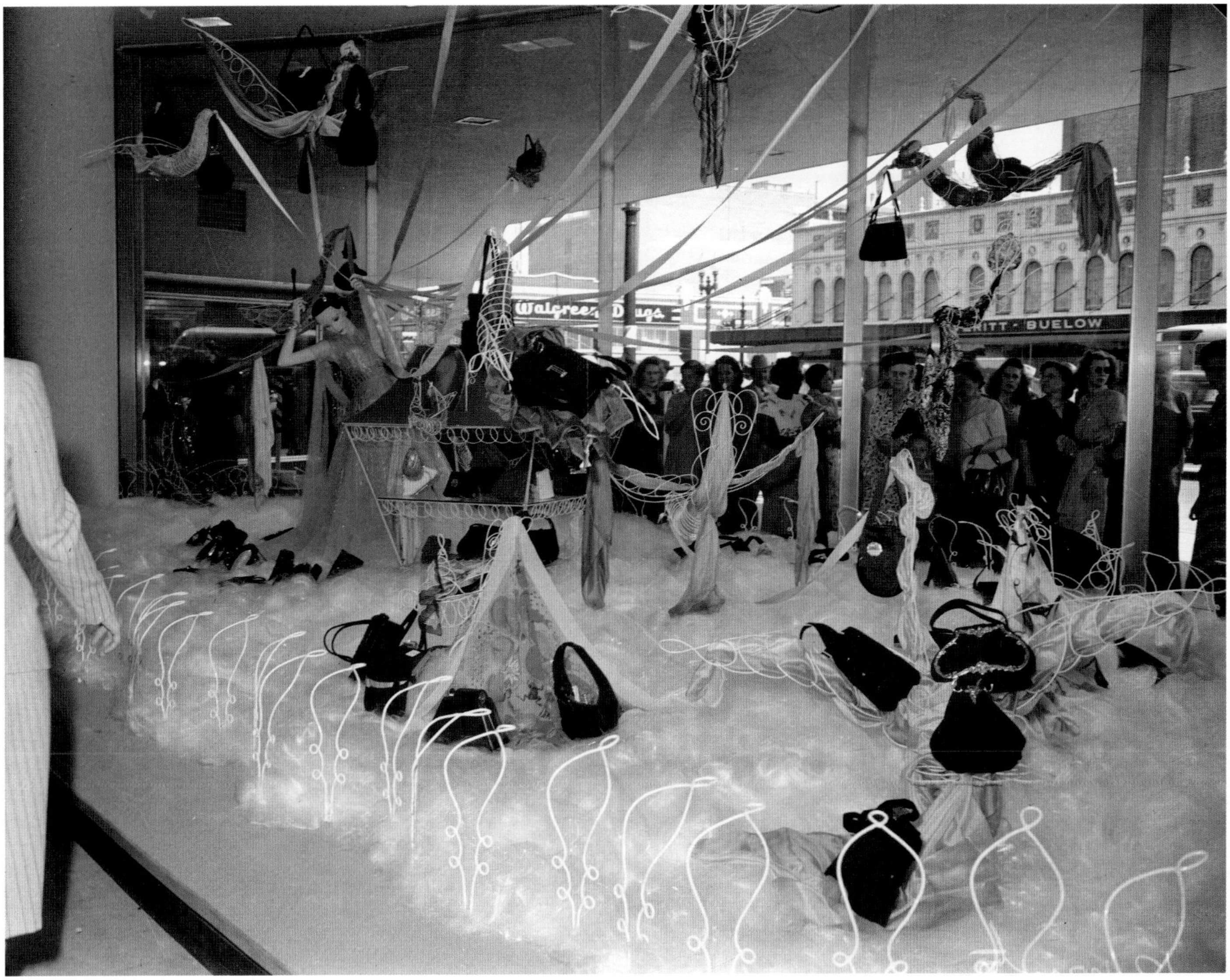

This display at Foley's (ca. 1948) could be viewed both inside and outside the store. Note the crowd of women on the sidewalk. Here, the atmosphere of dreamy surrealism that was sometimes sought in window displays of the period is achieved in every respect. The flying and stationary handbags and scarves appear as elements of women consumers' fondest, and most surreal, dreams. The mannequin at the left seems to be almost in a swoon, overcome by all of the available choices.

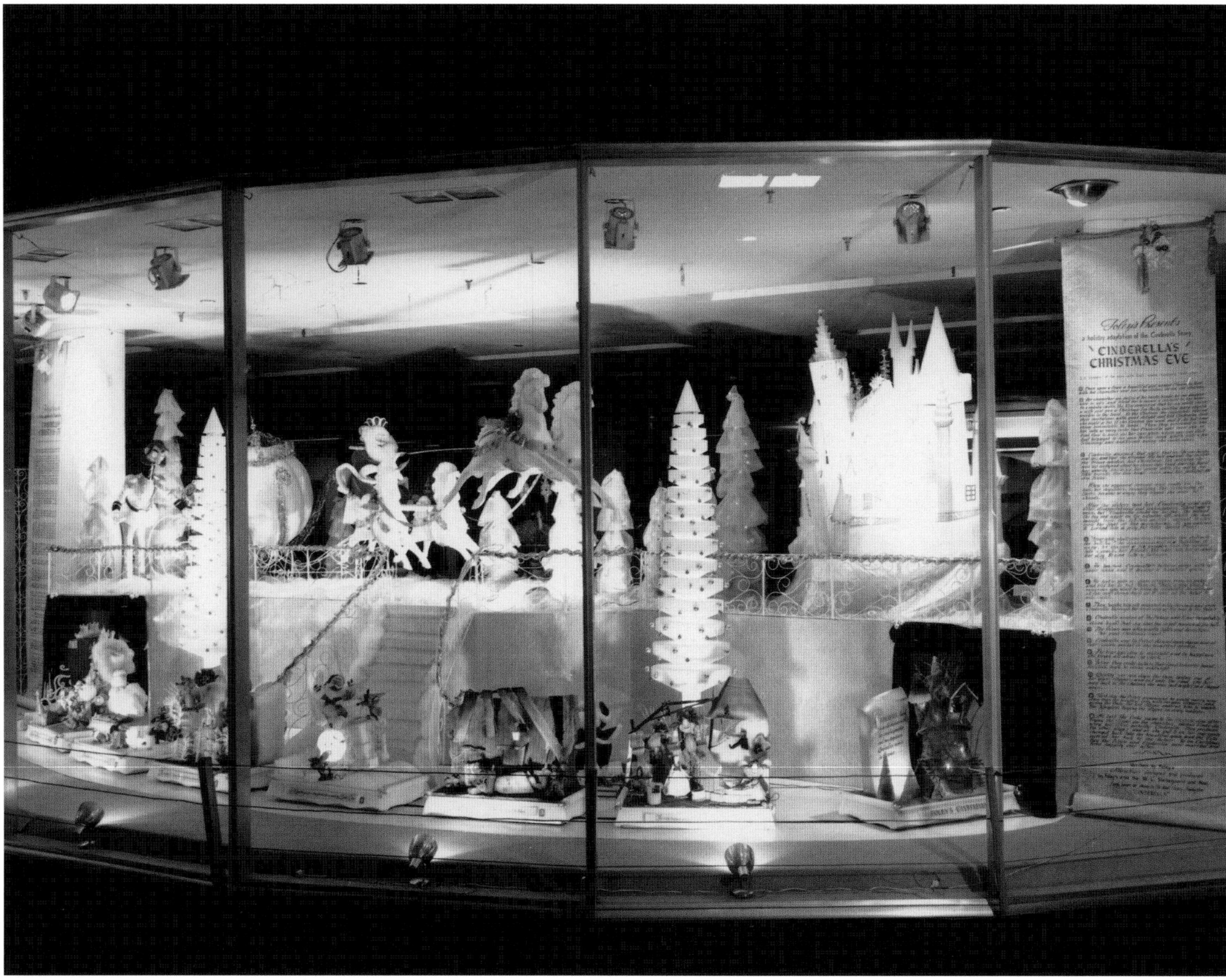

"Cinderella's Christmas Eve" was the theme of this Foley's window for the Christmas 1949 season. Such displays were intended to draw families downtown with the hope that they would stay and do some shopping. Thousands of Houstonians traveled downtown each Christmas season to see the lights, decorations, and show windows. The tradition was a ritual for many years until the "energy crisis" of late 1973 dimmed the downtown lights in an attempt to conserve energy; the lighting displays never again achieved their original luster, as the nation's economy slowed and downtown stores closed, moved to the suburbs, or cut back on displays as cost-cutting measures.

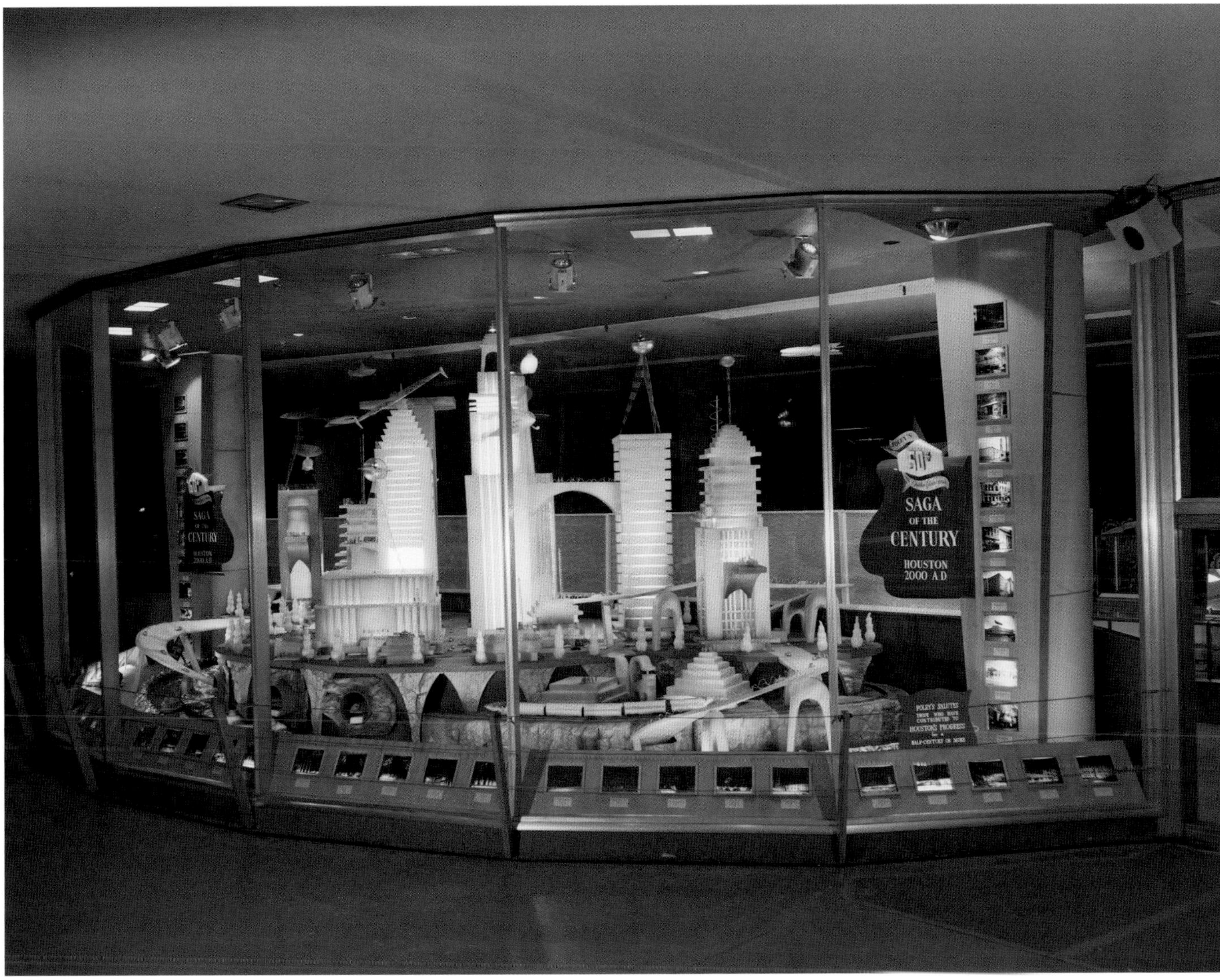

This model of Houston in the year 2000 was constructed for Foley's Saga of the Century celebration in 1950, which was the year of Foley's fiftieth anniversary. It was displayed in the Vista Window at Foley's Main Street entrance. Even before the beginning of the Space Age, many Houstonians already thought of the city as being at the forefront of progress and modernity. When Foley's new store opened in 1947, it was billed from the beginning as the "Store of Tomorrow." This display, publicized as a "blueprint for the future," contained a model of Foley's that gave the store six additional floors in 2000.

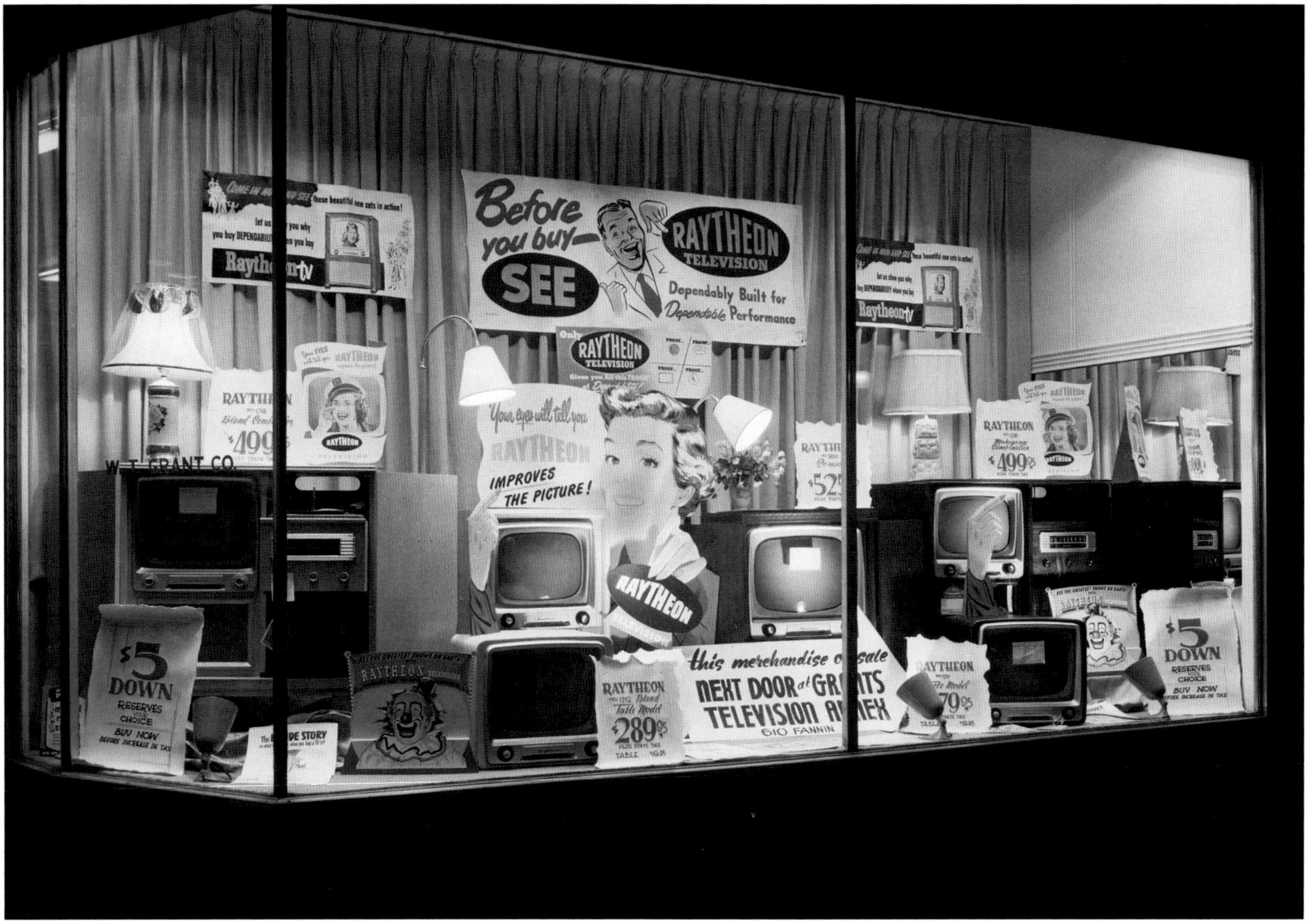

A display of Raytheon television sets for the W. T. Grant Department Store in 1951. Nothing was hyped more during the late 1940s and 1950s than television sets. Grant's store even had a "television annex" adjacent to its downtown store to display the huge number of sets in its inventory.

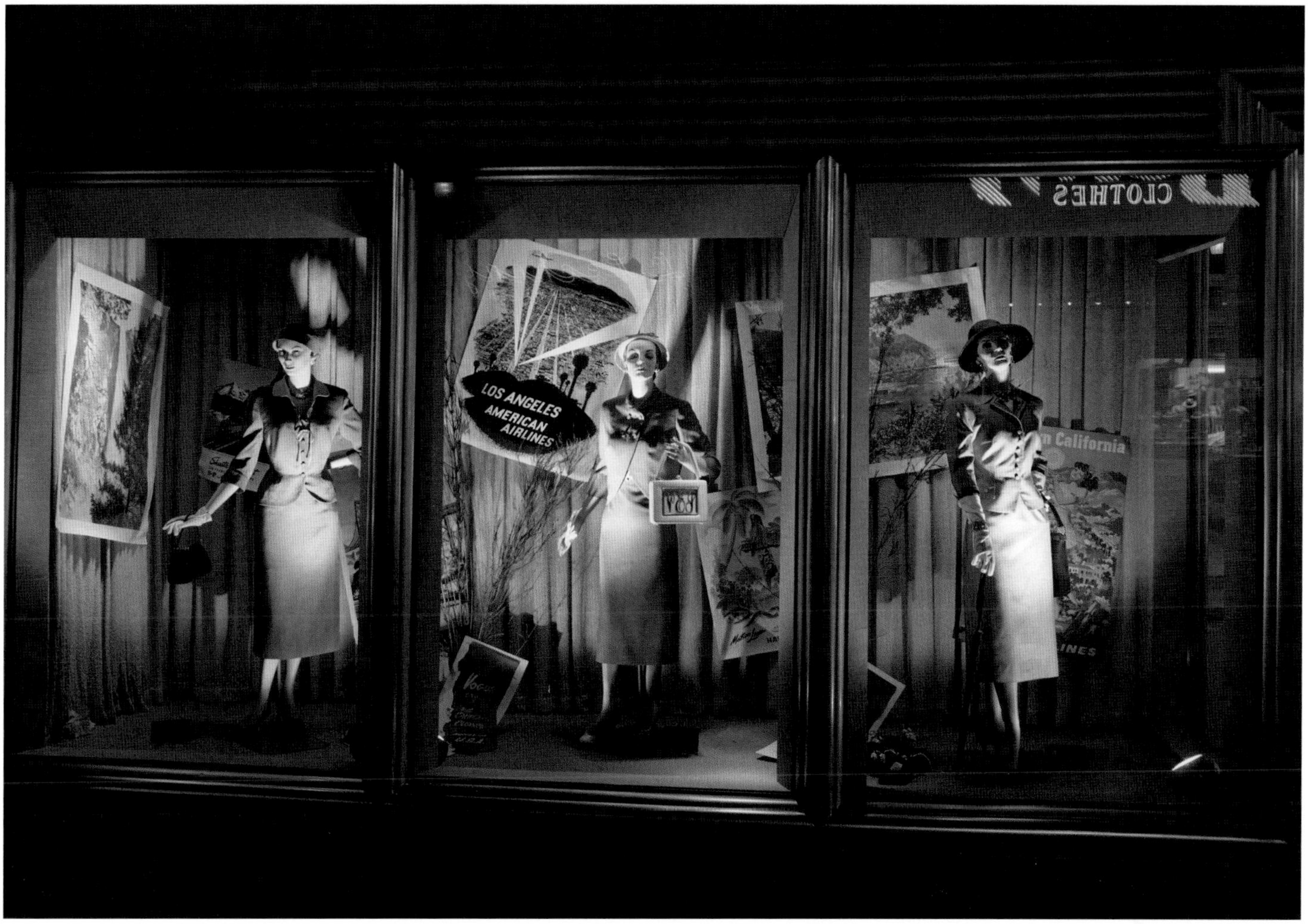

Travel-themed window at Battlestein's Department Store, April 1954. In addition to presenting the traveling outfits worn by the mannequins, the window also promoted travel to Southern California via American Airlines. Battlestein's, at 812 Main Street, opened at this location in 1950.

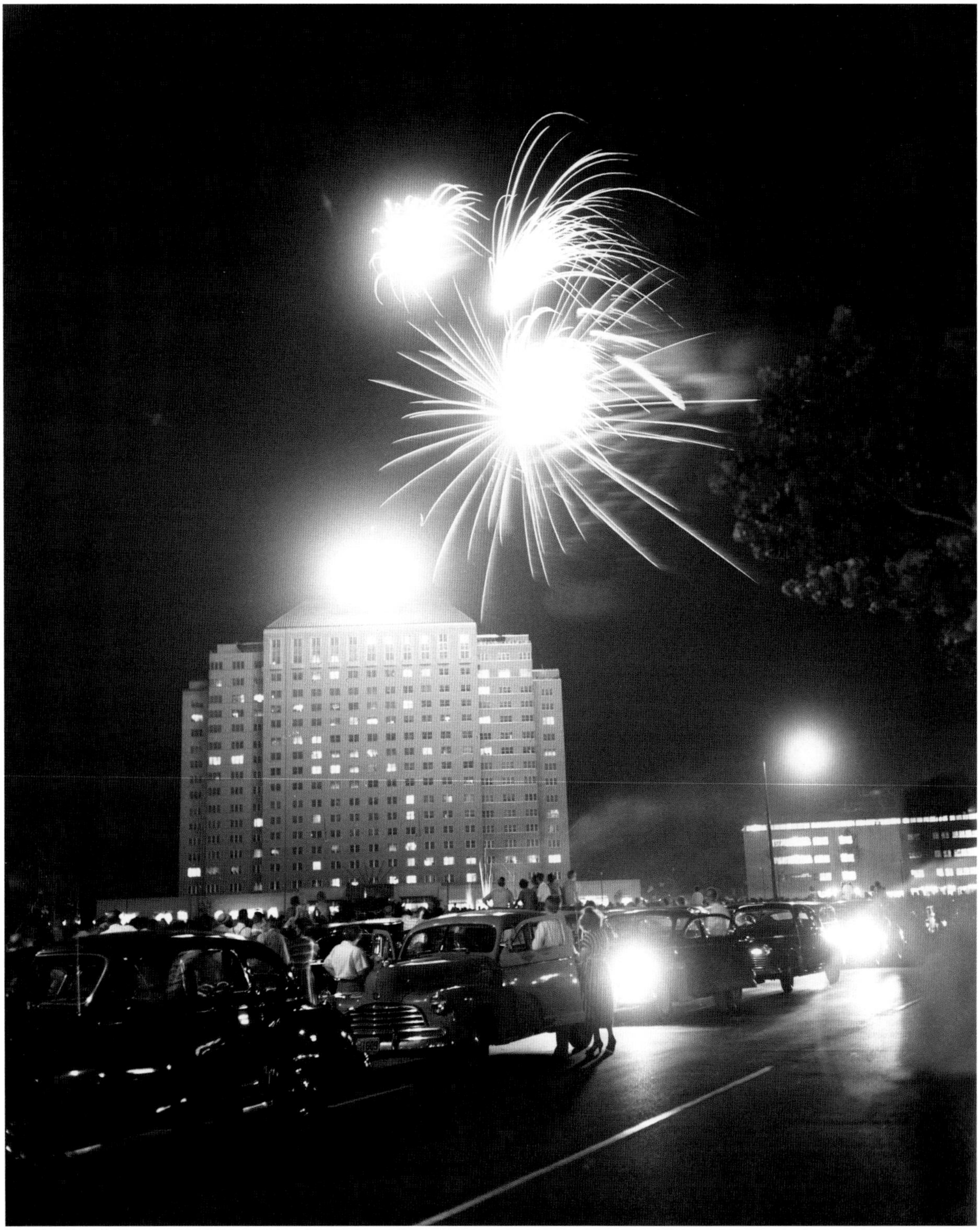

A huge fireworks display took place on the opening night of Houston's famed Shamrock Hotel, March 17, 1949.

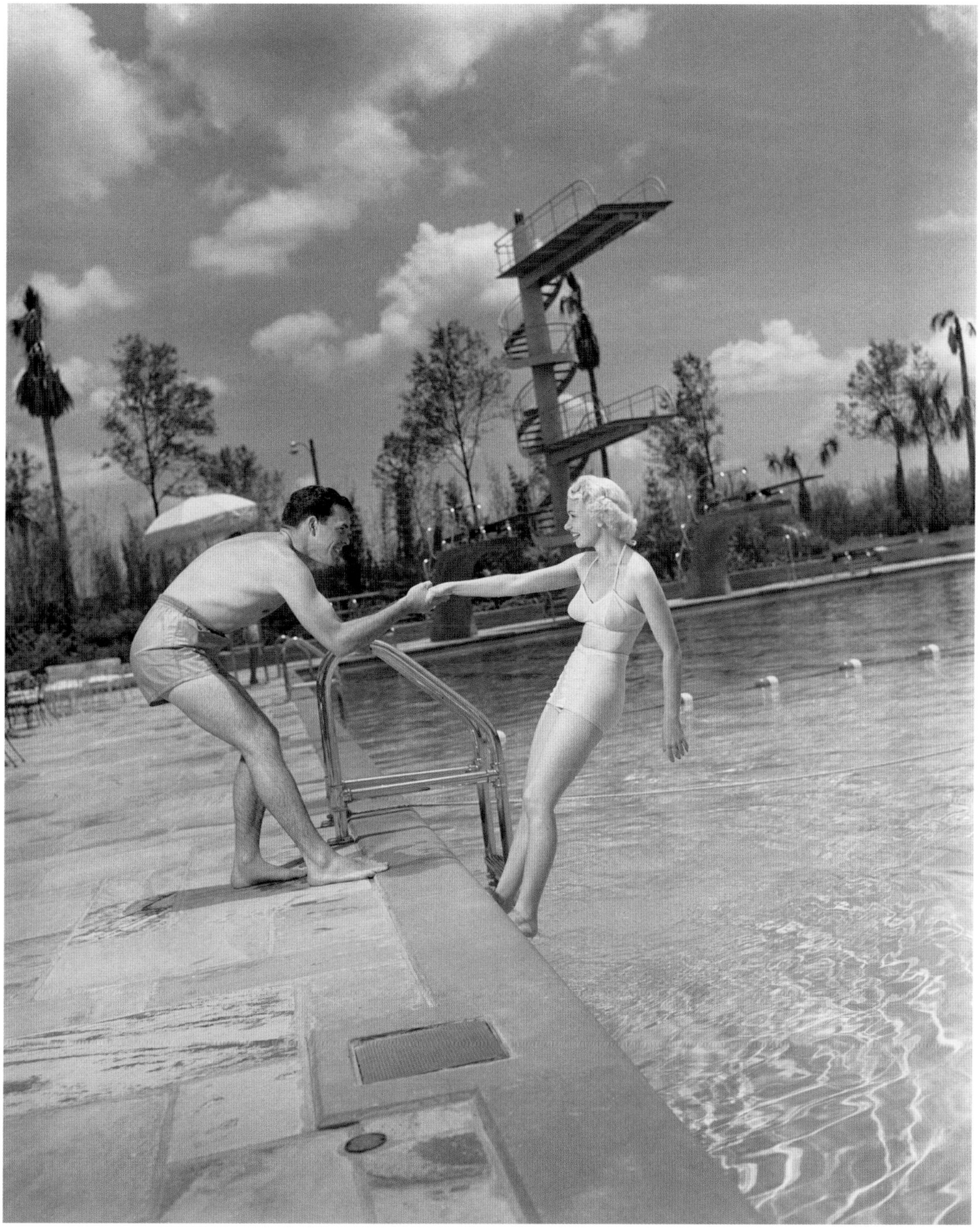

Two models pose at the Shamrock Hotel pool, May 1949. This photo was taken for *Hotel Manager,* a hotel trade journal. Bailey took this shot at a slightly skewed angle, giving viewers the illusion of being involved in the scene. Depending on your perspective, one might imagine either being pulled out of or being pulled into the pool.

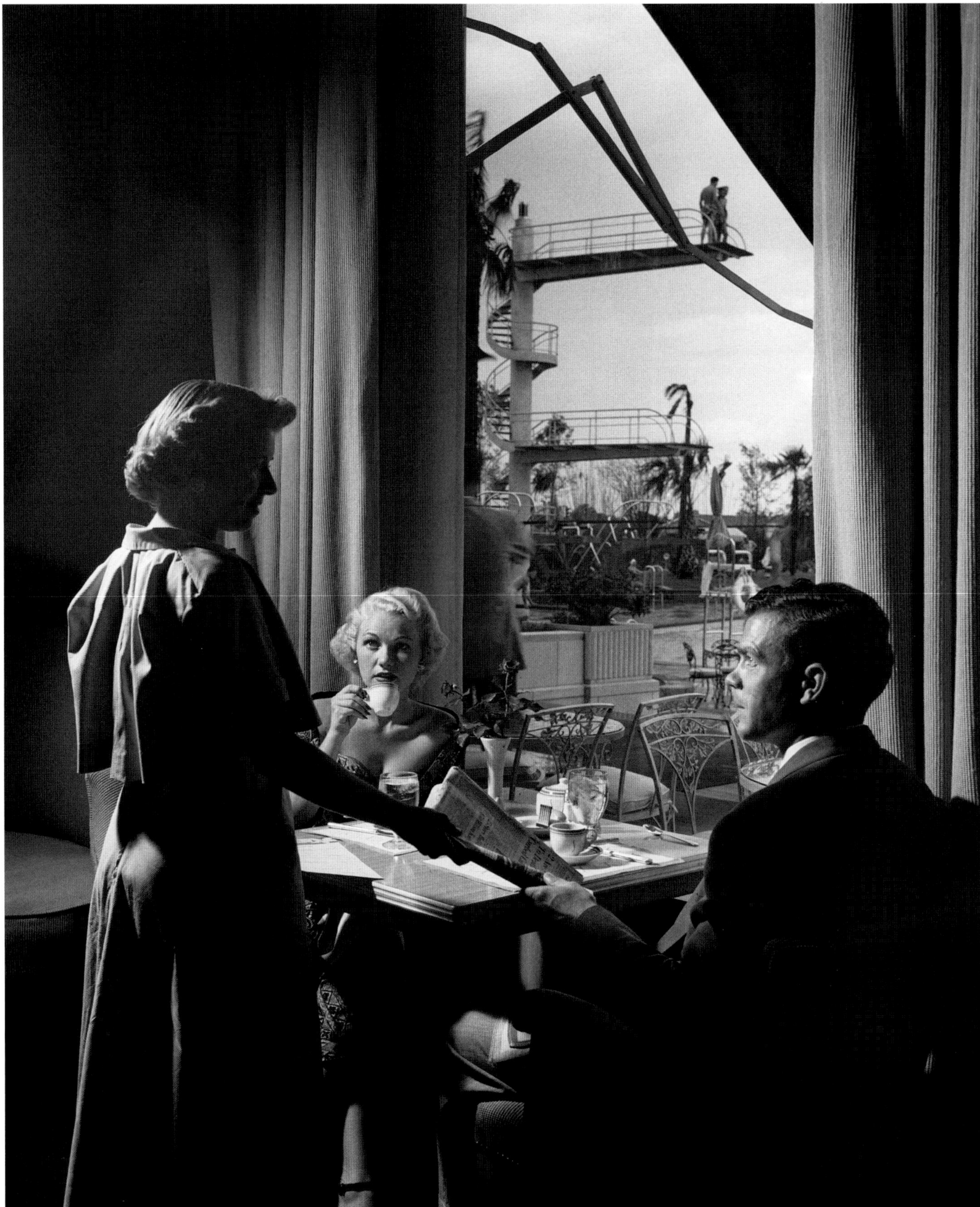

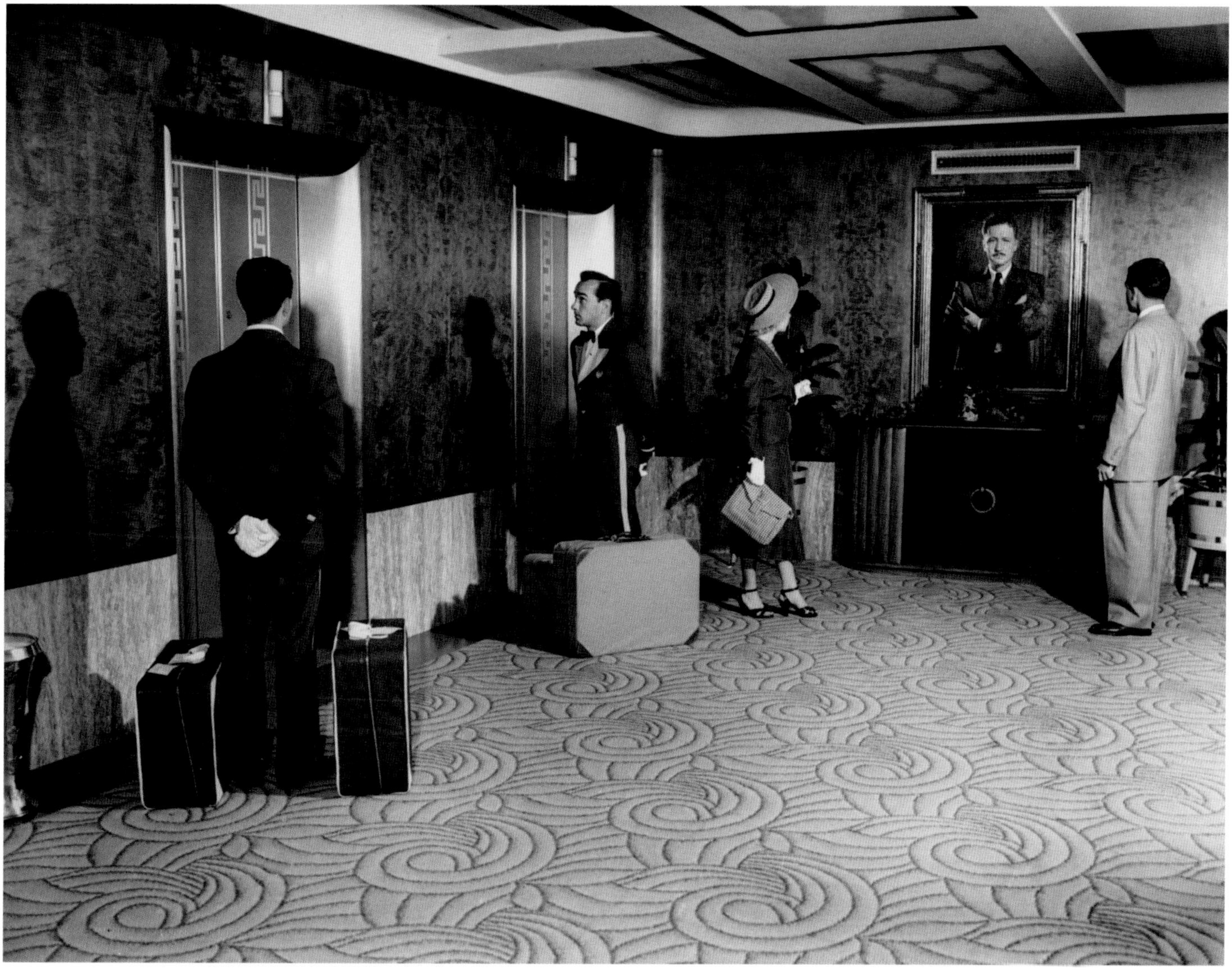

Facing: Guests dine at the newly opened Shamrock Hotel in May 1949. Bailey stylishly framed the shot to include the Shamrock's Art Deco diving board and part of its famous pool, the world's largest at the time. This photo was taken for publication in *Hotel Manager* magazine.

Above: Two guests at the Shamrock Hotel, ca. 1949, wait in the elevator lobby. They stand suitably awed before the portrait of Glenn McCarthy, developer and owner of the Shamrock, which dominated one wall of the lobby.

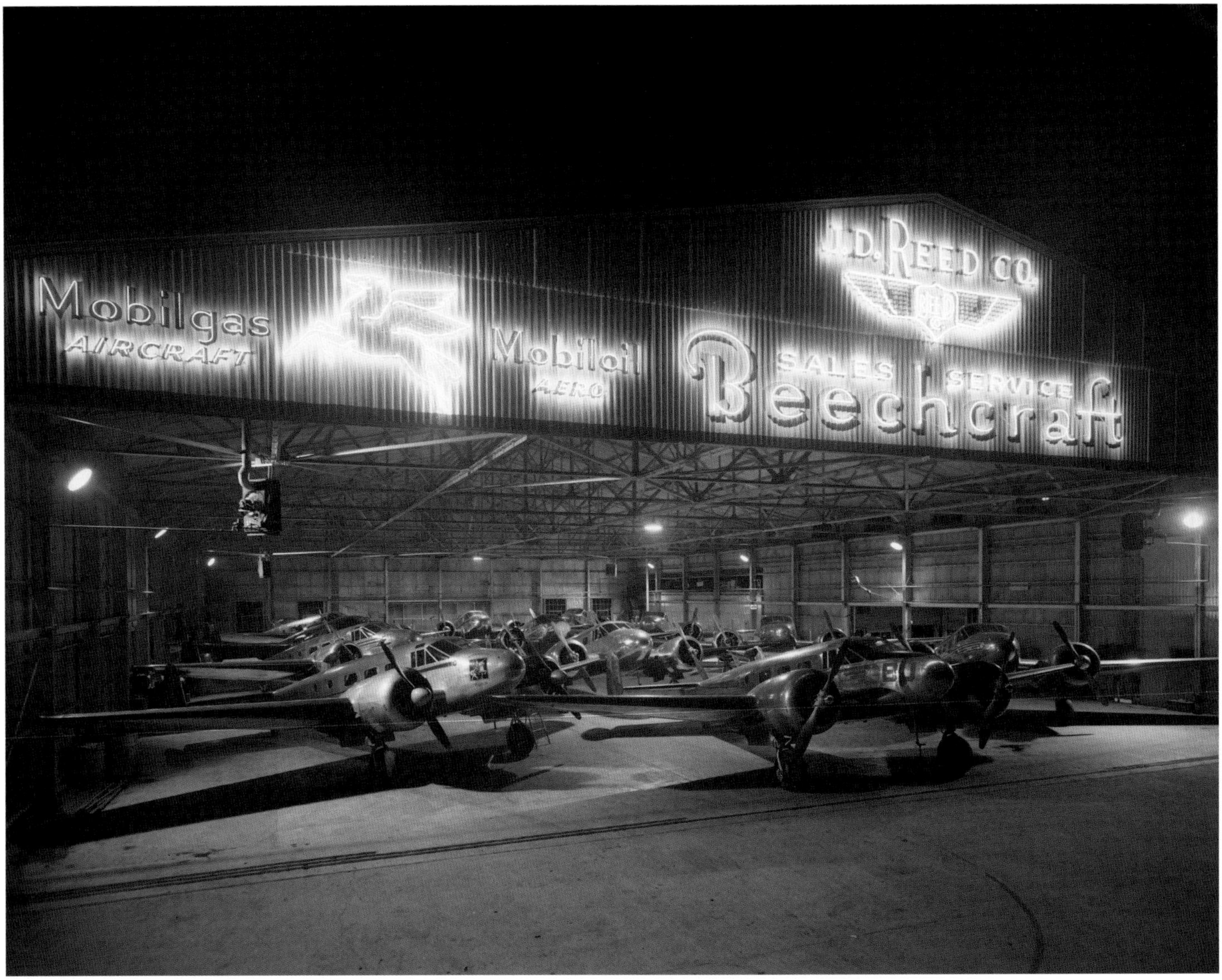

The J. D. Reed Co. owned and operated this Beechcraft aircraft sales and service facility. This nighttime shot was taken in January 1947, not long after the company opened for business. Its hangar was located at Houston Municipal Airport (now Hobby Airport).

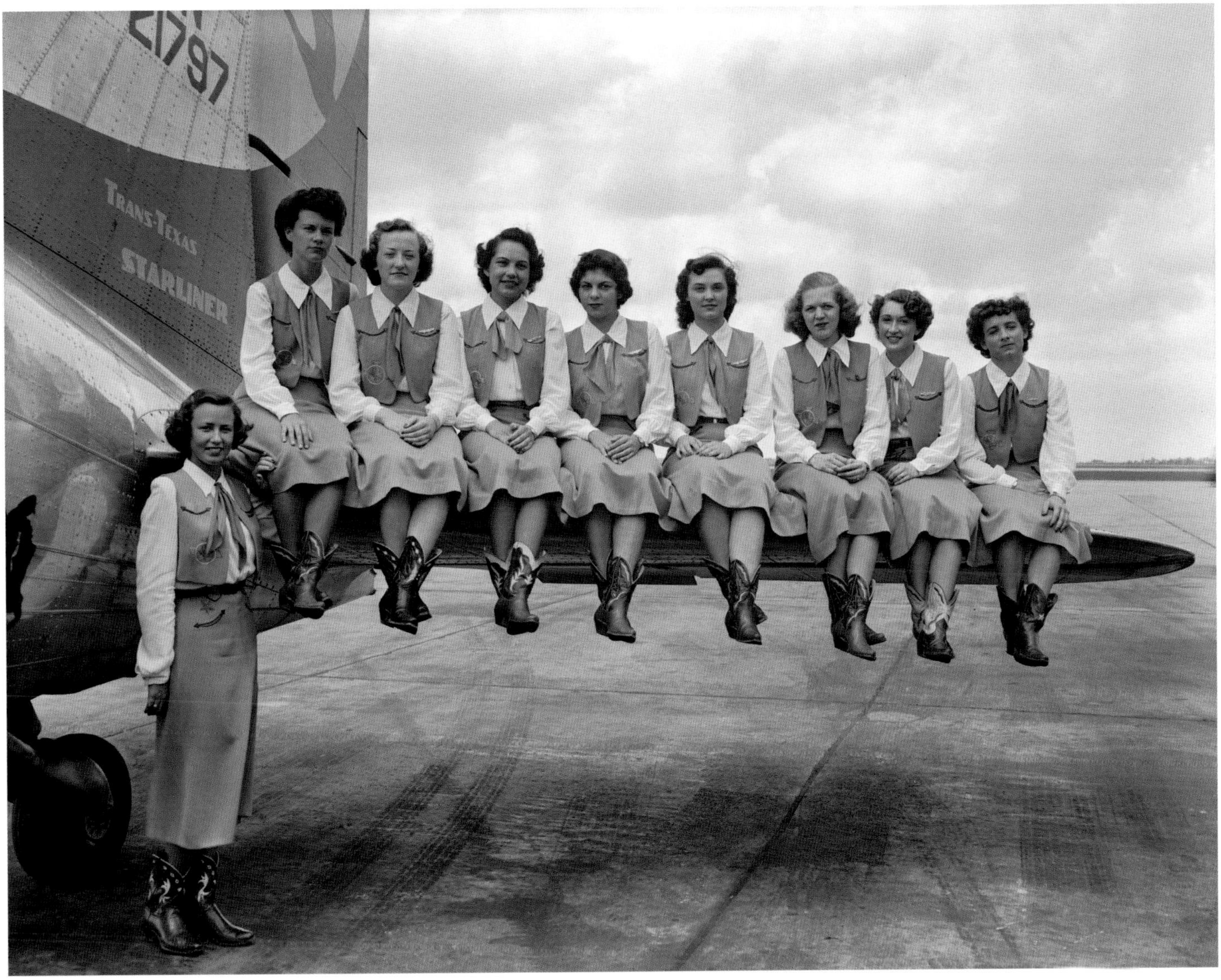

Trans-Texas Airways flight attendants in May 1949. Founded as Aviation Enterprises in 1944, the airline changed its name to Trans-Texas Airways in 1947. The airline named the Douglas DC–3 aircraft it used for all of its flights "Starliners." Dallas and Houston were the airline's hub cities, and it operated only within Texas.

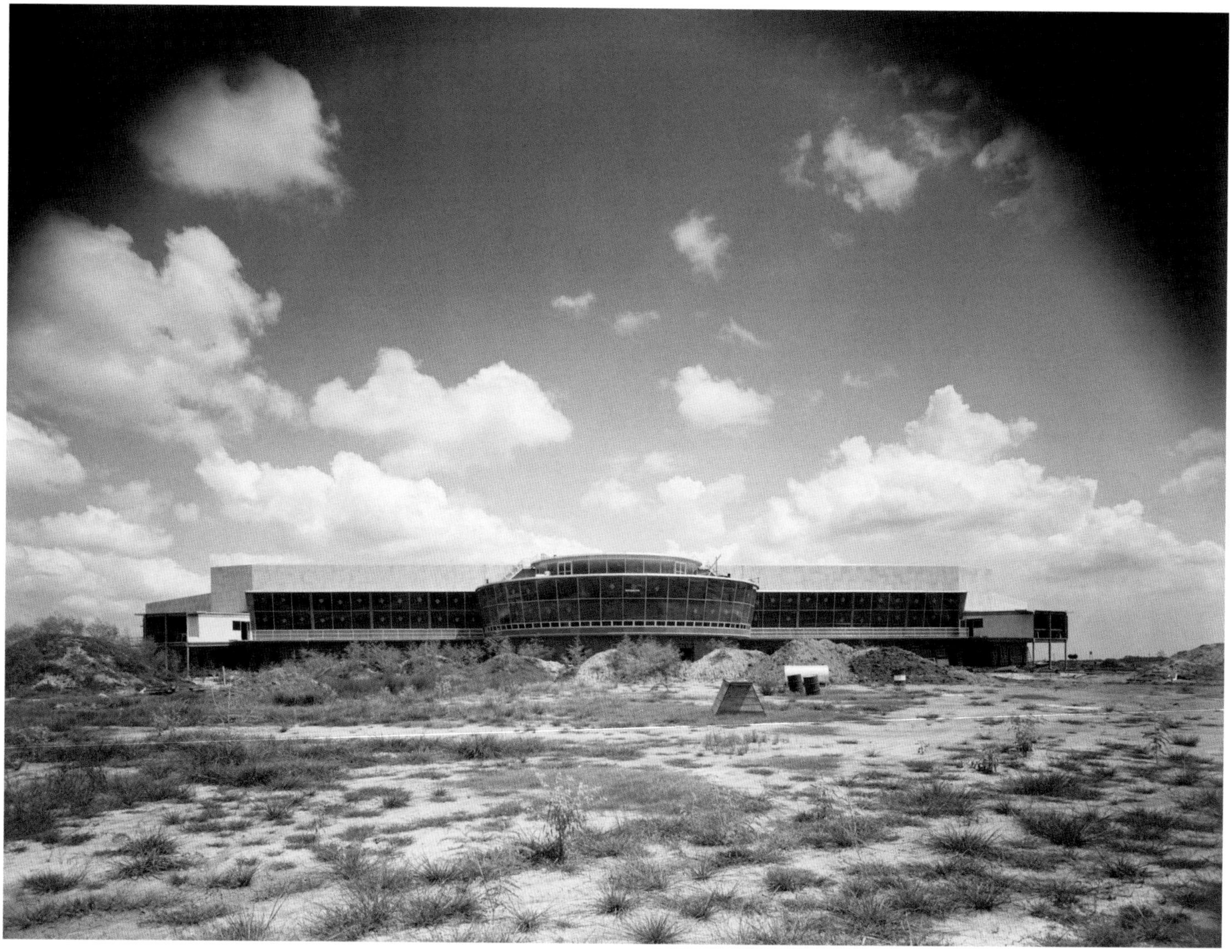

Houston's Municipal Airport (now Hobby Airport) terminal during construction in 1953. Designed by Wyatt C. Hedrick, the terminal cost five million dollars and was hailed by the *Houston Chronicle* as "a functional and beautiful eyeful."

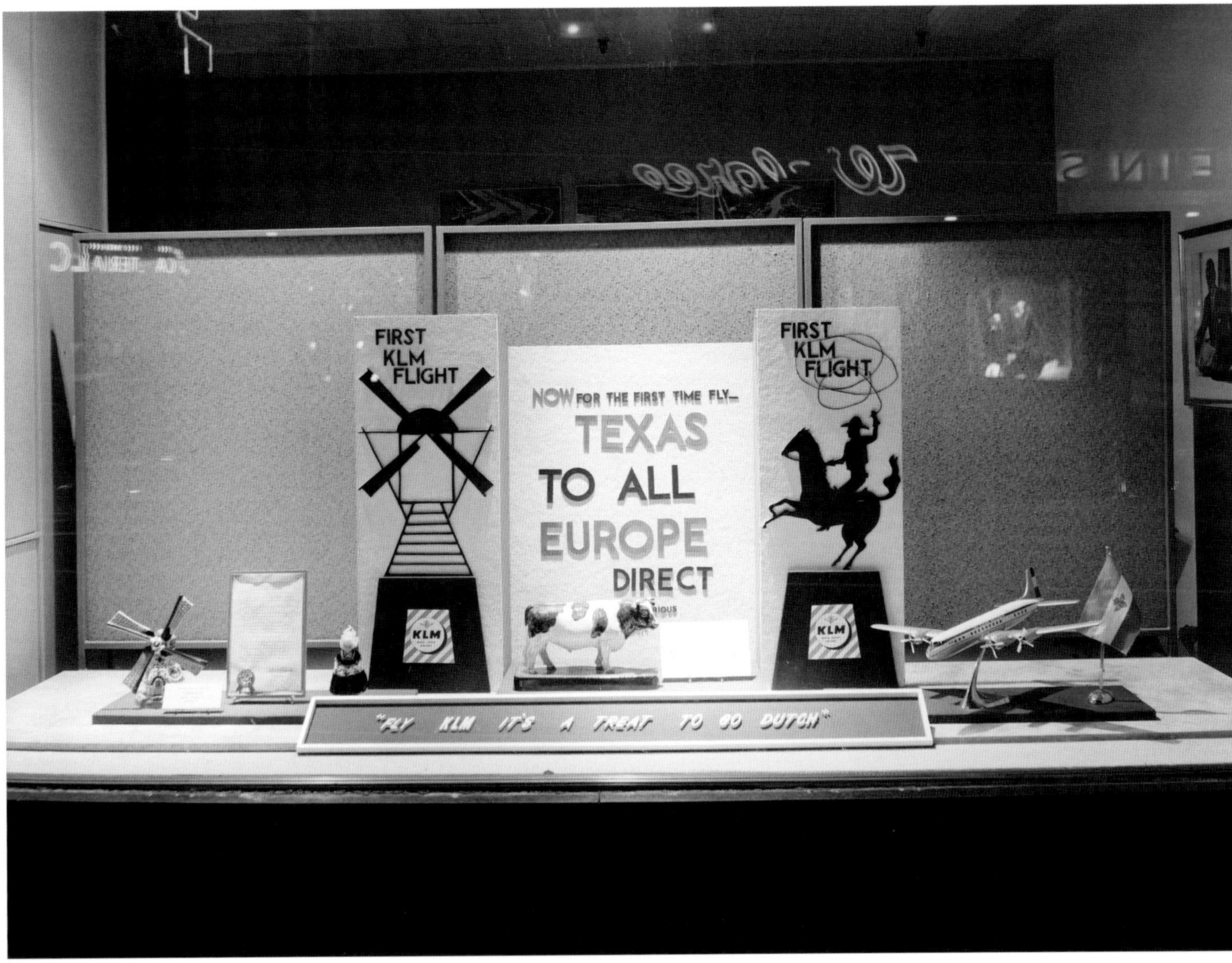

The Smart Shop featured this KLM (Royal Dutch Airlines) window advertising Houston's first direct flights to Europe from Houston International Airport (later Hobby Airport), which took place September 3, 1957. Houston was anxious to embrace direct international flights as confirmation to the rest of the world of its importance.

In 1956, Houston became the first city in the United States to have an operating monorail system, a prototype demonstration model built by Monorail Incorporated. This still was taken from color footage shot by Bailey Studios, almost certainly on February 8, 1956, when the Skyway Trailblazer monorail car was first demonstrated for the press and public. The film may be the only surviving color footage of the monorail in operation; it is possible that it was the only color footage filmed that day, since none of Houston's network affiliates had local color capabilities of their own at the time.

The still shows the monorail progressing along its 961-foot track. The model system's track was constructed in the privately developed Arrowhead Park near the intersection of Old Spanish Trail and South Main. Following a mixed reception in Houston after several months of operations, the monorail was dismantled and reassembled in Dallas's Fair Park, where it began operations at the State Fair of Texas in autumn 1956. Decades later, when Houston's traffic situation had become increasingly worse, voters approved additional funds for dealing with the city's traffic problems in a specially held 1988 election. Subsequent studies concluded that the construction of a monorail system was the best answer to Houston's traffic woes, and the city began drawing up plans for the monorail's construction, with Mayor Kathy Whitmire embracing the idea. However, in the 1991 mayoral election, Whitmire was defeated by Bob Lanier, who had made opposition to the monorail system one of the keystones of his campaign, and the monorail concept was shelved.

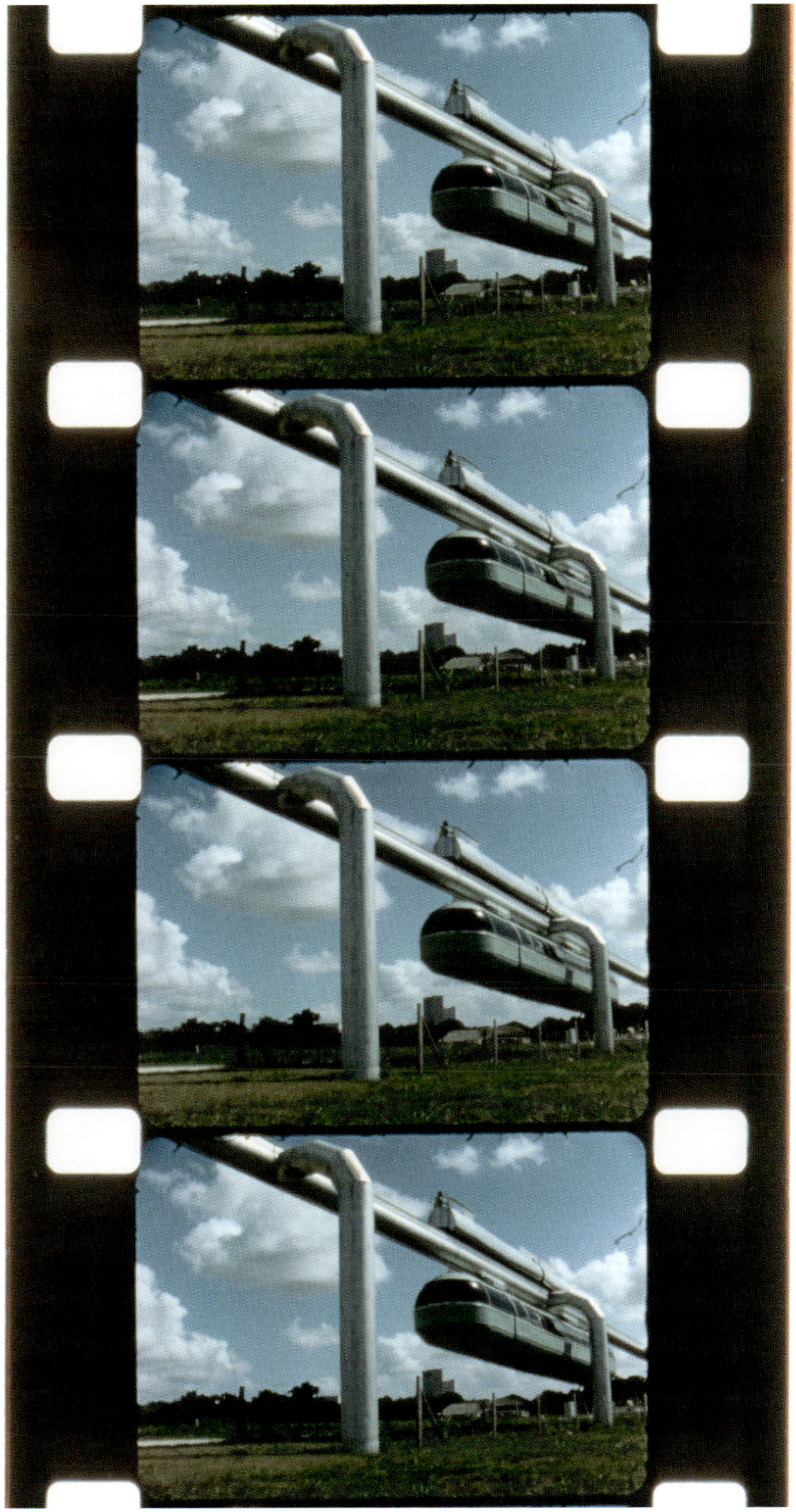

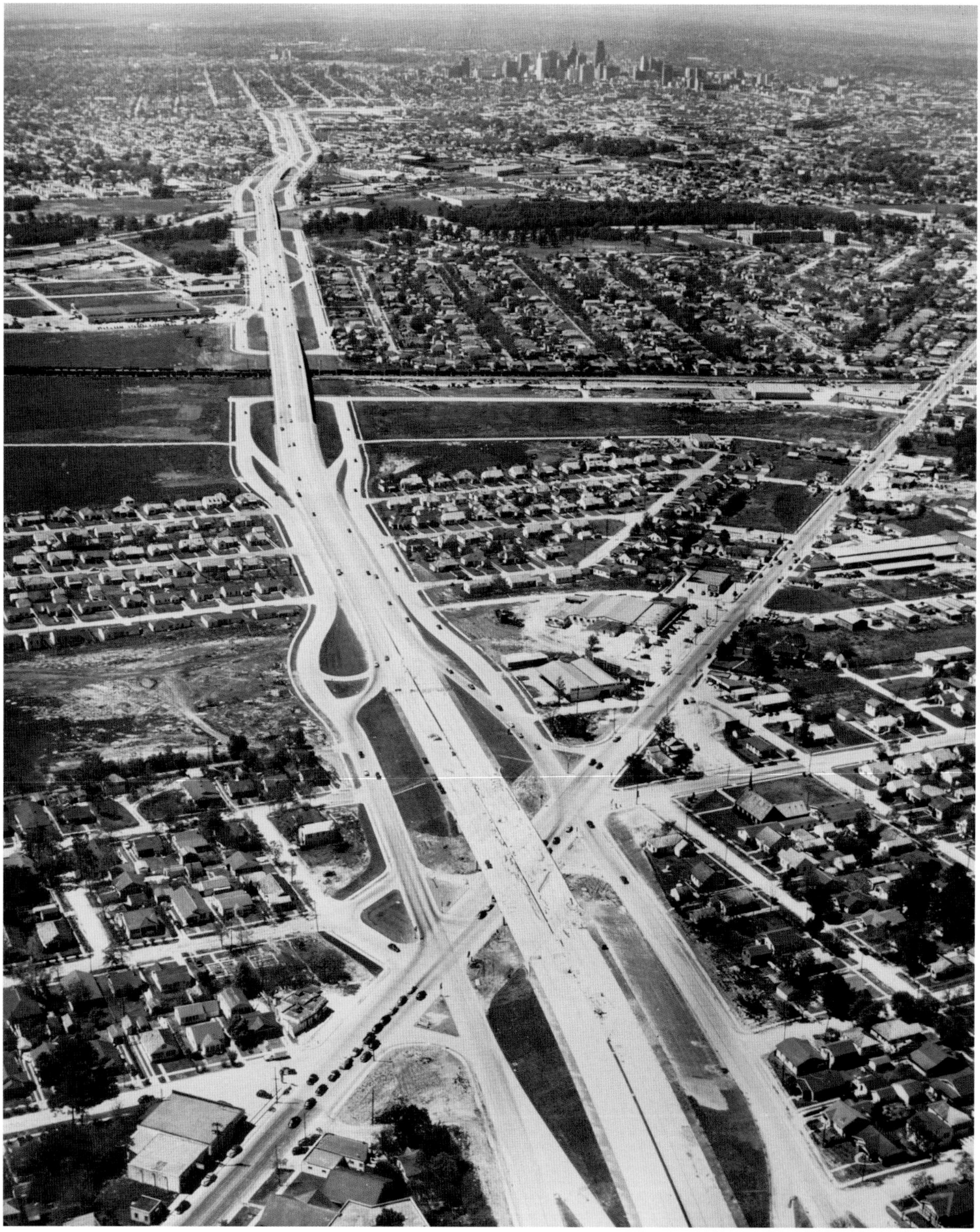

Aerial view of the Gulf Freeway, ca. 1950. The completion of the freeway enabled the spread of suburbia along its route, with tract housing occupying many of the agricultural fields and ranches that had once existed just beyond Houston's city limits. Planning for the freeway's capacity and any suburban growth that might take place following its completion was totally inadequate. In 1950, the number of cars using the Gulf Freeway had already exceeded the projections for car usage in 1960.

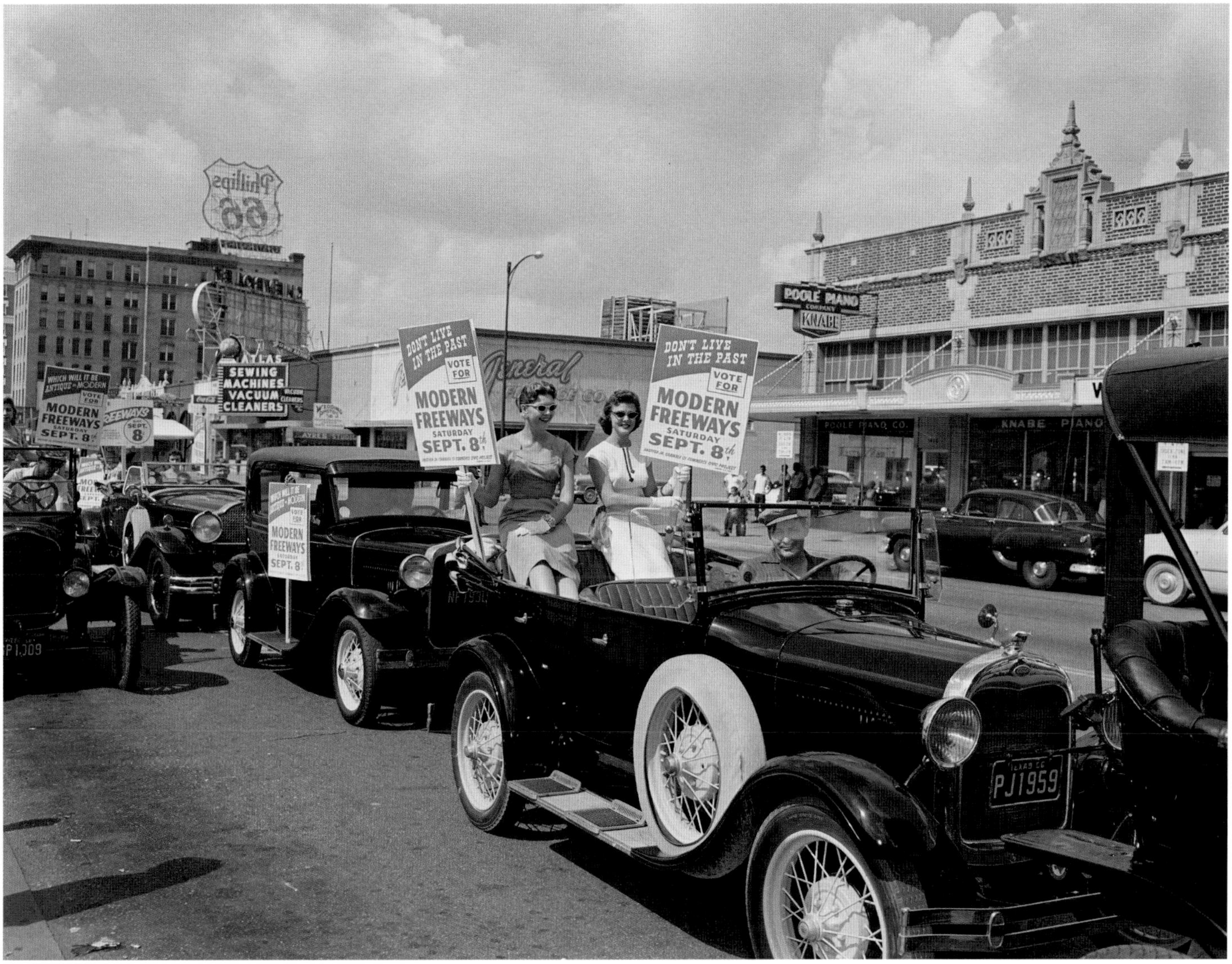

This motorcade demonstration was held in support of an upcoming Harris County bond election intended to provide 1.5 million dollars in additional funding for the expansion of the county's, and Houston's, freeway system by purchasing the right-of-way for future freeways. The election was scheduled for September 8, 1956, at a time when virtually all freeways were considered good by the vast majority of Houstonians and Americans, and the bond was ultimately approved by voters.

The expansion of the Houston area's freeways coincided with the building of America's Interstate Highway System. President Eisenhower signed the Federal-Aid Highway Act of 1956 on June 29 that year, and this marked the beginning of what was, at the time, the world's longest and largest system of highways.

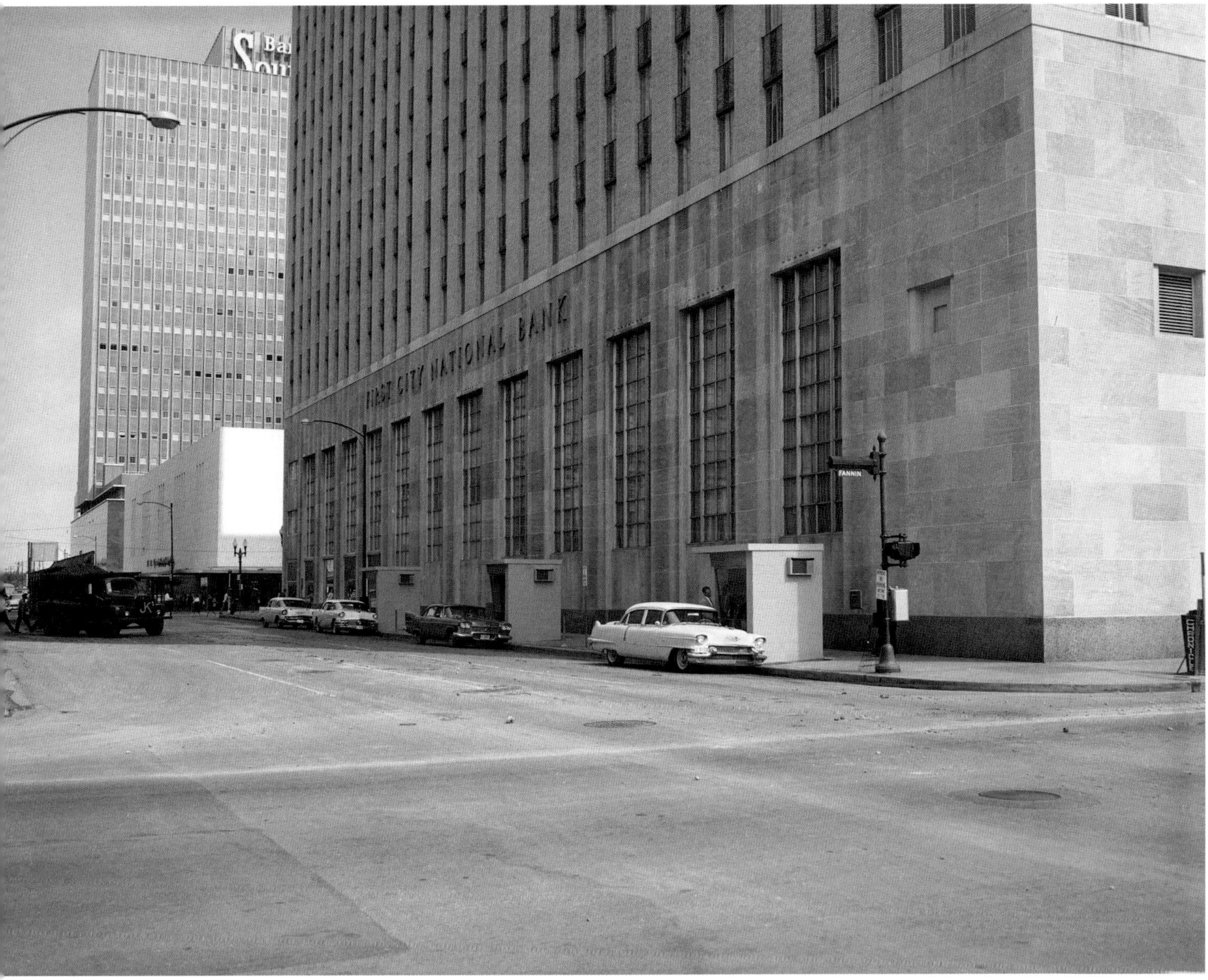

Drive-in windows at First City National Bank in 1959. Few innovations represented the complete dominance of the car culture in Houston better than drive-in, sometimes known as drive-through, bank windows. Conducting business inside the bank came to be viewed as passé, so most banks rapidly added drive-in windows during the 1950s. Some banks were even constructed as drive-in banks only.

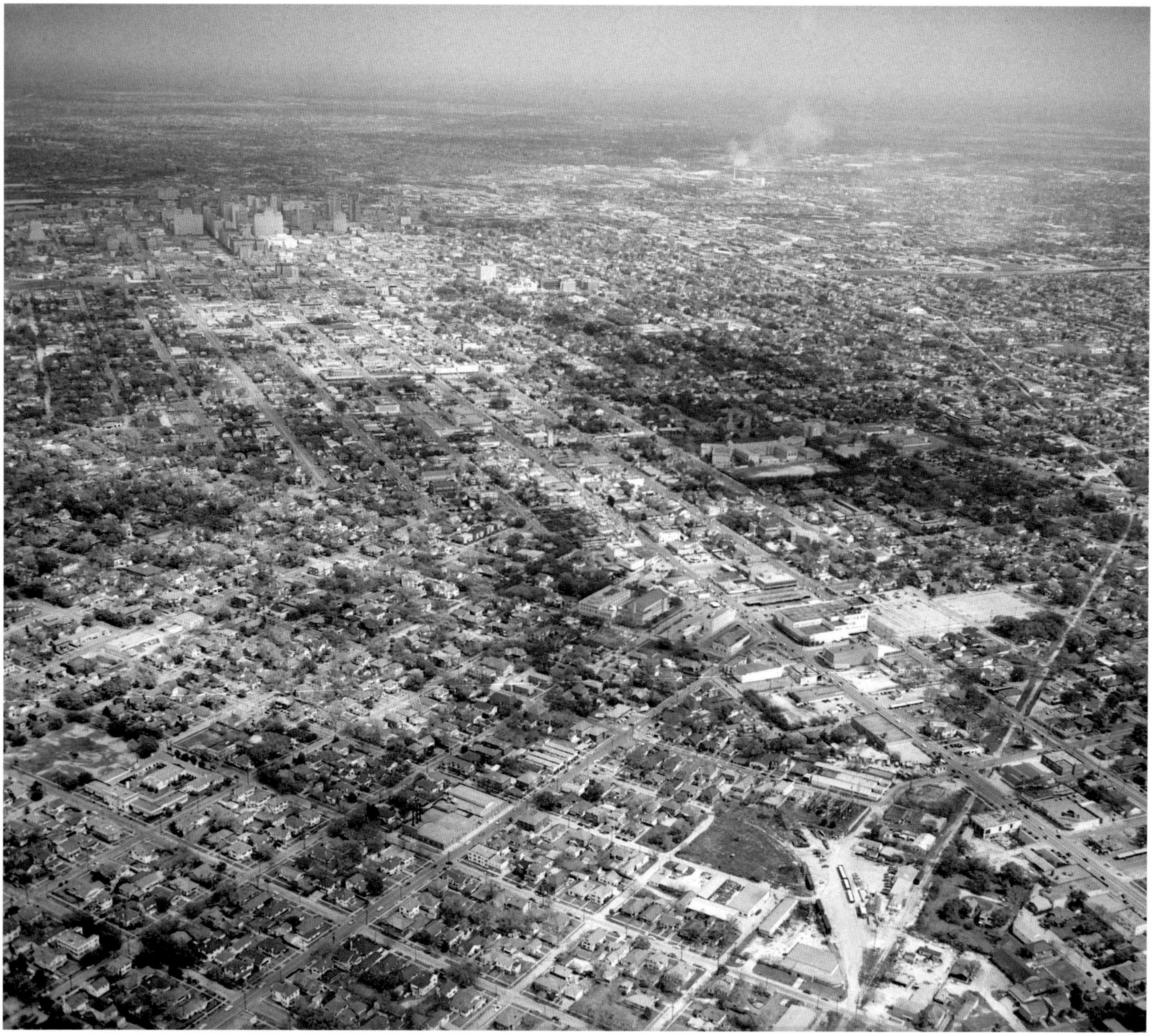

This aerial view of Houston looking north toward downtown was taken in 1953. The photograph clearly shows the city's first principal commercial growth pattern along South Main, away from the downtown area.

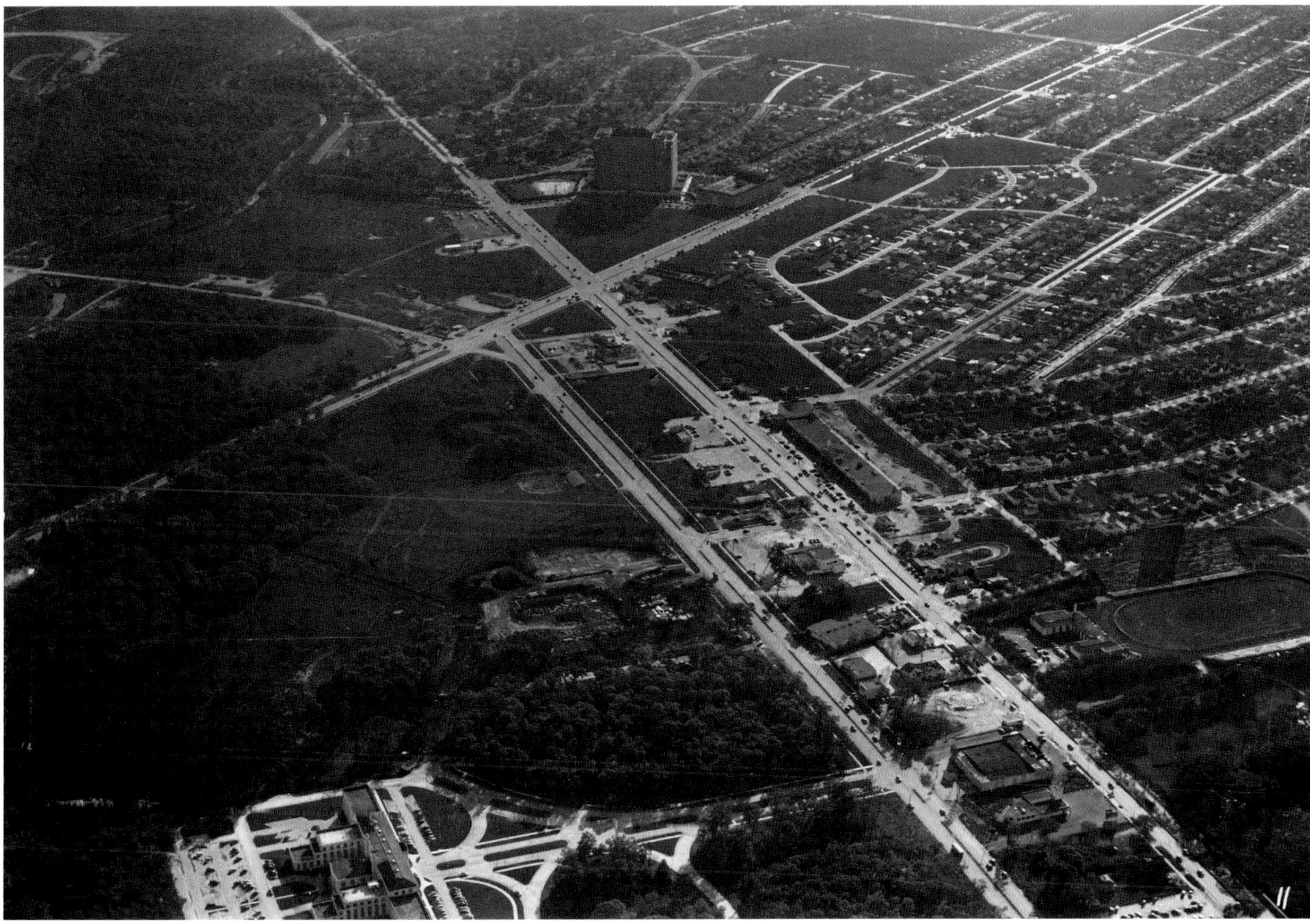

This view clearly shows just how undeveloped the area southwest of downtown, adjacent to the intersection of Main and Holcombe, remained in early 1950. The Shamrock Hotel, completed in 1949, is at the mid-rear of the picture. At the time, many Houstonians thought that Shamrock Hotel developer Glenn McCarthy had lost his sense for successful business transactions when he sited the hotel so far from downtown.

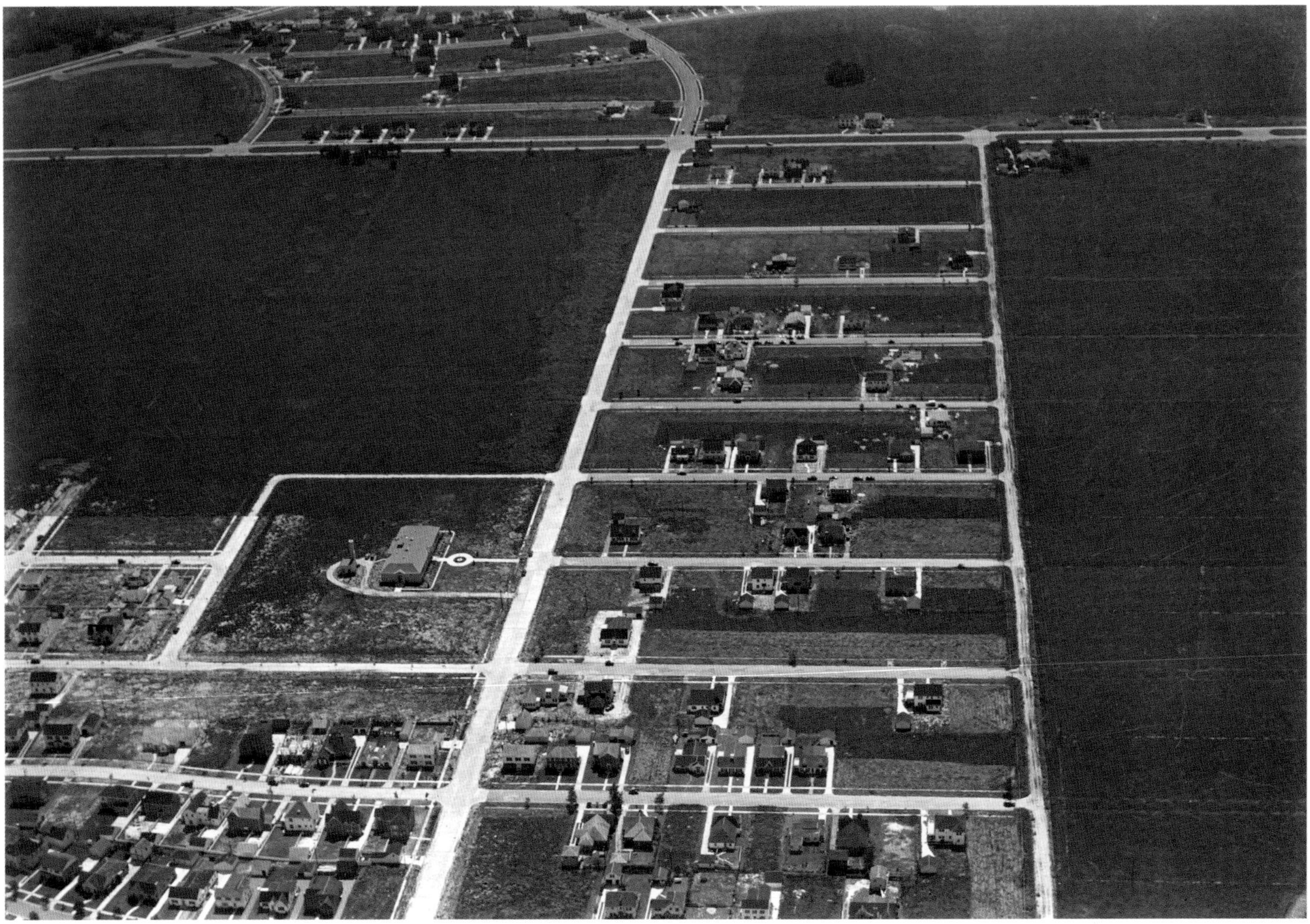

Houston suburban houses in an unidentified area, ca. 1950. This photo shows a simple suburban growth pattern, repeated in hundreds of other postwar cities across the nation following the development of the Interstate Highway System. Developers platted a tract of land and then had streets graded and paved, with the lots laid out in a monotonous grid pattern, as shown above. The first homes were then constructed, according to the same pattern, as shown; eventually the gradual "infill" of the homes followed on remaining lots.

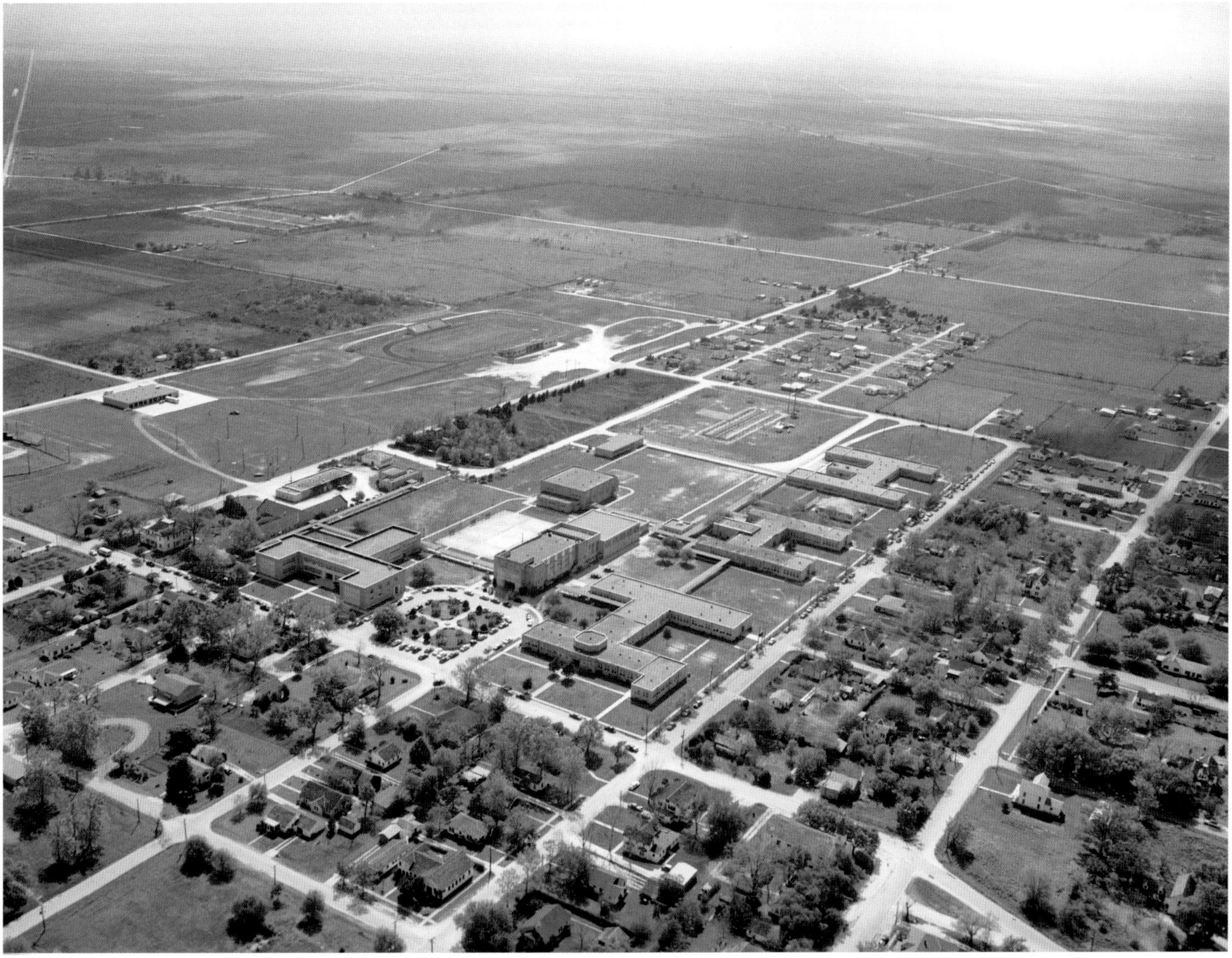

Aerial view of Alvin High School and surrounding homes in Alvin, Texas, ca. 1953. Bailey photographed a variety of scenes in this and several nearby communities. The photo is one of a series of exterior and interior photographs that Bailey shot of the Art Deco–style Alvin High School soon after its completion. As many towns and institutions have lost or destroyed records over the years, photographs in the Bailey collection may be the only surviving documentation. With the passage of time and the ever-increasing expansion of Houston's city limits, many of the small towns and communities that Bailey photographed have become virtual suburbs, or "bedroom communities," of Houston.

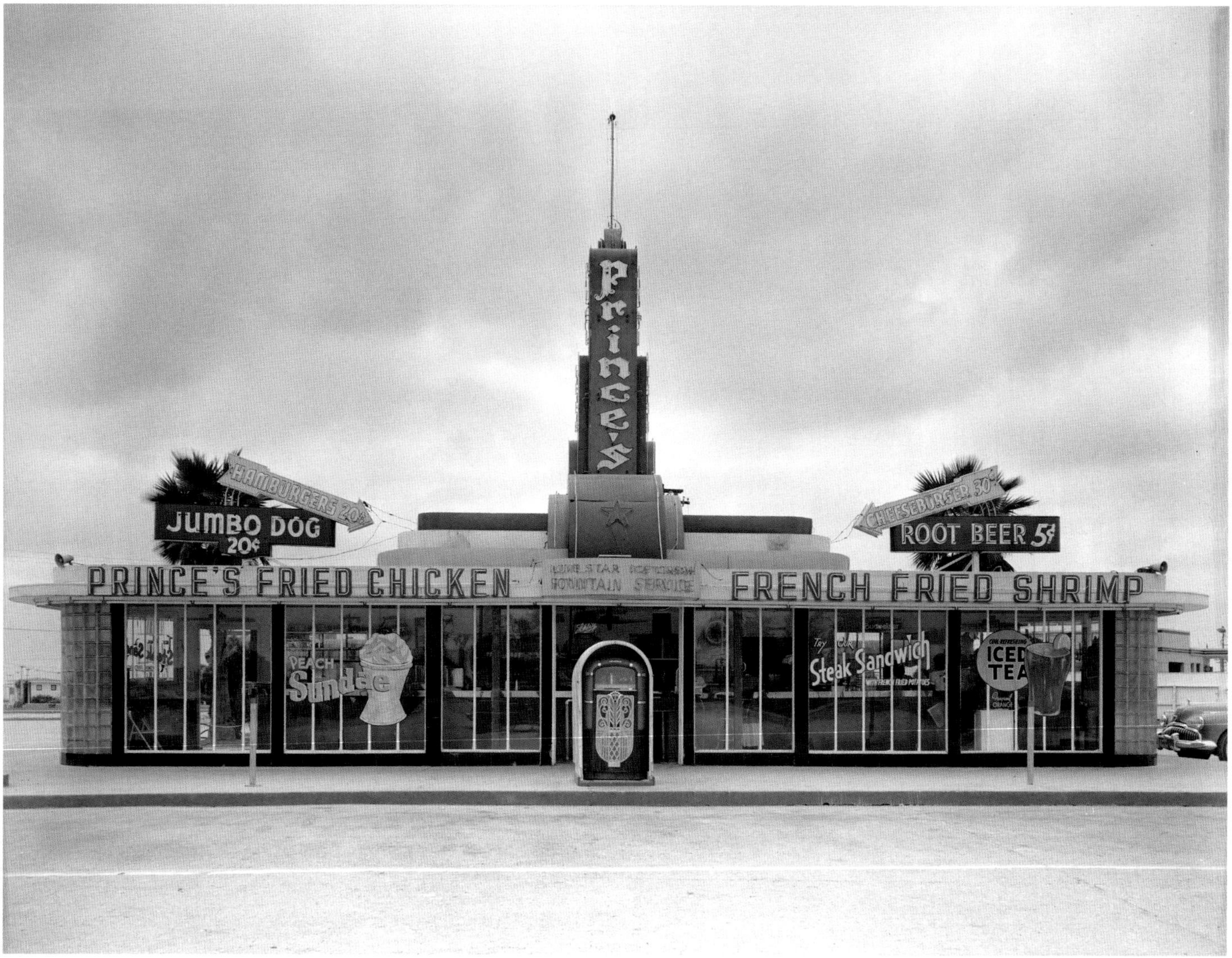

In 1949, this location of the popular Prince's Drive In chain featured an outdoor jukebox for its customers.

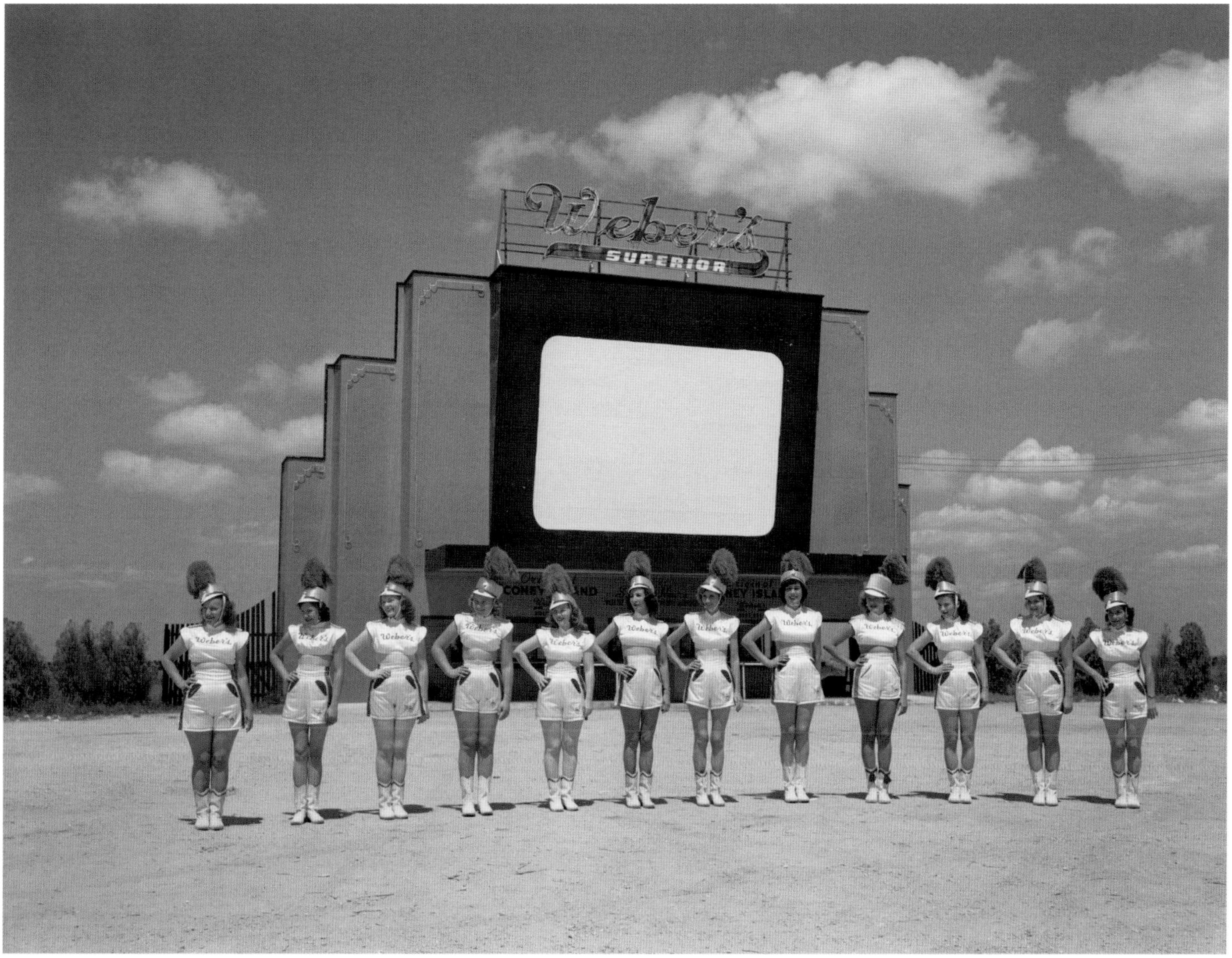

Weber's Superior Root Beer commissioned this photo of carhops in front of the company's own drive-in movie theater screen on South Main in 1950. Admission to Weber's Drive-in Theatre was free, but patrons were expected to buy refreshments from the carhops. Carhops became a staple not only at drive-in restaurants but also at many drive-in movie theater in the 1950s.

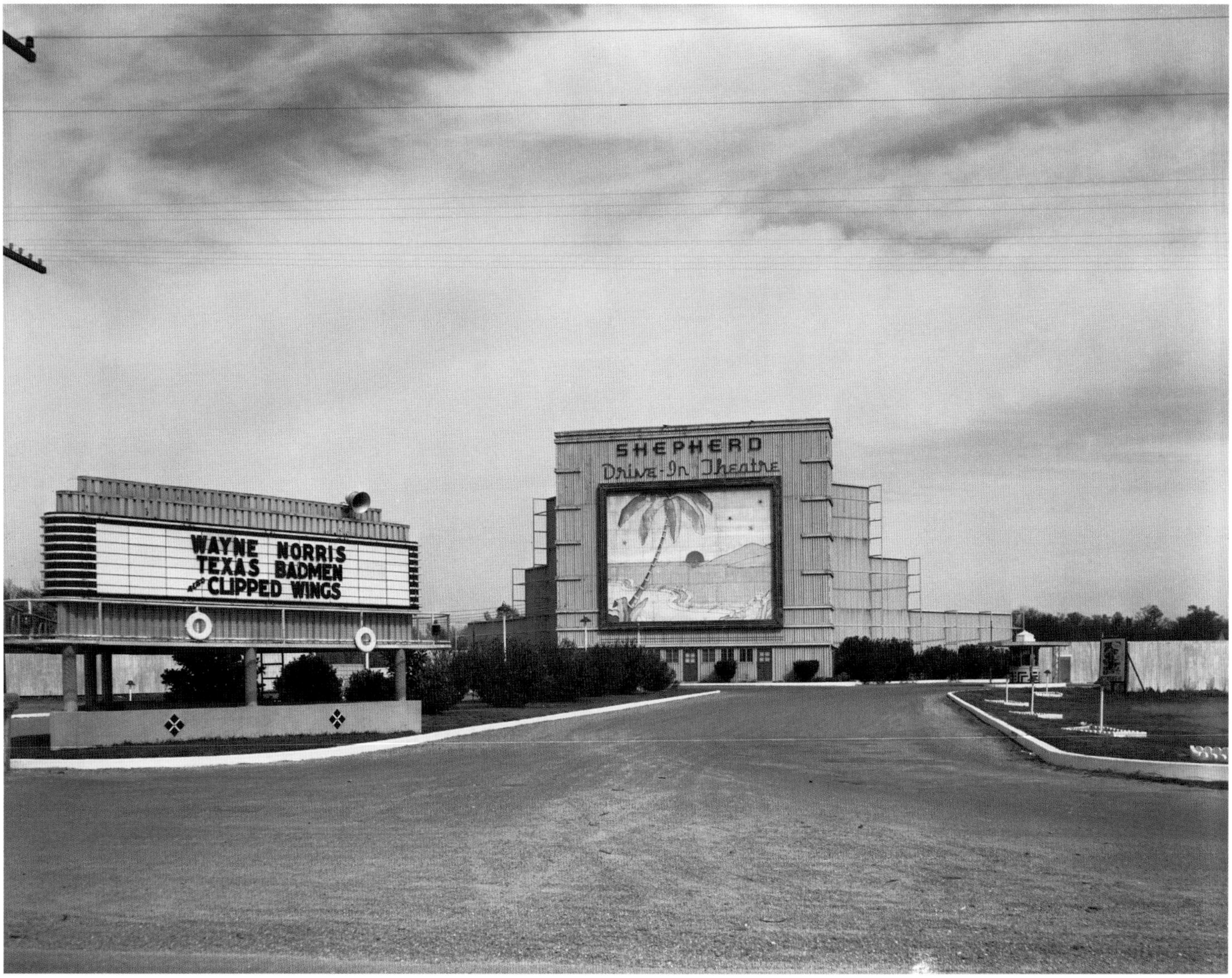

The Shepherd Drive-In Theatre in 1954. The Shepherd opened May 23, 1947, at 6004 North Shepherd. It has since been demolished. In an automobile-enamored city like Houston, drive-ins flourished after World War II.

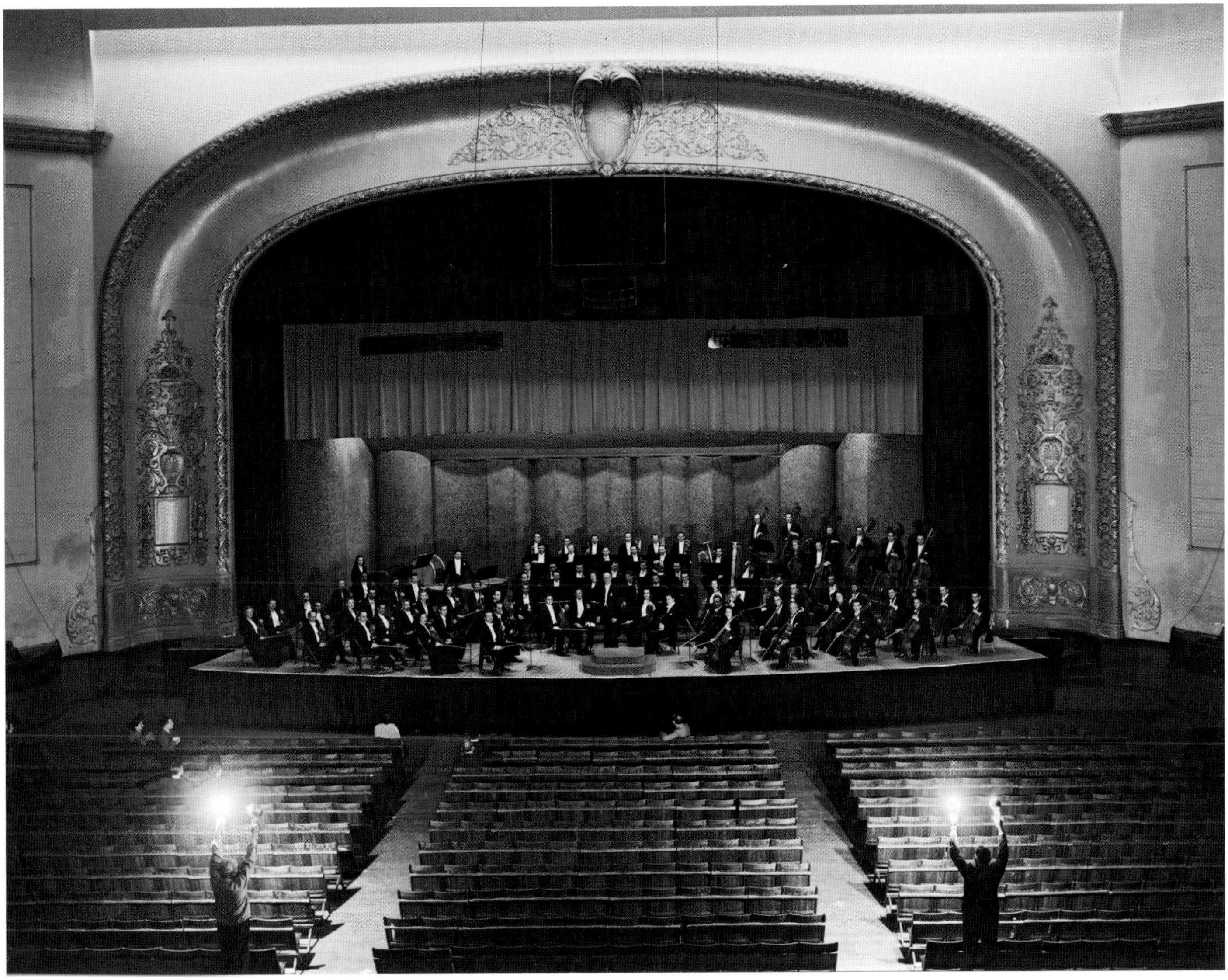

The Houston Symphony Orchestra on the stage of the Houston Municipal Auditorium, often known simply as City Auditorium, in 1949. The City Auditorium was demolished in 1963 and replaced by Jones Hall, completed in 1966, on the same site. Note the two men at left and right foreground, who are providing additional lighting for the photographer.

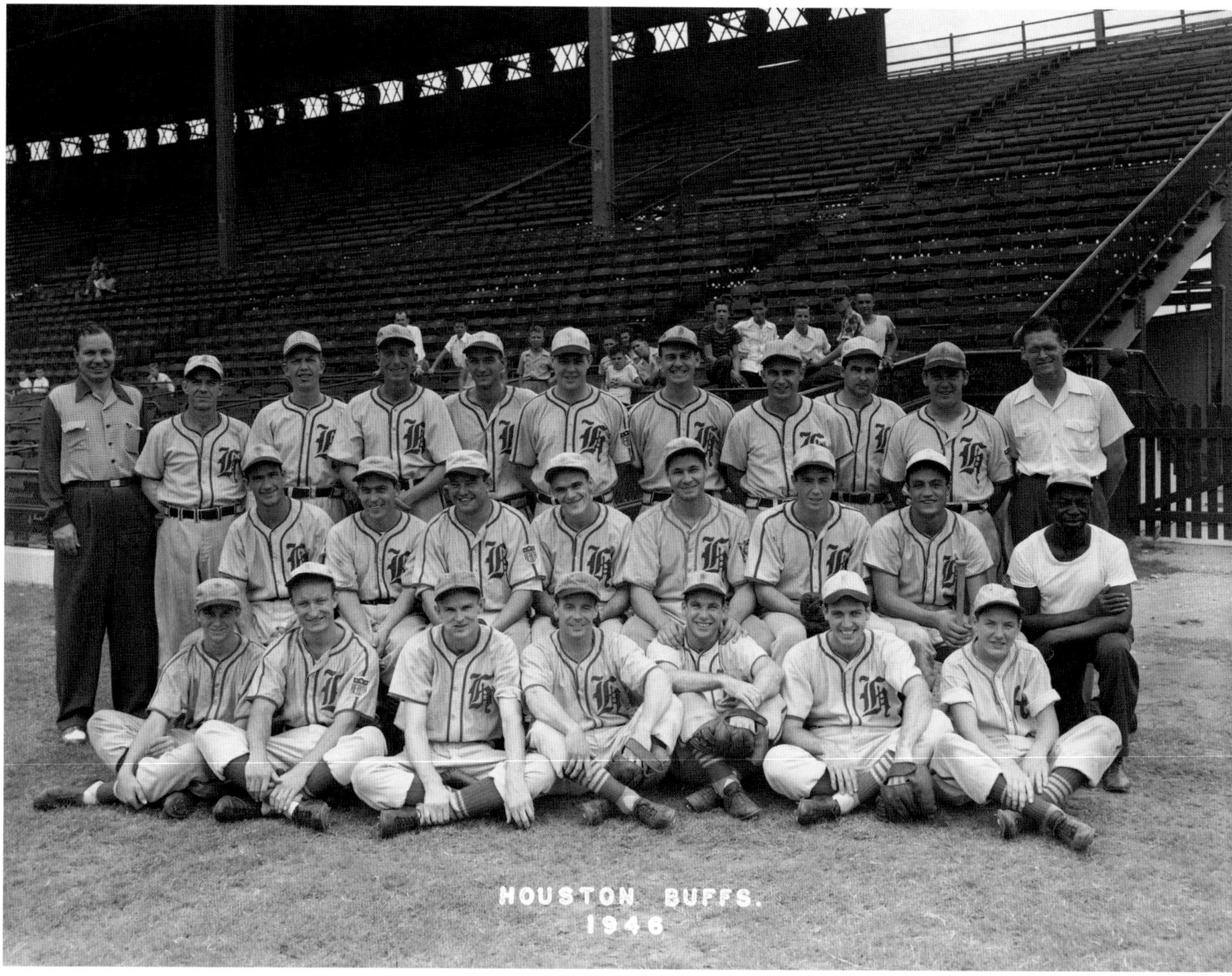

The Houston Buffaloes, usually known by their fans simply as the "Buffs," baseball team in 1946. The team was officially designated as the Houston Buffs in 1959, but only two years later the team was dissolved so that Houston could join a major league, beginning in 1962 with the National League's Houston Colt .45s.

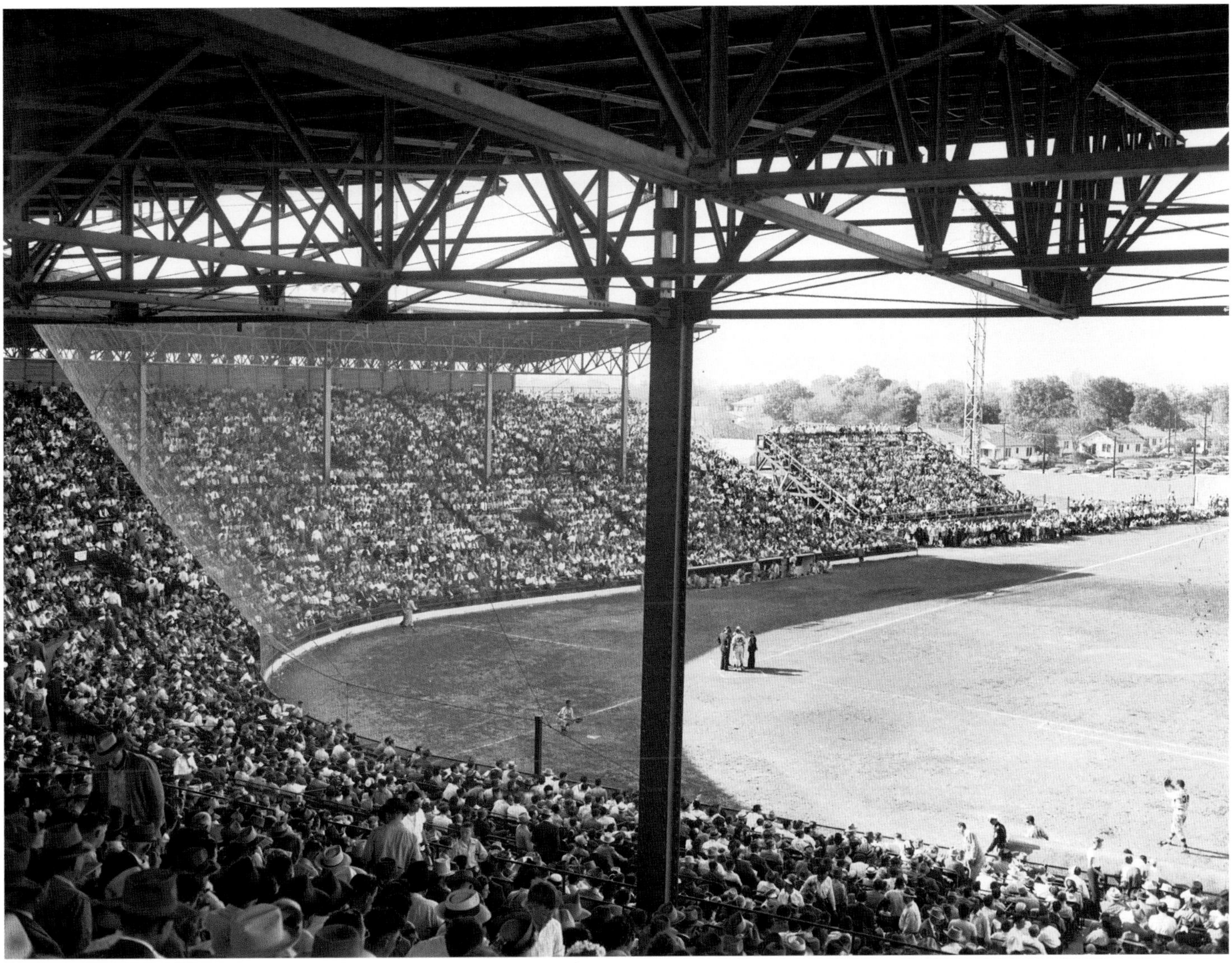

A photo of the huge crowd that turned out at Buff Stadium on April 7, 1947, to see Stan Musial of the St. Louis Cardinals play. The Cardinals had owned a majority stake in the Houston Buffs since 1920, and the affiliation between the two teams continued until 1959. The stadium was located on the site of the latter-day Finger's Furniture Store on the Gulf Freeway at Cullen Blvd.

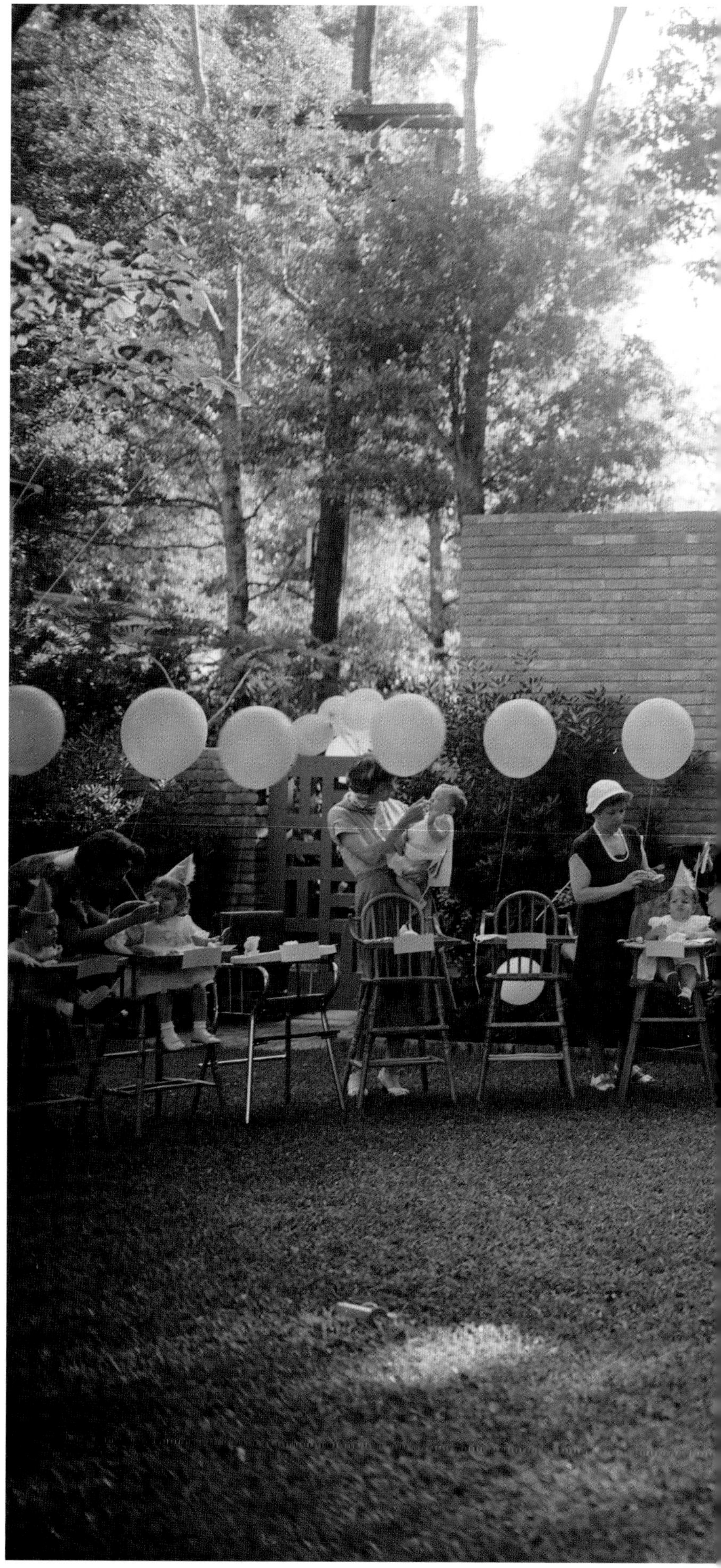

Few photos in the Bailey collection so clearly show the impact of the post–World War II "baby boom" like this shot of a children's birthday party taken in May 1953. Between 1946 and 1961, some seventy-six million births were recorded in the United States, and much of America's economy and popular culture rapidly became dependent on the spending and influence generated by boomers and their parents.

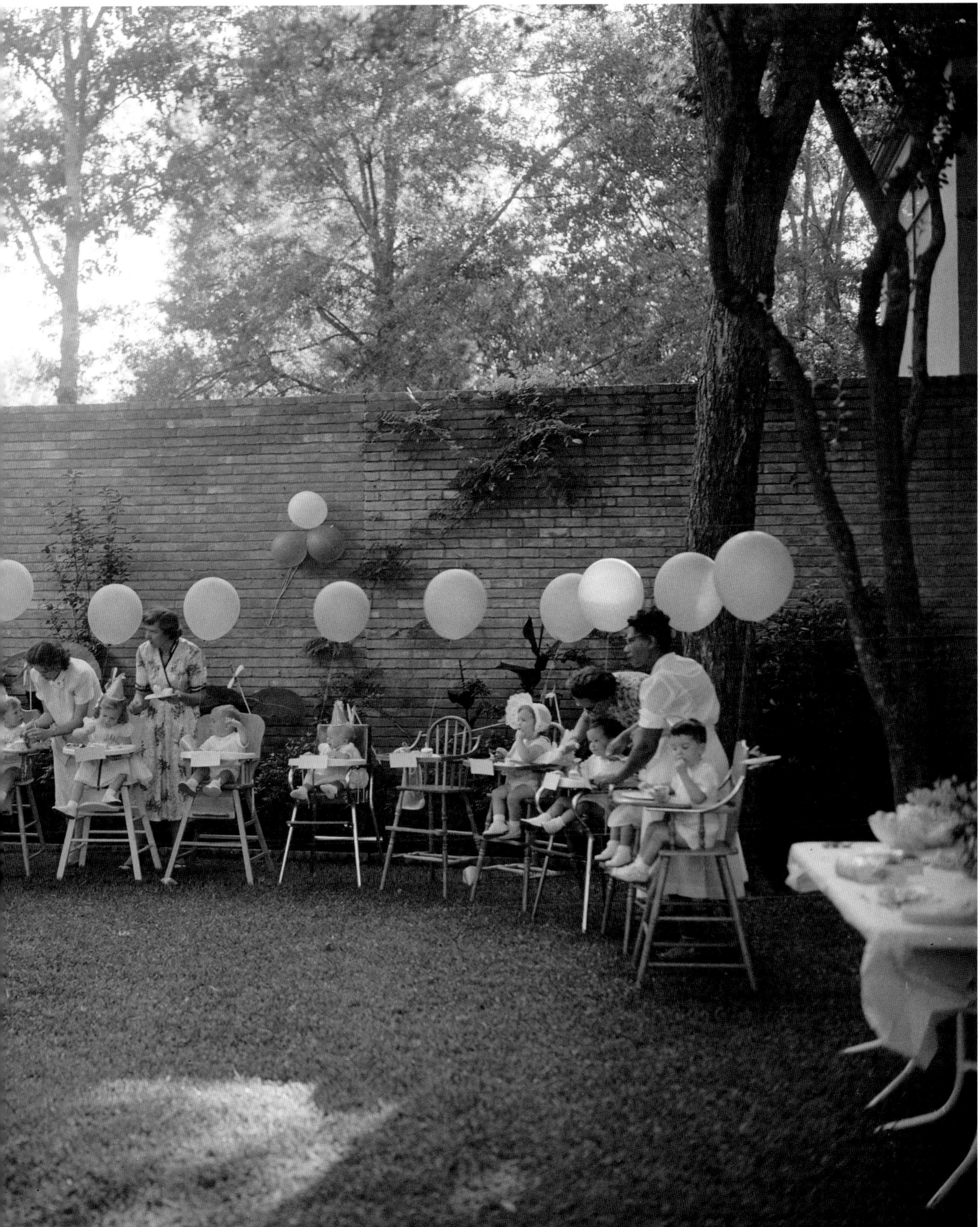

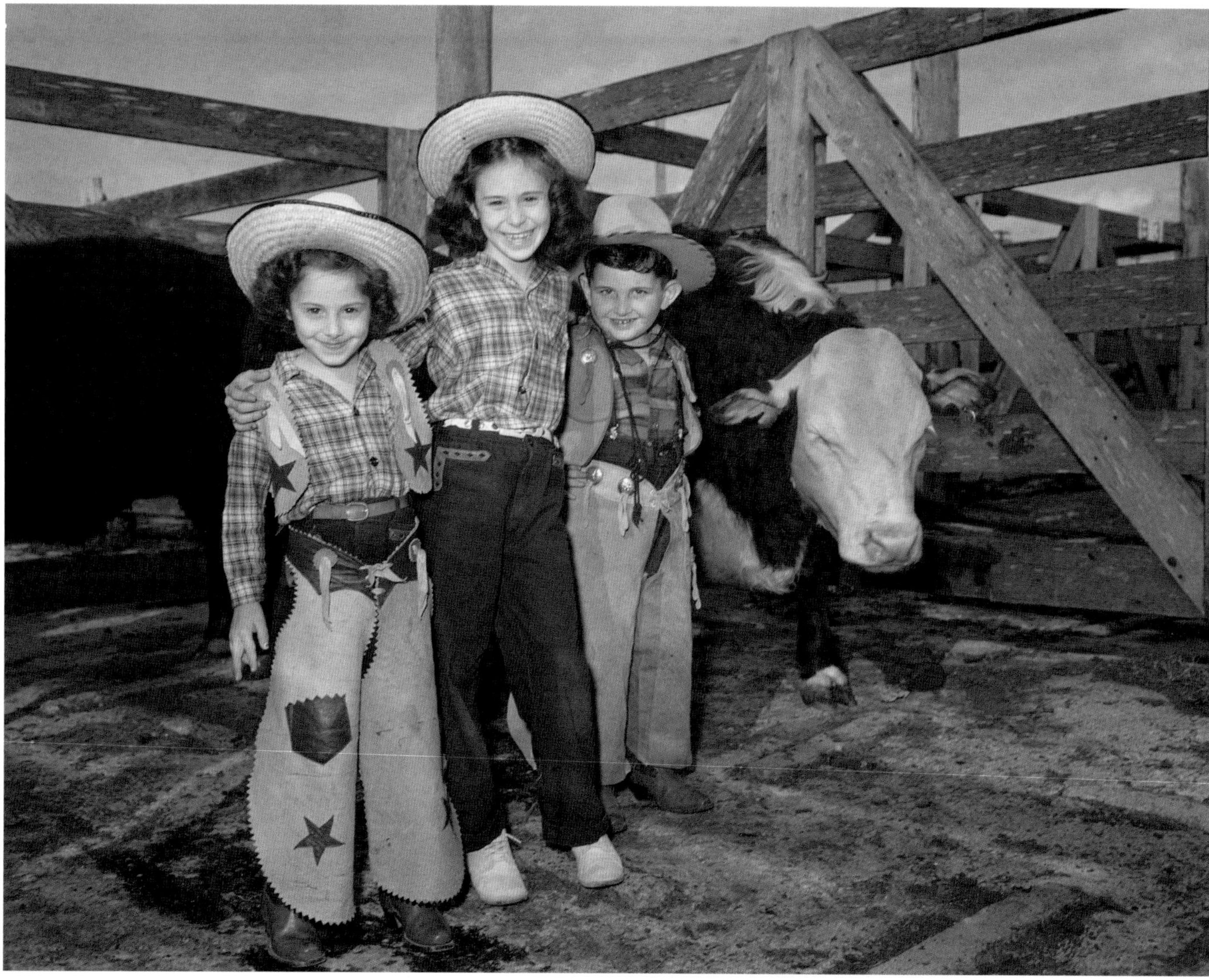

These children were posed with livestock during the February 1947 Fat Stock Show in this photograph taken for the Studewood Food Market. Innumerable children from the Houston area, and many from the rest of the state as well, have annually looked forward to the Houston Rodeo since its inception. The rodeo is still held annually.

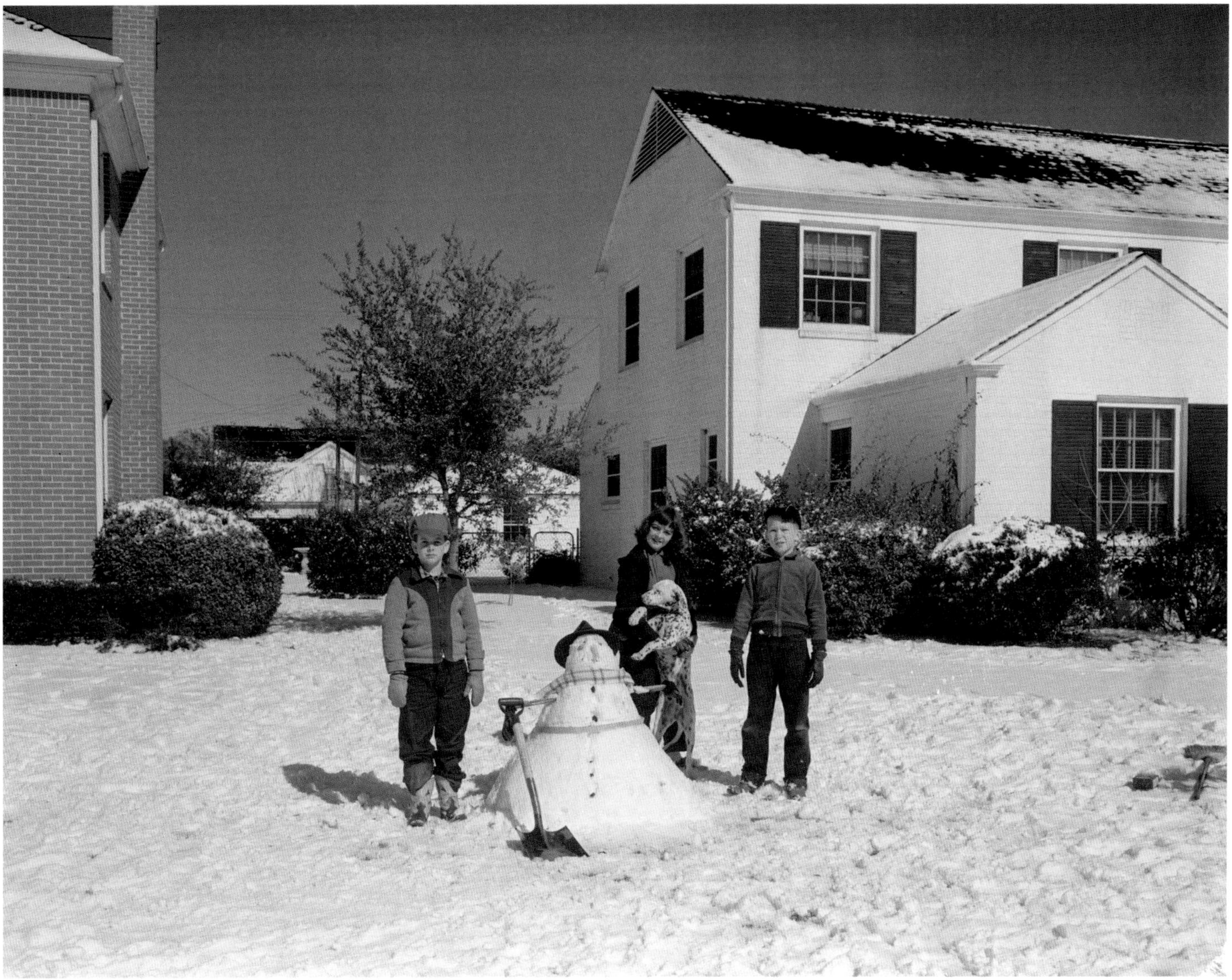

This scene of children and their snowman was taken in the River Oaks area of Houston following a rare snowfall in 1949. Any snowfall was considered to be major event in Houston, and each time it snowed, Bailey took a number of shots commissioned by families and businesses.

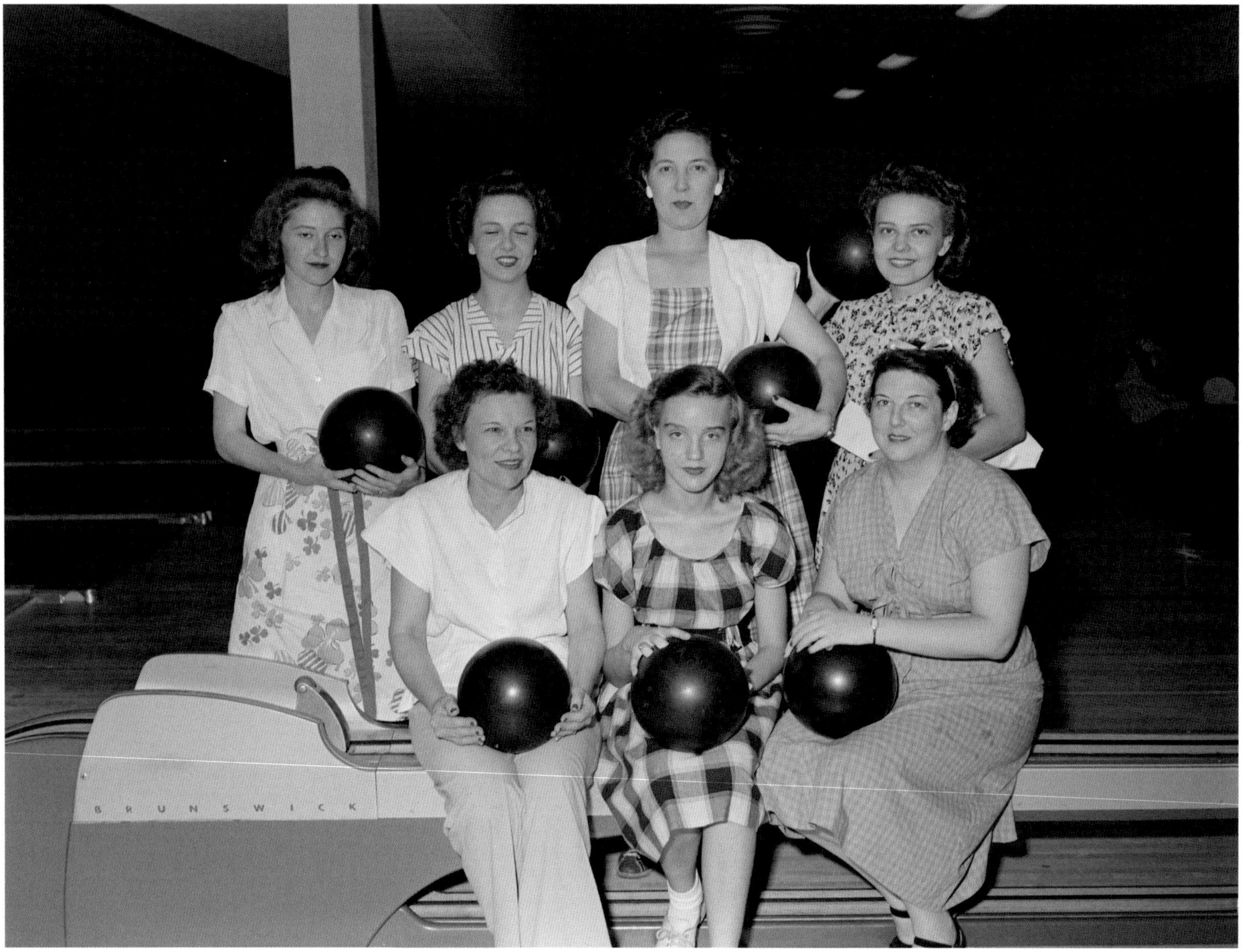

Women's bowling team made up of Foley's employees (ca. 1947). Foley's Department Store provided and sponsored dozens of clubs for employees to participate in during their leisure time.

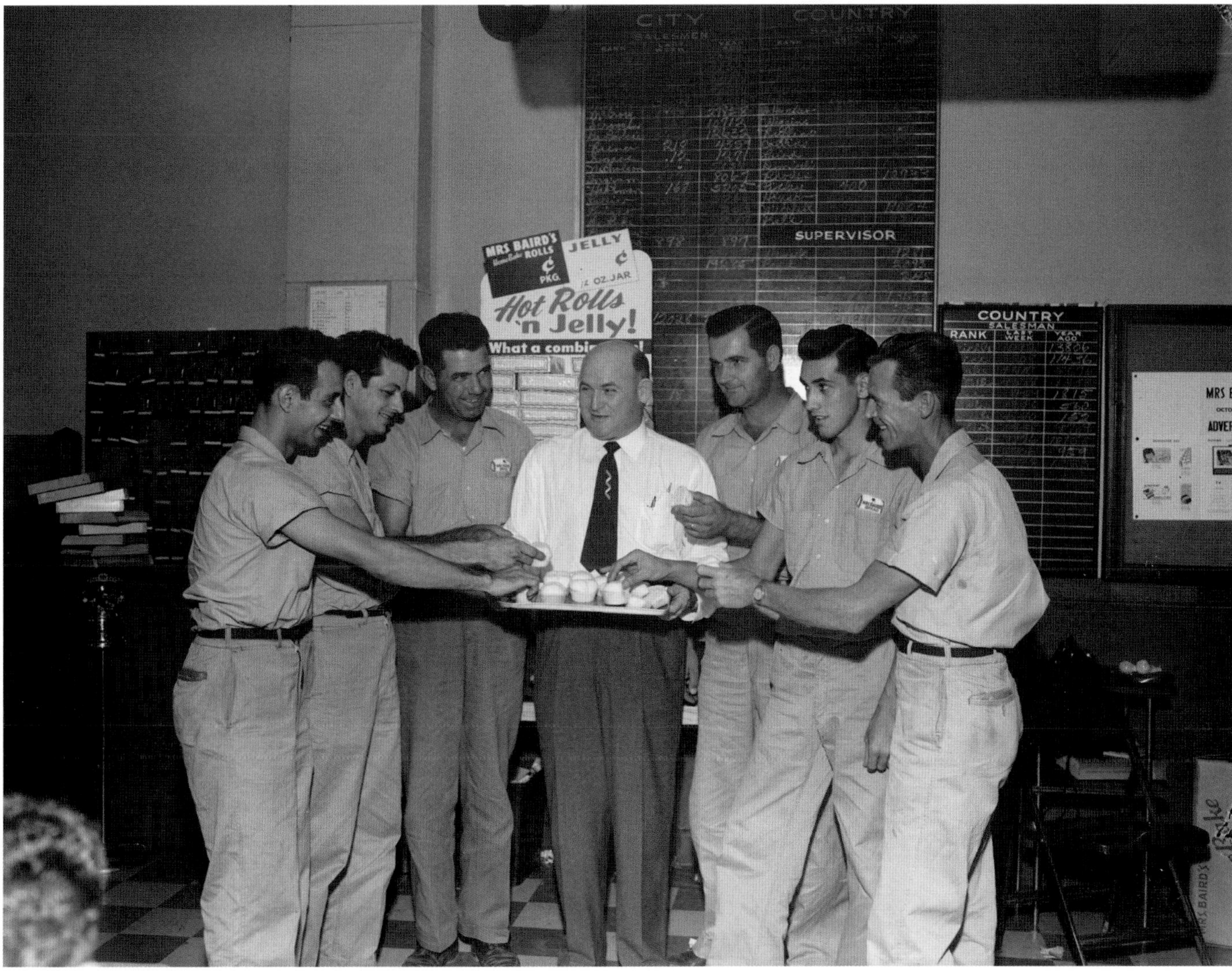

Mrs. Baird's Bakery employees sample the bakery's rolls in this 1954 scene. The bakery was located at 1925 West Gray. Few Houstonians who grew up nearby or drove their car anywhere near Mrs. Baird's while the baking was going on will ever forget the wonderful smell that wafted across the neighborhood.

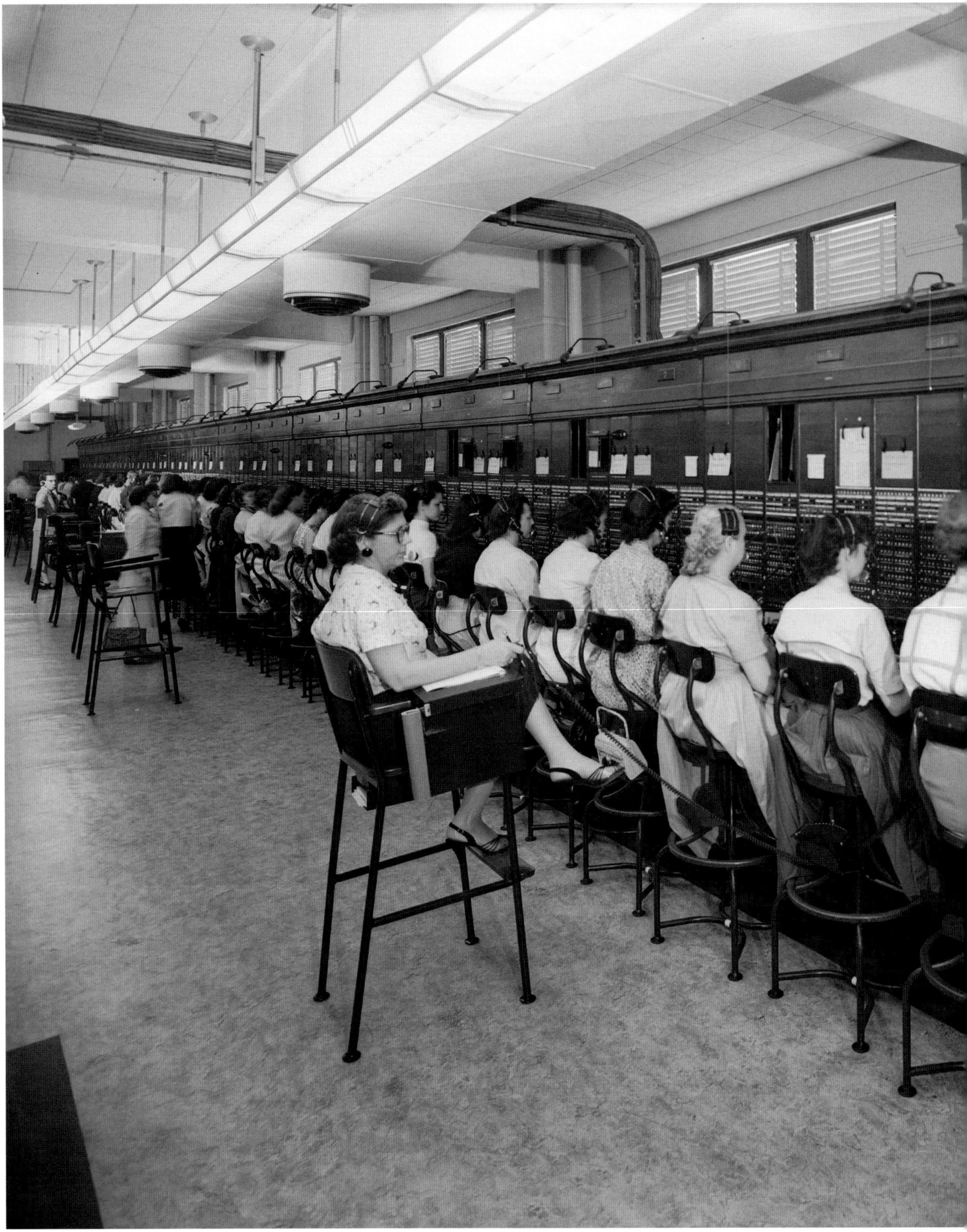

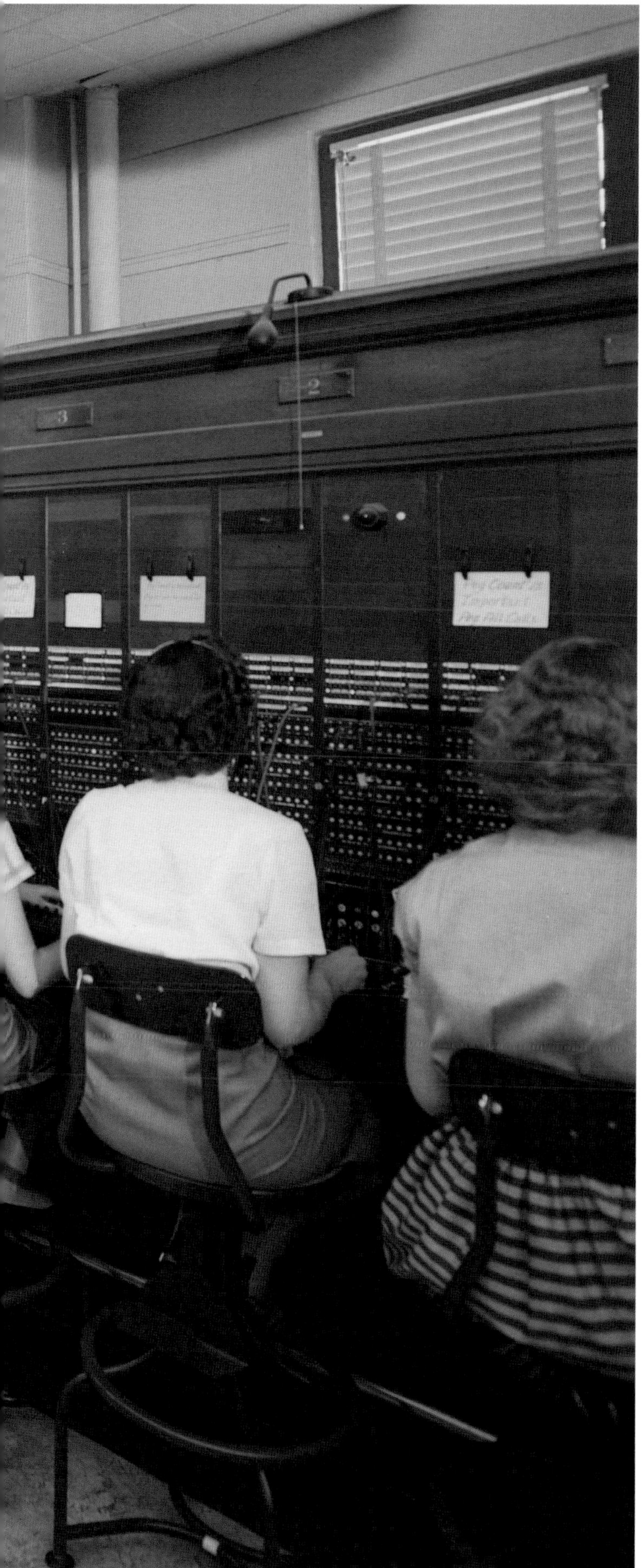

Line of Southwestern Bell telephone operators, ca. 1955. The telephone industry was one of the first major employers of women. This photo shows an example of the huge amount of human labor that went into maintaining communication industries prior to the digital age.

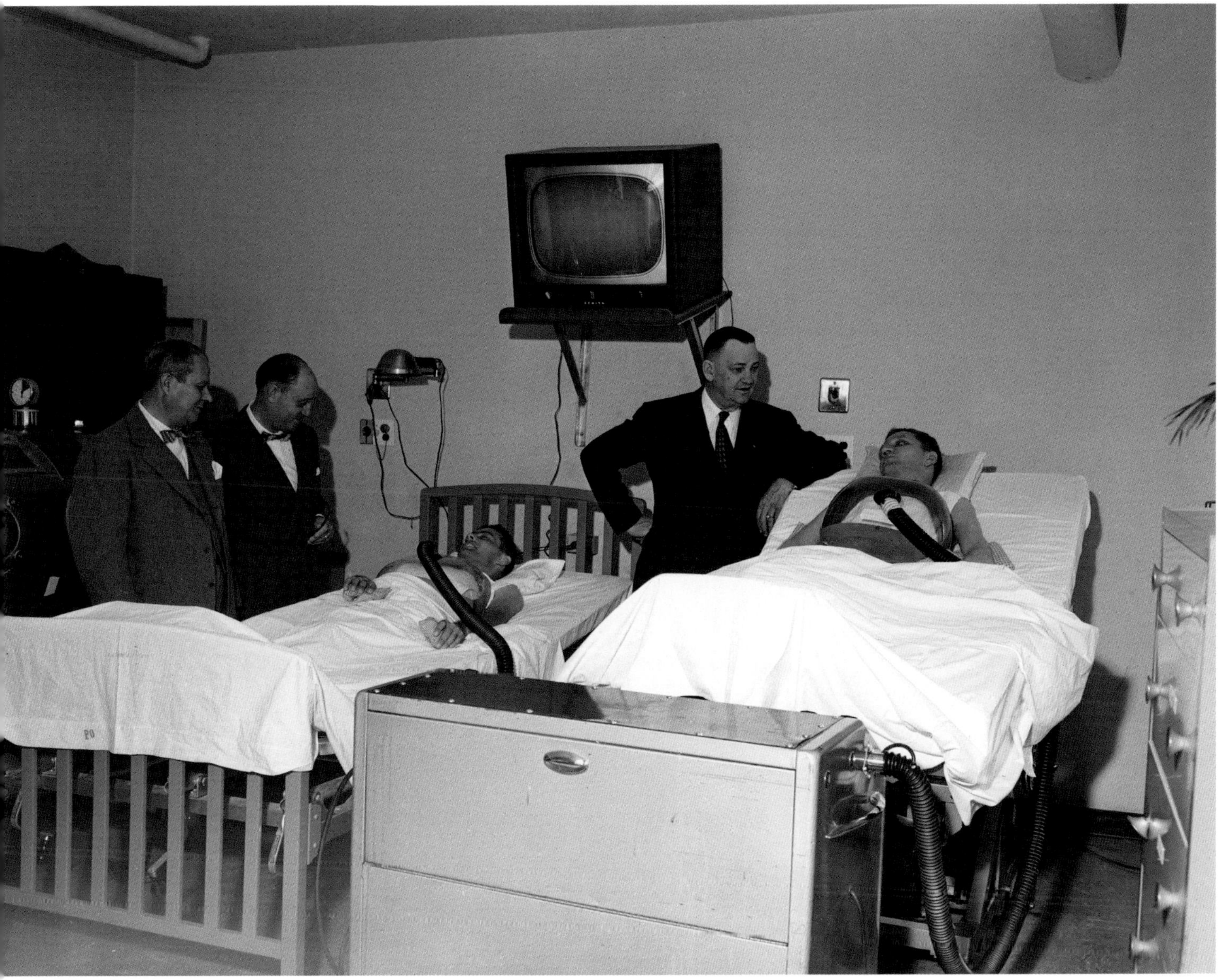

Two young patients with visitors in the polio ward of the Jefferson Davis Hospital in November 1952. Sadly, that same year Dr. Jonas Salk began experiments with his polio vaccine, but he was not able to announce the successful results of the vaccine's field trials until 1955. Like every other American city, Houston was both horrified and stricken by the nationwide polio epidemics that took place in the twentieth century on a scale previously unknown. This photo was commissioned by the Harris County Polio Foundation.

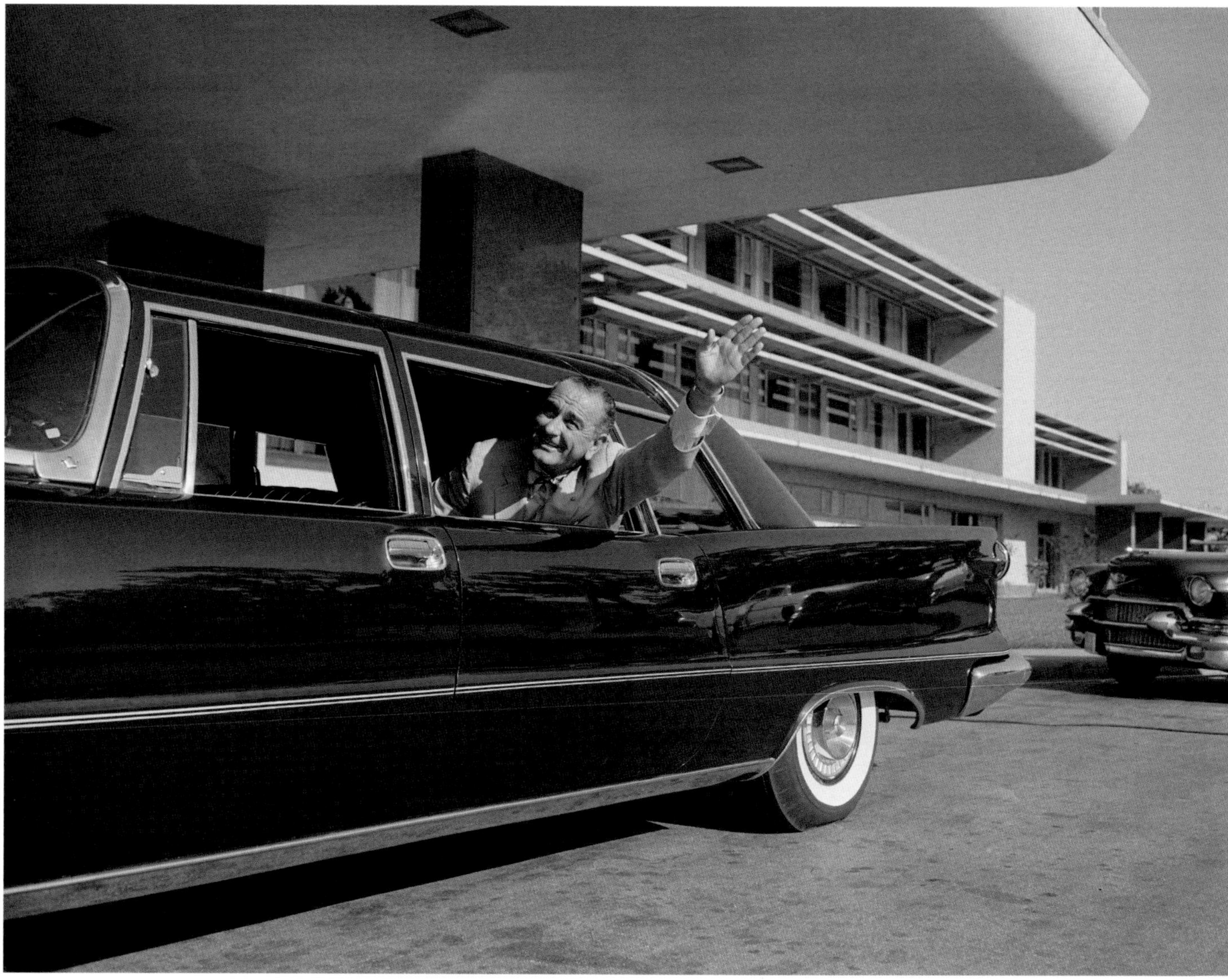

Then US Senate majority leader Lyndon Johnson is shown here during a June 1958 visit to Texas Children's Hospital. Texas Children's was dedicated in 1953 and admitted its first patient in February 1954; it is today the largest pediatric hospital in the world.

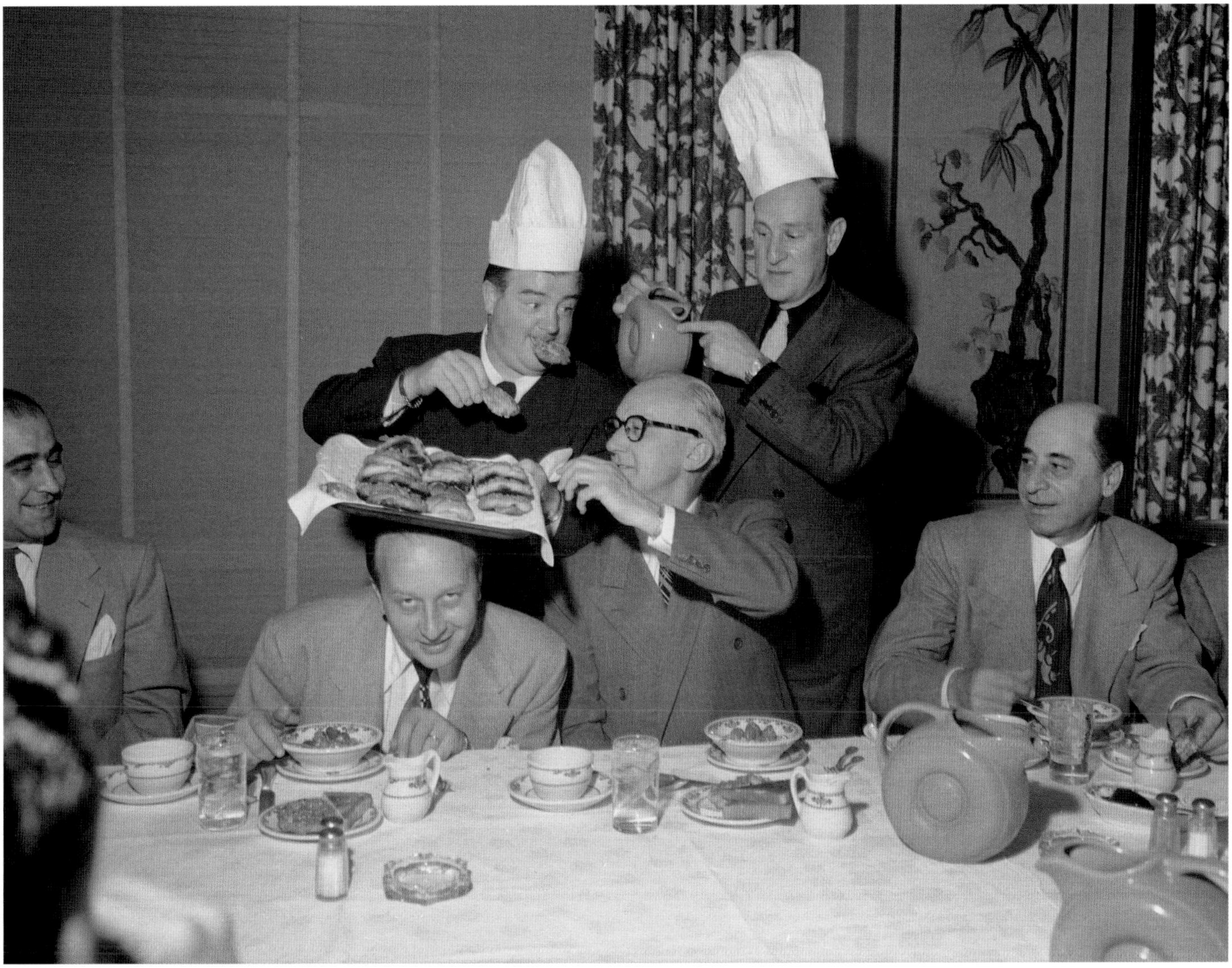

As part of their contract commitments, stars were often required to make multiple appearances at a variety of venues during their promotional tours. In this April 1948 scene, comedians Bud Abbott and Lou Costello (standing) entertain banquet guests, probably executives from the Interstate Theatre chain.

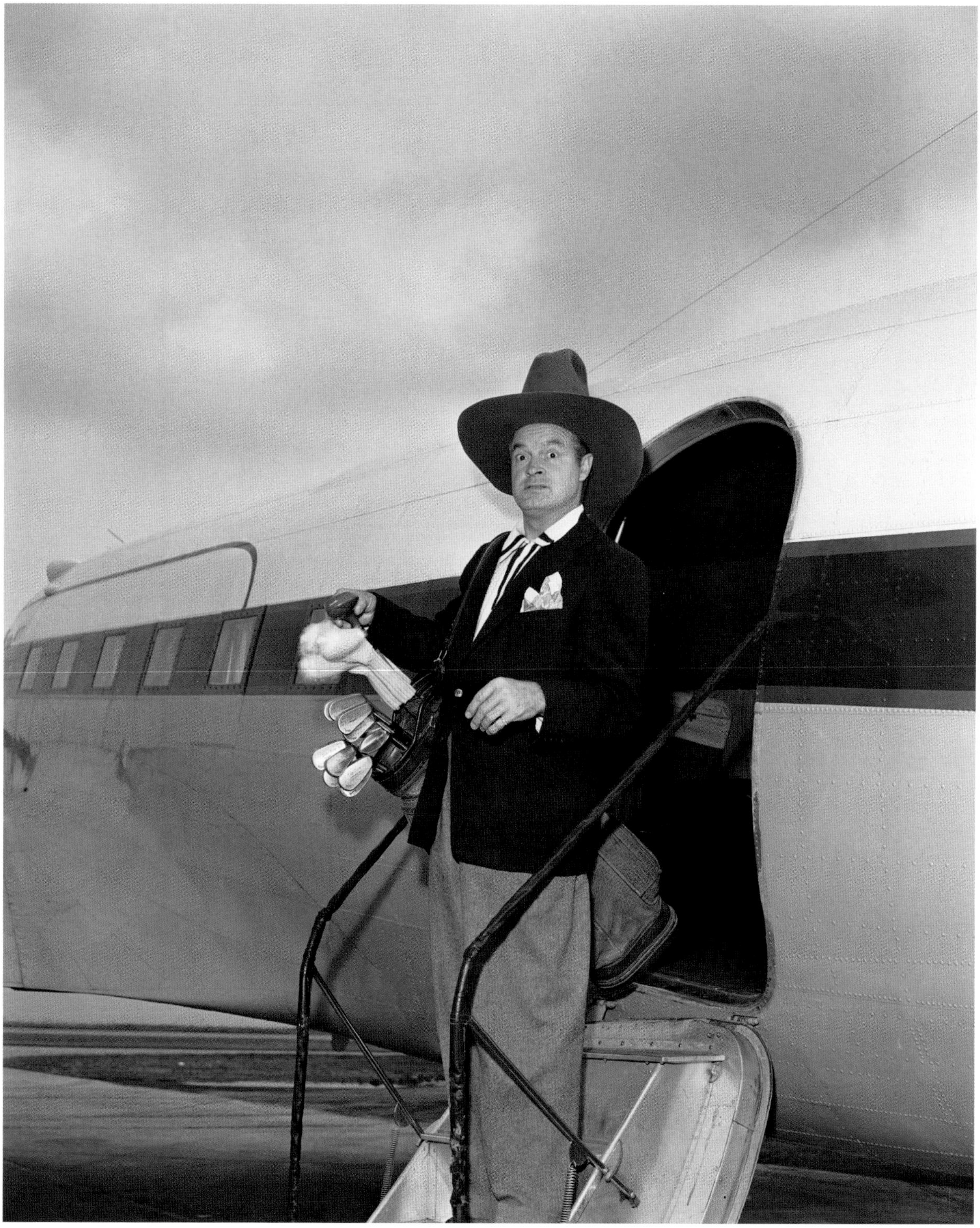

Comedian Bob Hope arrives at the Houston airport, ca. 1951, complete with ten-gallon hat and golf clubs in tow.

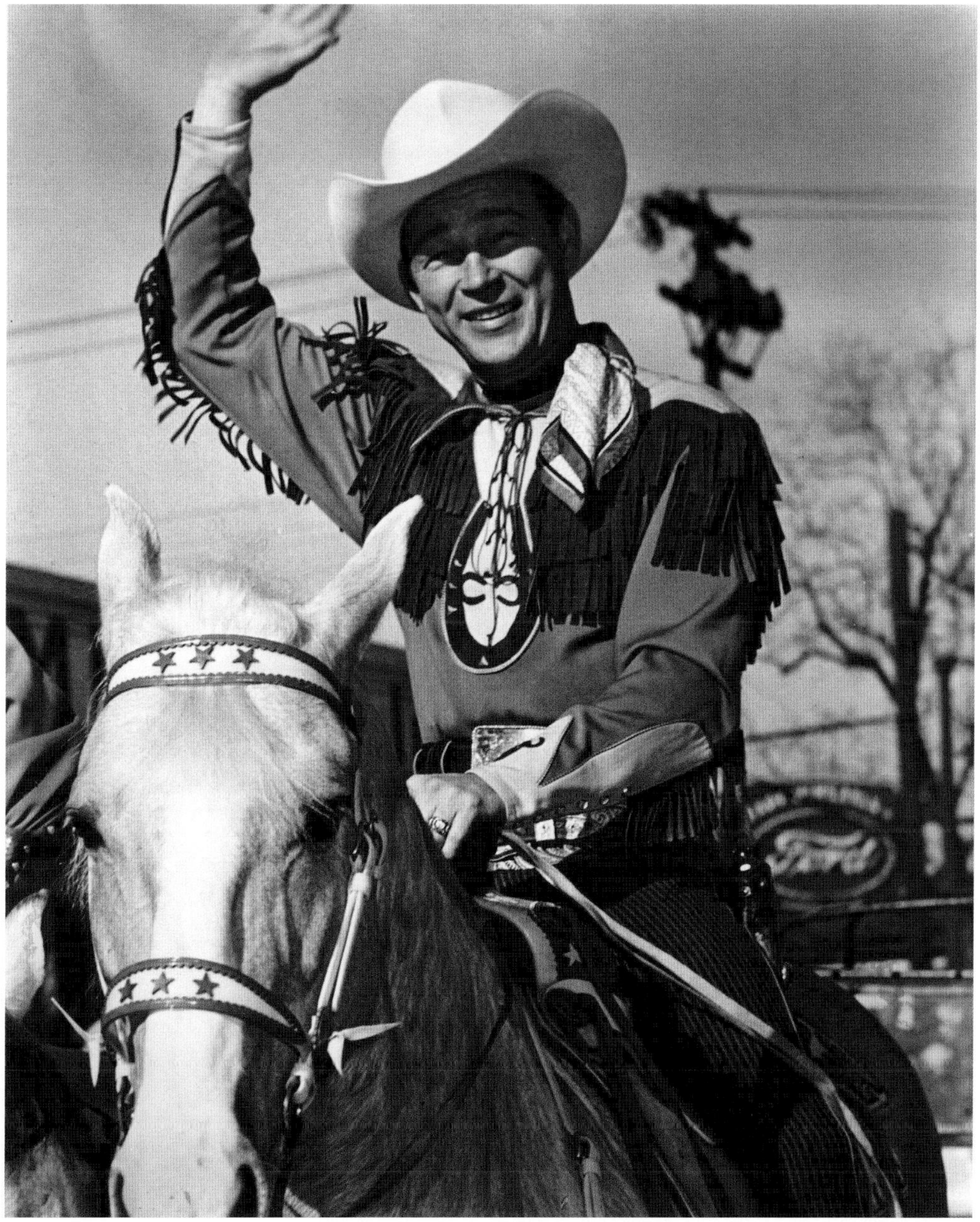

Roy Rogers riding Trigger in the Houston Fat Stock Show and Livestock Exposition's parade of March 1952. This was the first of eight Houston Rodeo appearances that the "King of the Cowboys" and his wife and co-star Dale Evans, the "Queen of the West," would make. Although Rogers had already appeared in films for many years, he was suddenly riding the wave of the new medium of television, his celebrity fueled by millions of young viewers. In just four years, from 1947 to 1951, retail sales of western-related children's clothing, books, records, toys, and other items reached 150 million dollars; almost all of these sales were related to television programming and commercials.

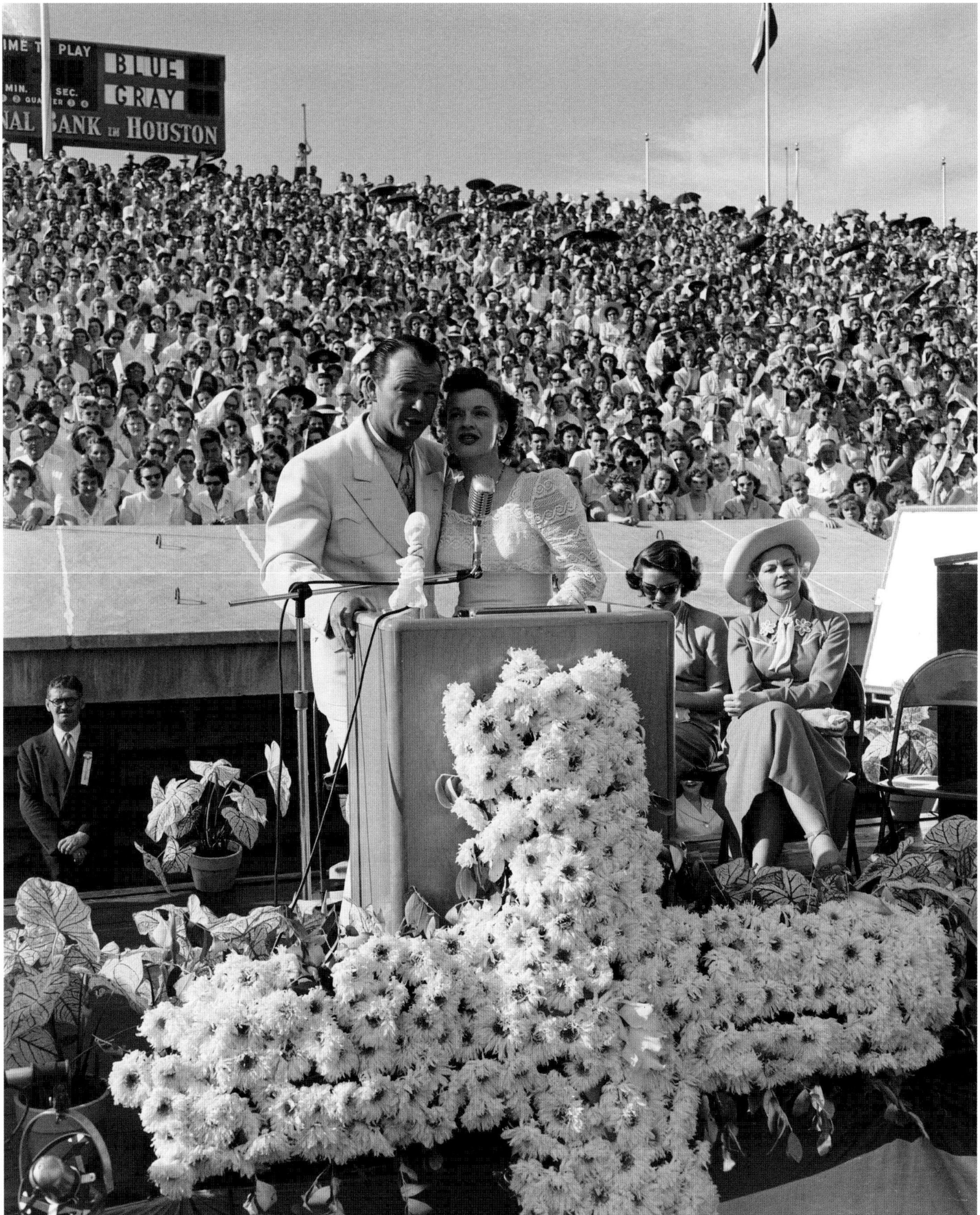

PLAY
BLUE
GRAY
MIN.
SEC.
BANK IN HOUSTON

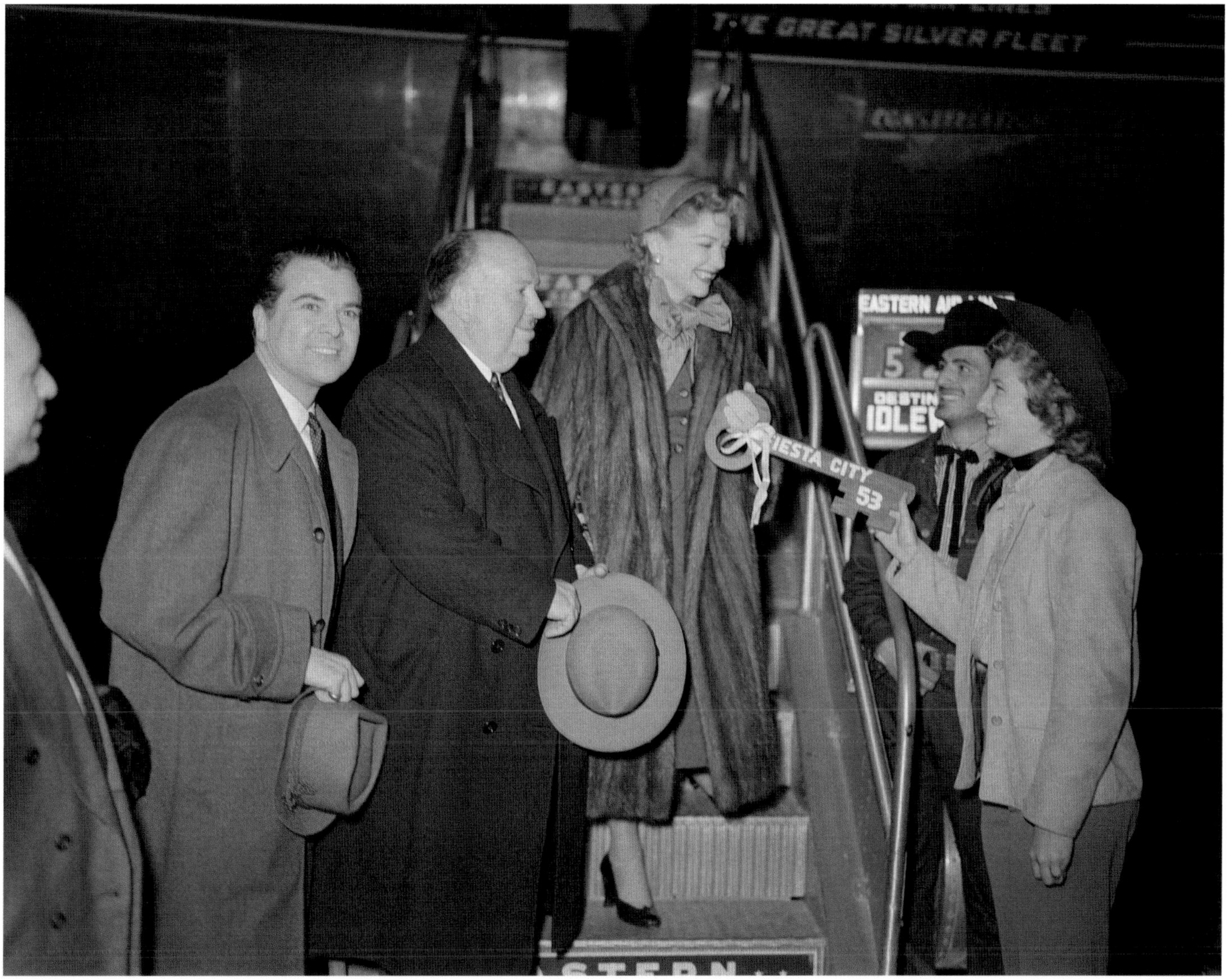

Facing: Roy Rogers and Dale Evans at a Billy Graham crusade held at Rice Stadium, in July 1952. The Rogerses often made personal appearances around the country in support of Christian evangelists and Christian causes. Some sixty thousand people turned out to hear Graham; the crusade was reported by the Rice Institute campus newspaper as being "the largest crowd ever to hear an evangelist."

Above: Actress Anne Baxter (on steps) and director Alfred Hitchcock received the key to the city on their arrival in Houston to promote what is today one of Hitchcock's least-known films, *I Confess* (1953).

126 *Houston skyline looking across Buffalo Bayou*: Lardas, *The Port of Houston*, 25–50.

133 *Aerial view of the Houston Ship Channel's Turning Basin*: Ibid., 39–64.

134 *View of the newly constructed Texas National Bank Building:* Fox, *Houston Architectural Guide*, 320.

136 *The Gulf Building at night, ca. 1956*: *Gulf Building Vertical File*, Houston Metropolitan Research Center; "Gulf Building," Houston Deco, accessed August 16, 2015, http://www.houstondeco.org/1920s/gulf.html.

138 *Aerial view of Friedman's Gambling Casino*: "Jakie Freedman Mansion Casino," Houston Architecture Information Forum (HAIF), accessed June 13, 2015; "Jake 'Jackie' Friedman aka Freedman," *Texas Mafia: Galveston*, Brix Central, accessed September 18, 2015.

139 *Texas City Disaster*: Arrington et al. *We Were There*, iv–xi.

143 *the nearly completed Foley's Department Store*: *Foley's Department Store Vertical File*, Houston Metropolitan Research Center; Desmond Fernandez, "Downtown Houston Macy's Store Imploded," ABC–13 Eyewitness News, accessed September 5, 2015, http://abc13.com/archive/9257218/; Yang Wang, "Macy's Building Comes Down with a Bang," *Houston Chronicle*, September 22, 2013, accessed August 12, 2015, http://www.chron.com/news/houston-texas/houston/article/Macy-s-building-comes-down-with-a-bang-4834076.php?cmpid=htx.

144 *Foley's Department Store on opening day*: *Foley's Department Store Vertical File*, Houston Metropolitan Research Center.

148 *Foley's enormous, 105-foot-wide Vista Window: Foley's Department Store Vertical File*, Houston Metropolitan Research Center; Burr, *Gods Like Us*, 180.

149 *display at Foley's:* For the influence of Surrealism's theories on the display of mannequins, see Muir, *Lionel Feininger*, 38–40.

151 *This model of Houston in the year 2000*: *Foley's Department Store Vertical File*, Houston Metropolitan Research Center.

153 *Battlestein's Department Store: Battlestein's Department Store Vertical File*, Courtesy HMRC, Houston Public Library.

159 *Trans-Texas Airways*: Trans-Texas Airways, accessed January 29, 2016, http://transtexasairways.com/index.html.

160 *Houston's Municipal Airport*: *Hobby Airport Vertical File*, Houston Metropolitan Research Center

161 *KLM (Royal Dutch Airlines) window*: "Years of Consolidation, 1955–1960," Houston History, accessed June 13, 2015, http://02db39d.netsolhost.com/decades/history5n.htm.

162 *operating monorail system*: "Back When Houston Had a Monorail," Houston Architecture Forums, accessed January 5, 2015, http://www.houstonarchitecture.com/haif/topic/5333-back-when-houston-had-a-monorail/; Strom, *Houston Lost and Unbuilt*, 160–163; J. R. Gonzales, "When Monorail came to Houston," *Bayou City History* (blog), *Houston Chronical*, October 22, 2008, accessed January 8, 2015, http://blog.chron.com/bayoucityhistory/2008/10/when-monorail-came-to-houston/.

164 *Aerial view of the Gulf Freeway, ca. 1950*: *Gulf Freeway Vertical File*, Houston Metropolitan Research Center.

165 *the expansion of the Houston area's freeways*: "Auto Tag is Ticket to Vote," *Baytown Sun*, September 1, 1956, p. 4, columns 2–6.

170 *Houston suburban houses*: There is a large body of scholarship regarding the enormous expansion and simultaneous homogenization of post–World War II suburban America. Both Tony Hiss's *The Experience of Place* and Kenneth Jackson's *Crabgrass Frontier* provide good histories of the overall experience of suburbanization and its effects on both American society and the natural environment.

173 *Weber's Superior Root Beer*: Welling, *Cinema Houston*, 203–227.

177 *huge crowd that turned out at Buff Stadium*: Frank Jackson, "Now Batting for the Houston Cardinals, No. 6, Stan Musial?" *The Hardball Times*, accessed July 8, 2015, http://www.hardballtimes.com/main/article/now-batting-for-the-houston-cardinals-no.6-stan-musial/.

178 *impact of the post–World War II "baby boom"*: Burr, *Gods Like Us*, 180.

180 *These children were posed with livestock*: "History," Houston Livestock Show and Rodeo, accessed August 3, 2015, http://www.rodeohouston.com/AboutUs/WhoWeAre/History.aspx.

182 *Women's bowling team made up of Foley's employees*: *Foley's Department Store Vertical File*, Houston Metropolitan Research Center.

187 *Two young patients with visitors*: Wooten, *The Polio Years in Texas*, 65, 68–69, 86.

188 *Then US Senate majority leader Lyndon Johnson*: "About Us: History," Texas Children's Hospital, accessed August 1, 2015, http://www.texaschildrens.org/About-Us/History/.

191 *Roy Rogers riding Trigger*: Burr, *Gods Like Us*, 188.

193 *Roy Rogers and Dale Evans at Billy Graham crusade*: Himes, *The Sword of the Lord*, 228.

193 *Actress Anne Baxter*: "I Confess," Internet Movie Database, accessed August 2, 2015.

1960 TO 1991

CITY OF THE FUTURE

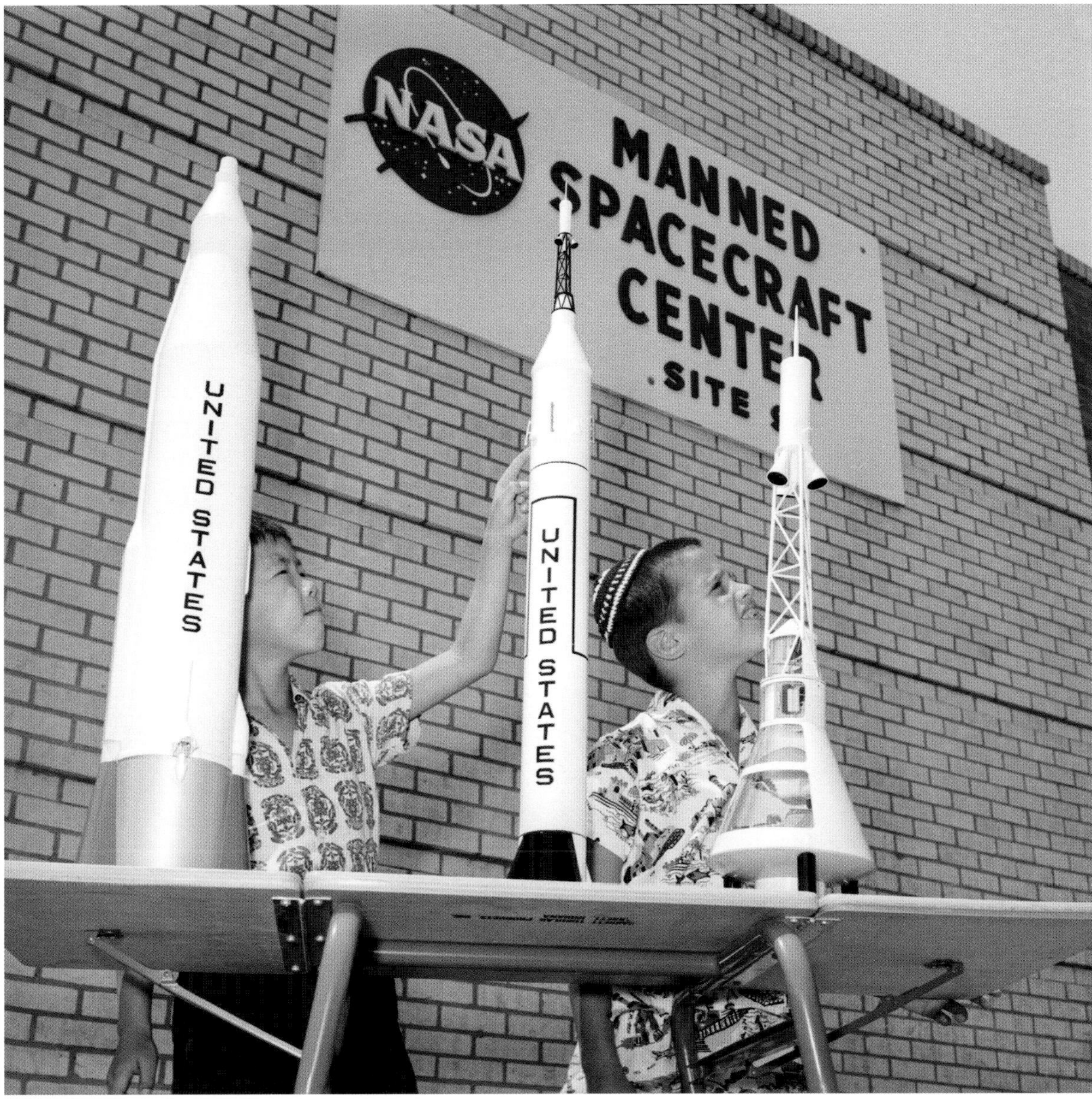

These children are inspecting early Mercury Program rocket and space capsule models at a NASA location in Houston in August 1962, prior to the completion of the Manned Spacecraft Center in Clear Lake, twenty-five miles southeast of Houston, in September 1963. In very little time, Houston came to be identified with the future and with spaceflight in the minds of many Americans, who heard American astronauts communicating with their Houston headquarters during televised spaceflights, beginning with the mission of Gemini IV in June 1964. While Houston had received national attention occasionally in its past, the establishment of the Manned Spacecraft Center was the first time in Houston's history that the city garnered international recognition.

Just two years before the Manned Spacecraft Center was completed, NASA administrator James Webb announced in September 1961 that Houston had been selected as the site for the operational command center of America's nascent manned spaceflight program. There was much grumbling by other out-of-state locations that had been reviewed during the selection process that Texas-born Vice President Lyndon B. Johnson, chairman of the National Aeronautics and Space Council, and US House representative Albert Thomas, another Texas native who served as chairman of the Independent Offices Subcommittee of the powerful House Appropriations Committee, might have exerted their enormous influence to obtain the NASA center for Houston.

NASA officials strenuously denied that any undue political influence was used during the site selection and always maintained that Houston was selected solely because the city and its surrounding area meshed so well with NASA's own site criteria. Following former President Johnson's death in January 1973, the center was renamed the Lyndon B. Johnson Space Center the following month.

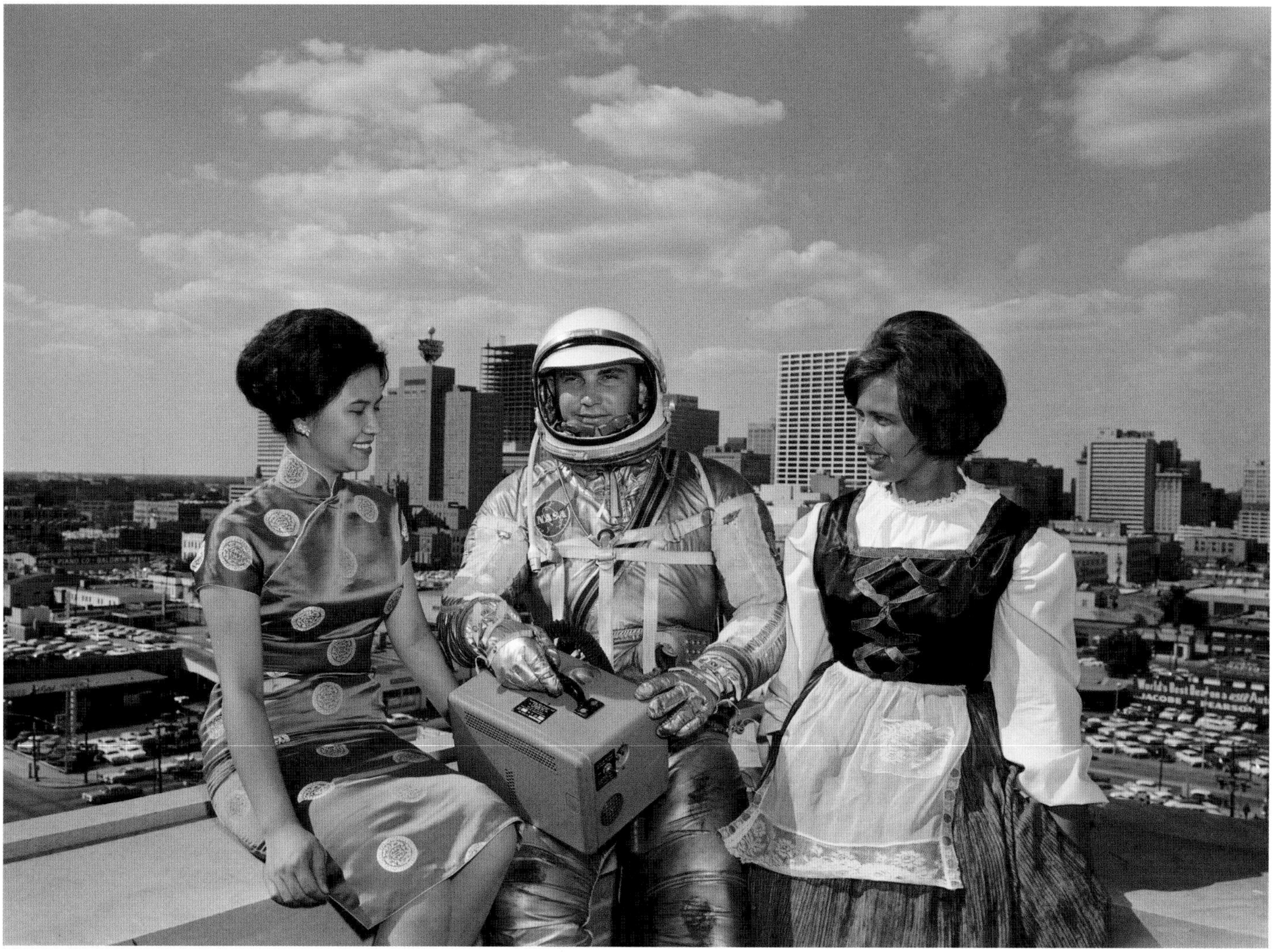

Male actor or model dressed as an astronaut, August 1962. The two women on either side of him represent Houston's international ties. The Space Age was new when this picture was taken, but Houston already had a very important role as NASA's official headquarters for manned spaceflight. Anything that could be even remotely space related was frequently used in local advertising.

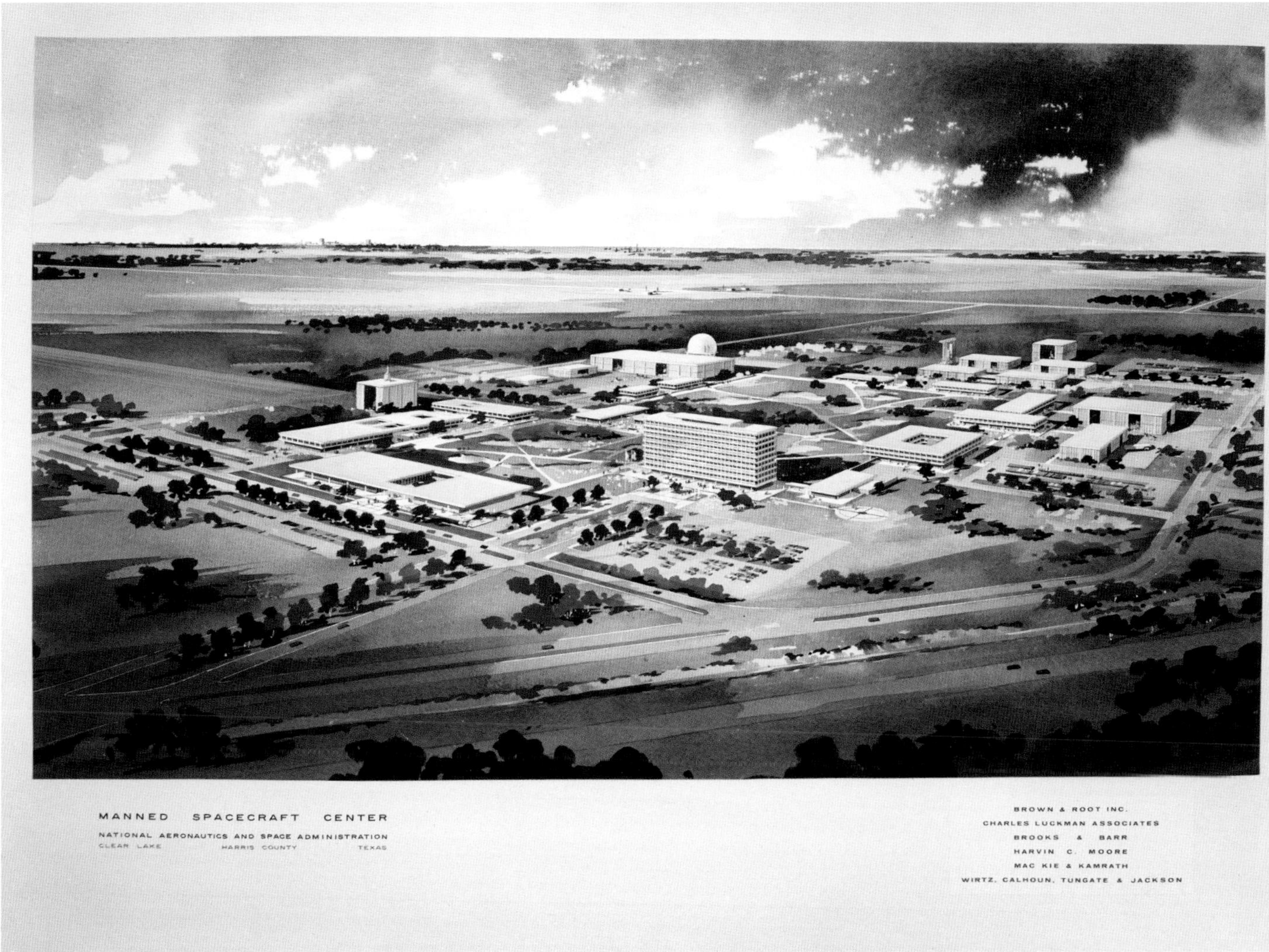

Architectural rendering of an aerial perspective view of the Manned Spacecraft Center. The drawing was photographed in January 1962 and is an example of the invaluable architectural records that are preserved in the Bailey collection.

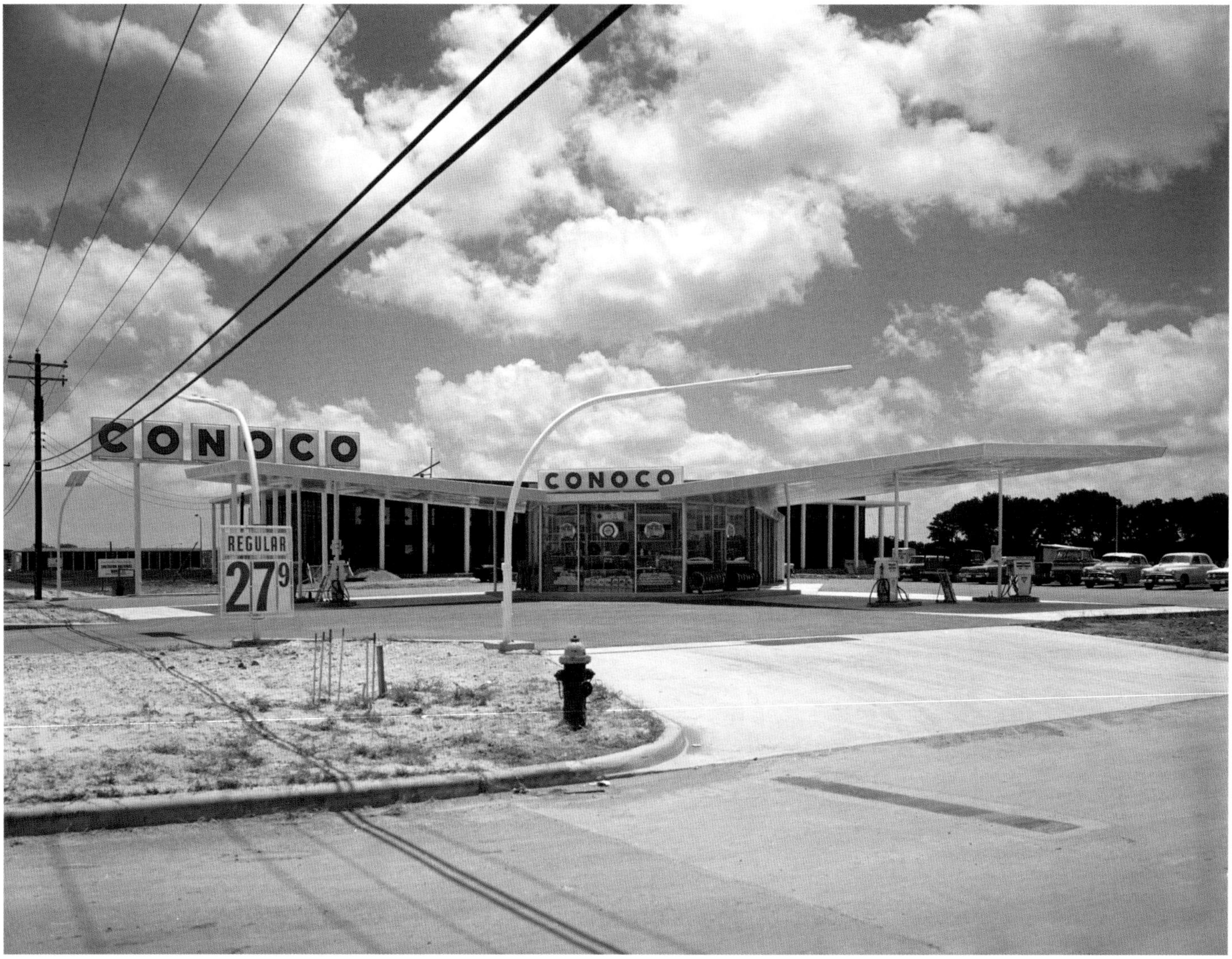

Houston's architecture was greatly affected by the city's affiliation with the Space Age. The swooping roof lines of this Clear Lake Conoco station, completed in 1964, were intended to evoke modernity and flight.

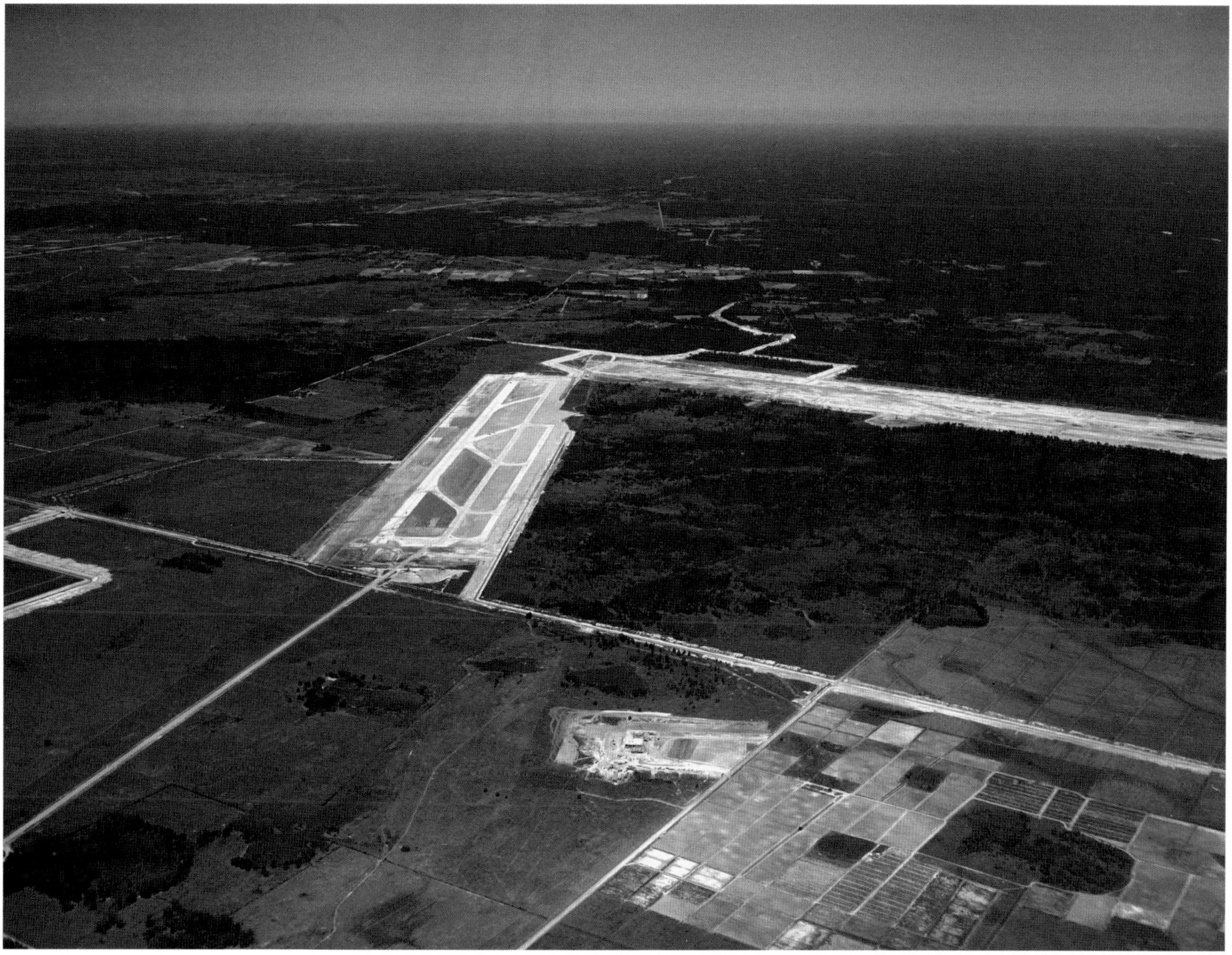

This view shows the construction progress of the Jetero Airport (today's George Bush Intercontinental Airport) in June 1964. The airport was completed in 1969. The name "Jetero" was meant to emphasize Houston's proud relationship with jet airplane travel.

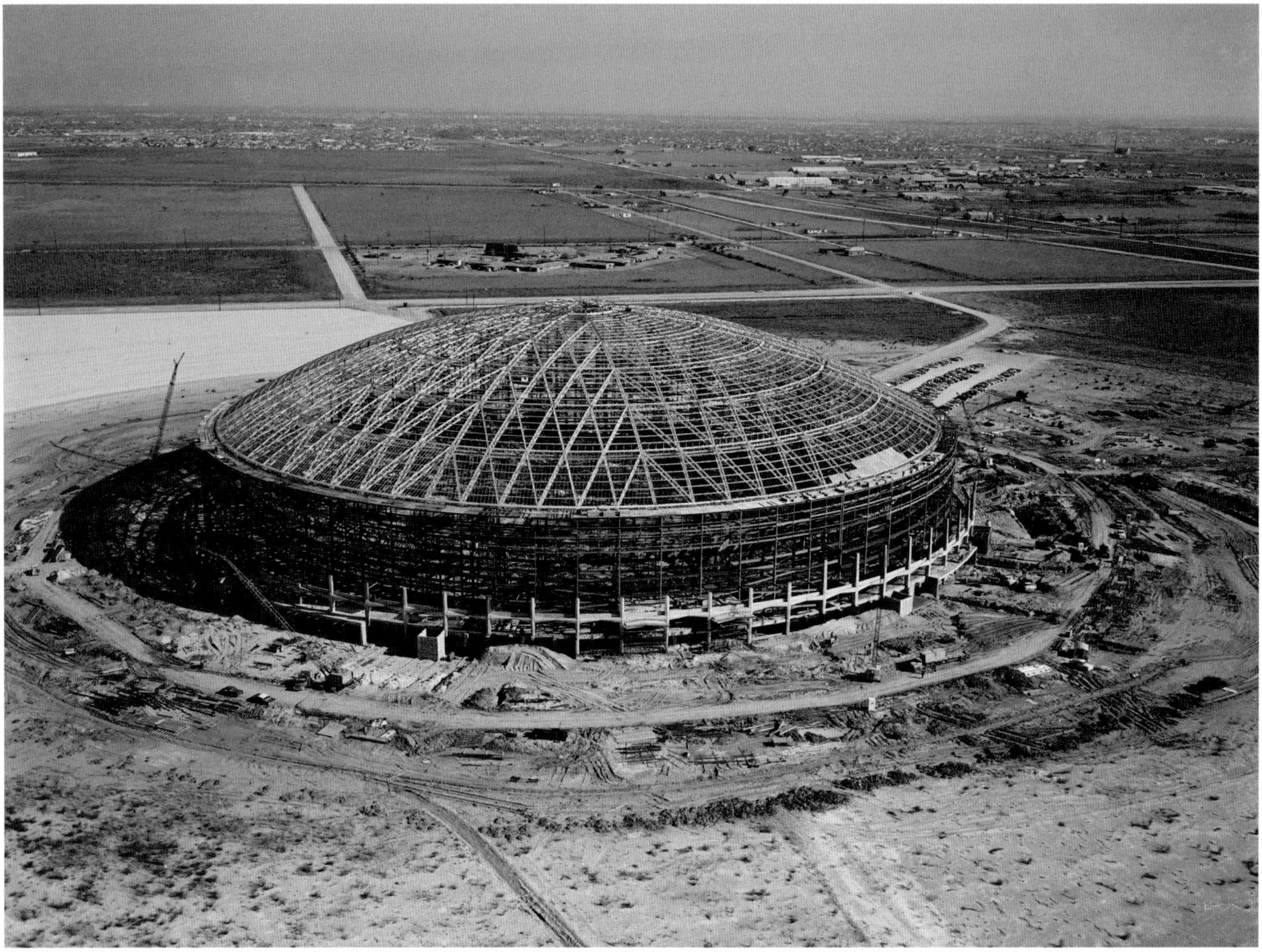

Aerial view of the Astrodome under construction, ca. 1964. The Harris County Domed Stadium, as it was formally known, opened in April 1965 and rapidly became one of the world's most recognizable structures. Despite the Astrodome's early reputation as the "Eighth Wonder of the World," in November 2013 Houston voters rejected a 213-million-dollar referendum to convert it into a state-of-the-art convention and exhibition center, and the stadium's future remains uncertain.

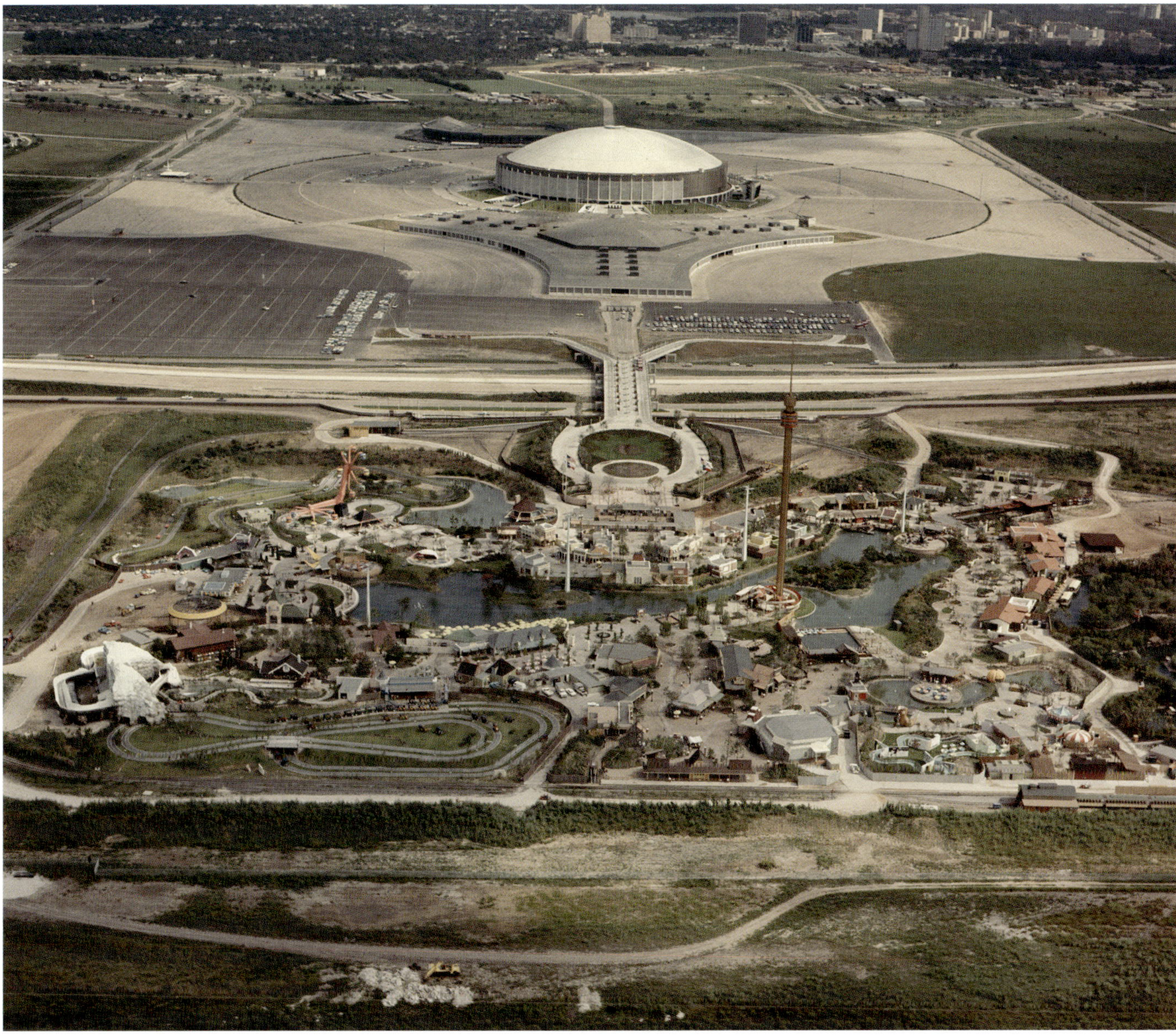

Aerial view of the Astrodome and the adjacent Astroworld amusement park in the foreground, ca. 1968. In keeping with the original space theme of the Astrodome, the entire complex was known as the Astrodomain. Astroworld opened in 1968 and remained in operation until October 30, 2005. Following its closure, it was demolished. Today, nothing remains of the once highly popular attraction.

Although the Astrodome is still extant, any current ideas for its use place the world-famous stadium in great danger of being either completely demolished or altered so much as to be almost unrecognizable. Along with the NASA headquarters, the world's first covered, completely air-conditioned sports stadium came to be identified with Houston in the early-to-mid 1960s, helping to cement the city's reputation as being on the cutting edge of technological and scientific innovation.

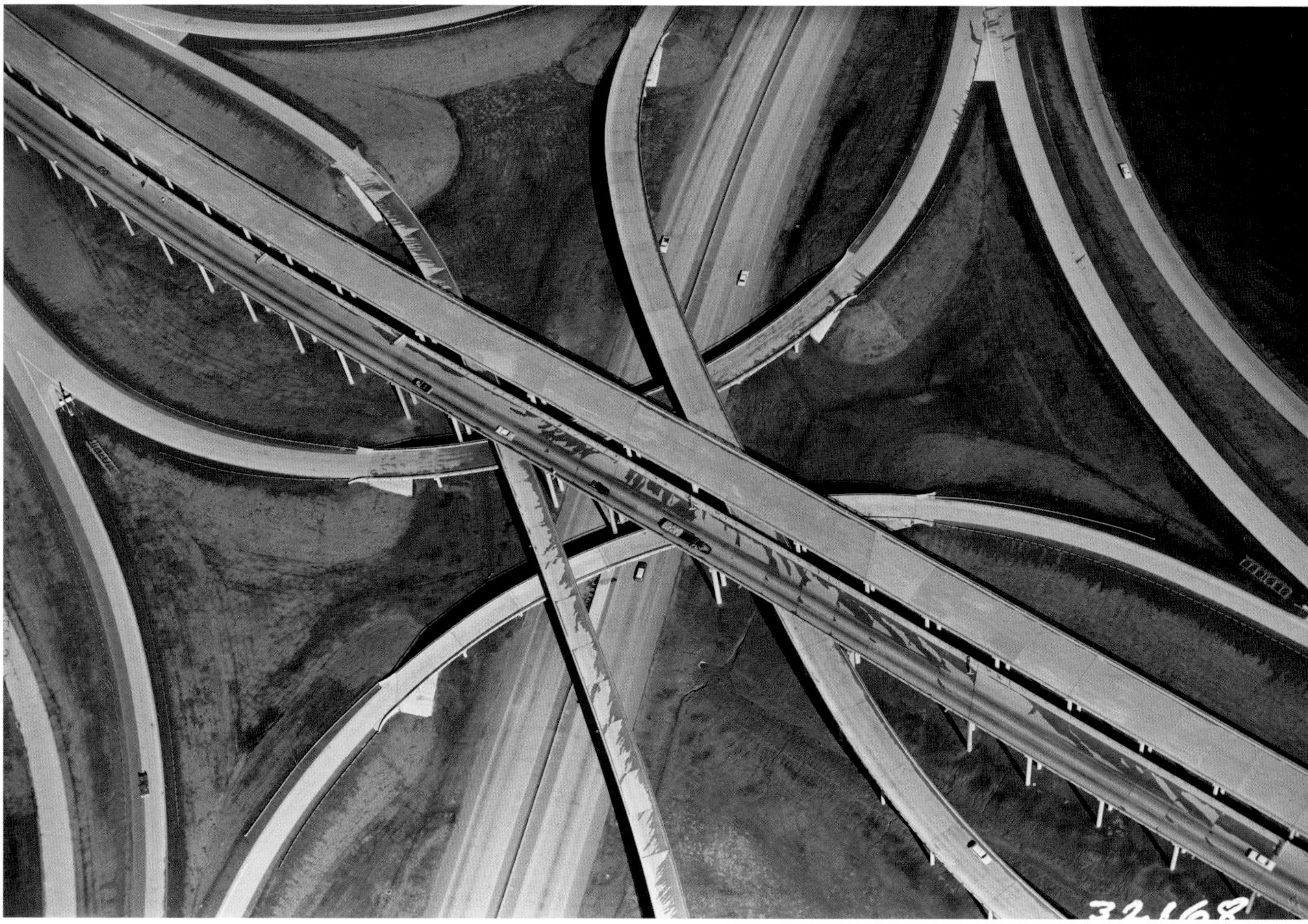

Above: A January 1963 aerial view of the intersection of Post Oak Road and the Southwest Freeway (US Highway 59). In postwar America, freeways were promoted as a tremendous improvement over the existing surface streets, which were often jammed with more cars than they were capable of handling efficiently. Bailey's photo celebrates highways and freeways, an attitude long adopted by many professional American photographers regarding the nation's industries and infrastructure.

Facing: In this publicity photo, Chevrolet was able to utilize a newly constructed freeway overpass to display its 1963 lineup of Corvair models, accompanied by their proud dealers and salesmen.

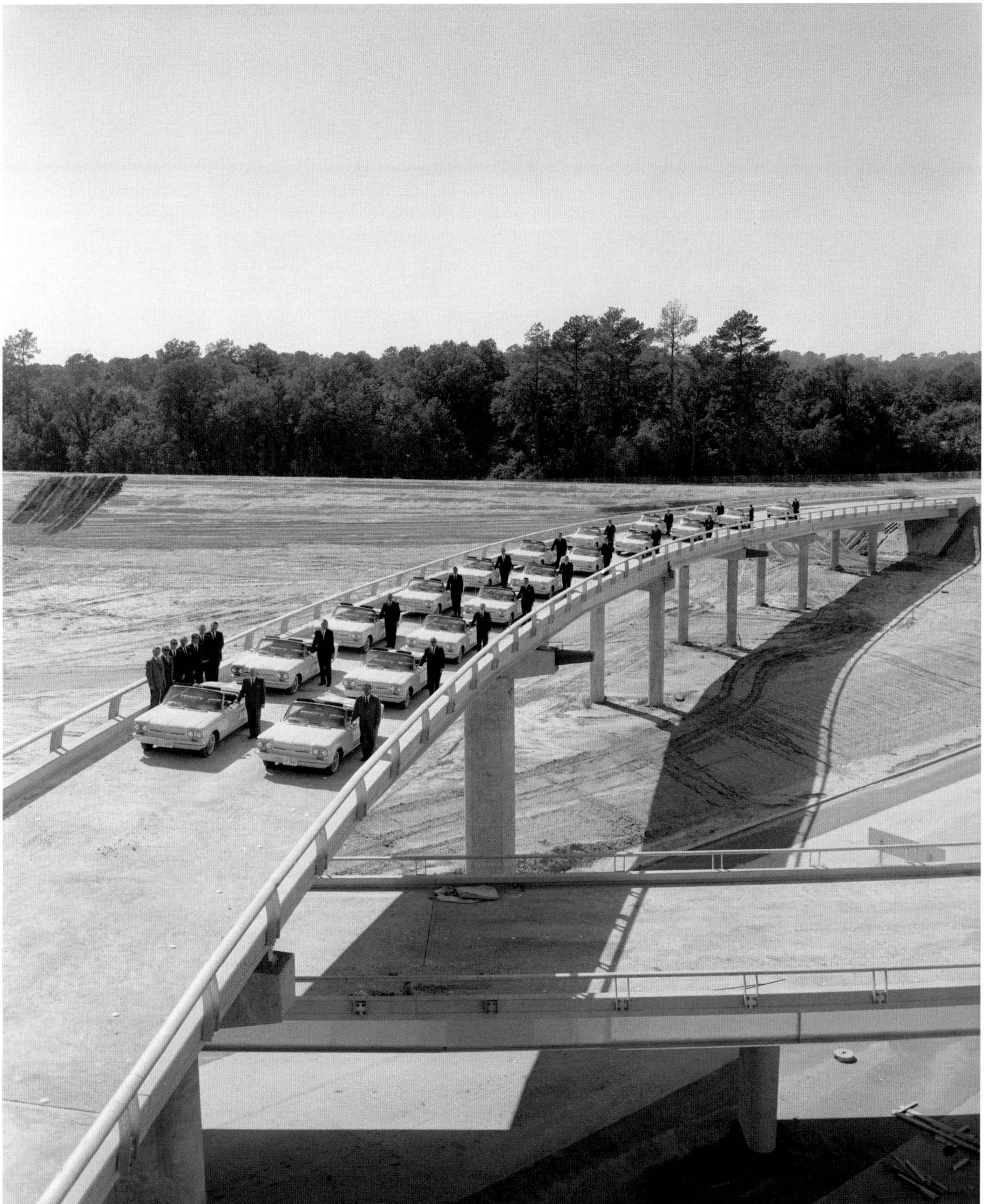

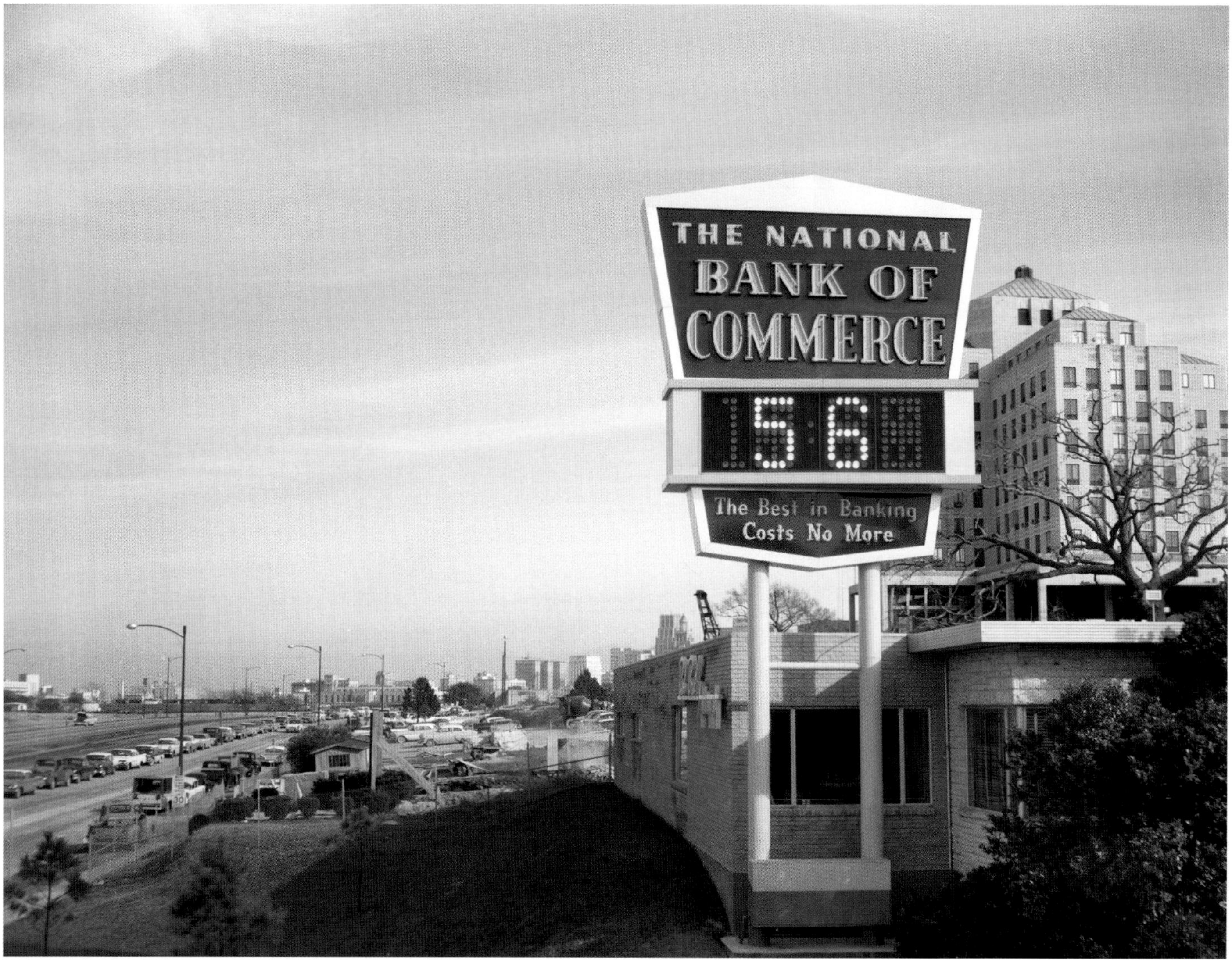

By the time this photo was taken in 1960, Houston was well known, if not notorious, for the great variety and large number of billboards and signs along its thoroughfares and highways. The National Bank of Commerce, like many other banks in Houston, employed a large, electric time and temperature sign for passing motorists. Allen Parkway can be seen to the left of the sign, and the now-demolished Jefferson Davis Hospital is in the right foreground.

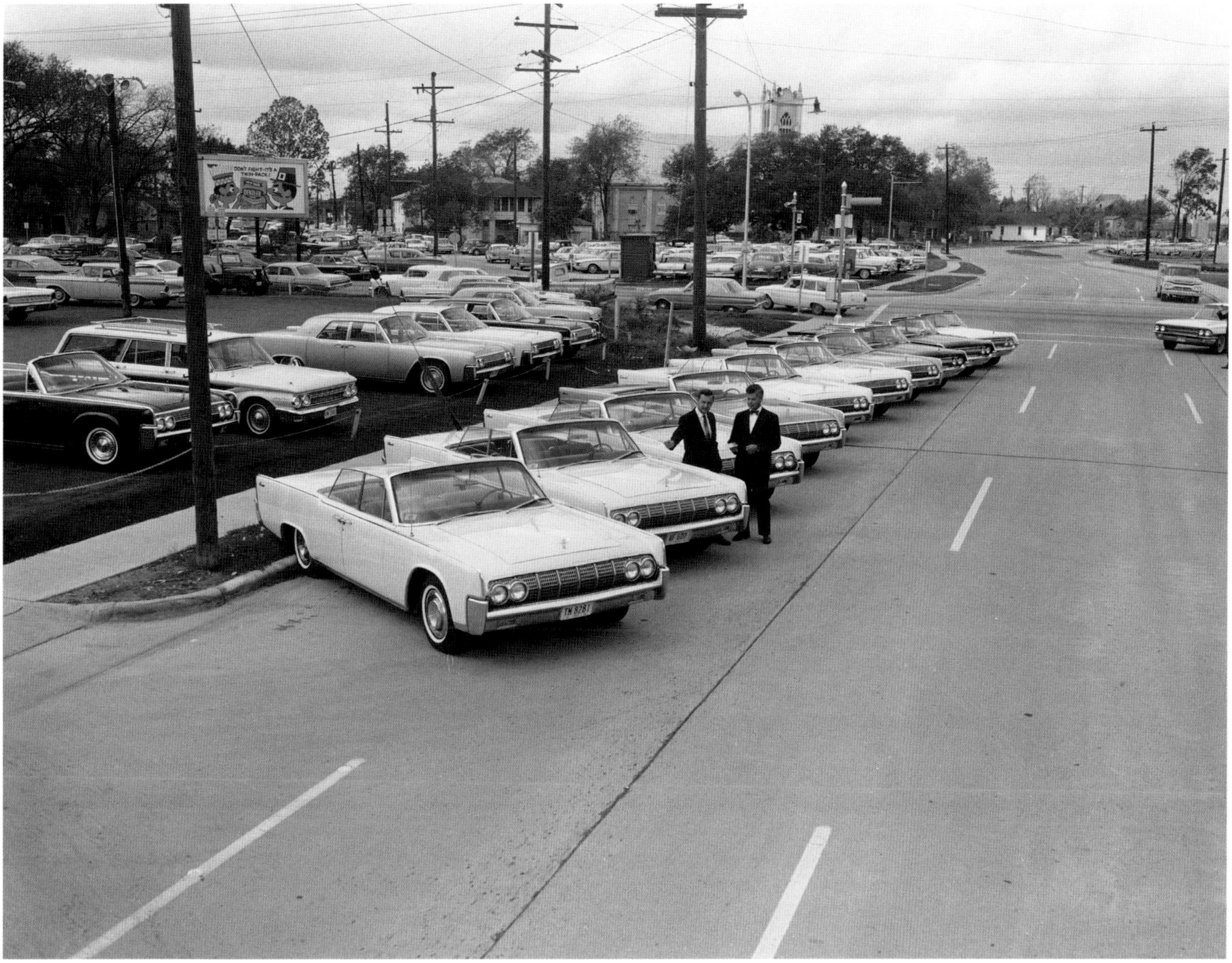

Cars to be used in President John F. Kennedy's motorcade, November 21, 1963, just one day before the president was assassinated in Dallas. President Kennedy arrived in Houston at the International Airport (now Hobby Airport) on the afternoon of November 21, after speaking in San Antonio earlier that day. The president's motorcade took him downtown to the Rice Hotel, and huge crowds turned out, both at the airport and along the route of the motorcade, in hopes of seeing the president, who was traveling with First Lady Jacqueline Kennedy; Vice President Johnson; and Johnson's wife, Lady Bird.

Later that evening, he attended a reception at the Rice Hotel for the League of United Latin American Citizens, where the first lady charmed the audience by addressing them in Spanish. Later that evening, he also made an appearance at a dinner held in the Sam Houston Coliseum in honor of Houston congressman Albert Thomas. The president left Houston that same evening for Fort Worth, where he spent his last night.

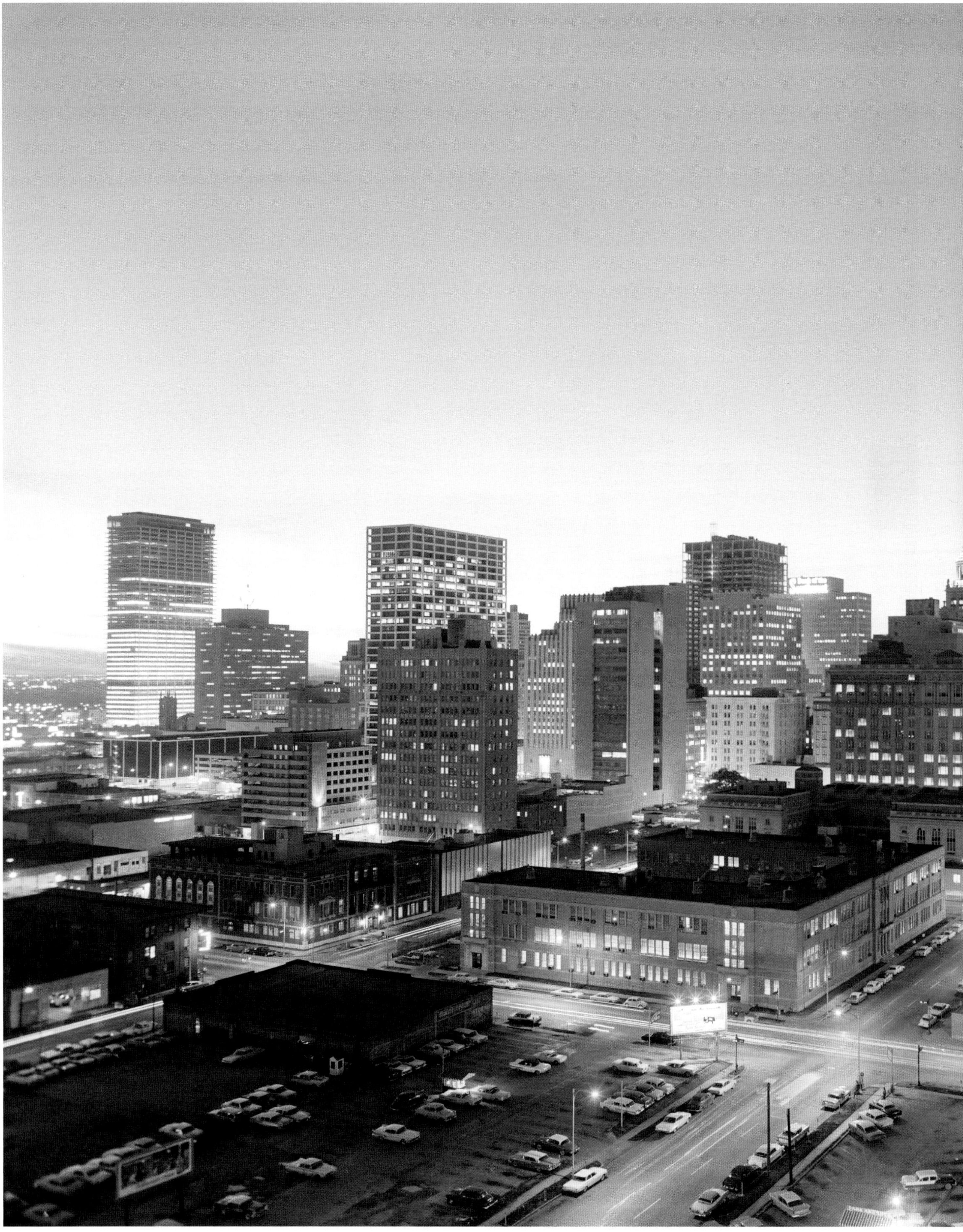

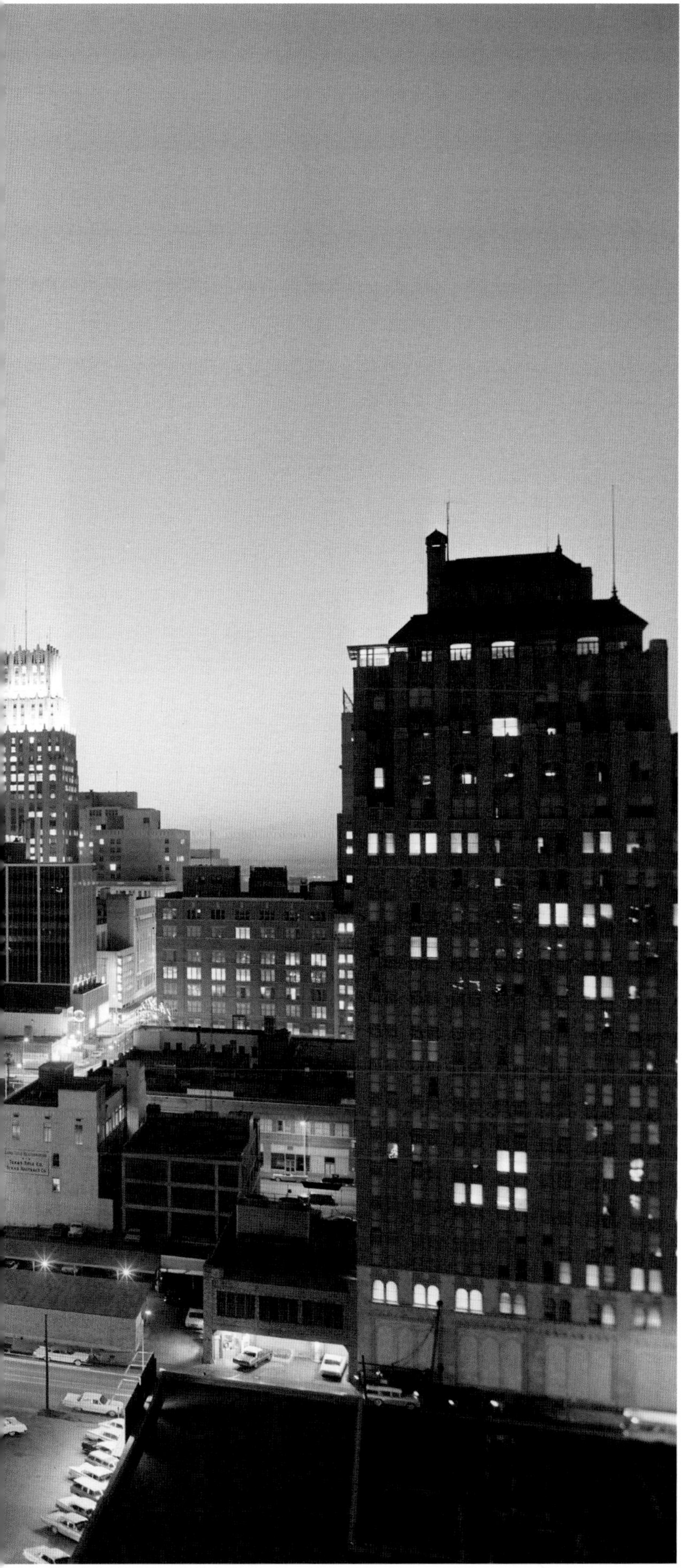

Houston's downtown skyline in early evening viewed from the World Trade Building on the east side of downtown, taken in September 1963. The World Trade Building was located at 1520 Texas Avenue.

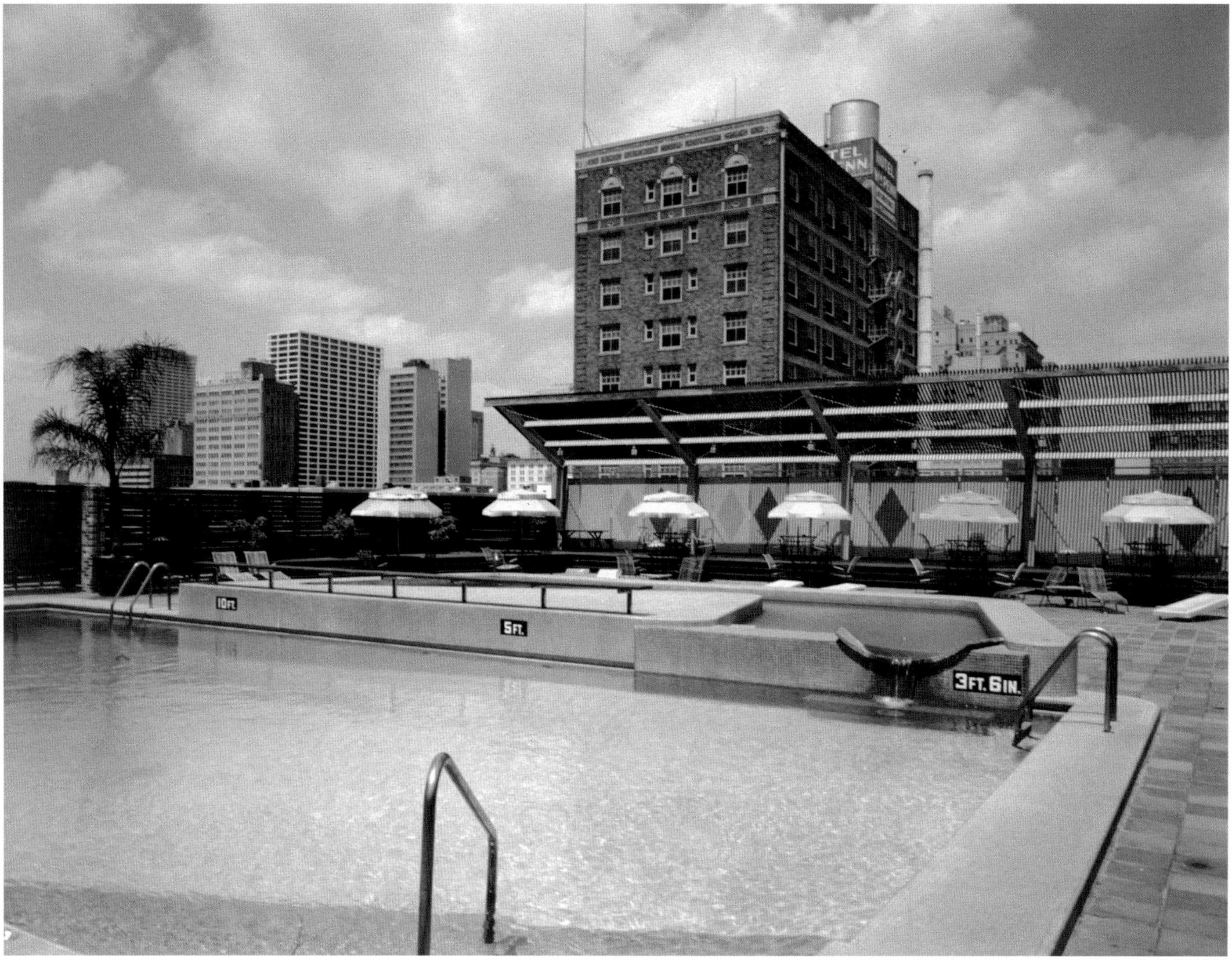

The Hotel Ben Milam's swimming pool, complete with potted palm, taken in January 1963. The Ben Milam had one of the few rooftop pools in Houston, likely added by the hotel in an effort to compete with the amenities offered by other downtown and suburban hotels and motels. The hotel originally catered mostly to travelers arriving in Houston by train; such travelers had all but disappeared by the mid-1950s, and hotels that once catered to rail passengers were forced to upgrade in order to compete for a different clientele.

This photo, together with many thousands of others, represents one of the great strengths of the Bailey collection: its vast documentation of Houston's lost architectural heritage. On December 9, 2012, the ten-story Hotel Ben Milam was imploded and totally razed to make way for a planned apartment complex. Like many other Houston buildings, the Ben Milam will now largely be known only through the images captured by Bob Bailey.

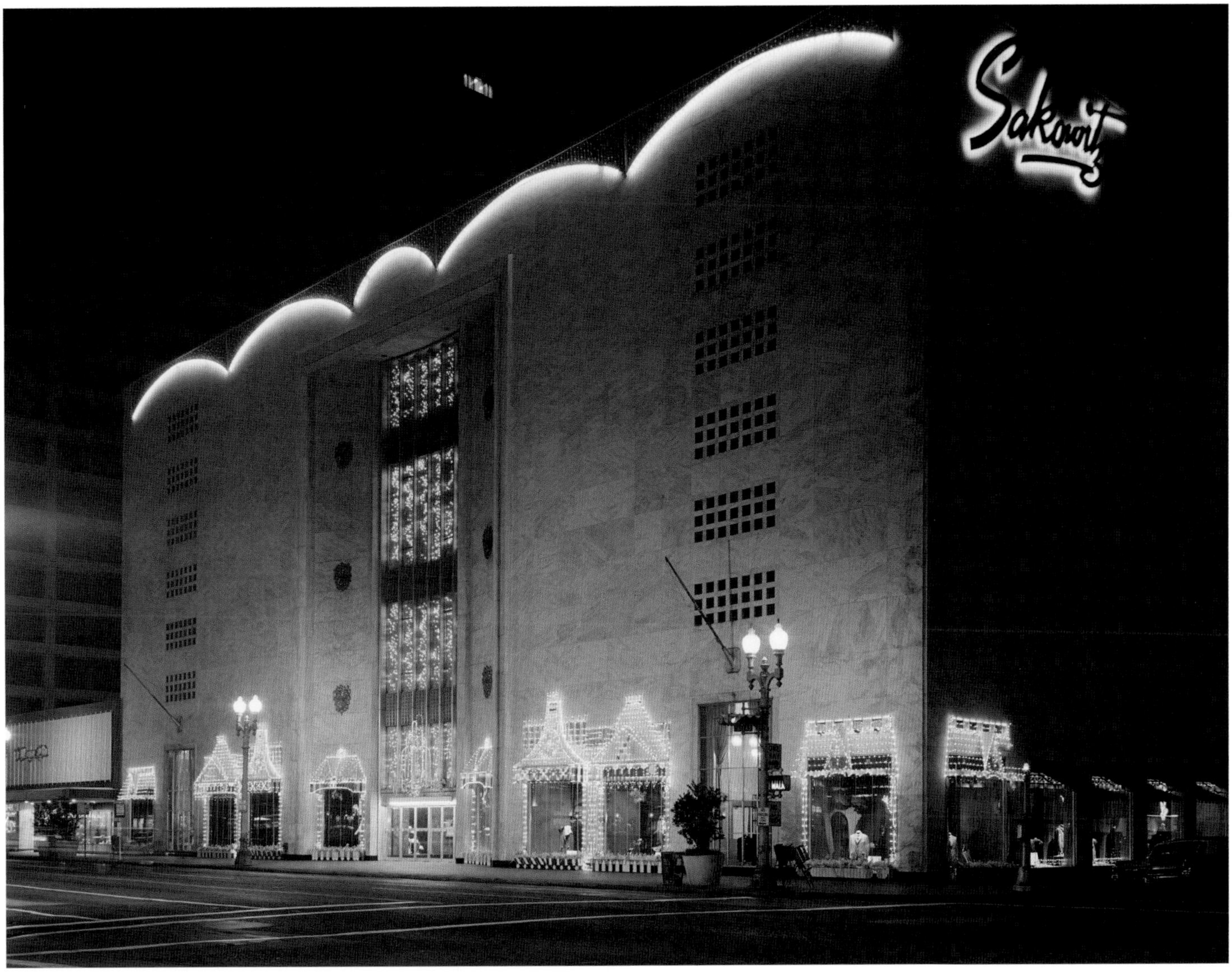

Sakowitz Brothers Department Store, 1111 Main, during the Christmas season, ca. 1966. Designed by Alfred Finn, the exterior was surfaced in white Vermont marble, and no details were spared with its interior design. In 1997, the interiors were gutted, and the once high-end department store was converted to a parking garage. The store was located directly across the street from Foley's.

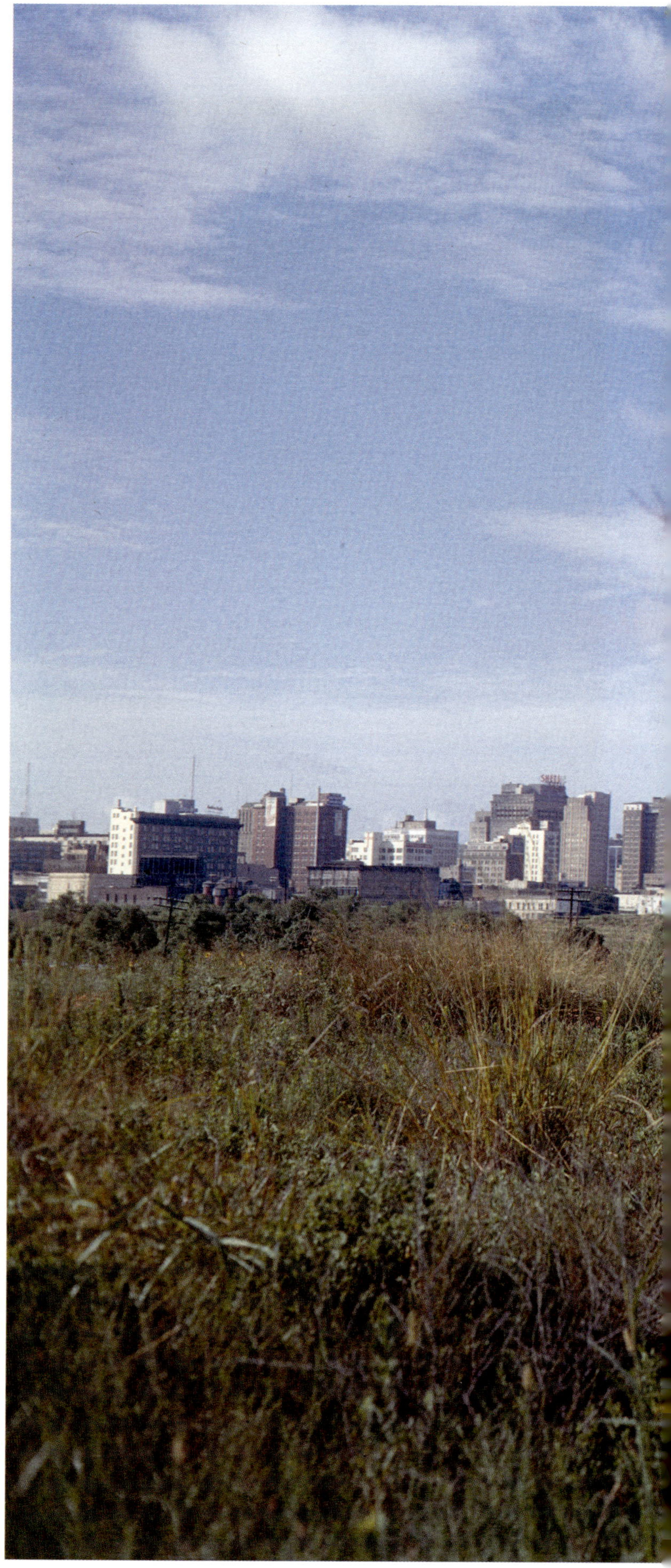

This image of Houston's skyline from August 1966 was taken for the Aylin Advertising Company from a now-rare vacant lot near downtown.

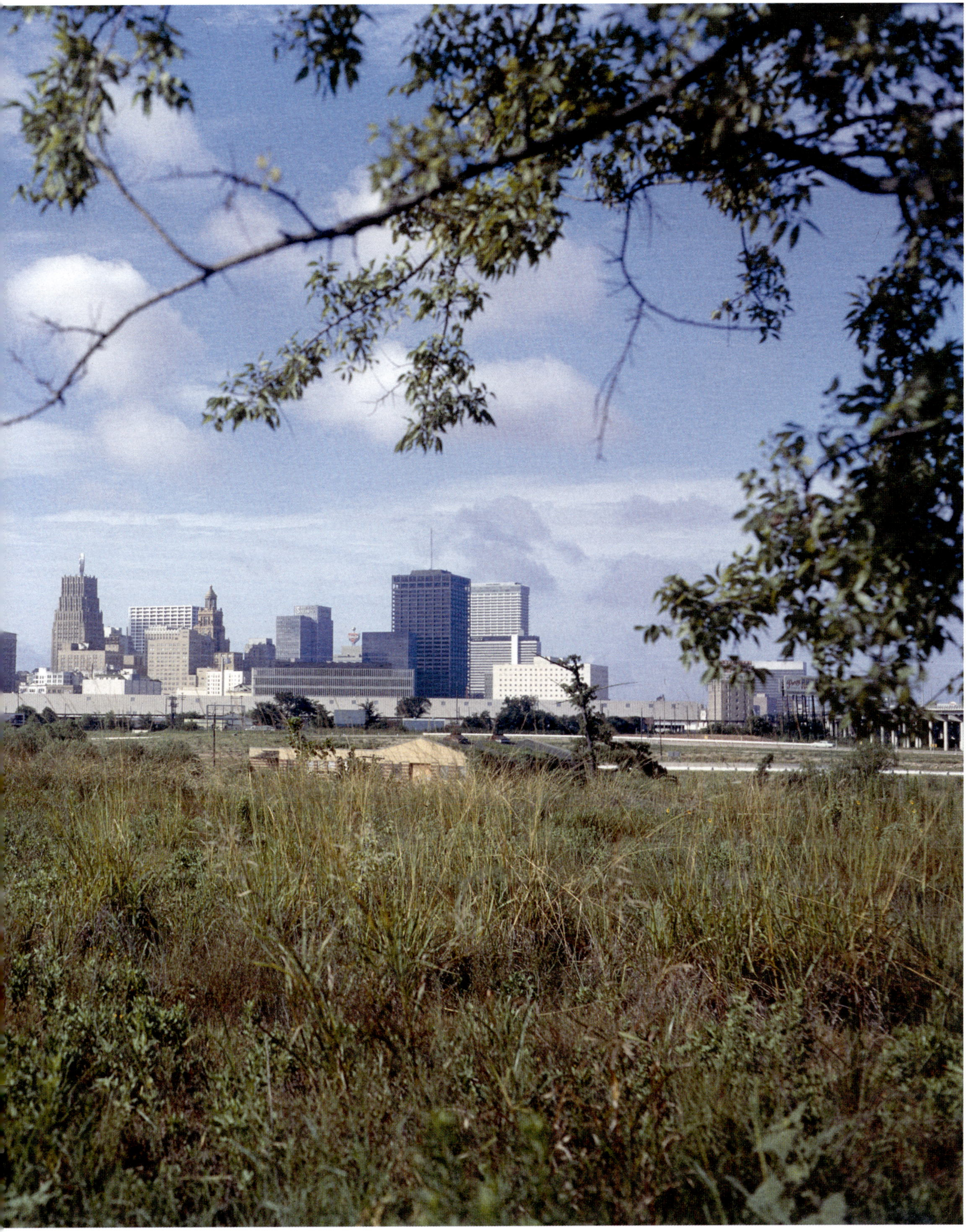

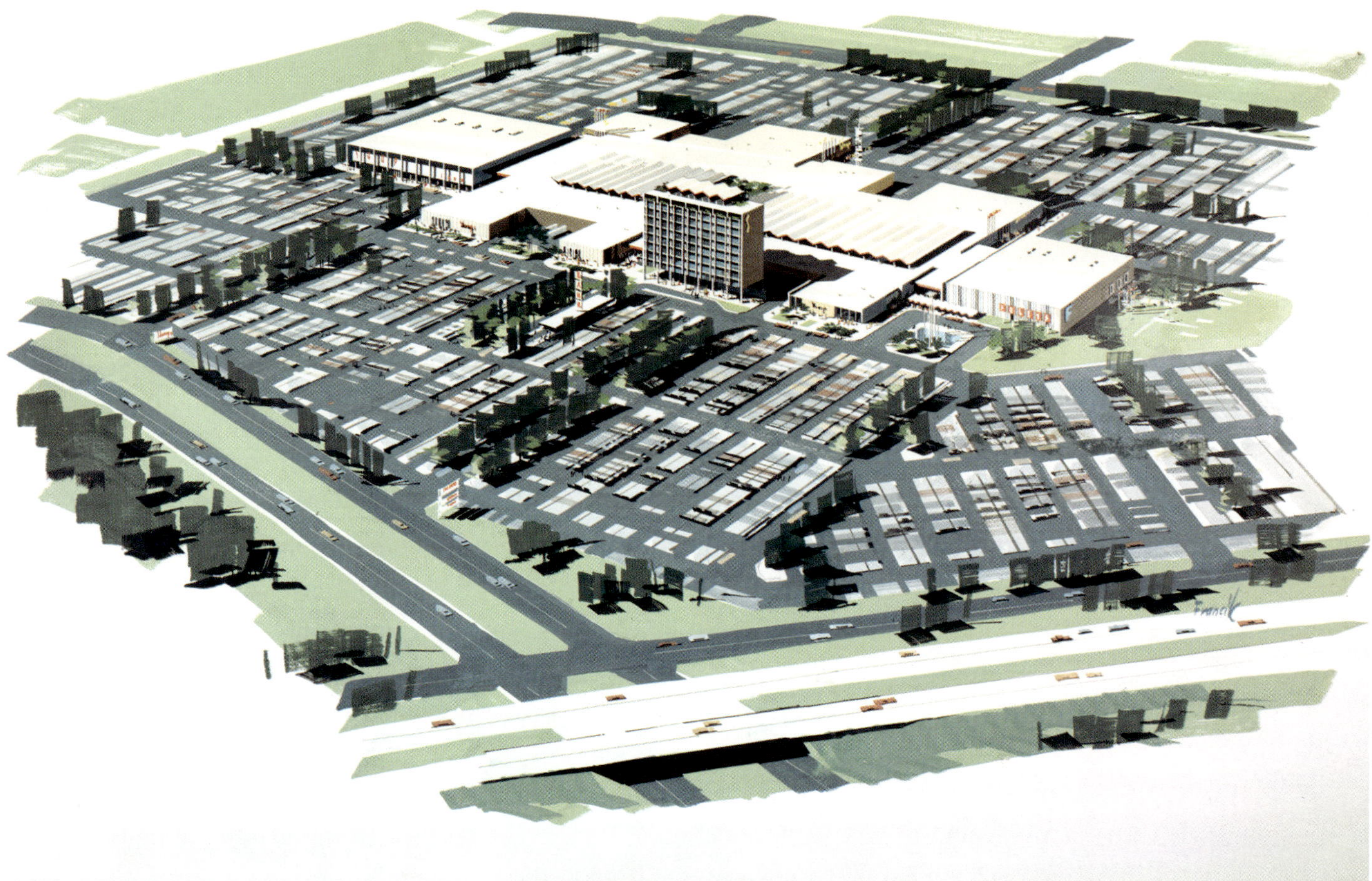

Architectural rendering of an aerial perspective of the Sharpstown Center, one of the first major commercial projects intended to draw both customers and potential residents to the new subdivision of Sharpstown, August 1961. At the time, the center was adjacent to much of Houston's suburban growth to the southwest of downtown.

The Bailey Studios photographed the architectural drawings of many Houston buildings in the days prior to easy copying services, and with many of these records lost or discarded during the years since, the Bailey collection sometimes represents the only known copies of original sets of drawings.

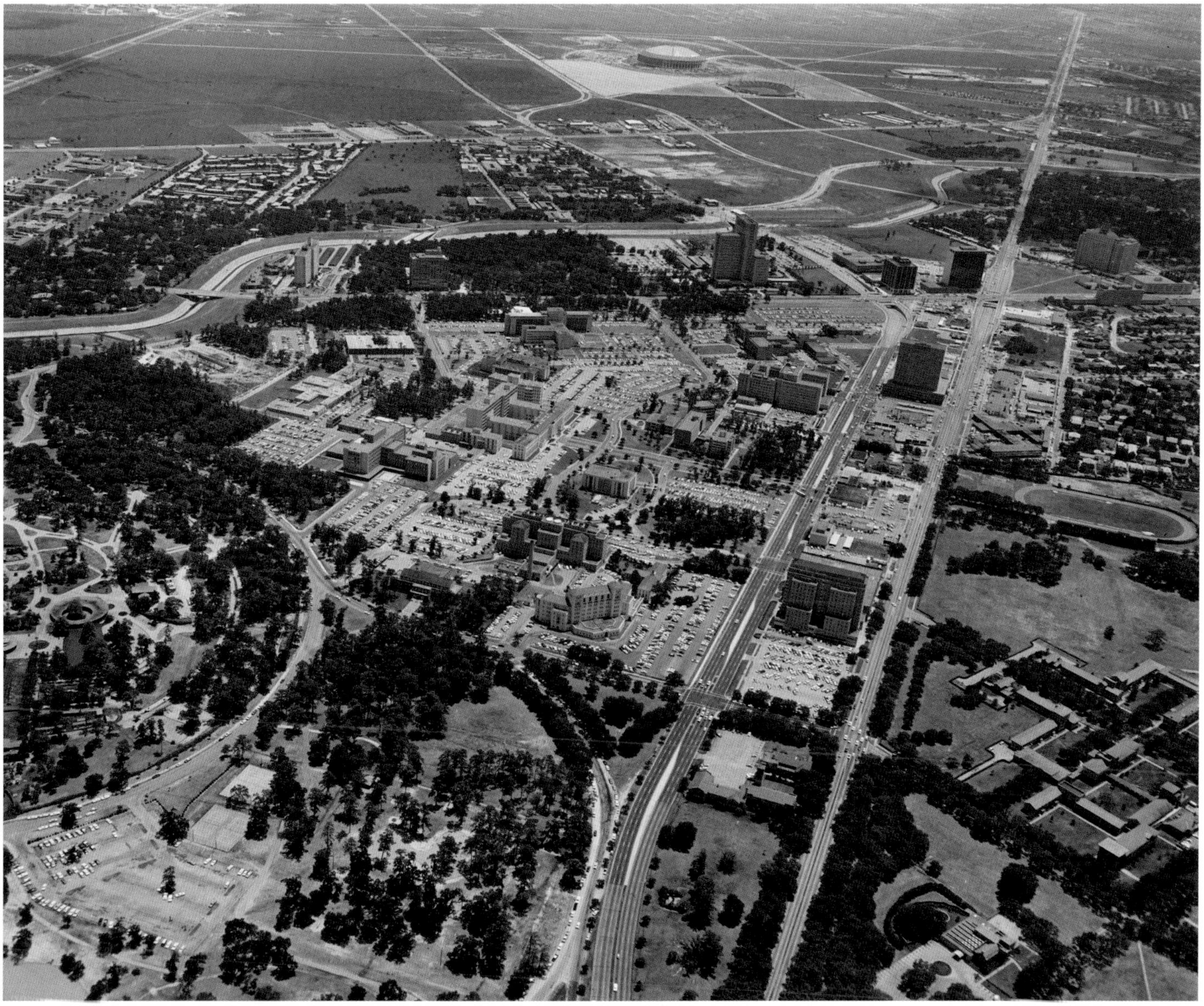

Houston's Texas Medical Center as it appeared in July 1964. The M. D. Anderson Foundation played a pivotal role in the creation of the Medical Center by sealing a partnership with the University of Texas for the center's oversight, which had been assigned by the state legislature. The foundation offered the university land for the center and matching funds, provided the Medical Center was established in Houston. Following the UT Regents' acceptance of the offer in August 1942, the center's first buildings were constructed on 134 acres of land that had formerly been part of Hermann Park, a deal that was approved by Houston voters. The Texas Medical Center was formally dedicated on February 26, 1948. By the time this photo was taken, the Texas Medical Center was already well on its way to being internationally known for its medical research, teaching, and breakthroughs in cancer treatment.

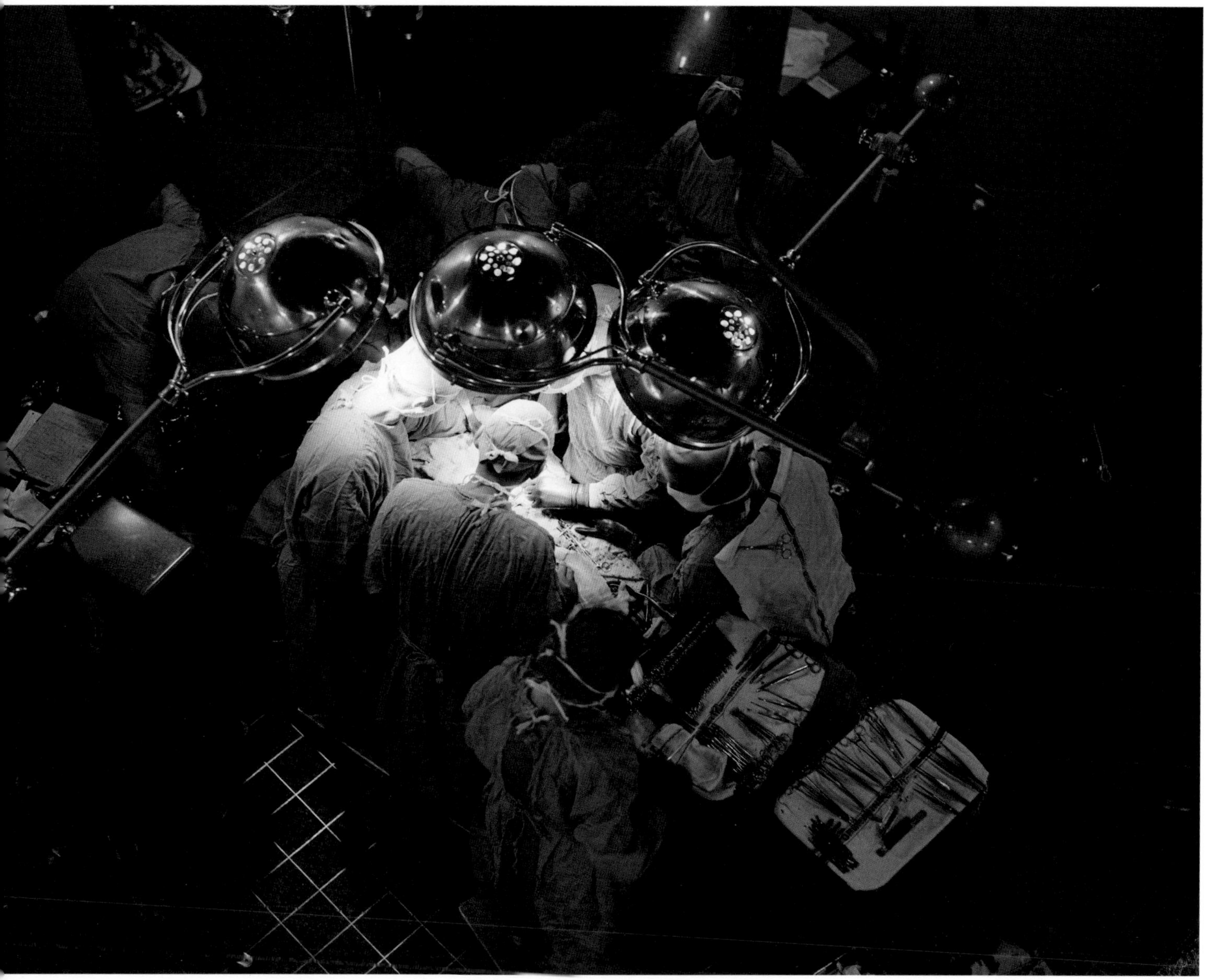

Doctors perform surgery at Hermann Hospital, ca. 1963. The medical breakthroughs made in the 1960s by Houston doctors added to the city's emerging image as a place where consistent advances were made in the fields of science and medicine.

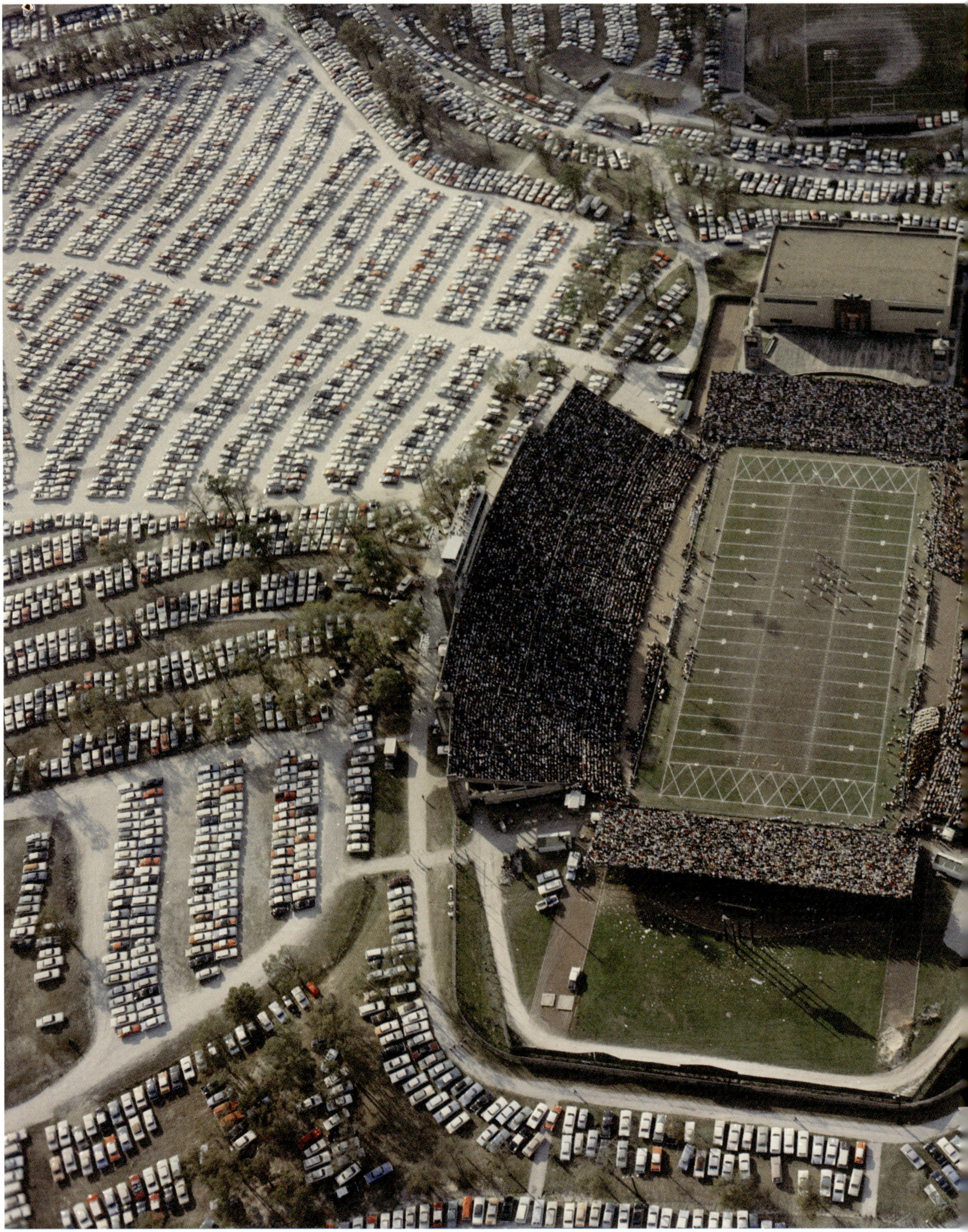

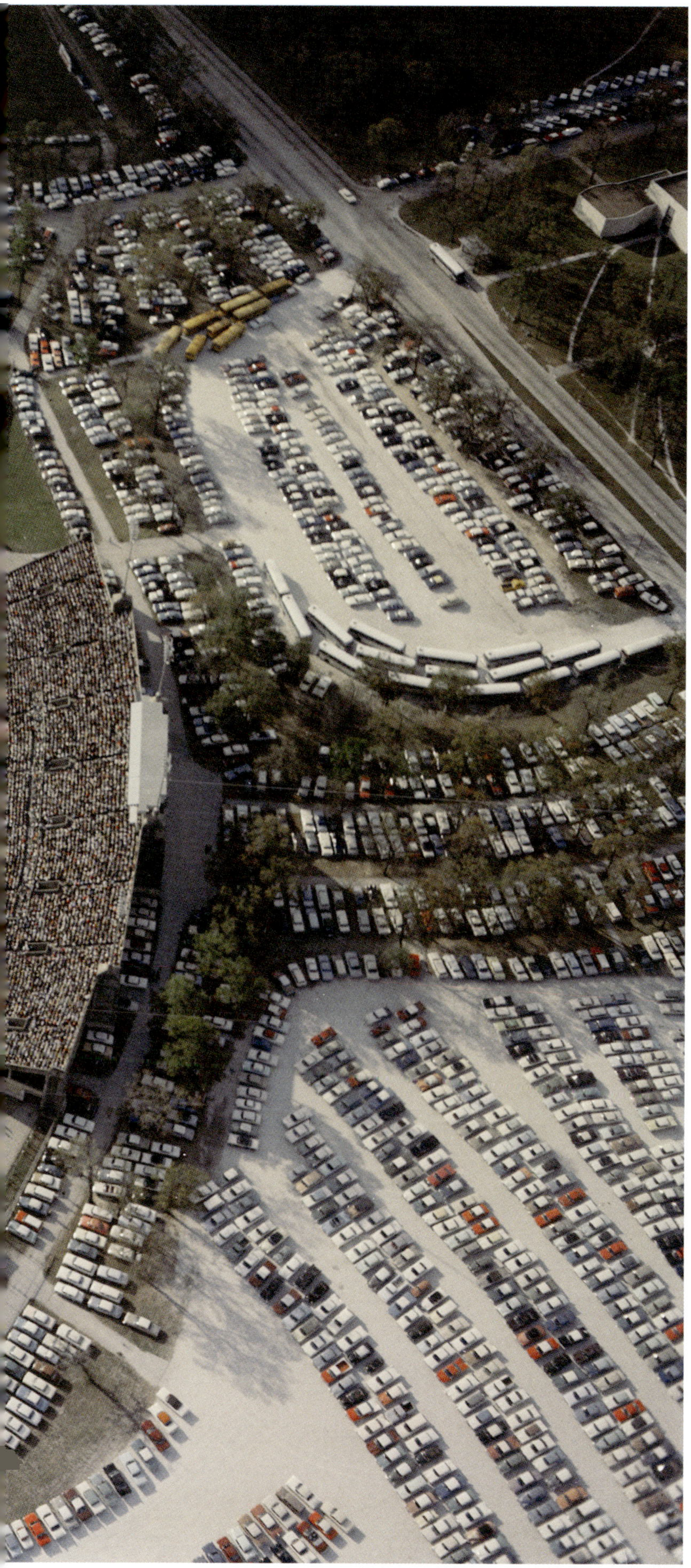

View of the Houston Oilers football team playing at the University of Houston's Jeppesen Stadium in December 1961. The image is dated December 14, so the game that was photographed was probably the December 3 match between the Oilers and the San Diego Chargers, the last home game of the 1961 season. The Oilers team was a charter member of the American Football League (AFL), which was founded in 1960, and won the AFL championships in both 1960 and 1961, although the team would never again win another national championship.

Oilers home games were played in Jeppesen Stadium from 1960 to 1964, when the team moved its games to Rice Stadium, where they played during the 1965–1967 seasons. The Oilers began playing at the Astrodome, the team's final Houston venue, at the start of the 1968 season. The Oilers relocated to Nashville, Tennessee, in 1997 and are today known as the Tennessee Titans.

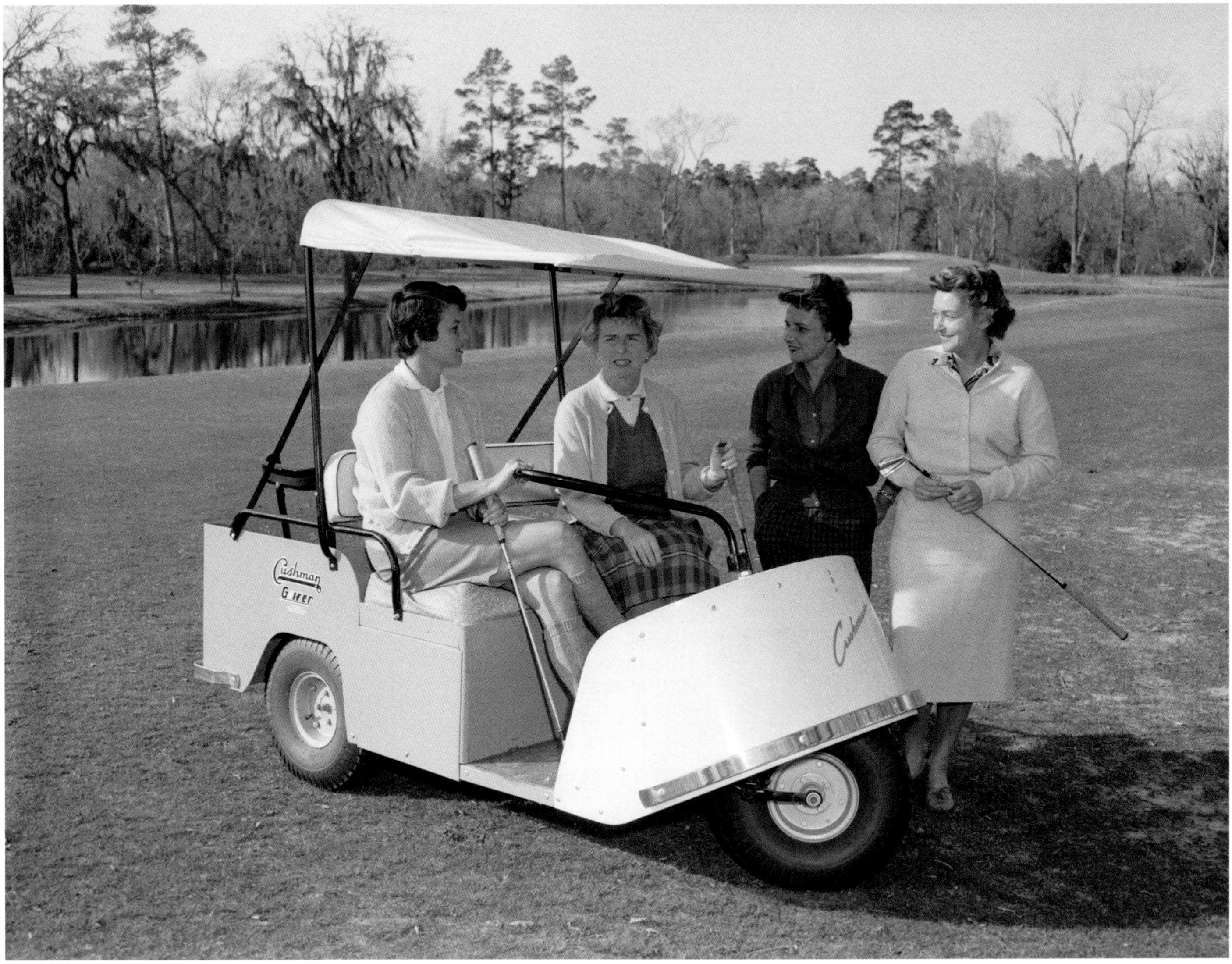

These golfers pose on the course for their portrait, possibly the Hermann Park Golf Course, in 1961.

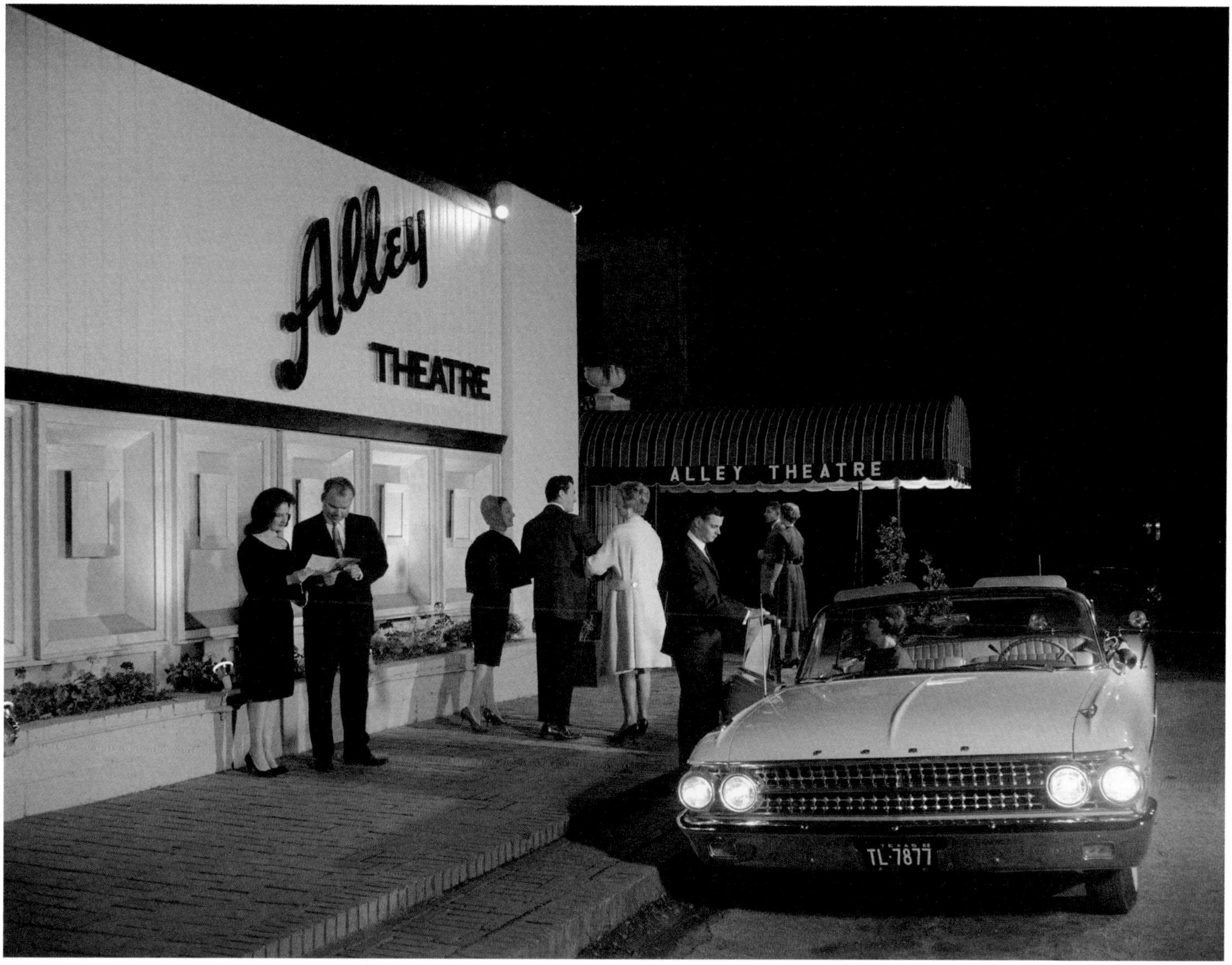

Theatergoers arrive at the Alley Theatre, ca. 1964. This former fan factory on Berry Street was acquired in 1948 as the theater's second home. Under the direction of its founder, Nina Vance, the Alley soon rose to national prominence and became one of the most important elements of Houston's cultural scene. The Alley relocated to its current location at 615 Texas Avenue in 1968.

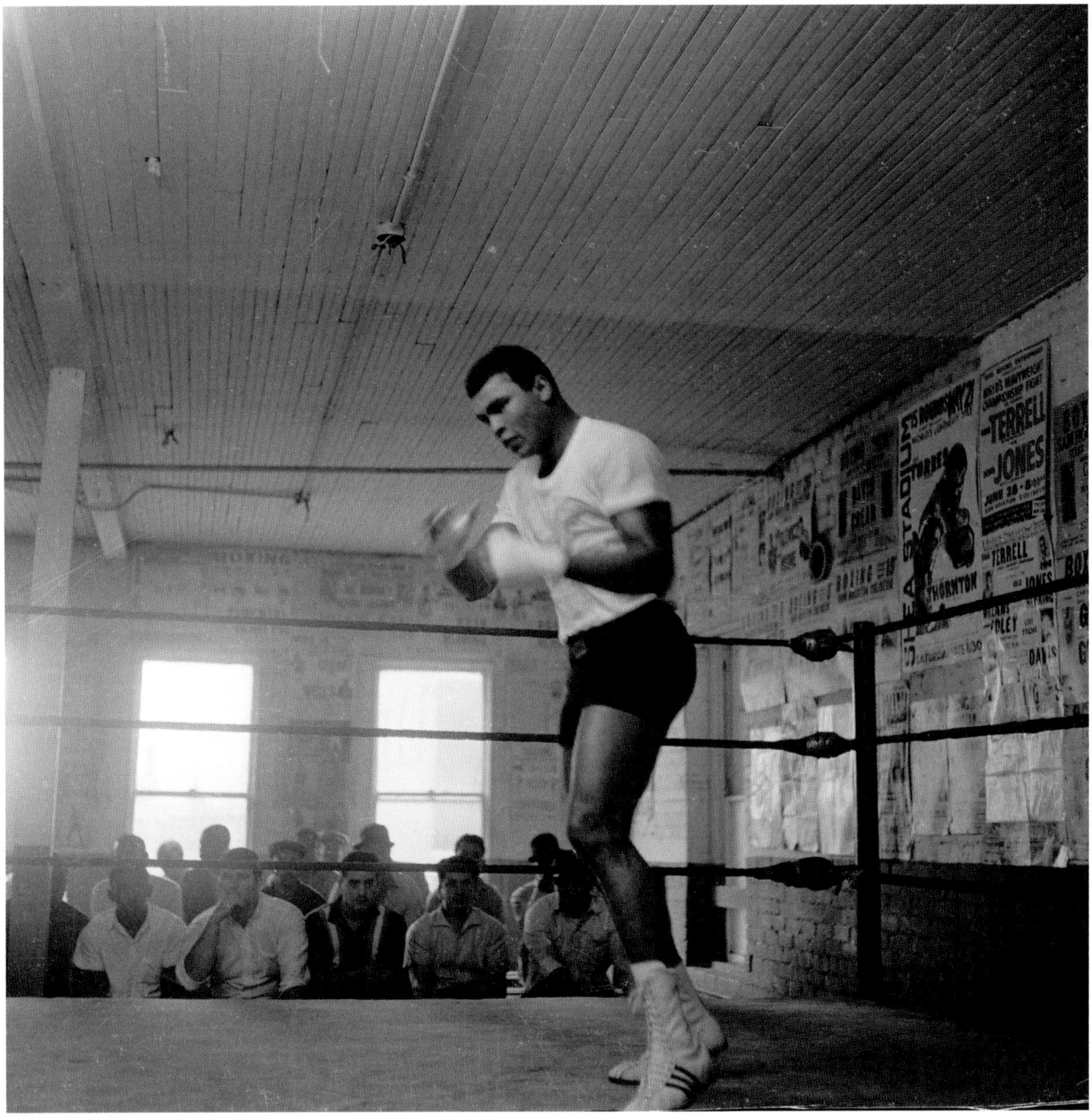

Muhammad Ali training in Houston in November 1966 for his upcoming heavyweight title bout with Cleveland Williams, which took place November 14, 1966, in the Astrodome. Ali won the match, which was stopped by the judges in the third round, retaining the World Heavyweight title. He would return to Houston again in April 1967, when he was arrested for refusing to be drafted into the US Army, asserting his right to conscientiously object to the Vietnam War. On June 20, 1967, Ali was unanimously convicted by a Houston jury of violating the US Selective Service laws, a conviction that was ultimately overturned by the US Supreme Court in 1971.

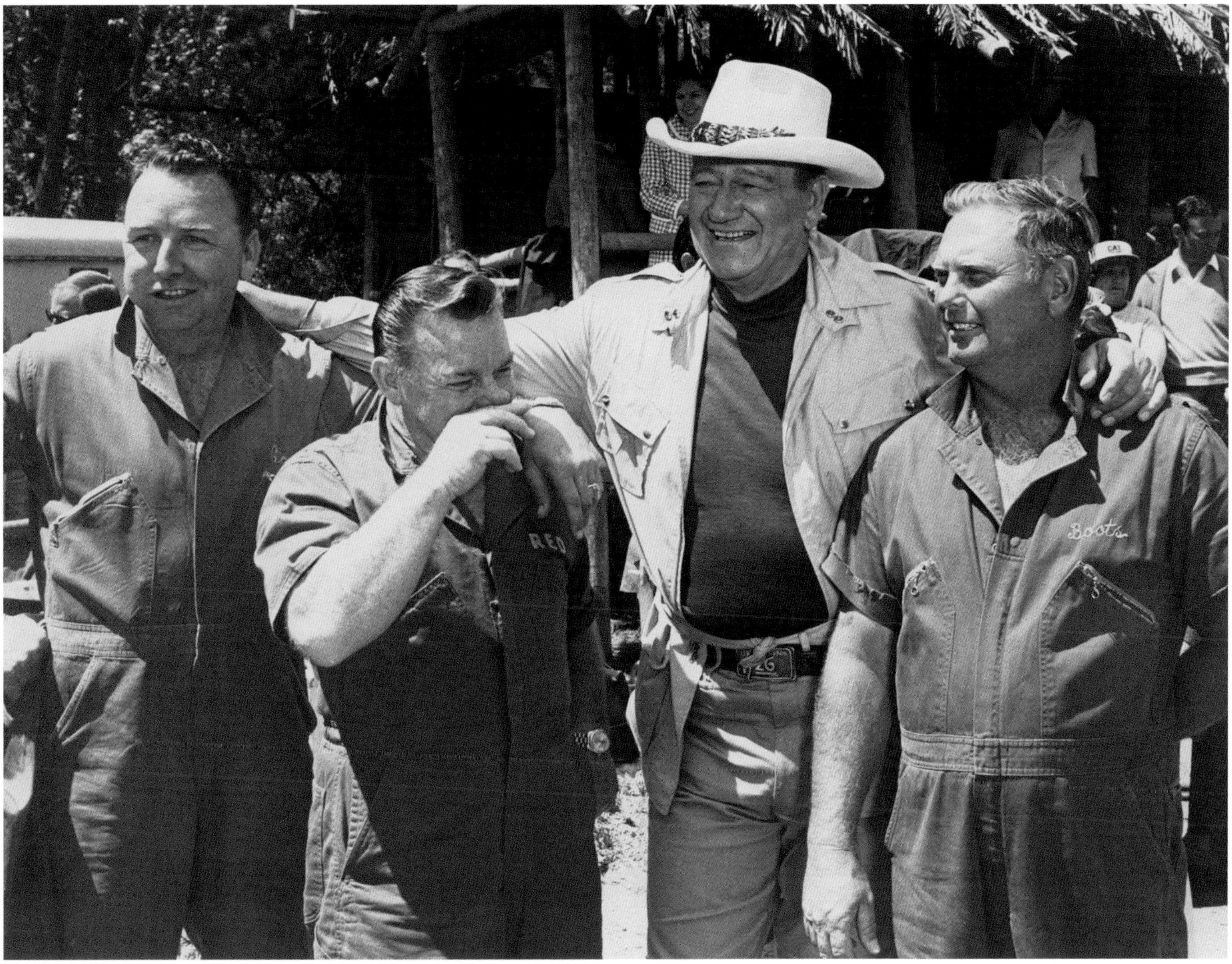

Actor John Wayne poses with world-famous oil well firefighter Red Adair (second from left) and two other firefighters, ca. 1968. Wayne, playing Adair, was filming *Hellfighters*, which was loosely based on Adair's successful extinguishing of an enormous Saharan gas field fire in 1962. That feat garnered Adair worldwide attention. The photo was probably taken before the film's completion and its American premiere on November 27, 1968. Adair was a native Houstonian, and portions of the movie were filmed in Baytown, Conroe, and Houston.

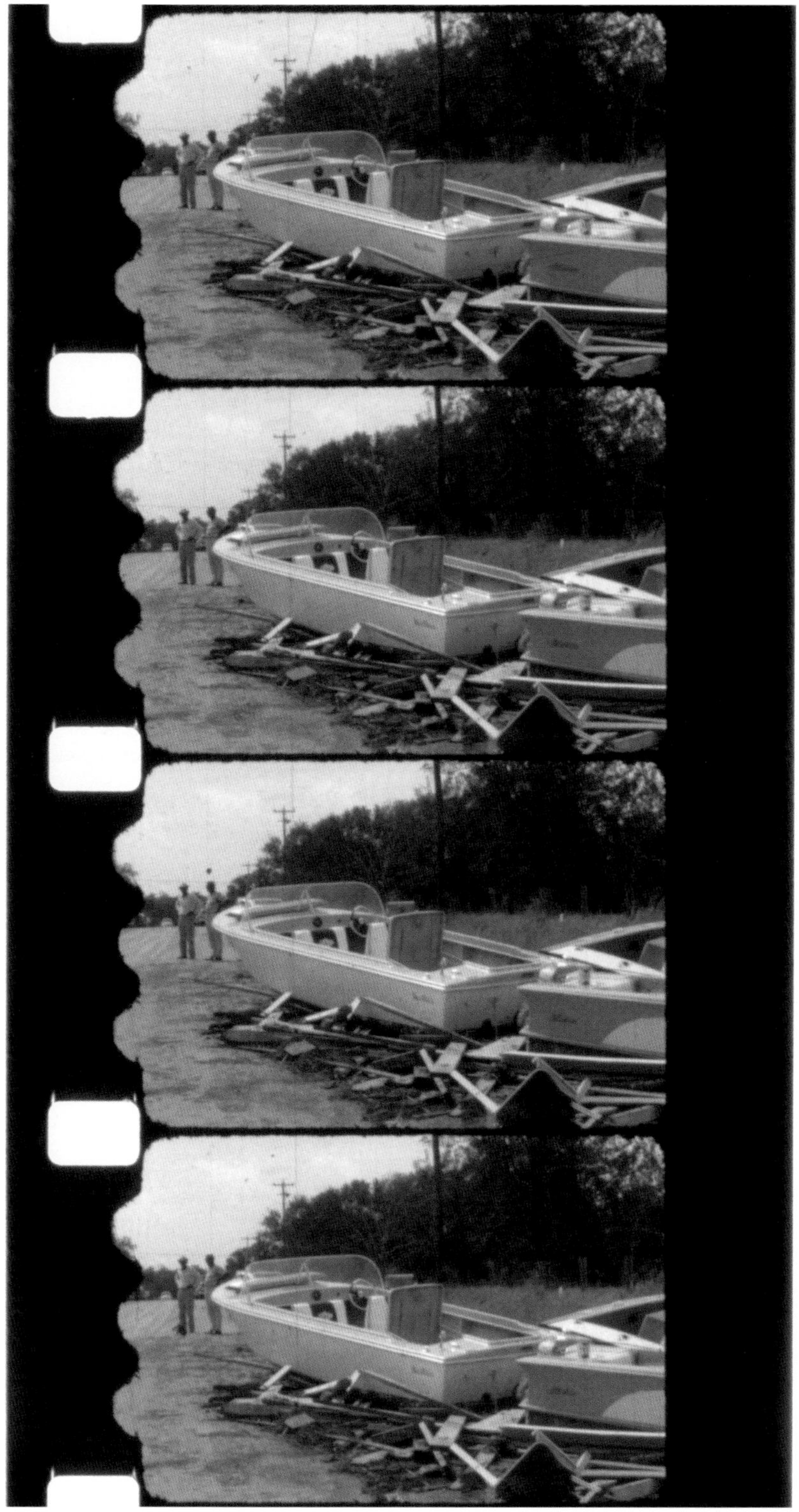

Two men inspect the wreckage of a boat that was washed ashore by Hurricane Carla in September 1961. This still is from a brief film that Bailey shot of scenes before and after the hurricane struck the Texas coast. Since Bailey owned a home in Clear Lake, the film was probably taken nearby. Carla made landfall at Port O'Connor, Texas, on September 11, and was ranked as a Category 5 storm. In Texas alone, the storm killed thirty-eight people and caused approximately three hundred million dollars in damages.

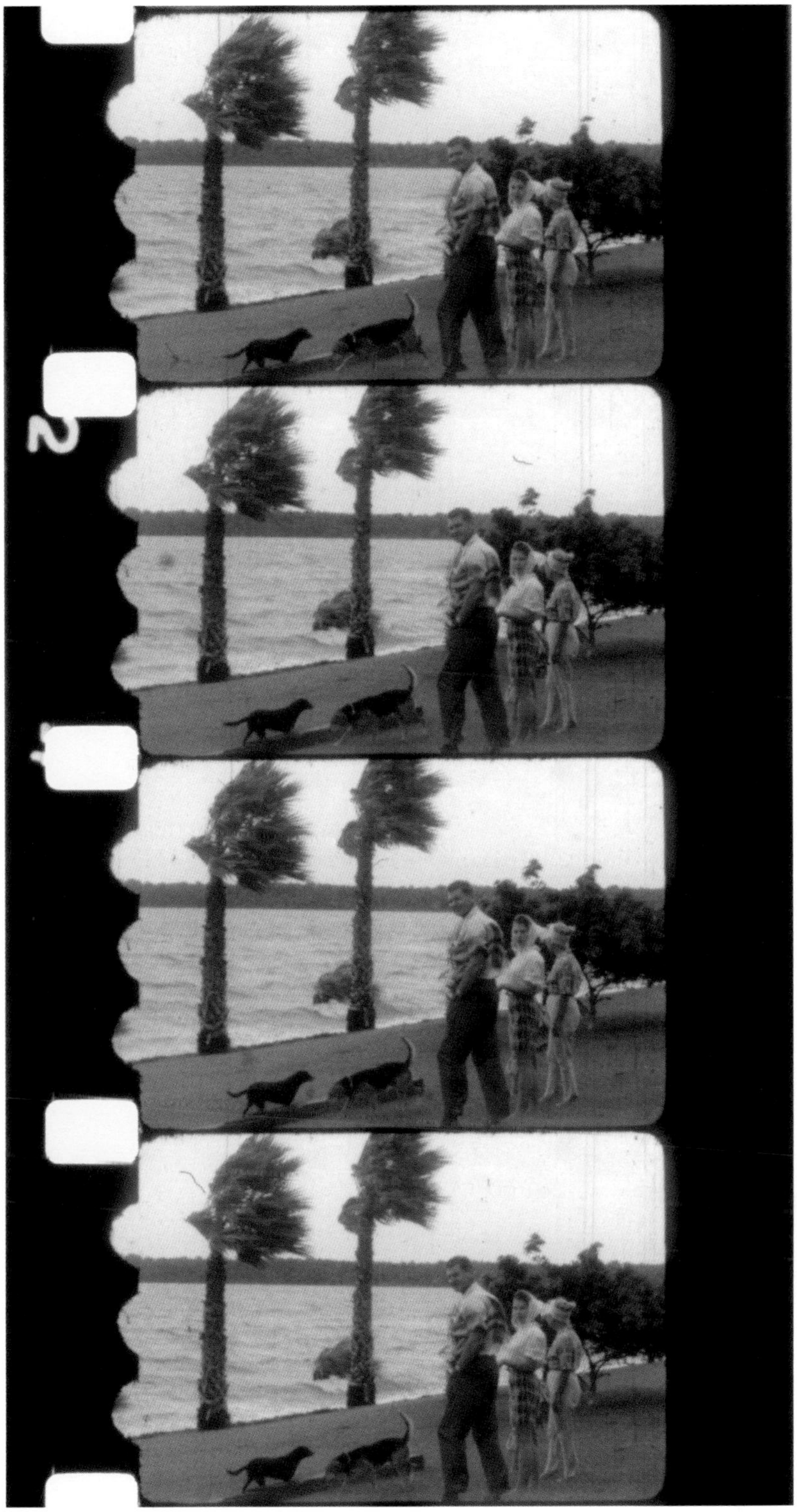

Another still from film shot by Bob Bailey as Hurricane Carla approached in September 1961. The people watching the rising water are unidentified but are likely standing along the shoreline of Clear Lake. Houston has experienced many hurricanes and tropical storms since its founding; the hurricanes of 1915 and 1943 were particularly destructive to the city. The city's residents seemed to take such storms in stride, as just another natural trial to be endured, much like heat and humidity. In Houston's earliest days, its detractors saw the recurring storms as just one more reason that the city should not have existed in the first place.

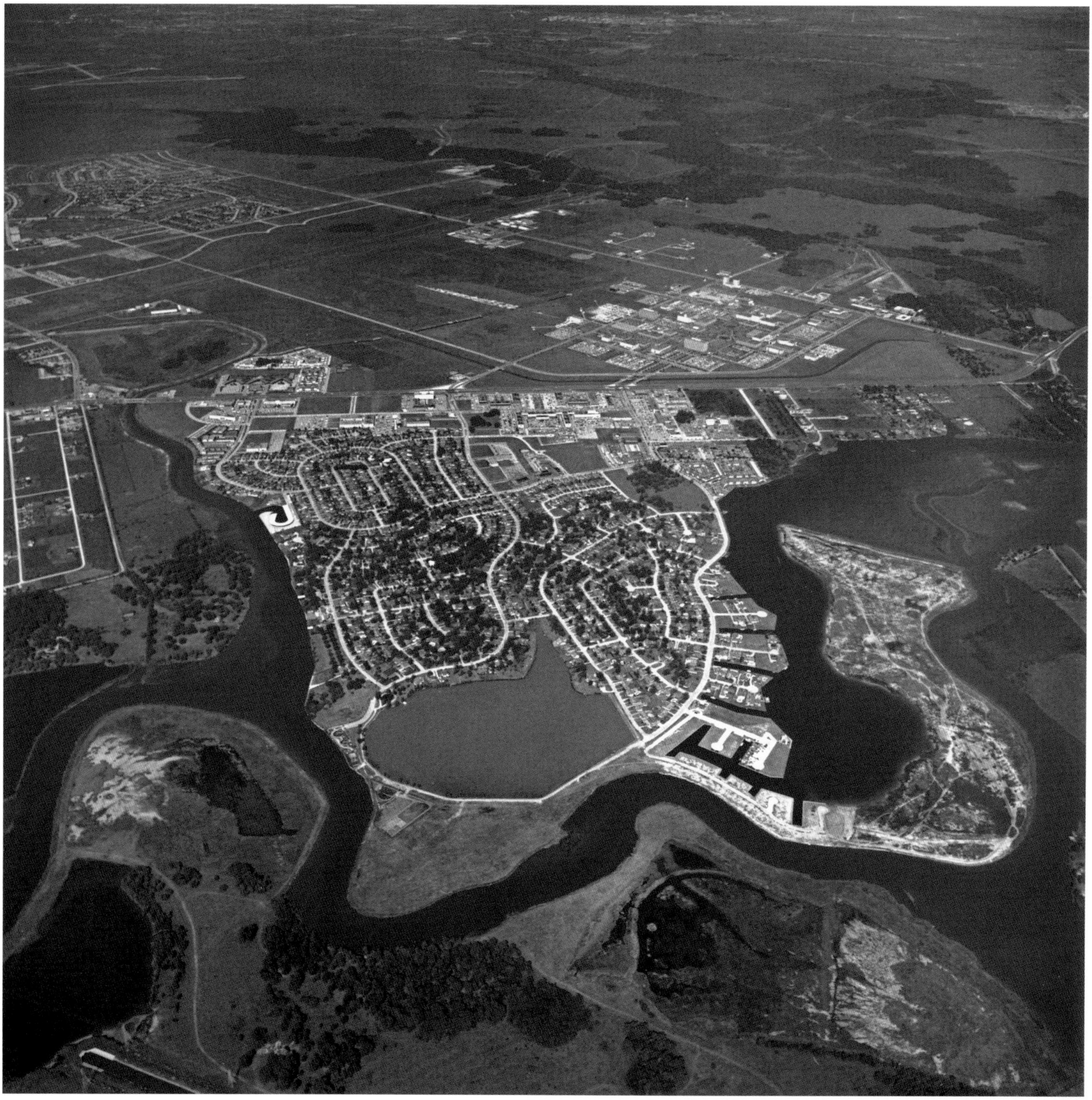

The planned community of Nassau Bay, October 1971. Nassau Bay was one of several communities developed to house the NASA workforce that immigrated to Houston to work at the Manned Spacecraft Center. The 570-acre development, which opened in 1964, was located across Farm Road 528 from what is today the Lyndon B. Johnson Space Center. Bob Bailey produced a promotional film for the community when it was still in its development phase; the film featured elaborate models of the complex.

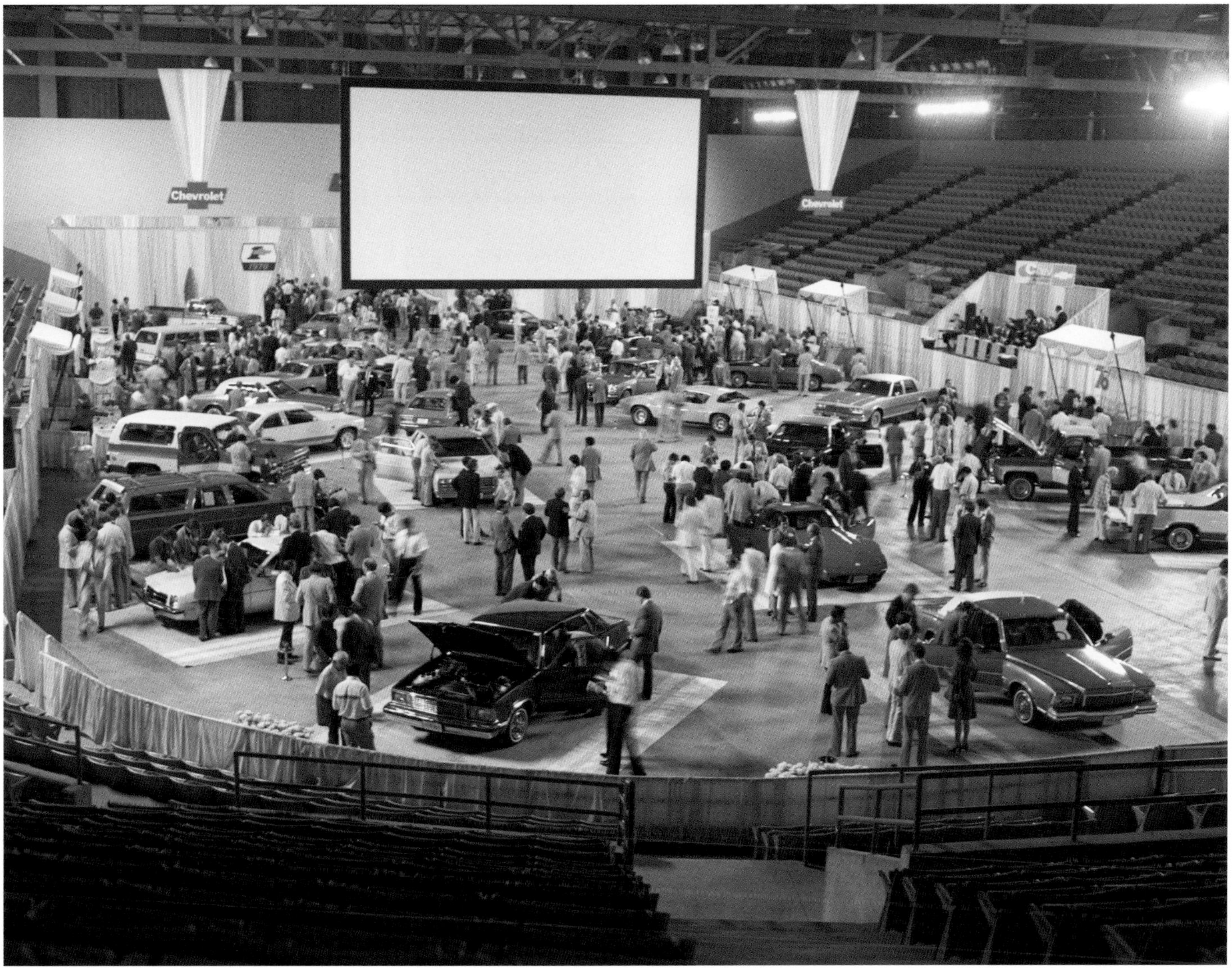

In September 1977, the introduction of new Chevrolet car models drew large crowds to this auto show. People gathered to see the latest 1978 models, blissfully unaware that gas rationing would occur again in just two years, ending many Americans' love affairs with some of the behemoth cars that Detroit was still churning out annually.

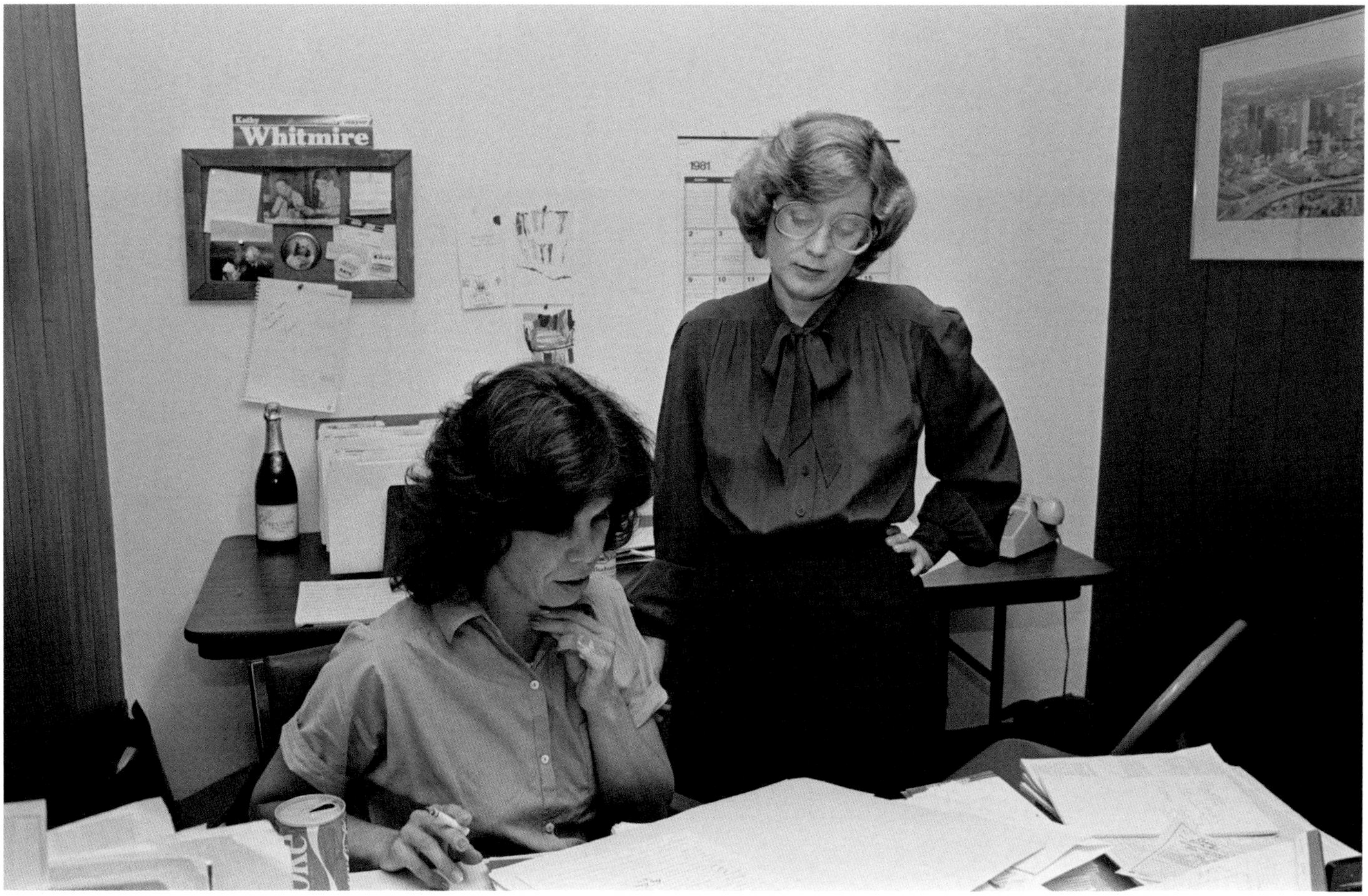

Kathy Whitmire confers with a volunteer in her campaign headquarters during her first run for mayor of Houston in 1981. She was serving as Houston's city controller at the time of her first mayoral campaign. Whitmire won the November 1981 election, the first woman ever to serve as mayor of Houston, and would go on to serve five consecutive two-year terms.

Whitmire's earlier election in 1977 as the city of Houston's controller made her the first woman in Houston's history to hold a citywide political office.

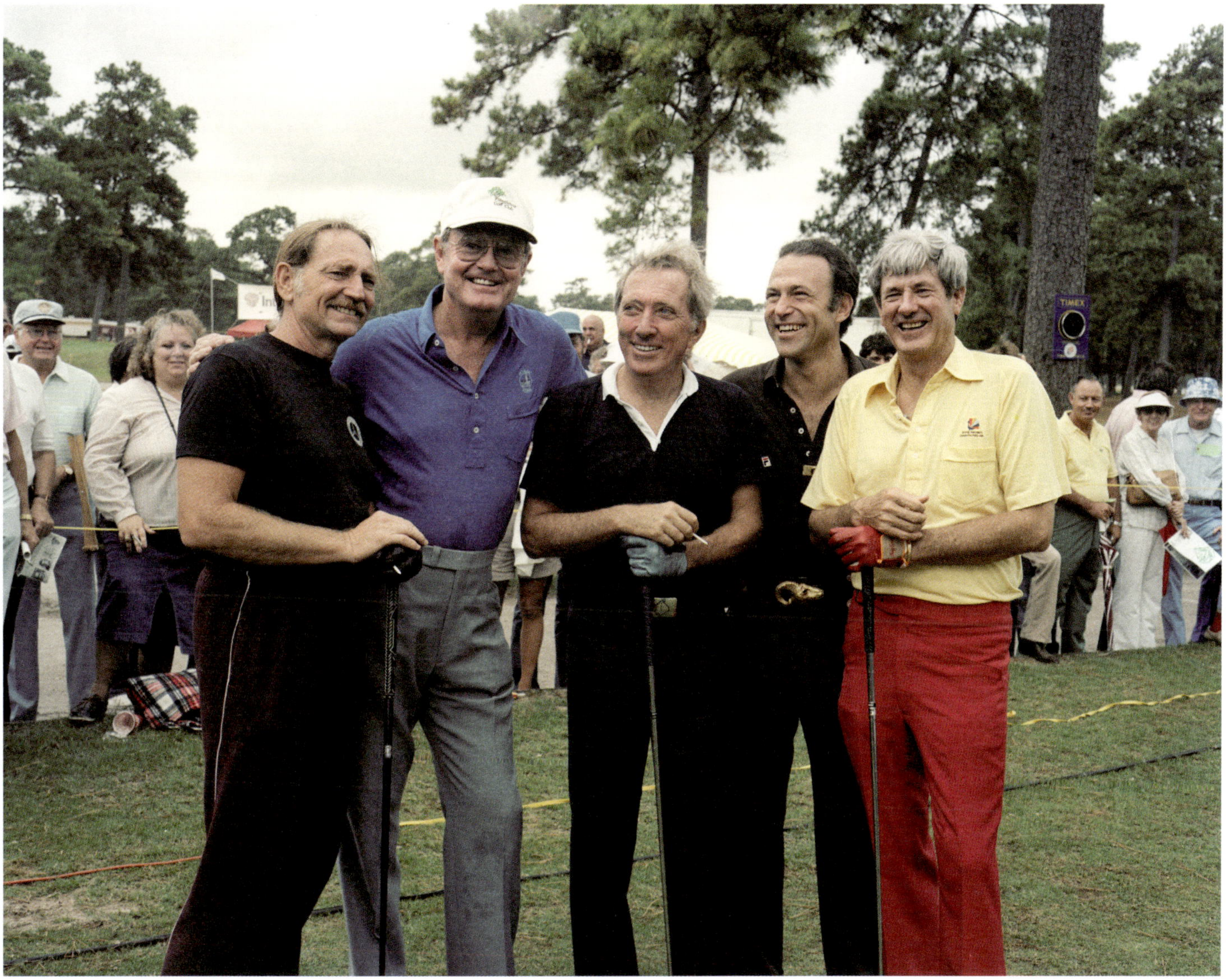

Group shot taken at the Doug Sanders Celebrity Energy Capital Classic golf tournament, which was held at Houston's Memorial Park Golf Course during October 8–10, 1982. From left to right, singer Willie Nelson, University of Texas Longhorns football coach Darrell K Royal, singer Andy Williams, department store owner Robert "Bobby" Sakowitz, and Doug Sanders, a former professional golfer who started the Celebrity Golf Classic tournament in Houston. Sanders later moved the tournament to Kingwood, a suburb of Houston, in 1988.

Youth summer soccer camp photographed on the steps of Rice University's Chemistry Lecture Hall, ca. 1979. The large size of the class indicates the surge in popularity that the sport enjoyed in Houston and the rest of the country during the 1970s and 1980s. The upsurge in soccer's popularity in the United States in the latter part of the twentieth century largely stemmed from the creation of the North American Soccer League, which operated from 1968 to 1984 and brought professional-league soccer to the attention of many Americans for the first time.

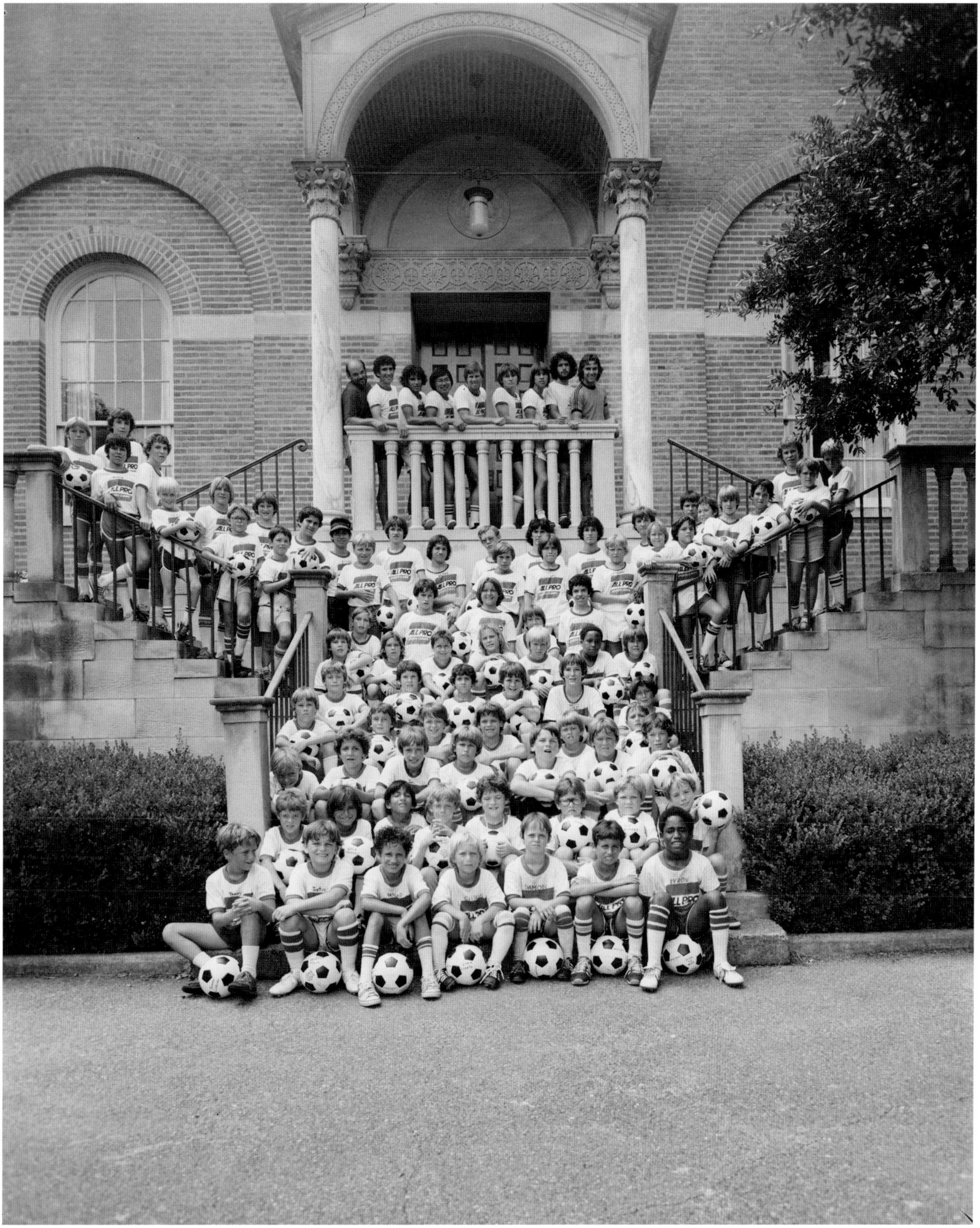
ALL PRO

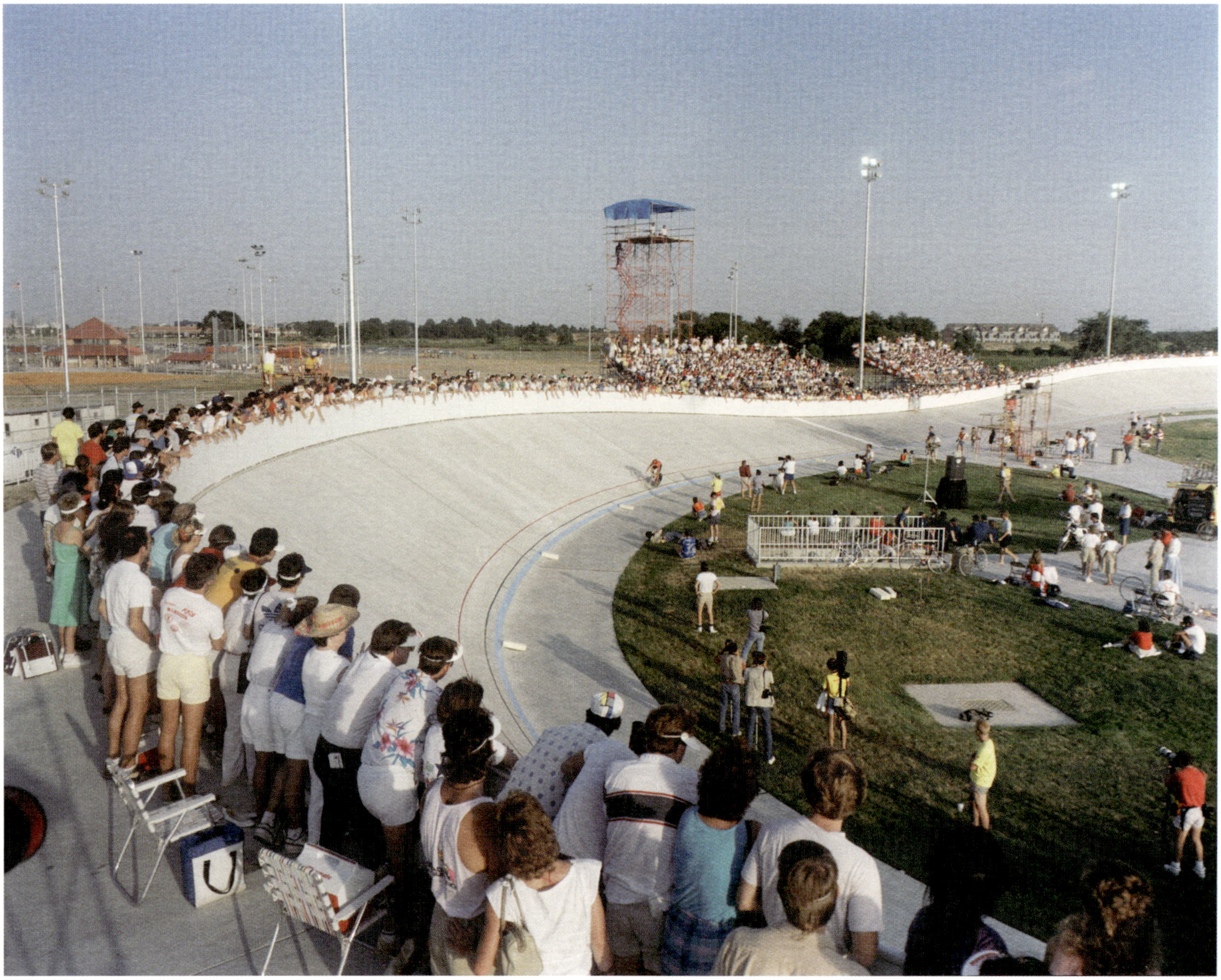

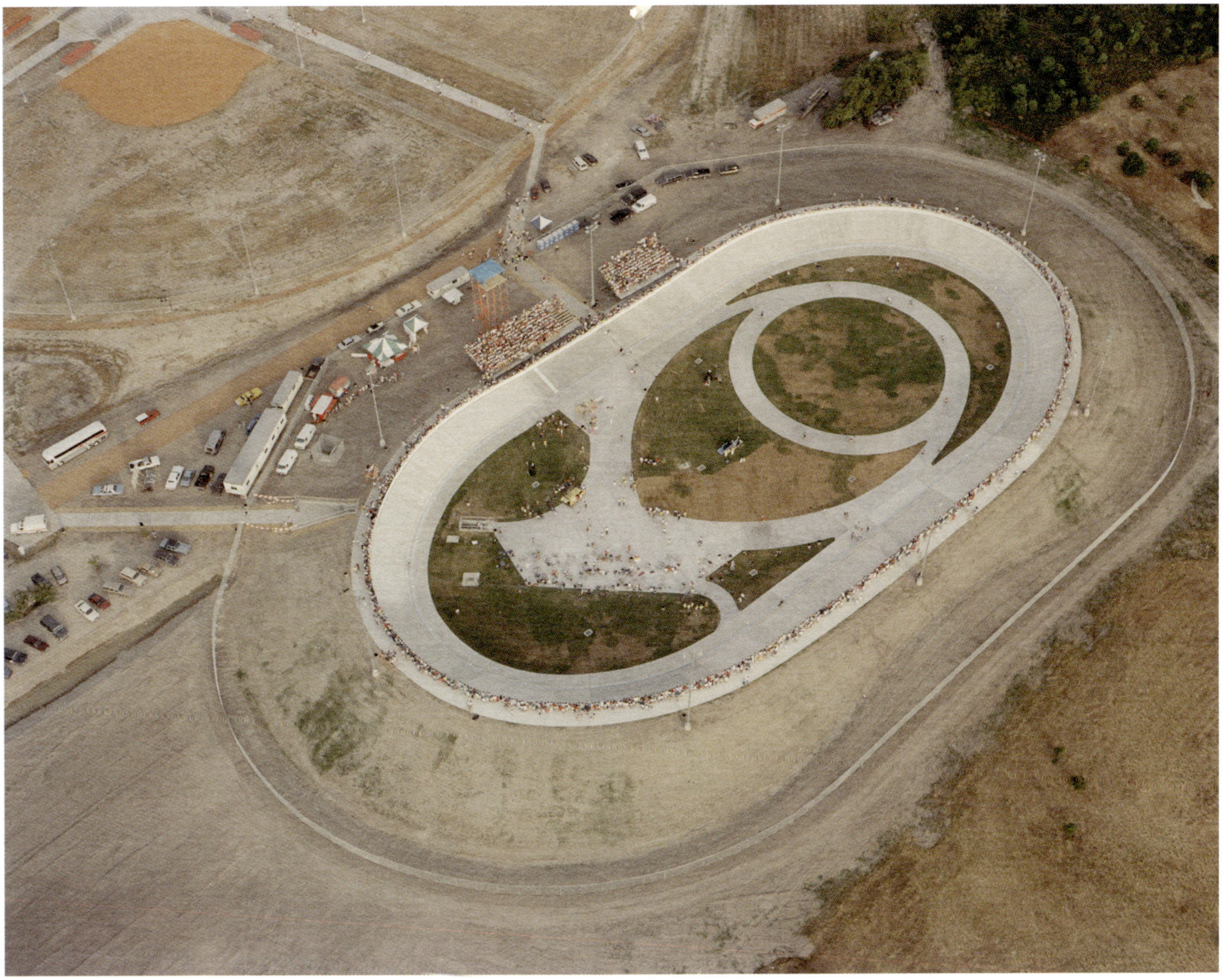

These two shots of Houston's Alkek Velodrome were both taken in July 1986, the same year the cycling facility opened. The city's first professional-level cycling facility was named in honor of Houston's Albert and Margaret Alkek Foundation. Like soccer, cycling became an increasingly popular sport in Houston during the 1970s and 1980s.

The velodrome was operated by Houston's Parks and Recreation Department until 2006, when its operations were transferred to the Greater Houston Cycling Foundation under a lease agreement.

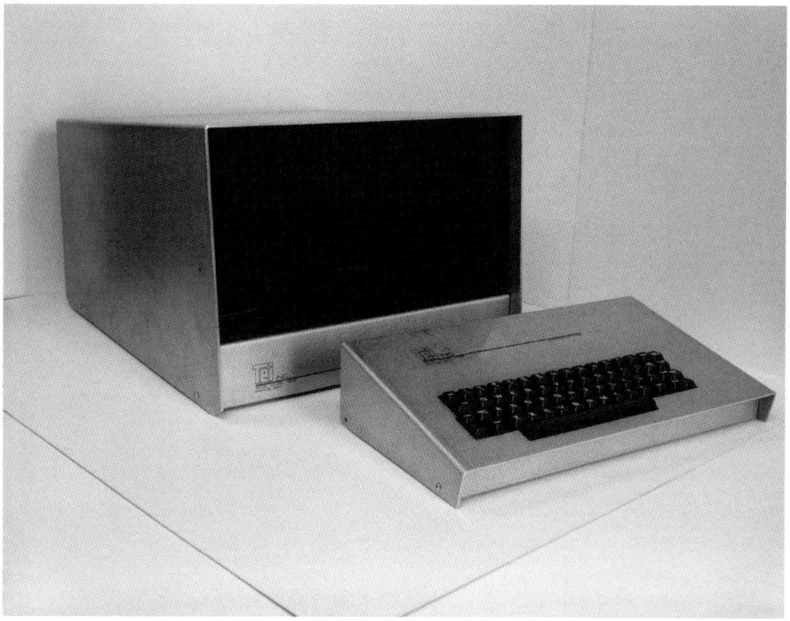

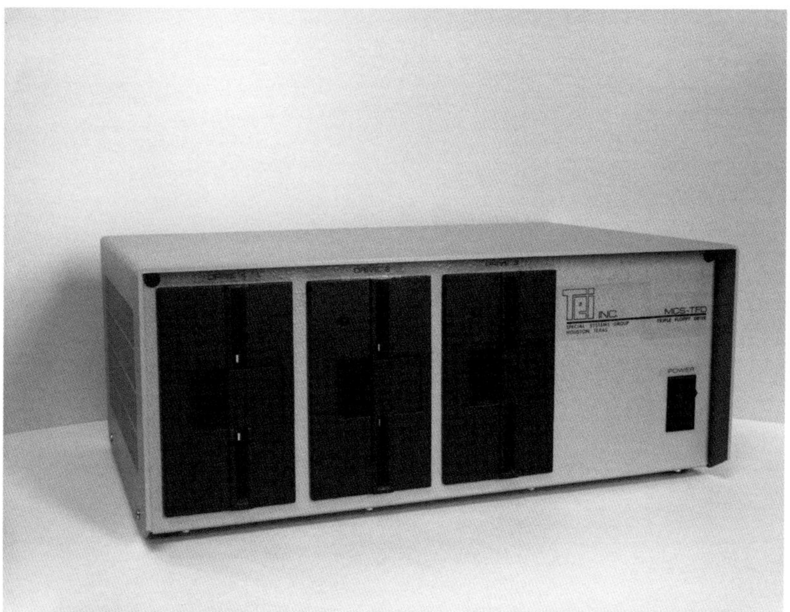

An early-model computer terminal and three-port floppy disk drive, ca. 1976, assembled by Houston's TEI, Inc., Special Systems Group. Houston's reputation as an entrepreneurial city with a huge technical knowledge base among its workforce attracted innovative computer start-up companies in the early stages of personal computer development. Only six years after this photo was taken, Compaq Computer Corporation was founded in Houston in February 1982 by three engineers who worked for Texas Instruments.

IBM had introduced the first personal computer in 1981; Compaq's signal achievement was to develop an IBM-compatible personal computer that was small enough to be transportable. Just three years after Compaq's founding, when Compaq stock was first sold publicly on the New York Stock Exchange in 1985, corporate sales rose to more than five hundred million dollars. In 1994, Compaq surpassed IBM as the largest manufacturer of personal computers in the world.

Compaq's headquarters was located in suburban northwest Houston, and its corporate campus ultimately grew to cover 150 acres. Its enormous success, said to be "unparalleled in the annals of American business history," was vital in establishing Houston's reputation as a high-technology center and in helping to end its image as a one-industry city, focused almost exclusively on energy development.

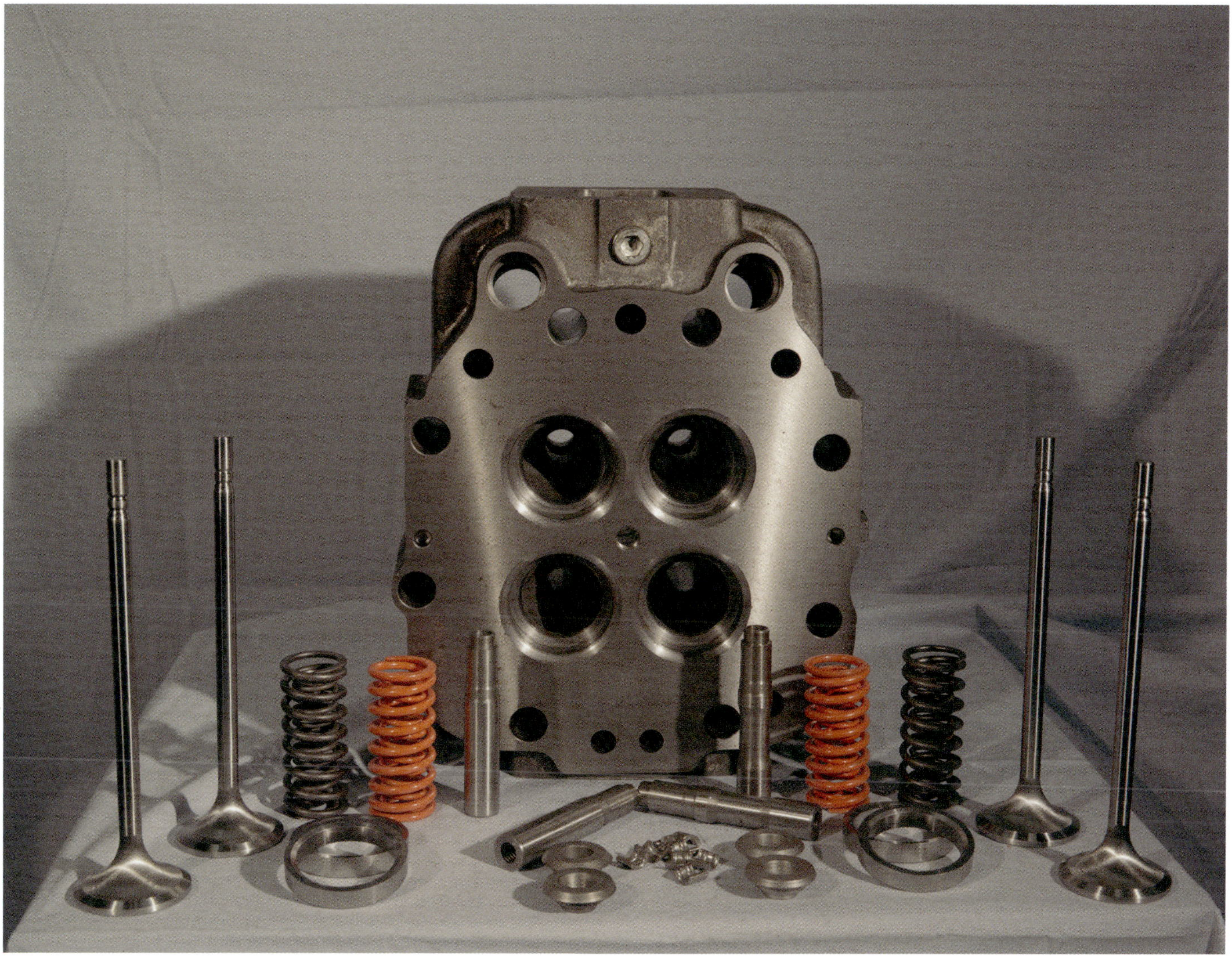

This photo of an engine block and its components was taken for Industrial Coastal Casting by Marvin Bailey, ca. 1987. Industrial photography of this type made up a sizeable percentage of the Bailey Studios' work throughout most of its existence.

The Houston First Savings and Loan Association Building, at Fannin and Capitol, ca. 1979. The Kress Department Store is at right. The now-demolished modernistic building was designed by Cameron Fairchild and opened in 1962.

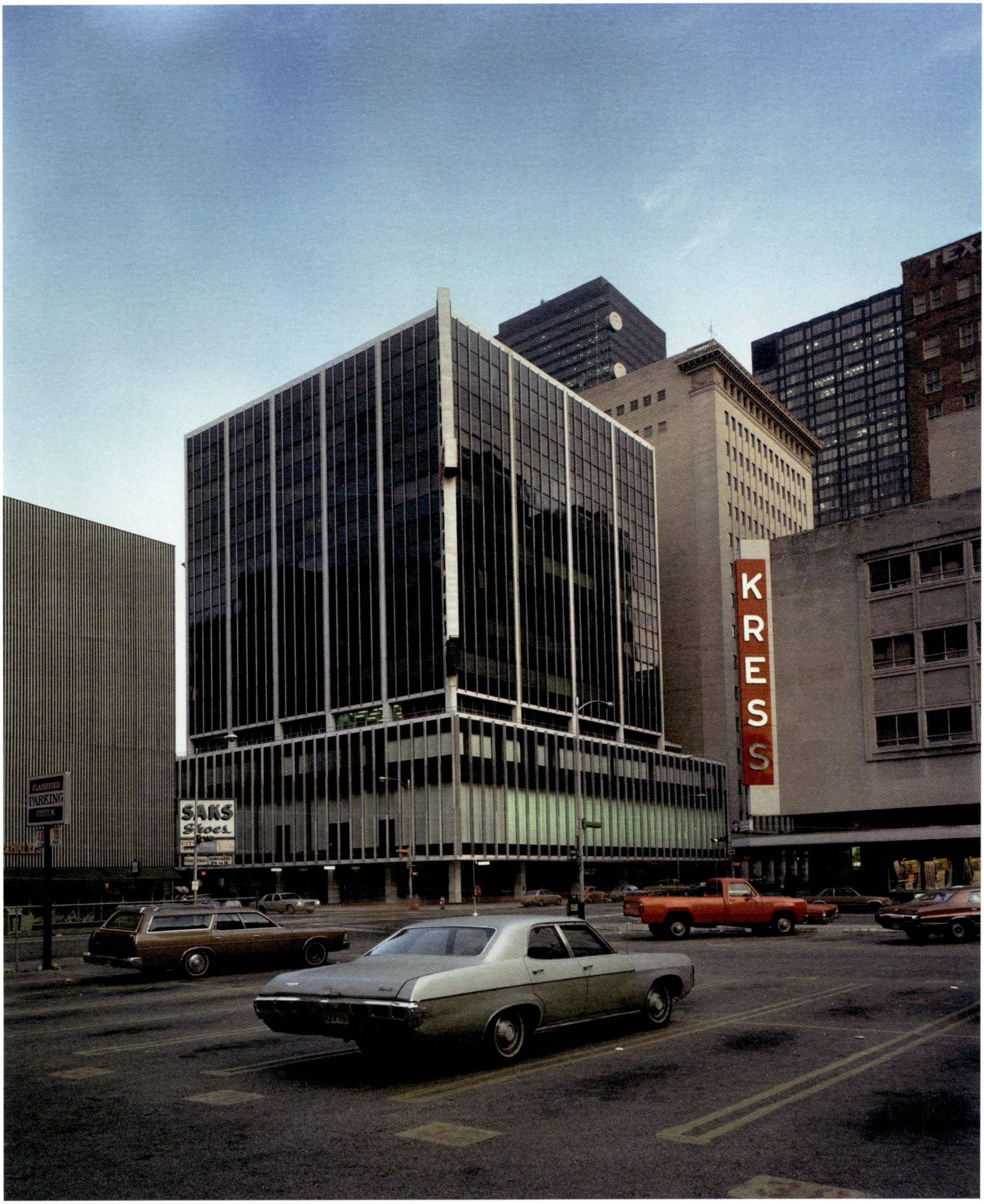
CLASSIFIED
PARKING
SYSTEM
SAKS
Shoes
KRESS

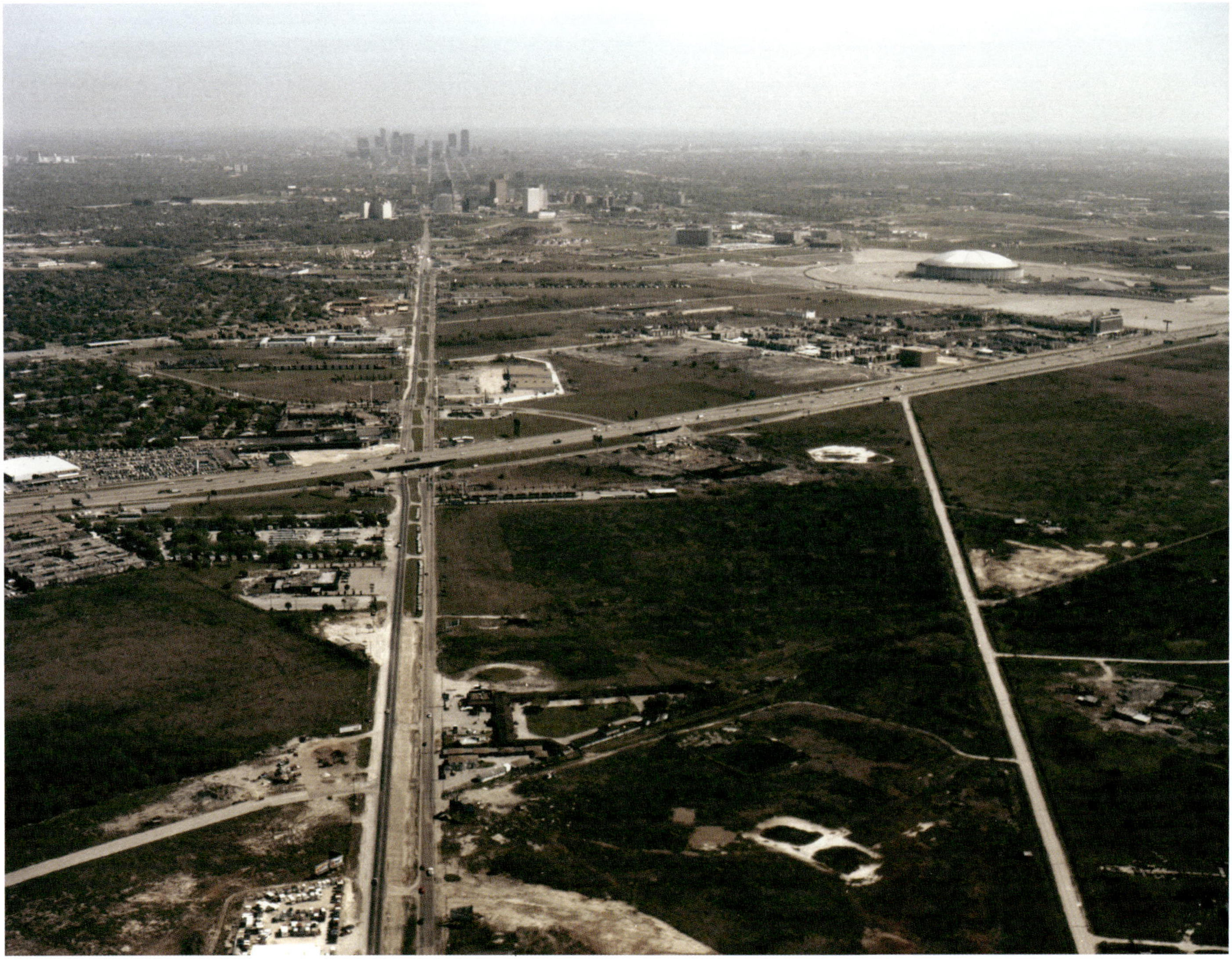

Above: Aerial photo taken from Houston's then largely undeveloped south side, looking north toward downtown, April 1979. The Astrodome can be seen at the right of the frame.

Facing: A beautifully composed early evening exterior shot of Maxim's Restaurant, located at 3207 Newcastle Street, taken by Marvin Bailey, ca. 1981. The Greenway Condominiums are in the background. Maxim's was Houston's preeminent fine dining restaurant for decades after its founding in 1949. In its 1999 "Best of the Century" issue, *Texas Monthly* designated Maxim's as the "Restaurant of the Century."

With typical Houston panache, its founder, Camille Bermann, named it after the famed Maxim's Restaurant in Paris, France, and proceeded to introduce fine French cuisine to Houston's elite. Maxim's was originally located downtown in Foley's Department Store garage building at Lamar and Milam. Maxim's never attempted to be trendy with its menu or style, and by the 1990s younger clientele stayed away, while the older patrons changed their allegiances to trendier restaurants, forcing the restaurant to close in 2001.

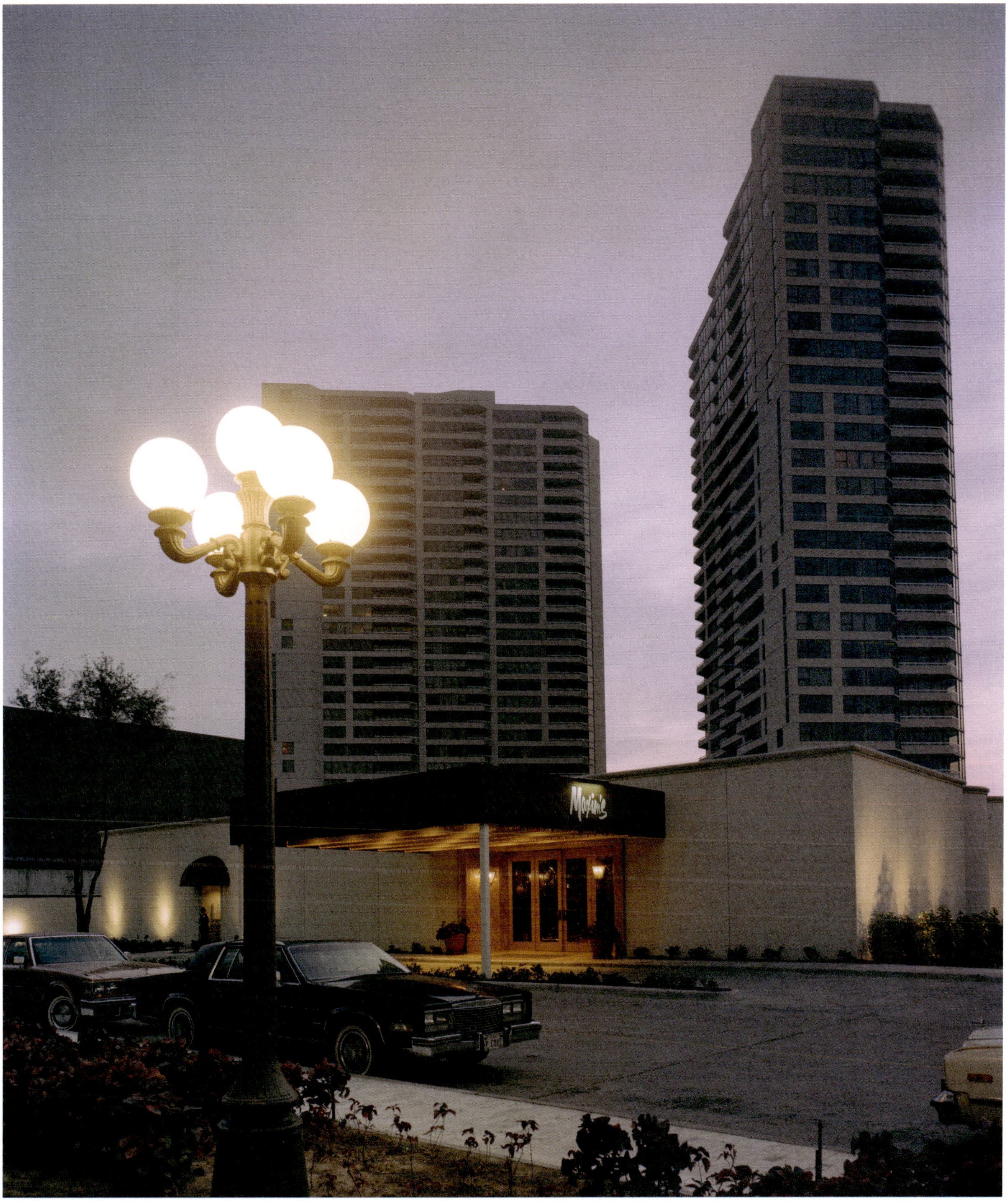
Maxim's

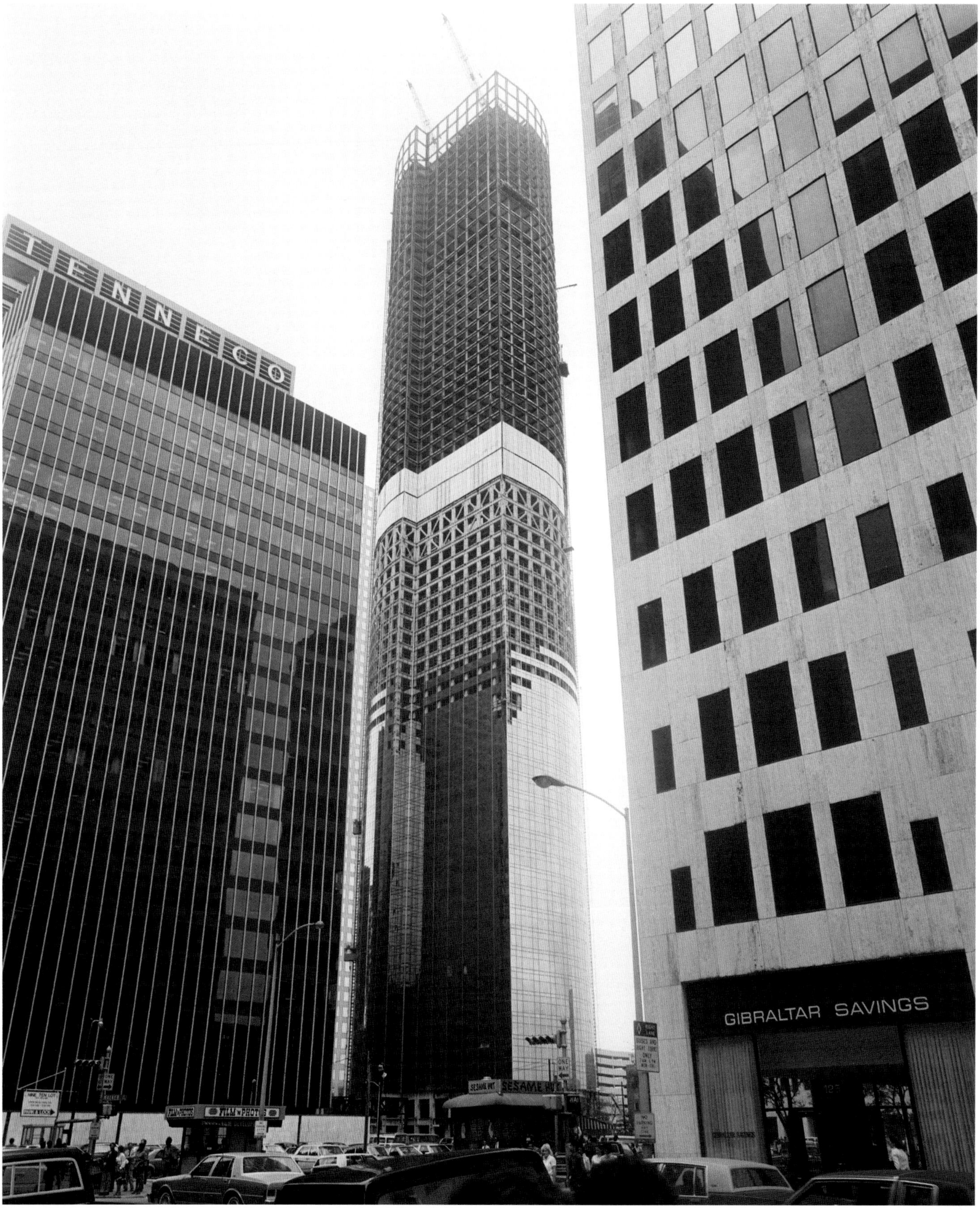
TENNECO
GIBRALTAR SAVINGS

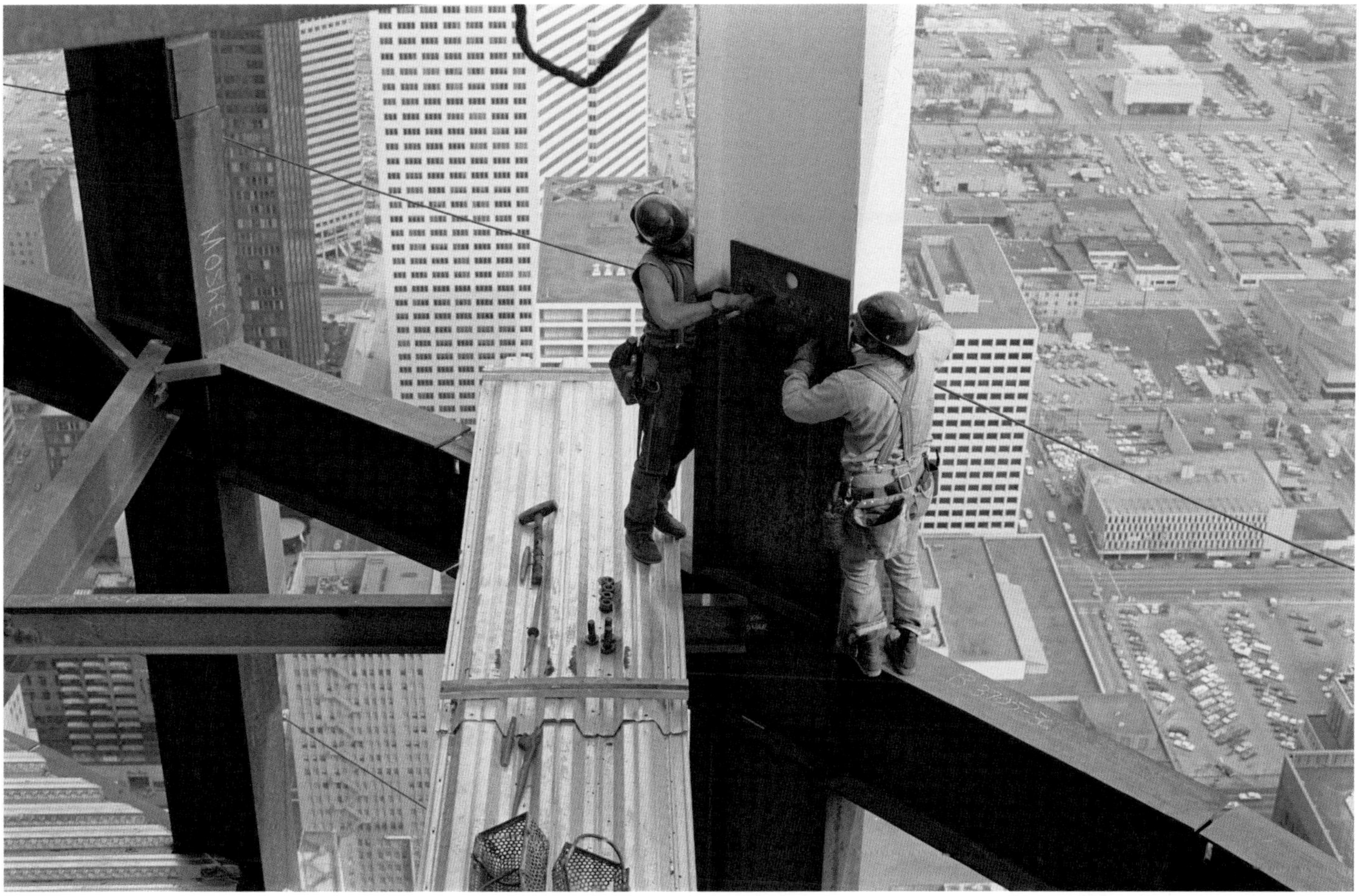

These two photos of Allied Bank Plaza, located downtown at 1000 Louisiana, show two perspectives of the building while it was under construction in 1982: a construction worker's dizzying on-site perspective and a street-level pedestrian view. When completed in 1983, at seventy-one stories it became and remains Houston's second-tallest building. It is known today as Wells Fargo Plaza.

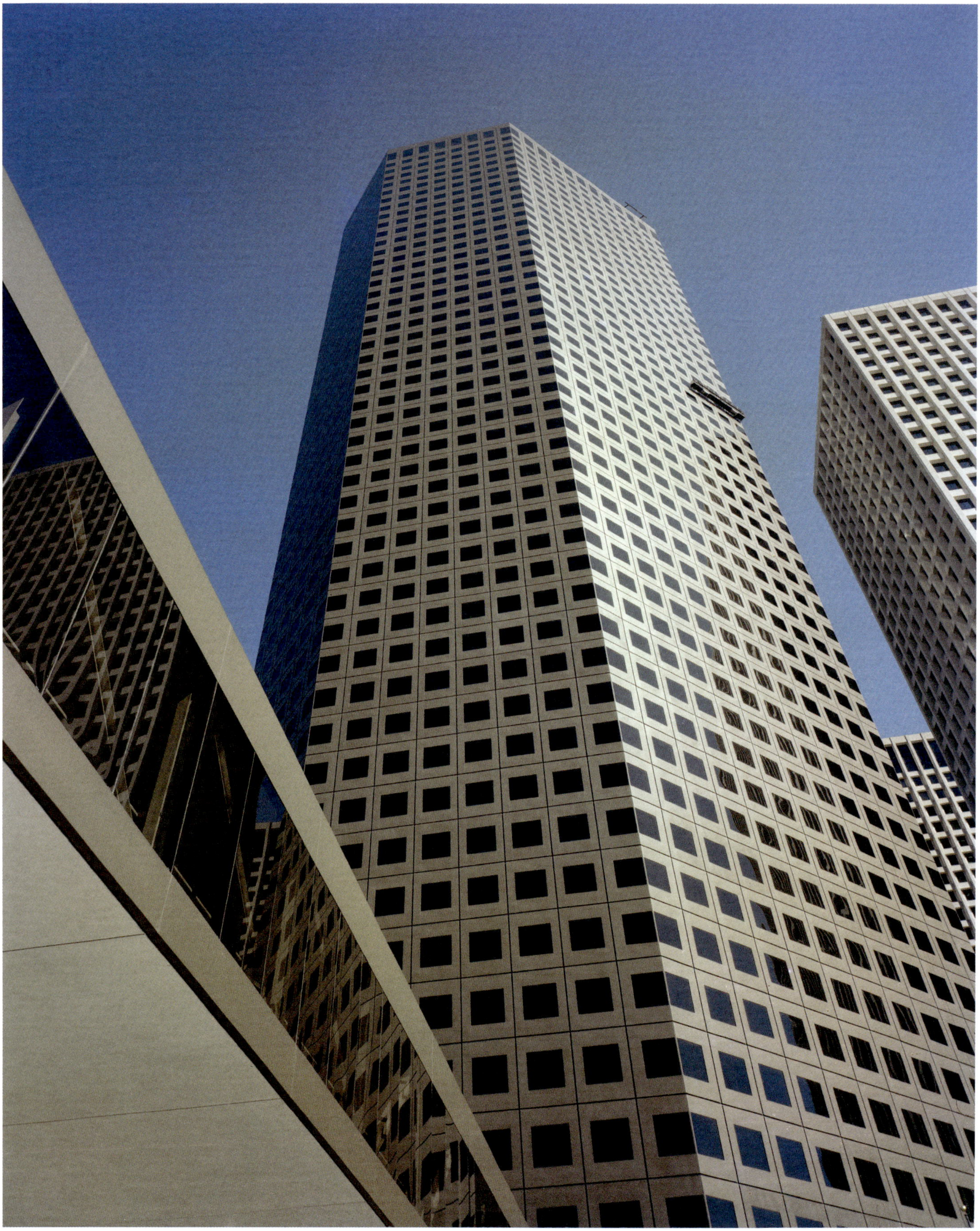

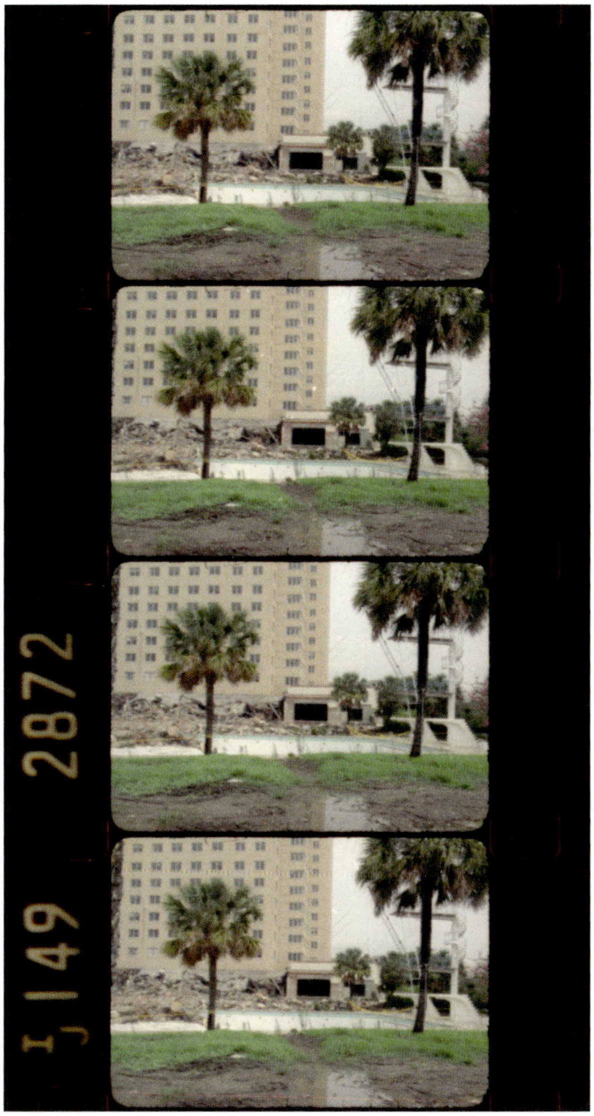

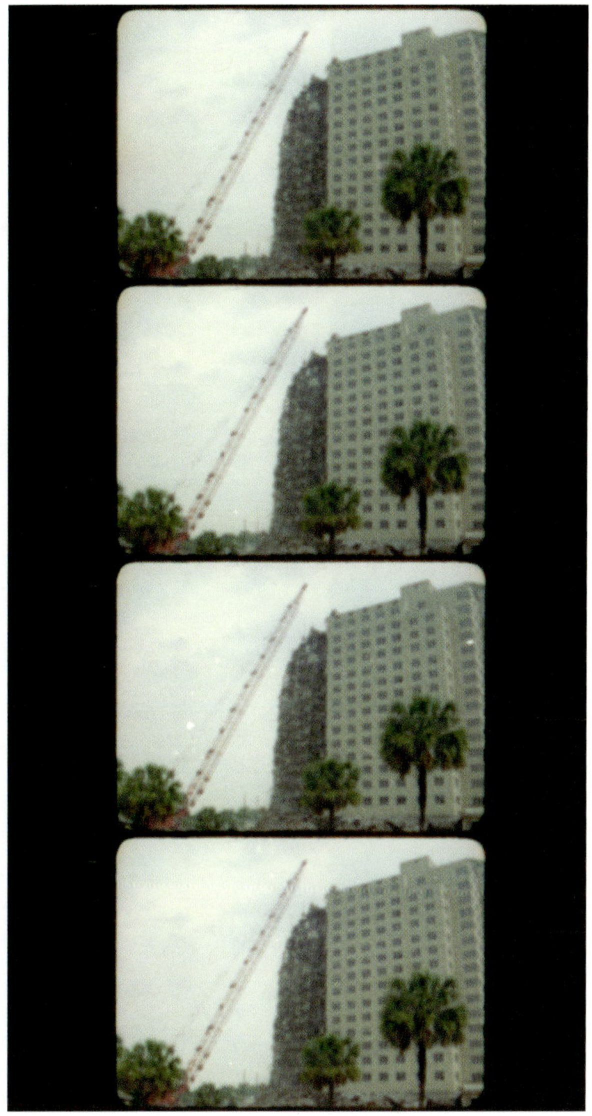

Facing: Exterior of Three Allen Center, ca. 1981. The third section of the Allen Center complex, designed by the firm of Lloyd Jones Brewer & Associates, was completed in 1980, following the construction of One Allen Center in 1972 and Two Allen Center in 1977. The three office buildings are connected to each other by pedestrian bridges. The fifty-story Three Allen Center is located at 333 Clay Street. Buildings four and five of the center were completed after the photo was taken, and the entire complex contains nearly three million square feet of office space.

Above: These stills are from film footage taken of the demolition of Houston's famed Shamrock Hotel. The much-loved Houston landmark was destroyed on June 1, 1987, generating sizeable public protests opposed to the landmark hotel's destruction. The Shamrock was developed by legendary Houston oil wildcatter Glenn McCarthy and opened on St. Patrick's Day 1949 with an onslaught of accompanying publicity, parades, and Hollywood stars flown in for the occasion. As early as 1955, McCarthy's streak of oil finds had ended, and he was forced to sell the Shamrock to Hilton Hotels Corporation. It remained in operation as a Hilton hotel until 1985, when it became the property of the Texas Medical Center until its 1987 demolition.

At the far right of the top still, the Moderne-style diving board of the Shamrock's famous swimming pool is still standing. It presided over what was widely publicized as the nation's largest swimming pool, with dimensions of 165 feet by 142 feet.

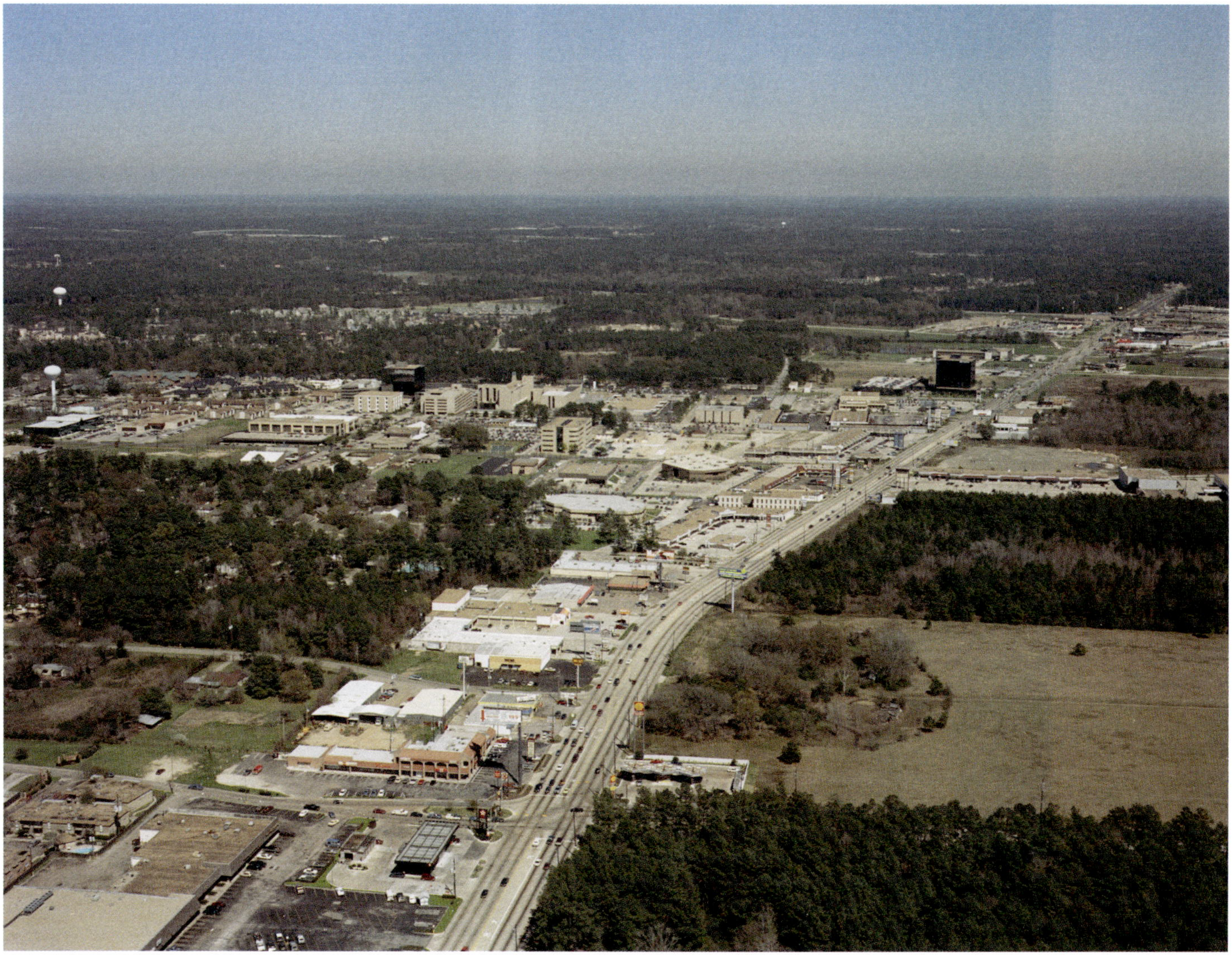

This 1991 view of a portion of FM Highway 1960 in northwest Houston shows a remarkable lack of development for a region that is now one of Houston's busiest and most densely populated areas. There was an early flurry of subdivision development in the area beginning in the late 1950s, and by 1970, some seventy thousand people lived in the area. During the next twenty years, the FM 1960 area, as it is known locally, maintained an increasing growth pattern.

However, a trend began during the 1970s and 1980s in which Houston's suburbs pushed out so far from the central city that developments in areas such as the FM 1960 region became exurbs stretching into adjacent counties. Sub-urban had become extra-urban with Houston's unlimited growth.

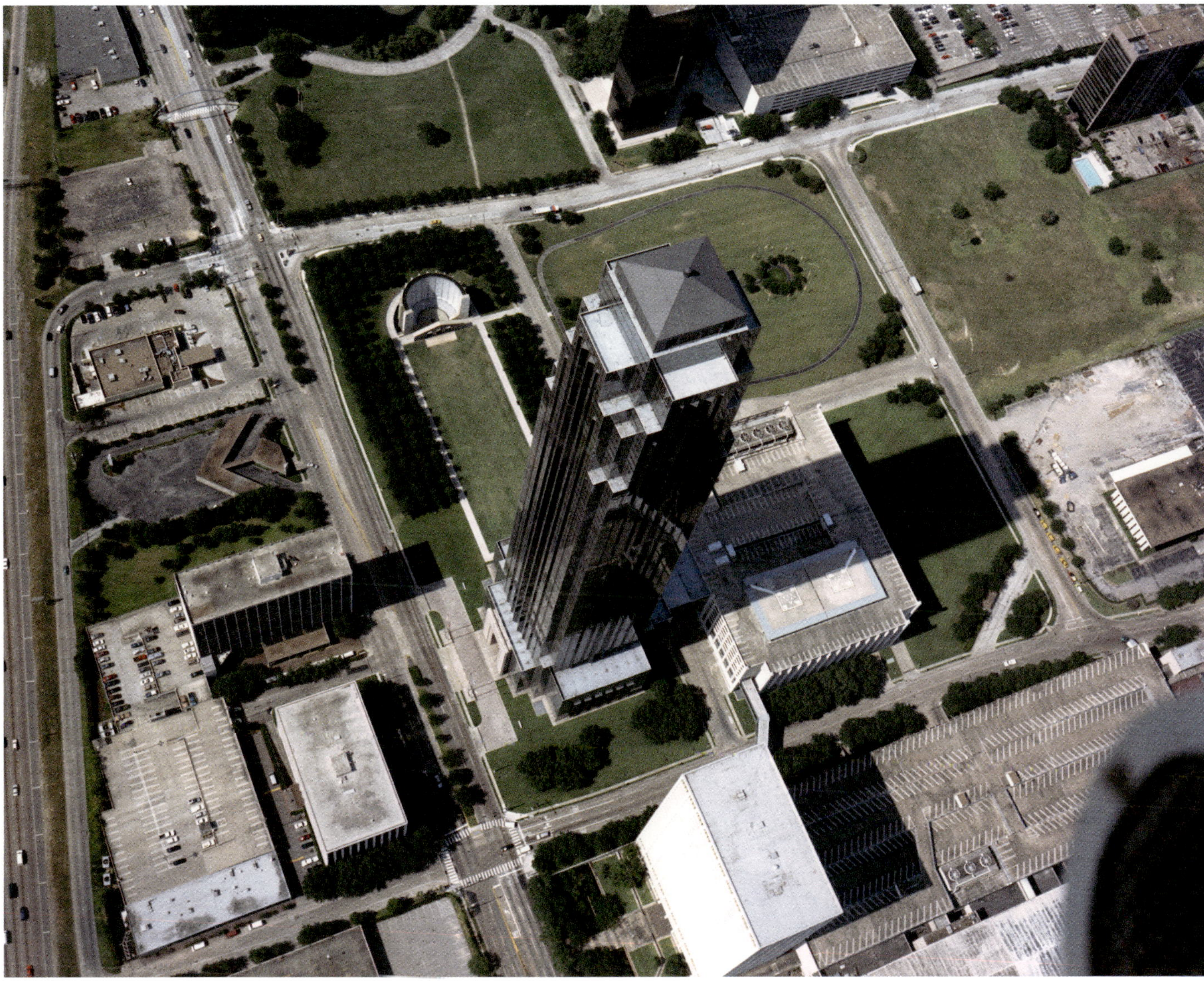

This aerial view of the sixty-four-story Transco Tower (now officially the Williams Tower, although the original name is still greatly in use by Houstonians) was photographed circa 1990. From the earliest years of the Bailey Studios, aerial photography had been one of the Studios' recognized areas of expertise, and this photograph is a clear confirmation that it still remained a strength of the studio more than sixty years later. Also visible in the picture is the footprint of Transco Park with its Transco Fountain, which opened in 1985. The park has since been re-designated as the Gerald D. Hines Waterwall Park.

The Transco Tower, designed by Philip Johnson and John Burgee and completed in 1983, almost immediately became an iconic symbol of Houston's shift westward from the downtown area, because it dominated the generally lower-slung skyline of the city's increasingly important Uptown district.

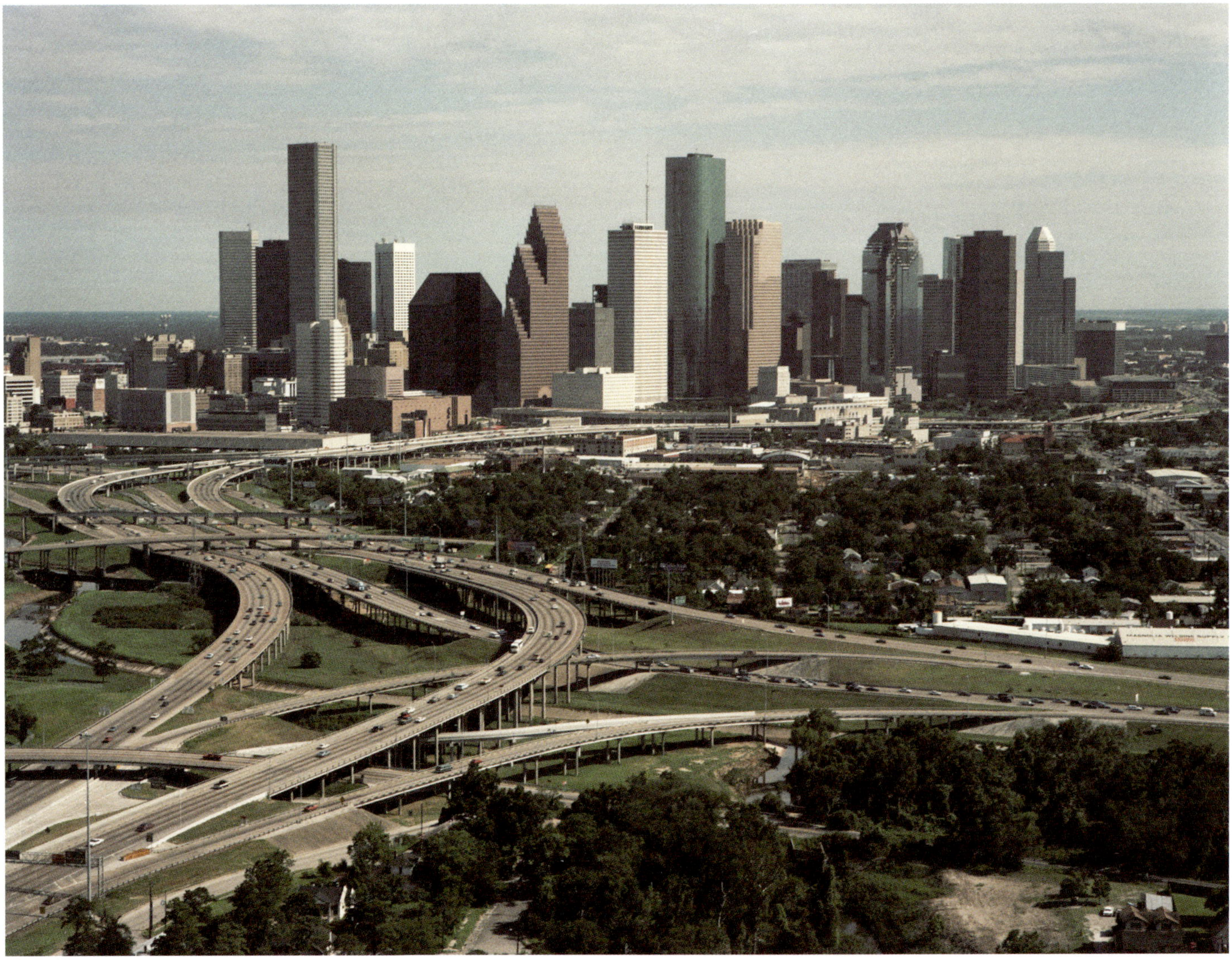

Houston skyline from the north, photographed in 1986 by Marvin Bailey. From 1980 to 1986, developers added an astonishing 88.9 million square feet of office space in downtown Houston, doubling the amount of office space that was available in 1979.

202 *Aerial view of the Astrodome under construction*: *Astrodome Vertical File*, Houston Metropolitan Research Center.

203 *Aerial view of the Astrodome and the adjacent Astroworld amusement park*: Ibid.; Strom, *Houston Lost and Unbuilt*, 124, 130.

207 *Cars to be used in President John F. Kennedy's motorcade*: J. R. Gonzales, "New Film Shows Kennedy's Nov. 1963 Visit to Houston," *Bayou City History* (blog), *Houston Chronicle*, February 22, 2011, accessed June 20, 2015, http://blog.chron.com/bayoucityhistory/2011/02/new-film-shows-kennedys-nov-1963-visit-to-houston/; "JFK: After 50 Years," *Houston Chronicle*, November 20, 2013, accessed June 20, 2015.

211 *Sakowitz Brothers Department Store*: *Sakowitz Department Store Vertical File*, Houston Metropolitan Research Center.

215 *Houston's Texas Medical Center as it appeared in July 1964*: Burleson and Burleson, *A Guide to the Texas Medical Center*; "A History of Innovation," Texas Medical Center, accessed July 21, 2015, http://www.texasmedicalcenter.org/about/history/; "The Texas Medical Center," accessed July 22, 2015, *Handbook of Texas Online*, Texas State Historical Association, https://www.tshaonline.org/handbook/online/articles/kct23.

219 *View of the Houston Oilers football team*: "Houston Oilers," *Sports Encyclopedia*, accessed September 18, 2015, http://www.sportsecyclopedia.com/nfl/tenhou/houoilers.html.

221 *Theatergoers arrive at the Alley Theatre*: "Alley Theatre," *Handbook of Texas Online*, Texas State Historical Association, Accessed July 8, 2015, https://tshaonline.org/handbook/online/articles/kla01.

222 *Muhammad Ali training in Houston*: Tex Maule, "Cruel Ali with All the Skills," *Sports Illustrated*, February 13, 1967, accessed July 21, 2015, https://web.archive.org/web/20130309201457/http://sportsillustrated.cnn.com/vault/article/magazine/MAG1079523/1/index.htm; Martin Waldron, "Clay Guilty in Draft Case," *New York Times*, June 20, 1967, accessed July 27, 2015, http://www.nytimes.com/learning/general/onthisday/big/0620.html; Hauser, *Muhammad Ali: His Life and Times*, 166–202.

223 *Actor John Wayne*: "Hellfighters," Internet Movie Database, accessed July 30, 2015.

224 *Two men inspect the wreckage of a boat that was washed ashore*: "Significant Weather, 1960s," *Texas Almanac*, Texas State Historical Association, accessed January 11, 2016, http://texasalmanac.com/topics/environment/significant-weather-1960s.

226 *The planned community of Nassau Bay, October 1971*: "History," Nassau Bay, accessed September 23, 2015, http://www.nassaubay.com/index.aspx?NID=291.

228 *Kathy Whitmire confers with a volunteer*: "Kathryn Jean Niederhofer Whitmire Facts," *Your Dictionary*, accessed July 25, 2015, http://biography.yourdictionary.com/kathryn-jean-niederhofer-whitmire.

229 *Doug Sanders Celebrity Energy Capital Classic golf tournament*: Alex Hecht, "The Burial and Resurrection (Maybe) of Doug Sanders," *Houston Press*, June 16, 1994, accessed October 4, 2015, http://www.houstonpress.com/news/the-burial-and-resurrection-maybe-of-doug-sanders-6572838; "Doug Sanders," Texas Golf Hall of Fame, accessed January 29, 2016, http://www.texasgolfhof.org/index.php/component/zoo/item/doug-sanders

233 *Houston's Alkek Velodrome*: "About the Velodrome," Alkek Velodrome, accessed October 4, 2015, http://www.houstoncycling.org/TrackInformation.php

234 *An early-model computer terminal*: "Compaq Computer Corporation," *Handbook of Texas Online*, Texas State Historical Association, accessed October 4, 2015, https://tshaonline.org/handbook/online/articles/dnc01; "Electronics Industry," *Handbook of Texas Online*, Texas State Historical Association, accessed August 2, 2015, https://www.tshaonline.org/handbook/online/articles/dne01; "Compaq Computer Corporation History," Funding Universe, accessed October 4, 2015, http://www.fundinguniverse.com/company-histories/compaq-computer-corporation-history/.

236 *The Houston First Savings and Loan Association Building*: Mod, *Building Modern Houston*, 94; J. R. Gonzales, "Downtown Houston by Air and by Color: The Houston First Saving Association Building," *Bayou City History* (blog), *Houston Chronicle*, August 5, 2013, accessed January 29, 2015, http://www.chron.com/life/gallery/Downtown-Houston-by-air-and-in-color-67653/photo-5005974.php.

238 *early evening exterior shot of Maxim's Restaurant*: Rob Walsh, "Top 9 Houston Restaurant Closings of the

Decade," *Houston Press,* January 6, 2010, accessed July 27, 2015, http://blogs.houstonpress.com/eat ing/2010/01/top_9_houston_restaurant_closi.php.

241 Allied Bank Building: *Allied Bank Building Vertical File,* Houston Metropolitan Research Center; "Welcome to Wells Fargo Plaza," Wells Fargo Plaza, accessed July 27, 2015, http://www.wellsfargoplaza.com/home.axis.

243 *Exterior of Three Allen Center, ca. 1981*: Fox, *Houston Architectural Guide,* 9.

243 *demolition of Houston's famed Shamrock Hotel*: *Shamrock Hotel Vertical File,* Houston Metropolitan Research Center.

244 *This 1991 view of a portion of FM Highway 1960*: Barbara Payne, "North Houston Rich History," 1960 Area, accessed October 4, 2015, http://www.1960area.com/history/.

245 *This aerial view of the sixty-four-story Transco Tower*: *Transco Tower Vertical File,* Houston Metropolitan Research Center; "Property Search: Williams Tower," accessed October 30, 2015, http://www.hines.com/property/detail.aspx?id=264.

BIBLIOGRAPHY

Anderson, Brian. "Visions of Monorail in Houston, 1955–1994." *Houston Review* 17, no. 1 (1995): 29–48.

Arrington, Tess, et al., eds. *We Were There: A Collection of the Personal Stories of Survivors of the 1947 Ship Explosions in Texas City, Texas, Commonly Referred to as the Texas City Disaster*. Texas City, TX: Mainland Museum of Texas City, 1997.

Baldwin, Gordon, and Martin Jurgens. *Looking at Photographs: A Guide to Technical Terms*. Los Angeles: Getty Publications, 2009.

Bogart, Michele H. *Artists, Advertising, and the Borders of Art*. Chicago: University of Chicago Press, 1995.

Burleson Clyde W., and Suzy Williams Burleson. *A Guide to the Texas Medical Center*. Austin: University of Texas Press, 1987.

Burr, Ty. *Gods Like Us: On Movie Stardom and Modern Fame*. Pantheon Books: New York, 2012.

Butterworth, Molly. "Streamlined Styling." *Modernism* 14, no. 3 (Fall 2011): 46–53.

Carroll, Michael. *Popular Modernity in America*. Albany, NY: SUNY Press, 2000.

Cohen, Lizabeth. *A Consumer's Republic: The Politics of Mass Consumption in Postwar America*. New York: Vintage Books, 2004.

Dailey, Victoria, Natalie Shivers, and Michael Dawson. *LA's Early Moderns: Art, Architecture, Photography*. Los Angeles: Balcony Press, 2003.

Droste, Magdalena. *Bauhaus: 1919–1933*. Los Angeles: Taschen, 2011.

Esperdy, Gabrielle. *Modernizing Main Street: Architecture and Consumer Culture in the New Deal*. Chicago: University of Chicago Press, 2008.

Ferriss, Hugh. *The Metropolis of Tomorrow*. Mineola, NY: Dover Publications, 1929.

Fox, Stephen. *Houston Architectural Guide*. Houston: Herring Press, 1999.

Franklin, Wayne, and Michael Steiner, eds. *Mapping American Culture*. Iowa City: University of Iowa Press, 1992.

Gide, Andre. *The Immoralist*. New York: Alfred A. Knopf, 1930.

Goldberg, Vicki, and Robert Silberman. *American Photography: A Century of Images*. San Francisco: Chronicle Books, 1999.

Gray, Lisa. "Houston's Last Ranch." *Houston Chronicle*, February 12, 2012. http://www.chron.com/life/gray/article/Gray-Houston-s-last-ranch-3356945.php

Greene, Melissa Fay. *The Photographs of Esther Bubley*. Washington, DC: The Library of Congress, 2010.

Hanson, Eric. "Remember When: Looking Back at a Younger Houston through the Lens of the Bailey Brothers." *Texas Magazine*, September 25, 1994, 8–11.

Hauser, Thomas. *Muhammad Ali: His Life and Times*. New York: Touchstone, 1991.

Haworth-Booth, Mark, ed. *Things: A Spectrum of Photography, 1850–2001*. London: Jonathan Cape, 2005.

Heiferman, Marvin, ed. *Photography Changes Everything*. New York: Aperture Foundation, 2012.

Himes, Andrew. *The Sword of the Lord: The Roots of Fundamentalism in an American Family*. Seattle: Chiara Press, 2011.

Hiss, Tony. *The Experience of Place: A New Way of Looking at and Dealing with Our Radically Changing Cities and Countryside*. New York: Knopf, 1990.

Hogan, Warren L., ed. *Hurricane Carla: A Salute to the News Media*. Houston: Leaman-Hogan Co., 1961.

Houston (Greater) City Directory (1930–1960). Dallas: Morrison & Fourmy Directory Co./R. L. Polk, Texas Directories Collection, Dolph Briscoe Center for American History. The University of Texas at Austin. Austin, Texas.

Houston (Greater) Yellow Pages (1957–1971). Dallas: Southwestern Bell, Texas Directories Collection, Dolph Briscoe Center for American History. The University of Texas at Austin. Austin, Texas.

Houston History. "The Decades." Accessed June 13, 2015. http://02db39d.netsolhost.com/.

Hudson, Leighton, ed. *Marcel Proust: The Critical Heritage*. London: Routledge, 2003.

Jackson, Kenneth. *Crabgrass Frontier: The Suburbanization of the United States*. New York: Oxford University Press, 1985.

Jeffrey, Ian. *How to Read a Photograph: Lessons from Master Photographers*. New York: Harry N. Abrams, Inc., 2008.

Kunstler, James Howard. *The Geography of Nowhere: The Rise and Decline of America's Man-Made Landscape*. New York: Touchstone Books, 1994.

Lardas, Mark. *The Port of Houston*. Charleston, SC: Arcadia Publishing, 2013.

Larkin, Jack. *Where We Worked: A Celebration of America's Workers and the Nation They Built*. Guildford, CT: Lyons Press, 2010.

Leach, William. *Land of Desire: Merchants, Power, and the Rise of a New American Culture*. New York: Vintage Books, 1994.

Longstreth, Richard. *The American Department Store Transformed, 1920–1960*. New Haven, CT: Yale University Press, 2010.

Marzio, Peter C. *The Democratic Art: Pictures for a 19th-Century America*. Boston: David R. Godine, Publisher, 1979.

McCauley, Elizabeth Anne. *Industrial Madness: Commercial Photography in Paris, 1848–1871*. New Haven, CT: Yale University Press, 1994.

McCombs, Kenneth M. *Commercial Photography*. Chicago: American Technical Society, 1951.

Mod, Anna. *Building Modern Houston*. Charleston, SC: Arcadia Publishing, 2011.

Muir, Laura. *Lionel Feininger: Photographs, 1928–1939*. Cambridge, MA: Harvard Art Museums, 2011.

Pfeiffer, Ingrid, and Max Hollein. *László Moholy-Nagy*. New York: Prestel, 2009.

Proust, Marcel. *Remembrance of Things Past, Vol. I, Swann's Way*. New York: The Modern Library, 1998.

Rice, Mark. *Through the Lens of the City: NEA Photography Surveys of the 1970s*. Jackson, MS: University Press of Mississippi, 2005.

Rosenblum, Naomi. *A World History of Photography*. New York: Abbeville Press Publishers, 2007.

Sandler, Martin W. *Photography: An Illustrated History*. New York: Oxford University Press, 2002.

Scardino, Barrie. "H2Ouston: How Water Shaped the Bayou City." *Cite: The Architecture and Design Review of Houston*, no. 46, Fall 1999–Winter 2000, 36–38.

Sharf, Frederic A. *Suburban America, 1930–1970: An Architectural Perspective*. Newbury, MA: Newbury Press, Inc., 2001.

Sibley, Marilyn McAdams. *The Port of Houston: A History*. Austin: University of Texas Press, 1968.

Smith, Joel. *The Life and Death of Buildings: On Photography and Time*. New Haven, CT: Yale University Press, 2011.

Sontag, Susan. *Regarding the Pain of Others*. New York: Picador, 2003.

Stephens, Hugh W. *The Texas City Disaster, 1947*. Austin: University of Texas Press, 1997.

Strom, Steven R. *Houston Lost and Unbuilt*. Austin: University of Texas Press, 2010.

———. "A Legacy of Civic Pride: Houston's PWA Buildings." *Houston Review* 17, no. 2 (1995).

———. "Modernism for the Masses." *Cite: The Architecture and Design Review of Houston* 62 (Fall 2004): 30–33.

———. "Remembering Houston: Online with the Bob Bailey Archives." *Cite: The Architecture and Design Review of Houston* 67 (Summer 2006).

Texas State Historical Association. *Handbook of Texas Online*. Austin: Texas State Historical Association, 1999. http://www.tshaonline.org/handbook/online.

Tuck, Kirk. *Commercial Photography Handbook: Business Techniques for Professional Digital Photographers*. Buffalo, NY: Amherst Media, Inc., 2010.

Vertical Files. Dolph Briscoe Center for American History. The University of Texas at Austin. Austin, Texas.

Vertical Files. Houston Metropolitan Research Center. Houston Public Library. Houston, Texas.

Watson, Roger, and Helen Rappaport. *Capturing the Light: The Birth of Photography, A True Story of Genius and Rivalry*. New York: St. Martin's Press, 2013.

Welling, David. *Cinema Houston: From Nickelodeon to Megaplex*. Austin: University of Texas Press, 2007.

Wooten, Heather Green. *The Polio Years in Texas: Battling a Terrifying Unknown*. College Station, TX: Texas A&M Press, 2009.

Wride, Tim B. *Retail Fictions: The Commercial Photography of Ralph Bartholomew Jr.* Los Angeles: Los Angeles County Museum of Art, 1998.

Yochelson, Bonnie, and Tracy A. Schmid. *Esther Bubley: On Assignment*. New York: Aperture Foundation, 2005.

INDEX

Page numbers in *italics* indicate photographs.